Search Engine Optimization

FOR

DUMMIES®

3RD EDITION

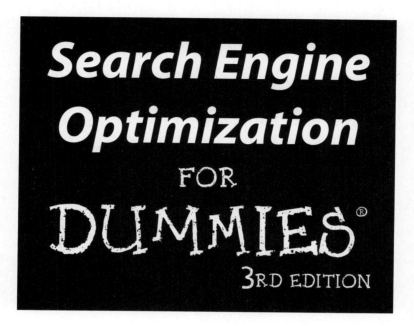

Search Engine Optimization

FOR

DUMMIES®

3RD EDITION

by Peter Kent

WILEY

Wiley Publishing, Inc.

Search Engine Optimization For Dummies® 3rd Edition

Published by
Wiley Publishing, Inc.
111 River Street
Hoboken, NJ 07030-5774

www.wiley.com

Copyright © 2008 by Wiley Publishing, Inc., Indianapolis, Indiana

Published by Wiley Publishing, Inc., Indianapolis, Indiana

Published simultaneously in Canada

For general information on our other products and services, please contact our Customer Care Department within the U.S. at 800-762-2974, outside the U.S. at 317-572-3993, or fax 317-572-4002.

For technical support, please visit www.wiley.com/techsupport.

Wiley also publishes its books in a variety of electronic formats. Some content that appears in print may not be available in electronic books.

Library of Congress Control Number: 2008927912

ISBN: 978-0-470-26270-2

Manufactured in the United States of America

10 9 8 7 6 5 4 3

WILEY

About the Author

Peter Kent is the author of numerous other books about the Internet, including *Pay Per Click Search Engine Marketing For Dummies*, the best-selling *Complete Idiot's Guide to the Internet*, and the most widely reviewed and praised title in computer-book history, *Poor Richard's Web Site: Geek Free, Commonsense Advice on Building a Low-Cost Web Site*. His work has been praised by *USA Today, BYTE,* CNN.com, *Windows Magazine, Philadelphia Inquirer,* and many others.

Peter has been online since 1984, doing business in cyberspace since 1991, and writing about the Internet since 1993. Peter's experience spans virtually all areas of doing business online, from editing and publishing an e-mail newsletter to creating e-commerce Web sites, from online marketing and PR campaigns to running a Web-design and -hosting department for a large ISP.

Peter was the founder of an e-Business Service Provider funded by one of the world's largest VC firms, Softbank/Mobius. He was VP of Web Solutions for a national ISP and VP of Marketing for a Web applications firm. He also founded a computer-book publishing company launched through a concerted online marketing campaign.

Peter now consults with businesses about their Internet strategies, helping them to avoid the pitfalls and to leap the hurdles they'll encounter online. He also gives seminars and presentations on subjects related to online marketing in general and search engine marketing in particular. He can be contacted at Consult@PeterKentConsulting.com, and more information about his background and experience is available at www.PeterKentConsulting.com.

Dedication

For Cheryl

Author's Acknowledgments

I'd like to thank all my clients, who have given me an opportunity to play with search-engine optimization in a wide variety of businesses. I'd also like to thank Kyle Looper, my Acquisitions Editor, and Blair Pottenger, Project Editor, who were surprisingly patient. And, of course, the multitude of Wiley staff involved in editing, proofreading, and laying out the book.

Publisher's Acknowledgments

We're proud of this book; please send us your comments through our online registration form located at www.dummies.com/register/.

Some of the people who helped bring this book to market include the following:

Acquisitions, Editorial, and Media Development

Project Editor: Blair J. Pottenger

Acquisitions Editor: Kyle Looper

Copy Editors: Brian Walls, Becky Whitney

Technical Editor: Paul Chaney

Editorial Manager: Kevin Kirschner

Media Development Project Manager: Laura Moss-Hollister

Media Development Assistant Producer: Angela Denny

Editorial Assistant: Amanda Foxworth

Sr. Editorial Assistant: Cherie Case

Cartoons: Rich Tennant (www.the5thwave.com)

Composition Services

Project Coordinator: Patrick Redmond

Layout and Graphics: Reuben W. Davis, Alissa D. Ellet, Stephanie D. Jumper

Proofreaders: Jessica Kramer, Bonnie Mikkelson

Indexer: Infodex Indexing Services, Inc.

Publishing and Editorial for Technology Dummies

Richard Swadley, Vice President and Executive Group Publisher

Andy Cummings, Vice President and Publisher

Mary Bednarek, Executive Acquisitions Director

Mary C. Corder, Editorial Director

Publishing for Consumer Dummies

Diane Graves Steele, Vice President and Publisher

Joyce Pepple, Acquisitions Director

Composition Services

Gerry Fahey, Vice President of Production Services

Debbie Stailey, Director of Composition Services

Contents at a Glance

Table of Contents

Introduction

Welcome to *Search Engine Optimization For Dummies,* 3rd Edition. What on earth would you want this book for? After all, can't you just build a Web site, and let your Web designer get the site into the search engines? Can't you simply pay someone $25 to register the site with thousands of search engines? I'm sure you've seen advertising stating, "We guarantee top-ten placement in a gazillion search engines!" and "We'll register you in 5,000 search engines today!"

Well, unfortunately, it's not that simple. (Okay, fortunately for me, because if it were simple, Wiley wouldn't pay me to write this book.) The fact is that search engine optimization is a little complicated. Not brain surgery complicated, but not as easy as "Give us 50 bucks and we'll handle it for you."

The vast majority of Web sites don't have a chance in the search engines. Why? Because of simple mistakes. Because the people creating the sites don't have a clue what they should do to make the site easy for search engines to work with. Because they don't understand the role of links pointing to their site, and because they've never thought about keywords. Because, because, because. This book helps you deal with those becauses and gets you not just one, but dozens, of steps ahead of the average Web-site Joe.

About This Book

This book demystifies the world of search engines. You find out what you need to do to give your site the best possible chance to rank well in the search engines.

In this book, I show you how to

- Make sure that you're using the right keywords in your Web pages.
- Create pages that search engines can read and will index how you want them to.
- Avoid techniques that search engines hate — things that can get your Web site penalized (knocked down low in search engine rankings).
- Build pages that give your site greater visibility in search engines.

✔ Get search engines and directories to include your site in their indexes and lists.

✔ Get search engines to display your site when people search locally.

✔ Encourage other Web sites to link to yours.

✔ Keep track of how your site is doing.

✔ Use pay-per-click advertising and shopping directories.

✔ And plenty more!

Foolish Assumptions

I don't want to assume anything, but I have to believe that if you're reading this book, you already know a few things about the Internet and search engines. I presume that you

✔ Have access to a computer that has access to the Internet.

✔ Know how to use a Web browser to get around the Internet.

✔ Know how to carry out searches at the Web's major search engines, such as Google and Yahoo!.

Of course, for a book like this, I have to assume a little. This is a book about how to get your Web site to rank well in the search engines. I have to assume that you know how to create and work with a site or at least know someone who can create and work with a site. In particular, you (or the other person) know how to

✔ Set up a Web site

✔ Create Web pages

✔ Load those pages onto your Web server

✔ Work with *HTML (HyperText Markup Language),* the coding used to create Web pages

In other words, you're not just using some kind of simple Web-page creation program that isolates you from the underlying HTML code and you, or your geek, understand a little about HTML and feel comfortable enough with it to insert or change HTML tags.

I don't go into a lot of complicated code in this book; this isn't a primer on HTML. But to do search engine work, you (or someone on your team) need to know what a <TITLE> tag is, for instance, and how to insert it into a page; how to recognize JavaScript (though not how to create or modify it); how to open a Web page in a text editor and modify it; and so on. You need basic HTML skills in order to optimize a site for the search engines. If you need more information about HTML, take a look at *HTML 4 For Dummies,* 5th Edition, by Ed Tittel and Mary Burmeister (Wiley Publishing, Inc.).

How This Book Is Organized

Like all good reference tools, this book is designed to be read when needed. It's divided into several parts: the basics, building search engine–friendly Web sites, getting your site into the search engines, what to do after the search engines index your site, search engine advertising, and the Part of Tens. If you just want to know how to find sites that will link to your Web site, read Chapter 15. If you need to understand the principles behind getting links to your site, read Chapter 14. If all you need is to figure out what keywords are important to your site, Chapter 5 is for you.

However, search engine optimization is a pretty complex subject, and all the topics covered in this book are interrelated. Sure, you can register your site with the search engines, but if your pages aren't optimized for the search engines, you may be wasting your time. You can create pages the search engines can read, but if you don't pick the right keywords, it's a total waste of time. So I recommend that you read everything in this book; it will make a huge difference in how well your pages are ranked in the search engines.

Part I: Search Engine Basics

In this part, I provide, yep, the basics — the foundation on which you can build your search engine optimization skills. Which search engines are important, for instance? In fact, what *is* a search engine? What's a *search directory?* And why am I using the term *search system?* In this part, you find out the basics of sensible site creation, discover how to pick the keywords that people are using to find your business, and discover how to do a few quick fixes to your site.

Part II: Building Search Engine–Friendly Sites

Do you have any idea how many sites are invisible to the search engines? Or, if they're not invisible, are built such that search engines can't see the information needed to index the site how the site owners would like?

Well, I don't know an exact number, but I do know that most sites aren't optimized for maximum search engine indexing. If you read Part II, you'll be way ahead of the vast majority of site owners and managers. You discover how to create techniques that search engines like and avoid the ones they hate. You also find out about tricks that some people use — and the dangers involved.

Part III: Adding Your Site to the Indexes and Directories

After you've created your Web site and ensured that the search engines can read the pages, somehow you have to get the *search systems* — the engines and directories — to include your site. That's hard if you don't know what you're doing. In this part, you find out which search systems are important, how to register, and how to find other search engines and directories that are important to your site. You also find out why registering sometimes doesn't work, and what to do about it.

Part IV: After You've Submitted Your Site

Your work isn't over yet. In this part, you find out why links to your site are so important and how to get other sites to link to you. You discover the shopping directories, such as Froogle and Shopping.com. I also explain the multi-billion-dollar search engine advertising business. You find out how to work with the hugely popular Google AdWords, Yahoo! Search Marketing, and MSN adCenter pay per click programs — and how to buy cheaper clicks. You also discover paid placement and other forms of advertising.

Part V: The Part of Tens

All *For Dummies* books have the Part of Tens. In this part, you find ten ways to keep up-to-date with the search engine business. You also find out about ten common mistakes that make Web sites invisible to search engines and ten services and tools that will be useful in your search engine campaign.

Appendix

Don't forget to check out the appendix, where you find information on copyright laws.

Icons Used in This Book

This book, like all *For Dummies* books, uses icons to highlight certain paragraphs and to alert you to particularly useful information. Here's a rundown of what those icons mean:

A Tip icon means I'm giving you an extra snippet of information that may help you on your way or provide some additional insight into the concepts being discussed.

The Remember icon points out information that is worth committing to memory.

The Technical Stuff icon indicates geeky stuff that you can skip if you really want to, although you may want to read it if you're the kind of person who likes to have the background info.

The Warning icon helps you stay out of trouble. It's intended to grab your attention to help you avoid a pitfall that may harm your Web site or business.

Don't forget to visit the Web sites associated with this book. At www.dummies.com/go/searchoptimization, you find all the links in this book (so you don't have to type them!), as well as a Bonus Chapter on how to power up your search engine skills. At www.SearchEngineBulletin.com, you find the aforementioned links along with additional useful information that didn't make it into the book.

Part I
Search Engine Basics

The 5th Wave   By Rich Tennant

"Well, heck — all the boy did was launch a search on the Web and up comes Tracy's retainer, your car keys, and my bowling trophy here on a site in Seattle!"

In this part . . .

The basics of search engine optimization are surprisingly, um, basic. In fact, you may be able to make small changes to your Web site that make a huge difference in your site's ranking in the search results.

This part starts with the basics. I begin by explaining which search engines are important. You may have heard the names of dozens of sites and heard that, in fact, hundreds of search engines exist. You'll be happy to hear that the vast majority of search results are provided by no more than four systems, and over 60 percent of all search results come from a single company, Google.

You also discover how to make some quick and easy changes to your Web site that may fix serious search engine problems for you. Comparatively, you may discover a significant (and common) problem in your site that must be resolved before you have any chance of getting into the search engines at all, let alone ranking well.

This part of the book also includes basic information on how to create a Web site that works well for both visitors and search engines, and you find out about one of the most important first steps you can take: carrying out a detailed keyword analysis.

Chapter 1

Surveying the Search Engine Landscape

In This Chapter

▶ Discovering where people search

▶ Understanding the difference between search sites and search systems

▶ Distilling thousands of search sites down to four search systems

▶ Understanding how search engines work

▶ Gathering tools and basic knowledge

*Y*ou've got a problem. You want people to visit your Web site; that's the purpose, after all — to bring people to your site to buy your product, or find out about your service, or hear about the cause you support, or for whatever other purpose you've built the site. So you've decided you need to get traffic from the search engines — not an unreasonable conclusion, as you find out in this chapter. But there are *so many* search engines! You have the obvious ones — Google, AOL, Yahoo!, and MSN — but you've probably also heard of others: HotBot, Dogpile, Ask.com, Netscape, EarthLink — even Amazon provides its A9 Web search box on many pages. There's also Lycos, InfoSpace, Mamma.com, and WebCrawler.

To top it all off, you've seen advertising asserting that for only $49.95 (or $19.95, or $99.95, or whatever sum seems to make sense to the advertiser), you, too, can have your Web site listed in hundreds, nay, thousands of search engines. You may have even used some of these services, only to discover that the flood of traffic you were promised turns up missing.

Well, I've got some good news. You can forget almost all the names I just listed — well, at least you can after you read this chapter. The point of this chapter is to take a complicated landscape of thousands of search sites and whittle it down into the small group of search systems that really matter. (Search sites? Search systems? Don't worry; I explain the distinction in a moment.)

If you really want to, you can jump to the "Where Do People Search" section (near the end of the chapter) to see the list of search systems you need to worry about and ignore the details. But I've found that when I give this list to someone, he or she looks at me like I'm crazy because they know that some popular search sites aren't on the list. This chapter explains why.

Investigating Search Engines and Directories

The term *search engine* has become the predominant term for *search system* or *search site,* but before reading any farther, you need to understand the different types of search, um, thingies that you're going to run across. Basically, you need to know about four thingies.

Search indexes or search engines

Search indexes or engines are the predominant type of search tools you'll run across. Originally, the term *search engine* referred to some kind of search index, a huge database containing information from individual Web sites.

Large search-index companies own thousands of computers that use software known as *spiders* or *robots* (or just plain *bots*) to grab Web pages and read the information stored in them. These systems don't always grab all the information on each page or all the pages in a Web site, but they grab a significant amount of information and use complex *algorithms* — calculations based on complicated formulae — to index that information. Google, shown in Figure 1-1, is the world's most popular search engine, closely followed by Yahoo! and MSN Live Search.

Index envy

Late in 2005, Yahoo! (www.yahoo.com) claimed that its index contained information for about 20 billion pages, along with almost 2 billion images and 50 million audio and video pages. Google (www.google.com) used to actually state on its home page how many pages it indexed — they reached 15 billion or so at one point — but decided not to play the "mine is bigger than yours" game with Yahoo!.

Figure 1-1:
Google, the world's most popular search engine, produced these results.

Search directories

A *search directory* is a categorized collection of information *about* Web *sites* instead of containing information *from* Web *pages*.

The most significant search directories are owned by Yahoo! (`dir.yahoo.com`) and the Open Directory Project (`www.dmoz.org`). (You can see an example of Open Directory Project information, displayed in Google — `dir.google.com` — in Figure 1-2.) Directory companies don't use spiders or bots to download and index pages on the Web sites in the directory; rather, for each Web site, the directory contains information, such as a title and description, submitted by the site owner. The two most important directories, Yahoo! and Open Directory, have staff members who examine all the sites in the directory to make sure they're placed into the correct categories and meet certain quality criteria. Smaller directories often accept sites based on the owners' submission, with little verification.

Here's how to see the difference between Yahoo!'s search results and the Yahoo! directory:

1. **Go to** `www.yahoo.com`.

2. **Type a word into the Search box.**

Figure 1-2:
Google also
has a
search
directory,
but it
doesn't
create the
directory
itself; it gets
it from the
Open
Directory
Project.

3. **Click the Search button.**

   The list of Web sites that appears is called the Yahoo! Search results.

4. **Look for Directory above the Search box.**

   Above the Search box you'll see either a <u>Directory</u> link or a <u>More</u> link that opens a drop-down menu with the Directory option inside the menu; either way, click Directory and you'll end up in Yahoo! directory. (You can also go directly to the directory by using `dir.yahoo.com`.)

Non-spidered indexes

I wasn't sure what to call these things, so I made up a name: *non-spidered indexes*. A number of small indexes, less important than major indexes (such as Google), don't use spiders to examine the full contents of each page in the index. Rather, the index contains background information about each page, such as titles, descriptions, and keywords. In some cases, this information comes from the meta tags pulled off the pages in the index. (I tell you about meta tags in Chapter 2.) In other cases, the person who enters the site into the index provides this information. A number of the smaller systems discussed in Chapter 12 are of this type.

Pay-per-click systems

Some systems provide *pay-per-click* listings. Advertisers place small ads into the systems, and when users perform their searches, the results contain some of these sponsored listings, typically above and to the right of the free listings. Pay-per-click systems are discussed in more detail in Chapter 18.

Keeping the terms straight

Here are a few additional terms that you'll see scattered throughout the book:

- ✔ **Search site:** This Web site lets you search through some kind of index or directory of Web sites, or perhaps both an index and directory. (In some cases, search sites known as *meta indexes* allow you to search through multiple indices.) Google.com, AOL.com, and EarthLink.com are all search sites. Dogpile.com and Mamma.com are meta-index search sites.

- ✔ **Search system:** This organization possesses a combination of software, hardware, and people that index or categorize Web sites — they build the index or directory you search through at a search site. The distinction is important because a search site might not actually own a search index or directory. For instance, Google is a search system — it displays results from the index that it creates for itself — but AOL.com and EarthLink.com aren't. In fact, if you search at AOL.com or EarthLink.com you actually get Google search results.

  Google and the Open Directory Project provide search results to hundreds of search sites. In fact, most of the world's search sites get their search results from elsewhere; see Figure 1-3.

Figure 1-3: Look carefully, and you'll see that many search sites get their search results from other search systems.

- **Search term:** This is the word, or words, that someone types into a search engine when looking for information.

- **Search results:** Results are the information (the results of your search term) returned to you when you go to a search site and search for something. As just explained, in many cases the search results you see don't come from the search site you're using, but from some other search system.

- **Natural search results:** A link to a Web page can appear on a search results page two ways: The search engine may place it on the page because the site owner paid to be there (pay-per-click ads), or it may pull the page from its index because it thinks the page matches the search term well. These free placements are often known as *natural search results;* you'll also hear the term *organic search results* and sometimes even *algorithmic search results*.

- **Search engine optimization (SEO):** Search engine optimization (also known as *SEO*) refers to "optimizing" Web sites and Web pages to rank well in the search engines — the subject of this book, of course.

Why bother with search engines?

Why bother using search engines for your marketing? Because search engines represent the single most important source of new Web site visitors.

You may have heard that most Web site visits begin at a search engine. Well, this isn't true, though many people continue to use these outdated statistics because they sound good — "80 percent of all Web site visitors reach the site through a search engine," for instance. However, in 2003, that claim was finally put to rest. The number of search-originated site visits dropped below the 50 percent mark. Most Web site visitors reach their destinations by either typing a *URL* — a Web address — into their browsers and going there directly or by clicking a link on another site that takes them there. Most visitors don't reach their destinations by starting at the search engines.

However, search engines are still extremely important for a number of reasons:

- The proportion of visits originating at search engines is still significant. Sure, it's not 80 percent, but with billions of searches each month, it's still a lot of traffic.

- According to a report by comScore, published in March of 2008, Internet users in the United States carry out almost 10 billion searches a month at the major search engines.

✔ comScore also reported that in August of 2007, 750 million people around the world carried out a total of 61 billion searches on the world's top search sites; that's almost three searches every day by 10 percent of the world's population.

✔ Of the visits that don't originate at a search engine, a large proportion are revisits — people who know exactly where they want to go. This isn't new business; it's repeat business. Most *new* visits come through the search engines — that is, search engines are the single most important source of new visitors to Web sites.

✔ It's also been well established for a number of years that most people researching a purchase begin their research at the search engines.

✔ Search engines represent an inexpensive way to reach people. Generally, you get more bang for your buck going after free search engine traffic than almost any other form of advertising or marketing.

Here's an example. One client of mine, selling construction equipment to the tune of $10,000 a month, rebuilt his site and began a combined natural-search and paid-search campaign, boosting sales to $700,000 a month in less than two years. It's hard to imagine how he could have grown his company, with relatively little investment, so quickly without the search engines!

Where Do People Search?

You can search for Web sites at many places. Literally thousands of sites, in fact, provide the ability to search the Web. (What you may not realize, however, is that many sites search only a small subset of the World Wide Web.)

However, *most* searches are carried out at a small number of search sites. How do the world's most popular search sites rank? That depends on how you measure popularity:

✔ Percentage of site visitors *(audience reach)*

✔ Total number of visitors

✔ Total number of searches carried out at a site

✔ Total number of hours visitors spend searching at the site

Each measurement provides a slightly different ranking. Although all provide a similar picture with the same sites generally appearing on the list, some are in slightly different positions.

The following list runs down the world's most popular search sites, based on one month of searches during August of 2007 — almost 8 billion searches — according to a Nielsen/NetRatings study. These statistics are for U.S. Internet users:

Google.com   53.6%

Yahoo.com   19.9%

MSN.com   12.9%

AOL.com   5.6%

Ask.com   1.7%

My Web Search   0.9%

BellSouth Search   0.5%

Comcast Search   0.4%

My Way   0.4%

SBC Yellow Pages Search   0.4%

Remember: This is a list of search sites, not search systems. In some cases, the sites own their own systems. Google provides its own search results, but AOL doesn't. (AOL gets its results from Google.) My Web Search is a meta-search engine getting results from Google, Yahoo!, and Ask.com.

The fact that some sites get results from other search systems means two things:

- ✔ **The numbers in the preceding list are somewhat misleading.** They suggest that Google has around 54 percent of all searches. But Google also feeds AOL its results — add AOL's searches to Google's, and you have 59.6 percent of all searches. Additionally, Google feeds Comcast and BellSouth (another 0.9 percent combined, according to NetRatings). Furthermore, My Web Search is a meta-search engine; therefore, if you search at My Web Search, you see results from Google, Yahoo!, MSN Live Search, and Ask.

- ✔ **You can ignore some of these systems.** At present, and for the foreseeable future, you don't need to worry about AOL.com. Even though it's one of the world's top search sites, you can forget about it. Sure, keep it in the back of your mind, but as long as you remember that Google feeds AOL, you need to worry about Google only.

Now reexamine the preceding list of the world's most important search sites and see what you can remove to get closer to a list of sites you care about. Check out Table 1-1 for the details.

Table 1-1	The Top Search Sites	
Search Site	*Keep It On the List?*	*Description*
Google.com	Yes	The big kid on the block. Lots of people search the Google index on its own search site, *and* it feeds many sites. Obviously, Google has to stay on the list.
Yahoo.com	Yes	Yahoo! is obviously a large, important site; keep it.
MSN.com (MSN Live Search)	Yes	Ditto; MSN Live Search creates its own index, and gets many searches.
AOL.com	No	Fuggetaboutit — AOL gets search results from Google (although it manipulates their appearance) and from the Open Directory Project.
Ask.com (previously known as AskJeeves.com)	Yes	It has its own search engine and feeds some other systems — MyWay, Lycos, and Excite. Keep it, though it's small.
MyWebSearch.com	No	This system simply searches through other systems' search indexes (Google, Yahoo!, and Ask). Forget it.
BellSouth Search	No	Results come from Google.
Comcast Search	No	Again, results come from Google, so forget it.
MyWay.com	No	MyWay uses data from Ask, so forget about it.
SBC Yellow Pages	No	These results come from the Yellow Pages, something we talk about in Chapter 13. For now, we can forget about this.

Based on the information in Table 1-1, you can whittle down your list of systems to four: Google, Yahoo!, MSN Live Search, and Ask. The top three search systems are all very important, with a small follower, Ask, which provides results to many smaller search sites. There's one more system I want to add to these four systems, though. Very few people search at the Open Directory Project (www.dmoz.org). However, this directory system feeds data to hundreds of search sites, including Google and AOL.

To summarize, five important systems are left:

- ✔ Google
- ✔ Yahoo!
- ✔ MSN Live Search
- ✔ Ask
- ✔ Open Directory Project

That's not so bad, is it? You've just gone from thousands of sites to five. Note, by the way, that the top three positions may shift around a little. Google had already lost a large proportion of its share (when I wrote the first edition of this book, Google had around three-quarters of the market— now it's probably a little over one-half), and then regained about 8 percent of the market between the second and third editions of this book.

Of course we may soon see some real changes in this profile. Microsoft is trying to buy Yahoo! If it succeeds, it seems likely that the two search indexes will be merged at some point. (After all, the main point of the proposed merger is to share — and thus cut — costs.)

Then there's Ask.com, which recently announced that it was no longer going head to head with Google — years of trying to gain market share got them nowhere — and was planning to focus on the search needs of married women. Perhaps more significantly, there are rumors that Ask may stop managing its own search index — and use Google's! Ask already uses Google's Pay Per Click ads (see Chapter 18), so extending its partnership with Google wouldn't be such a surprise. So, who knows, we may soon see just two major search indexes: the Yahoo!/MSN index and the Google/Ask/and-everything-else index.

Now, some of you may be thinking, "Aren't you missing some sites? What happened to HotBot, Mamma.com, WebCrawler, Lycos, and all the other systems that were so well known a few years ago?" A lot of them have disappeared or have turned over a new leaf and are pursuing other opportunities.

For example, Northern Light, a system well known in the late 1990s, now sells search software. And in the cases where the search sites are still running, they're generally fed by other search systems. Mamma.com, Dogpile, and MetaCrawler get search results from the top four systems, for instance, and HotBot gets results from MSN Live Search and LyGo, a new service from Lycos.

AltaVista, the first big search index, is now owned by Yahoo! and is really just a different Web design displaying Yahoo! search results. The same goes for AllTheWeb, for the geeks among you who remember it. If the search site you remember isn't mentioned here, it's either out of business, being fed by someone else, or simply not important in the big scheme of things.

When you find a new search system, look carefully on the page near the search box, or on the search results page — perhaps at the bottom of the page in the copyright message — and you may find where the search results are coming from.

You'll also want to work with some other search systems, as you find out in Chapters 12 and 13. In some cases, you need to check out specialty directories and indexes related to the industry in which your Web site operates, or submit your site to Web directories in order to build links back to your site. But the preceding systems are the important ones for every Web site.

Google alone provides well over 60 percent of all search results (down from 75 percent just a year or two ago). Get into *all* the systems on the preceding list, and you're in front of probably more than 96 percent of all searchers. Well, perhaps you're in front of them. You have a chance of being in front of them, anyway, if your site ranks highly (which is what this book is all about).

Search Engine Magic

Go to Google and search for the term *personal injury lawyer*. Then look at the blue bar below the Google logo, and you see something like this:

```
Results 1 - 10 of about 19,800,000 for personal injury
          lawyer
```

This means Google has found almost 20 million pages that contain these three words. Yet, somehow, it has managed to rank the pages. It's decided that one particular page should appear first, and then another, and then another, and so on, all the way down to page 19,800,000. (By the way, this has to be one of the wonders of the modern world: Search engines have tens of thousands of computers, evaluating 20 billion pages or more, and returning the information in a fraction of a second.)

How do they do it?

How on earth does Google do it? How does it evaluate and compare pages? How do other search engines do the same? Well, I don't know *exactly*. Search engines don't want you to know how they work (or it would be too easy to create pages that exactly match the search system, "giving them what they want to see"). But I can explain the general concept.

When Google searches for your search term, it begins by looking for pages containing the exact phrase. Then it starts looking for pages containing the words close together. Then it looks for pages that have the pages scattered around. This isn't necessarily the order in which a search engine shows you pages; in some cases, pages with words close together (but not the exact phrase) appear higher than pages with the exact phrase, for instance. That's because search engines evaluate pages according to a variety of criteria.

Search engines look at many factors. They look for the words throughout the page, both in the visible page and in the HTML source code for the page. Each time they find the words, they are *weighted* in some way. A word in one position is worth more than a word in another position. A word formatted in one way is worth more than a word formatted in another. (You read more about this in Chapter 5.)

There's more, though. Search engines also look at links pointing to pages, and use those links to evaluate the referenced pages: How many links are there? How many are from popular sites? What words are in the link text? You read more about this in Chapters 14 and 15.

Stepping into the programmers' shoes

There's a lot of conflicting information out there about SEO. Some of it's good, some of it's not so good, and some of it's downright wrong. When evaluating a claim about what search engines do, I sometimes find it useful to step into the shoes of the people building the search engines; I try to think, "what would make sense" from the perspective of the programmers who write the code that evaluates all these pages.

Consider this: Say, you search for *personal injury lawyer*, and the search engine finds one page with the term in the page's title (between the <TITLE> and </TITLE> tags, which you read more about in Chapters 2 and 6), and another page with the term somewhere deep in the page text. Which do you think is likely to match the search term better? If the text is in the title, doesn't that indicate that page is likely to be, in some way, related to the term? If the text is deep in the body of the page, couldn't it mean that the page isn't directly related to the term, that it's related to it in some incidental or peripheral manner?

Considering SEO from this point of view makes it easier to understand how search engines try to evaluate and compare pages. If the keywords are in the links pointing to the page, the page must be relevant to those keywords; if the keywords are in headings on the page, that must be significant; if the keywords appear frequently throughout the page, rather than just once, that must mean something. Suddenly, it all makes sense.

By the way, in Chapter 7, I discuss things that search engines don't like. You may hear elsewhere all sorts of warnings that may or may not be correct. Here's an example: I've read that using a refresh meta tag to automatically push a visitor from one page to another will get your site penalized, and may even get your site banned from the search engine. You've seen this situation: You land on a page on a Web site, and there's a message saying something like "We'll forward you to page *x* in five seconds, or you can click <u>here</u>." The theory is that search engines don't like this, and they may punish you for doing this.

Now, does this make any sense? Aren't there good reasons to sometimes use such forwarding techniques? Yes, there are. So why would a search engine punish you for doing it? They don't. They probably won't index the page that is forwarding a visitor — based on the quite reasonable theory that if the site doesn't want the visitor to read the page, they don't need to index it — but you're not going to get punished for using it.

Remember that the search engine programmers aren't interested in punishing anyone, they're just trying to make the best choices between billions of pages. Generally, search engines use their "algorithms" to determine how to rank a page, and try to adjust the algorithms to make sure "tricks" are ignored. But they don't want to punish anyone for doing something for which there might be a good reason, even if the technique could also be used as a trick.

What would the programmers do? I like to use this as my "plausibility filter" when I hear someone make some unusual or even outlandish claim about how search engines function.

Gathering Your Tools

You need several tools and skills to optimize and rank your Web site. I talk about a number of these in the appropriate chapters, but I want to cover a few basics before I move on. It goes without saying that you need

- ✔ Basic Internet knowledge
- ✔ A computer connected to the Internet
- ✔ A Web site
- ✔ One of these two things:
  - Good working knowledge of HTML
  - Access to a geek with a good working knowledge of HTML

Which path should you take? If you don't know what HTML means (HyperText Markup Language), you probably need to run out and find that geek. *HTML* is the code used to create Web pages, and you need to understand how to use it to optimize pages. Discussing HTML and how to upload pages to a Web site is beyond the scope of this book. If you're interested in finding out more, check out *HTML 4 For Dummies,* 5th Edition, by Ed Tittel and Mary Burmeister, and *Creating Web Pages For Dummies,* 8th Edition, by Bud E. Smith and Arthur Bebak (both published by Wiley Publishing, Inc.).

✔ Toolbars

Install the Google toolbar in your Web browser . . . and perhaps the Yahoo!, MSN Live Search, and Ask.com toolbars, too. And, maybe, the Alexa toolbar. (Before you complain about spyware, I explain in a few moments.) You may want to use these tools even if you plan to use a geek to work on your site. They're simple to install and open up a completely new view of the Web. The next two sections spell out the details.

Search toolbars

I definitely recommend the Google toolbar, which allows you to begin searching Google without going to the Web site first (if you use the Firefox Web browser, the built-in Search Engine box does the same). You might also want to use the Yahoo!, MSN Live Search, and Ask.com toolbars Additionally, these toolbars have plenty of extras: auto form fillers, tabbed browsing, desktop search, spyware blockers, translators, spell checkers, and so on. I'm not going to describe all these tools, as they aren't directly related to SEO, but they're definitely useful.

You really don't need all of them, but hey, here they are if you really want to experiment. You can find these toolbars here:

✔ toolbar.google.com

✔ toolbar.yahoo.com

✔ toolbar.msn.com

✔ toolbar.ask.com

Unfortunately, all these toolbars require Microsoft Windows and the Internet Explorer browser or Firefox browser (the MSN toolbar only works in Internet Explorer); that's most of you but, I realize, not all. You can see the Google and Yahoo! toolbars, along with the Alexa toolbar (at the bottom left of the browser window), in Figure 1-4. Don't worry; you don't have to have all this clutter on your screen all the time. Right-click a blank space on any toolbar, and you can add and remove toolbars temporarily; simply open a toolbar when you need it. I leave the Google toolbar on all the time, and open the others now and then.

Figure 1-4:
The toolbars provide useful information for search engine campaigns; the Google bar's PageRank button is shown open.

TIP

One thing I do find frustrating about these systems is the pop-up blockers. Yes, they can be helpful, but often they block pop-up windows that I want to see; if you find that you click a link and it doesn't open, try Ctrl+clicking (which may temporarily disable the pop-up blocker), or disable the blocker on the toolbar.

I refer to the Google toolbar here and there throughout this book because it provides you with the following useful features:

✔ A way to search Google without going to `www.google.com` first

✔ A quick view of the Google PageRank, an important metric that I explain in Chapter 14

✔ A quick way to see if a Web page is already indexed by Google

✔ A quick way to see some of the pages linking to a Web page

TIP

Geek or no geek

Many readers of this book's first edition are business people who don't plan to do the search engine work themselves (or, in some cases, realize that it's a lot of work and need to find someone with more time or technical skills to do the work). However, having read the book, they understand far more about search engines and are in a better position to find and direct someone. As one reader-cum-client told me, "There's a lot of snake oil in this business," so his reading helped him understand the basics and ask the right questions of search engine optimization firms.

The Google toolbar has a number of other useful features, but the preceding features are the most useful for the purposes of this book. Turn on the PageRank button after installing the toolbar:

1. **Click the Settings button, and then choose Options from the menu that appears.**

2. **Click the More tab in the Toolbar Options dialog box.**

3. **Enable the PageRank and Page Info check box and click OK.**

Alexa toolbar

Alexa is a company owned by Amazon.com, and a partner with Google and Microsoft. It's been around a long time, and millions of people around the world use it. Every time someone uses the toolbar — Sparky, as it's now known — to visit a Web site, the toolbar sends the URL to Alexa, allowing the system to create an enormous database of site visits. The toolbar can provide traffic information to you; you can quickly see how popular a site is and even view a detailed traffic analysis, such as an estimate of the percentage of Internet users who visit the site each month.

Work with the Alexa toolbar for a while, and you'll quickly get a feel for site popularity. A site ranks 453? That's pretty good. 1,987,123? That's a sign that hardly anyone visits the site. In addition, it provides a quick way to find information about who owns the site on which the current page sits, and how many pages link to the current page. You can find the Alexa toolbar (refer to Figure 1-4), at `toolbar.alexa.com`.

I've been criticized for recommending the Alexa toolbar in earlier editions of this book: Some people claim it is spyware. Some anti-spyware programs even search for the toolbar and flag it as spyware, though others don't. As I mention, the toolbar sends the URLs you're visiting. However, Alexa states on the site (and I believe them) that "The Alexa Toolbar contains no advertising and does not profile or target you." I know for sure that it doesn't display ads. Alexa doesn't steal your usernames and passwords, as is occasionally claimed. Alexa does gather information about where you visit, but it doesn't know who you are, so does it matter? Decide for yourself.

Chapter 2

Your One-Hour Search Engine–Friendly Web Site Makeover

A few small changes can make a big difference in your site's position in the search engines. So instead of forcing you to read this entire book before you can get anything done, this chapter helps you identify problems with your site and, with a little luck, shows you how to make a significant difference through quick fixes.

It's possible that you may not make significant progress in a single hour, as the chapter title promises. You may identify serious problems with your site that can't be fixed quickly. Sorry, that's life! The purpose of this chapter is to help you identify a few obvious problems and, perhaps, make some quick fixes with the goal of really getting something done.

Is Your Site Indexed?

It's important to find out whether your site is actually in a search engine or directory. Your site doesn't come up when someone searches at Google for *rodent racing?* Can't find it in the Yahoo! Directory? Have you ever thought that perhaps it simply isn't there? In the next several sections, I explain how to find out if your site is indexed in a few different systems.

Some of the systems into which you want to place your Web site aren't household names. If I mention a search system that you don't recognize, page to Chapter 1 to find out more about it.

Google

I'll start with the behemoth: Google. Here's the quickest and easiest way to see what Google has in its index. Search Google, either at the site or through the Google toolbar (see Chapter 1) for the following:

```
site:domain.com
```

Don't type the `www.` piece, just the domain name. For instance, say your site's domain name is *RodentRacing.com*. You'd search for this:

```
site:rodentracing.com
```

Google returns a list of pages it's found on your site; at the top, on the blue bar, you see something like this:

```
Results 1 - 10 of about 256 from rodentracing.com
```

That's it — quick and easy. You know how many pages Google has indexed on your site, and can even see which pages.

This indexed number can fluctuate greatly — a site that has 350,000 pages indexed today may have 200,000 pages next week; then 300,000, and so on. And it seems that, sometimes, Google has a bug in this search syntax — it returns much lower numbers than it should. Just one of the irritations of the SEO business. In particular Google's index numbers dropped dramatically late in 2007 and early in 2008 for many sites (perhaps most), and then recovered in March of 2008. Sites that had several hundred thousand indexed pages dropped below a hundred thousand, for instance . . . then recovered. These sorts of fluctuations are common (though the one late in 2007 was extreme).

Here's another way to see what's in the index, in this case a particular page in your site. Open your browser and load a page at your site. Then follow these steps:

1. **Click the PageRank button on the Google toolbar.**

   As I suggest in Chapter 1, I'm assuming that you've downloaded the Google toolbar — available at `toolbar.google.com` — and installed it in your browser. If you don't have the toolbar, don't worry; I explain a non-toolbar method in a moment.

2. **Choose Cached Snapshot of Page from the drop-down list that
   appears.**

   If you're lucky, Google loads a page showing you what it has in its cache,
   so you know Google has indexed the page (see Figure 2-1). If you're
   unlucky, Google tells you that it has nothing in the cache for that page.
   That doesn't necessarily mean Google hasn't indexed the page, though.

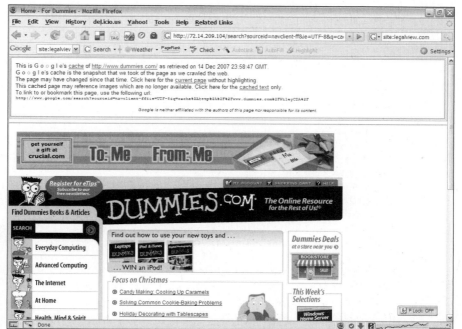

Figure 2-1:
A page
stored in the
Google
cache.

A *cache* is a temporary storage area in which a copy of something is placed.
In the context of the Web, a cache stores a Web page. Google, Yahoo!, MSN
Live Search, and Ask.com keep a copy of many of the pages they index, and
all but Yahoo! even tell you the date that they indexed the cached pages.

If you don't have the Google toolbar, you can instead go to Google
(www.google.com) and type the following into the Google search box:

```
cache:http://yourdomain.com/page.htm
```

Replace *yourdomain.com* with your actual domain name, and *page.htm* with
the actual page name, of course. When you click Search, Google checks to see
if it has the page in its cache.

What if Google doesn't have the page? Does that mean your page isn't in Google? No, not necessarily. Google may not have gotten around to caching it. Sometimes Google grabs a little information from a page but not the entire page.

By the way, you can open a cached page saved by Google, Yahoo!, or MSN Live Search directly from the results page when searching; look for the Cached or Cached Page link after a search result.

You can search for a Web site at Google another way, too. Simply type the domain name into the Google search box and click Search. Google returns just that site's home page at the top of the results. If you want to use the search box on the Google toolbar to do this, type the domain name and then click the binoculars G Search button. (If you type the domain name and press Enter, Google simply redirects your browser to the specified domain name.)

Yahoo! and MSN Live Search

And now, here's a bonus. The search syntax I used to see what Google had in its index for RodentRacing.com — `site:rodentracing.com` — not only works on Google, but also on Yahoo! and MSN Live Search. That's right, type the same thing into any of these search sites and you see how many pages on the Web site are in the index — with one caveat. MSN Live Search's results are a little flaky. For instance, it may show, say 750 results, but as you move through the results pages MSN Live Search then shows a different number, 546 perhaps. Sometimes that number increases, sometimes it decreases. MSN Live Search has been acting like this for years, so it may — or may not — be fixed at some point.

Yahoo! Directory

You must check whether your site is listed in the Yahoo! Directory. You have to pay to get a commercial site into the Yahoo! Directory, so you may already know if you're listed there. Perhaps you work in a large company and suspect that another employee may have registered the site with Yahoo!. Here's how to find out:

1. **Point your browser to** `dir.yahoo.com`.

   This takes you directly to the Yahoo! Directory search page.

2. **Type your site's domain name into the Search text box.**

   All you need is *yourdomain.com*, not `http://www.` or anything else.

3. **Ensure that the Directory option button is selected, and then click Search.**

   If your site is in the Yahoo! Directory, your site's information appears on the results page. You may see several pages, one for each category in which the site has been placed (though in most cases a site is placed into only one category).

Open Directory Project

You should also know if your site is listed in the Open Directory Project (www.dmoz.org). This is a large directory of Web sites, actually owned by AOL although volunteer run; it's very important, because its data is "syndicated" to many different Web sites, providing you with many links back to your site (you find out about the importance of links in Chapter 14).

If your site isn't in the directory, it should be. Just type the domain name, without the www. piece. If your site is in the index, the Open Directory Project will tell you. If it isn't, you'd better register it; see Chapter 12.

Taking Action If You're Not Listed

First, if your site isn't in Yahoo! Directory or the Open Directory Project, you have to go to those systems and register your site. See Chapter 12 for information. What if you search for your site in the search engines and can't find it? If the site isn't in Google, Yahoo!, and MSN Live Search, you have a huge problem.

Here are two possible reasons your site isn't being indexed in the search engines:

✔ **The search engines haven't found your site yet.** The solution is relatively easy, though you won't get it done in an hour.

✔ **The search engines have found your site, but can't index it.** This is a serious problem, though in some cases you can fix it quickly.

For the lowdown on getting your pages indexed in search engines — to ensure that the search engines can find your site — see the section, "Getting Your Site Indexed," later in this chapter. To find out how to make your pages search engine–friendly — to ensure that when found, your site will be indexed well — check out the upcoming "Examining Your Pages" section. But first, let's see how to check if your site *can* be indexed.

Is your site invisible?

Some Web sites are virtually invisible. A search engine might be able to find the site (by following a link, for instance). But when it gets to the site, it can't read it or, perhaps, can read only parts of it. A client of mine, for instance (before he was a client), built a Web site that had only three visible pages; all the other pages, including those with product information, were invisible.

How does a Web site become invisible? I talk about this subject in more detail in Chapter 7, but here's a brief explanation:

- ✔ The site is using some kind of navigation structure that search engines can't read, so they can't find their way through the site.
- ✔ The site is creating dynamic pages that search engines choose not to read.

Unreadable navigation

Many sites have perfectly readable pages, with the exception that the *searchbots* — the programs search engines use to index Web sites — can't negotiate the site navigation. The searchbots can reach the home page, index it, and read it, but they can't go any farther. If, when you search Google for your pages, you find only the home page, this is likely the problem.

Why can't the searchbots find their way through? The navigation system may have been created by using JavaScript, and because search engines ignore JavaScript, they don't find the links in the script. Look at this example:

```
<SCRIPT TYPE="javascript" SRC="/menu/menu.js"></SCRIPT>
```

In one site I reviewed, this was how the navigation bar was placed into each page: The page called an external JavaScript, held in menu.js in the menu subdirectory. Search engines won't read menu.js, so they'll never read the links in the script.

Try these simple ways to help search engines find their way around your site, whether or not your navigation structure is hidden:

- ✔ **Create more text links throughout the site.** Many Web sites have a main navigation structure and then duplicate the structure by using simple text links at the bottom of the page. You should do the same.
- ✔ **Add a sitemap page to your site.** This page contains links to most or all of the pages on your Web site. Of course, you also want to link to the sitemap page from those little links at the bottom of the home page.

Dealing with dynamic pages

In many cases, the problem is that the site is *dynamic* — that is, a page is created on the fly when a browser requests it. The data is pulled from a database, pasted into a Web page template, and sent to the user's browser. Search engines sometimes won't read such pages (though this is nowhere near as serious a problem as it was a few years ago), for a variety of reasons explained in detail in Chapter 7.

How can you tell if this is a problem? Take a look at the URL in the browser's location bar. Suppose that you see something like this:

```
http://www.yourdomain.edu/rodent-racing-
          scores/march/index.php
```

This address is okay. It's a simple URL path made up of a domain name, two directory names, and a filename. Now look at this one:

```
http://www.yourdomain.edu/rodent-racing/scores.php?prg=1
```

The filename ends with `?prg=1`. This *parameter* is being sent to the server to let it know what information is needed for the Web page. If you have URLs like this, with just a single parameter, they're probably okay, especially for Google; however, a few smaller search engines may not like them. Here's another example:

```
http://yourdomain.com/products/index.html?&DID=18&CATID=13
          &ObjectGroup_ID=79
```

This one may be a real problem, depending on the search engine. This URL has too much weird stuff after the filename:

```
?&DID=18&CATID=13&ObjectGroup_ID=79
```

That's three parameters — `DID=18`, `CATID=13`, and `ObjectGroup_ID=79` — and that's too many. Some systems *cannot* or *will not* index this page. (My feeling is that Google tends to index "deeper" into dynamic sites than, for instance, Yahoo!.)

Another problem is caused by *session IDs* — URLs that are different every time the page is displayed. Look at this example:

```
http://yourdomain.com/buyAHome.do;jsessionid=07D3CCD4D9A6A
          9F3CF9CAD4F9A728F44
```

Each time someone visits this site, the server assigns a special ID number to the visitor. That means the URL is never the same, so Google won't index it.

Search engines may choose not to index pages with session IDs. If the search engine sees links to a page that appears to have a session ID, it doesn't know whether the URL changes between sessions or whether many different URLs point to the same page. Search engines don't want to overload the site's server and don't want garbage in their indexes.

If you have a clean URL with no parameters, the search engines should be able to get to it. If you have a single parameter in the URL, it's probably fine. Two parameters may not be a problem, although they're more likely to be a problem than a single parameter. Three parameters may be a problem with some search engines. If you think you have a problem, I suggest reading Chapter 7.

Picking Good Keywords

Getting search engines to recognize and index your Web site can be a problem, as the first part of this chapter makes clear. Another huge problem — one that has little or nothing to do with the technological limitations of search engines — is that many companies have no idea what *keywords* (the words people are using at search engines to search for Web sites) they should be using. They try to *guess* the appropriate keywords, without knowing what people are really using in search engines.

In Chapter 5, I explain keywords in detail, but here's how to do a quick keyword analysis:

1. **Point your browser to** `https://adwords.google.com/select/KeywordToolExternal`.

    You see the Google AdWords Keyword Tool. AdWords is Google's PPC (pay per click) division. See Chapter 18 for more about PPC.

2. **In the search box, type a keyword you think people may use to search for your products or services.**

3. **In the *captcha,* or challenge-response box, type the security word shown.**

4. **Click the Get Keyword Ideas button.**

    The tool returns a list of keywords, showing you how often that term and related terms are used by people searching on Google and partner sites. See Figure 2-2.

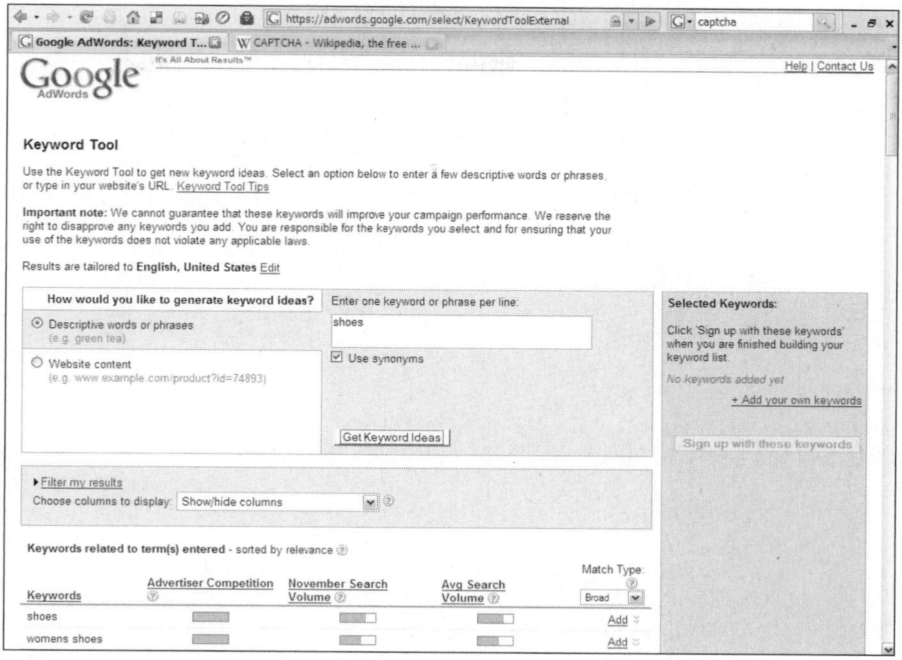

Figure 2-2:
The Google
AdWords
Keyword
Tool
provides a
quick way
to check
keywords.

You may find that the keyword you guessed is perfect. Or you may discover better words, or, even if your guess was good, find several other great keywords. A detailed keyword analysis almost always turns up keywords or keyword phrases you need to know about.

Don't spend a lot of time on this task. See if you can come up with some useful keywords in a few minutes and then move on; see Chapter 5 for details about this process.

Examining Your Pages

Making your Web pages "search engine–friendly" was probably not uppermost in your mind when you sat down to design your Web site. That means your Web pages — and the Web pages of millions of others — probably have a few problems in the search engine–friendly category. Fortunately, such problems are pretty easy to spot; you can fix some of them quickly, but others are more troublesome.

Using frames

In order to examine your pages for problems, you need to read the pages' source code; remember, I said you'd need to be able to understand HTML! In order to see the source code, choose View➪Source in your browser.

When you first peek at the source code for your site, you may discover that your site is using frames. (Of course, if you built the site yourself, you already know whether it uses frames. However, you may be examining a site built by someone else.) You may see something like this in the page:

```
<HTML>
<HEAD>
</HEAD>
    <FRAMESET ROWS="20%,80%">
        <FRAME SRC="navbar.html">
        <FRAME SRC="content.html">
    </FRAMESET>
<BODY>
</BODY>
</HTML>
```

When you choose View➪Source or View➪Page Source in your browser, you're viewing the source of the *frame-definition document,* which tells the browser how to set up the frames. In the preceding example, the browser creates two frame rows, one taking up the top 20 percent of the browser and the other taking up the bottom 80 percent. In the top frame, the browser places content taken from the `navbar.html` file; content from `content.html` goes into the bottom frame.

Framed sites don't index well. The pages in the internal frames get *orphaned* in search engines; each page ends up in search results alone, without the navigation frames with which they were intended to be displayed.

Framed sites are bad news for many reasons. I discuss frames in more detail in Chapter 7, but here are a few quick fixes:

✔ Add `TITLE` and `DESCRIPTION` tags between the `<HEAD>` and `</HEAD>` tags. (To see what these tags are and how they can help with your frame issues, check out the next two sections.)

✔ Add `<NOFRAMES>` and `</NOFRAMES>` tags between the `<BODY>` and `</BODY>` tags, and place 200 to 300 words of keyword-rich content between the tags. The `NOFRAMES` text is designed to be displayed by browsers that can't work with frames, and search engines will read this text, although they won't rate it as high as normal text (because many designers have used `NOFRAMES` tags as a trick to get more keywords into a Web site, and because the `NOFRAMES` text is almost never seen these days, as almost no users have browsers that don't work with frames).

✔ Include a number of links, in the text between the NOFRAMES tags, to other pages in your site to help search engines find their way through.

Looking at the TITLE tags

TITLE tags tell a browser what text to display in the browser's title bar, and they're very important to search engines. Quite reasonably, search engines figure that the TITLE tags may indicate the page's title — and therefore, its subject.

Open your site's home page and then choose View⇨Source in your browser to see the page source. A window opens, showing you what the page's HTML looks like. Here's what you should see at the top of the page:

```
<HTML>
<HEAD>
<TITLE>Your title text is here</TITLE>
```

Here are a few problems you may have with your TITLE tags:

✔ **They're not there.** Many pages simply don't have TITLE tags. If not, you're not giving the search engines one of the most important pieces of information about the page's subject matter.

✔ **They're in the wrong position.** Sometimes you find the TITLE tags, but they're way down in the page. If they're too low in the page, search engines may not find them.

✔ **There are *two* sets.** Now and then I see sites that have two sets of title tags on each page; in this case, the search engines will probably read the first and ignore the second.

✔ **They're there, but they're poor.** The TITLE tags don't contain the proper keywords.

Your TITLE tags should be immediately below the <HEAD> tag and should contain useful keywords. Have around 40 to 60 characters between the <TITLE> and </TITLE> tags (including spaces) and, perhaps, repeat the primary keywords once. If you're working on your Rodent Racing Web site, for example, you might have something like this:

```
<TITLE>Rodent Racing Info. Rats, Mice, Gerbils, Stoats,
          all kinds of Rodent Racing</TITLE>
```

Find out more about keywords in Chapter 5.

Examining the DESCRIPTION tag

The DESCRIPTION tag is important because search engines often index it (under the reasonable assumption that the description describes the contents of the page) and, in many cases, may use the DESCRIPTION tag to provide the site description on the search results page.

Different search engines use the DESCRIPTION tag in different ways; in fact, the search engine giant, Google, has changed the way in which it uses the DESCRIPTION tag.

A while back Google wasn't using the DESCRIPTION tag to provide the description in the search results. Instead, it typically found the search words in the page, grabbed a snippet of information from around the words, and used that as the description. Starting sometime in 2007, though, Google changed this and began working with the DESCRIPTION tag. These seem to be the rules:

1. If all the keywords you search for are found in the DESCRIPTION tag, then the description shown in the search results page comes from the DESCRIPTION tag.

2. If some of the keywords are in the DESCRIPTION tag, then part of the DESCRIPTION tag is used and the rest of the search results come from within the page.

3. If none of the keywords are in the DESCRIPTION tag, then the DESCRIPTION tag isn't used in the search results.

In some cases, Google and MSN Live Search may grab the description from the Open Directory Project, while Yahoo! may use the description from the Yahoo! Directory.

Open a Web page, and then open the HTML source (select View↷Source from your browser's menu), and take a quick look at the DESCRIPTION tag. It should look something like this:

```
<META NAME="description" CONTENT="your description goes
        here">
```

Sites often have the same problems with DESCRIPTION tags as they do with TITLE tags. The tags aren't there, are hidden away deep down in the page, are sometimes duplicated, or simply aren't very good.

Place the DESCRIPTION tag immediately below the TITLE tags (see Figure 2-3) and create a keyworded description of up to 250 characters (again, including spaces). Here's an example:

```
<META NAME="description" CONTENT="Rodent Racing - Scores,
       Schedules, everything Rodent Racing. Whether
       you're into mouse racing, stoat racing, rats,
       or gerbils, our site provides everything you'll
       ever need to know about Rodent Racing and
       caring for your racers.">
```

Figure 2-3:
A clean
start to your
Web page,
showing the
TITLE and
DESCRIP
TION tags.

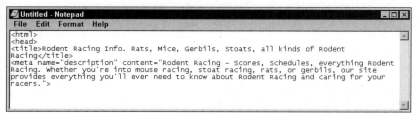

Sometimes Web developers switch the attributes in the tag, putting the
CONTENT= before the NAME=, like this:

```
<META CONTENT="your description goes here"
       NAME="description">
```

Make sure that your tags do *not* switch the tag attributes. I don't know if the
order of the attributes causes a problem for Google or the other big search
engines (probably not), but it does confuse some smaller systems. There's no
reason to do it, so don't.

Giving search engines something to read

You don't necessarily have to pick through the HTML code for your Web page
to evaluate how search engine–friendly it is. You can find out a lot just by
looking at the Web page in the browser. Determine whether you have any text
on the page. Page *content* — text that search engines can read — is essential,
but many Web sites don't have any page content on the front page and often
have little or any on interior pages. Here are some potential problems:

✔ Having a (usually pointless) Flash intro on your site

✔ Embedding much of the text on your site into images, rather than relying
on readable text

✔ Banking on flashy visuals to hide the fact that your site is light on content

✔ Using the wrong keywords; Chapter 5 explains how to pick keywords

If you have these types of problems, they can often be time consuming to fix. (Sorry, you may run over the one-hour timetable by several weeks.) The next several sections detail ways you might overcome the problems.

Eliminating Flash

Huh? What's Flash? You've seen those silly animations when you arrive at a Web site, with a little *Skip Intro* link hidden away in the page. Words and pictures appear and disappear, scroll across the pages, and so on. You create these animations with a product called Macromedia Flash.

I suggest that you kill the Flash intro on your site. They don't *hurt* your site in the search engines (unless of course you're removing indexable text and replacing it with Flash), but they don't help either, and I rarely see a Flash intro that actually serves any purpose. In most cases, they're nothing but an irritation to site visitors. (The majority of Flash intros are created because the Web designer likes playing with Flash.)

Replacing images with real text

If you have an image-heavy Web site, in which all or most of the text is embedded onto images, you need to get rid of the images and replace them with real text. If the search engine can't read the text, it can't index it.

It may not be immediately clear whether text on the page is real text or images. You can quickly figure it out a couple of ways:

- ✔ Try to select the text in the browser with your mouse. If it's real text, you can select it character by character. If it's not real text, you simply can't select it — you'll probably end up selecting an image.

- ✔ Right-click the text — if you see menu options, such as Save Image and Copy Image — then you know it's an image, not text.

Using more keywords

The light-content issue can be a real problem. Some sites are designed to be light on content, and sometimes this approach is perfectly valid in terms of design and usability. However, search engines have a bias for content; that is, for text they can read. (I discuss this issue in more depth in Chapter 9.) In general, the more text — with the right keywords — the better.

Using the right keywords in the right places

Suppose that you do have text, and plenty of it. But does the text have the right keywords? The ones discovered with the Google AdWords Keyword Tool earlier in this chapter? It should.

Where keywords are placed and what they look like is also important. Search engines use position and format as clues to importance. Here are a few simple techniques you can use — but don't overdo it!

- ✔ Use particularly important keywords — those that people are using to search for your products and services — near the top of the page.

- ✔ Place keywords into <H> (heading) tags.

- ✔ Use bold and italic keywords; search engines take note of this.

- ✔ Put keywords into bulleted lists; search engines also take note of this.

- ✔ Use keywords multiple times on a page, but don't use a keyword or keyword phrase too often. If your page sounds really clumsy through over-repetition, it may be too much.

Ensure that the links between pages within your site contain keywords. Think about all the sites you've visited recently. How many use links with *no* keywords in them? They use buttons, graphic navigation bars, short little links that you have to guess at, *click here* links, and so on. Big mistakes.

I don't object to using the words *click here* in links. Some writers have suggested that you should never use *click here* because it sounds silly and people know they're supposed to click. I disagree, and research shows that using the words can sometimes increase the number of clicks on a link. The bottom line is that, for search engine purposes, you should rarely, if ever, use a link with only the words *click here* in the link text; you should include keywords in the link.

When you create links, include keywords in the links wherever possible. If, on your rodent-racing site, you're pointing to the scores page, don't create a link that says *To find the most recent rodent racing scores, click here* or, perhaps, *To find the most recent racing scores, go to the scores page*. Instead, get a few more keywords into the links, like this: *To find the most recent racing scores, go to the rodent racing scores page.* That tells the search engine that the referenced page is about *rodent racing scores*.

Getting Your Site Indexed

So your pages are ready, but you still have the indexing problem. Your pages are, to put in bluntly, just *not in the search engine!* How do you fix that problem?

For Yahoo! Directory and the Open Directory Project, you have to go to those sites and register directly, but before doing that, you should read Chapter 12. With Google, Yahoo! Web Search, MSN Live Search, and Ask.com, the process is a little more time consuming and complicated.

The best way to get into the search engines is to have them *find* the pages by following links pointing to the site. In some cases, you can ask or pay the search engines to come to your site and pick up your pages, but you face two main problems with this:

- ✔ If you ask search engines to index your site, they probably won't do it. And if they do come and index your site, it may take weeks or months. Asking them to come to your site is unreliable.

- ✔ If you pay search engines to index your site, you have to pay for every URL you submit. The problem with paying, of course, is that you have to pay.

If you want to submit your site to the search engines for indexing, read Chapter 11, where I provide all the details.

So how do you get indexed? The good news is that you can often get indexed by some of the search engines *very* quickly. I'm not talking about a full-blown link campaign here, with all the advantages I describe in Chapters 14 through 16. You simply want to get search engines — particularly Google, Yahoo!, MSN Live Search, and Ask.com — to pick up the site and index it.

Find another Web site to link to your site, right away. Call several friends, colleagues, and relatives who own or control a Web site, and ask them to link to your site. Of course, you want sites that are already indexed by search engines. The searchbots have to follow the links to your site.

When you ask friends, colleagues, and relatives to link to you, specify what you want the links to say. No *click here* or company name links for you. You want to place keywords into the link text. Something like *Visit this site for all your <u>rodent racing needs - mice, rats, stoats, gerbils, and all other kinds of rodent racing</u>*. Keywords in links are a powerful way to tell a search engine what your site is about.

After the sites have links pointing to yours, it can take from a few days to a few weeks to get into the search engines. With Google, if you place the links right before Googlebot indexes one of the sites, you may be in the index in a few days. I once placed some pages on a client's Web site on a Tuesday and found them in Google (ranked near the top) on Friday. But Google can also take several weeks to index a site. The best way to increase your chances of getting into search engines quickly is to get as many links as you can on as many sites as possible.

You should also create an XML sitemap, submit that to Google, Yahoo!, and MSN Live Search, and add a line in your `robots.txt` file that points to the sitemap so that search systems — such as Ask.com — that don't provide a way for you to submit the sitemap can still find it. You find out all about that in Chapter 11.

Chapter 3

Planning Your Search Engine Strategy

*T*here's much to find out about generating traffic from search engines, and sometimes it's hard to see the forest for the trees. As you discover in this book, there are page optimization and link strategies and index submissions and directory submissions and electronic press releases and blogs and this and that — it goes on and on. Before you jump right in, I need to discuss the big picture (to give you an idea of how all this fits together) and help you decide what you should do when (to help you plan your strategy). In this chapter, I show you how a search engine campaign works overall.

Don't Trust Your Web Designer

Let me start with a warning: Don't rely on your Web designer to manage your SEO project. In fact, I know that many of you are reading this book because you did just that, and have realized the error of your ways.

Here's one of the more egregious cases I've run across. The owner of a small e-commerce store came to me for help; he had paid a Web-design firm $5,000 to build his site, and before beginning he had asked them to make sure that the site was search engine–friendly. Unfortunately, that means different things to different people, and to the design firm it didn't mean much. The site they built definitely was *not* optimized for search engines. The owner asked the firm what it was planning to do about the search engines. They told him it would cost him $5,000.

Big doesn't always equal better

By the way, don't imagine that because you're working with a large Web-design team with extensive programming experience that they understand search engines. In fact, it's sometimes the more sophisticated design teams that get into the most trouble, building complex sites that simply won't work well with search engines. I consult with companies big and small, so I've advised large design teams made up of very good programmers. I can assure you that large, sophisticated teams often know as little as the independent Web designer who's been in business a few months.

This unusual case is more egregious than most, but the first part — that your Web-design firm says it will handle the search engines, and then doesn't — is *very* common. When I hire a Web designer to build a site for me, I explain exactly what I want. And you should do the same. (Thus, this book can help you even if you never write a line of HTML code.)

The problem is twofold:

- ✔ Web designers pretty much *have* to say they understand search engines, because all their competitors are saying it.
- ✔ Many Web designers think they *do* understand, but typically, it's at an "add some meta tags and submit to the search engines" level. It won't work.

Sorry, Web designers. I don't want to be rude, but this is a simple fact, attested to by many, many site owners out there. I've seen it over and over again. Not trusting your Web designer or team — even if they claim they know what they're doing — is probably the first step in your search engine strategy!

Understanding the Limitations

You've probably received spam e-mails guaranteeing top-ten positions for your Web site in the search engines. You've probably also seen claims that you'll be ranked in hundreds or thousands of search engines. Most of this is nonsense — background noise that creates an entirely false picture. As one of my clients put it, "There's a lot of snake oil out there!" Here are the facts.

Top two in four

Sometimes, it's easy to get a very high position in the search systems. But usually, it isn't. A client wanted to be positioned in Google for six important key phrases. I built some pages, ensured that Google knew where those pages were (find out how to do this in Chapter 11), and

waited. In just four days, the client didn't just have a top-ten position or even just a number-one position, but the top *two* positions for five of the six key phrases. But this situation is very unusual. More commonly, the game takes much more work and much more time.

Typically, getting a high position isn't that easy. You try a couple of techniques, but they don't seem to work. So you try something else, and maybe you achieve a little success. Then you try another thing. Search engine optimization can often be *very* labor intensive, and you may not see results for weeks, and more likely, months.

The degree of work required depends on the competitiveness of the keywords you're going after. Some keywords are incredibly competitive: *mortgage, insurance, attorney, real estate,* and so on, are highly competitive, with millions of people wanting some of the action. Other phrases are very easy — such as *rodent racing,* for instance. If you're in the rodent-racing business, you're in luck because you can probably rank right at the top very easily!

Although how search engines function is based on science, search engine optimization is more art than science. Why? Because search engines don't want outside parties to know exactly how they rank sites. You have to just experiment. Ranking a site can be very difficult, and tremendously laborious. After all, why should it be easy? There is huge competition, so it *can't* always be easy. If it were easy for your site, then it would be easy for your competitors' sites, wouldn't it? And, after all, there can only ever be one number one.

Eyeing the Competition

Some search terms are incredibly competitive. That is, many, many sites are competing for the top positions. Other search terms are far less competitive. How can you tell just how competitive your search terms are? Let me show you a few ways to figure it out:

✔ **Search for your terms.** This is not a terribly good method, but so commonly recommended that I want to explain it. Go to Google and search for a few of your terms. (I discuss keywords in more detail in Chapter 5.) For instance, search for *personal injury lawyer.* You see a blue bar containing something like this:

```
Results 1 - 10 of about 19,800,000 for personal injury
    lawyer
```

This tells you that almost 20 million pages match the search terms in the Google index. Actually, most of these pages don't match well. Most of the pages don't actually have the term *personal injury lawyer.* Rather, as explained earlier, they have the words *personal, injury,* and *lawyer* scattered around the page.

✔ **Search for your terms by using quotation marks.** Type search terms in quotation marks, like this: *"personal injury lawyer."* This time, Google searches for the exact phrase and comes back with a different number. When I searched, it came back with 3,700,000 because Google ignores all the pages with the words scattered around the page, and returns only pages with the exact phrase.

Unfortunately, in recent months, when I originally wrote this section, Google clearly had some bugs in its basic search syntax. Searching for *personal injury lawyer* was showing a smaller number than searching for *"personal injury lawyer,"* which is clearly incorrect. There are obviously many more pages with the words *personal injury lawyer* somewhere in the page than pages with the exact phrase *"personal injury lawyer".* During final review of this book, this bug seemed to have been fixed; just be aware that these odd little idiosyncrasies can happen now and then.

Here's the problem with these two techniques: Although they show you how commonly used the words are, they don't show you how well the pages are optimized. Remember, you're not competing against every page with these terms; you're really competing with pages that were optimized for search engines. There may be millions of pages with the term, but if none of them have been optimized, you can take your new-found SEO knowledge, create your own optimized pages, and have a good chance of ranking well.

So here's another quick technique I like to use — a simple way to get a feel for competitiveness in a few seconds. (If you use the Google toolbar, you might want to click the Highlight button so the words you search for are highlighted in color on the results page, not just bolded.) Search for a term, and then scan down the page looking for the number of

✔ **PPC ads on the page:** For instance, in Figure 3-1 you see search results for the phrase *personal injury attorney.* As you look down the page, you see three PPC ads at the top of the page, and then more ads all the way down the right side of the page. Lots of PPC ads indicate lots of interest in the phrase. If people are spending money on PPC ads, many are also probably spending money on SEO.

✔ **Bold and highlighted words on the page:** You'll also notice that Google bolds the words that you searched for (and, if you're using Highlight on the Google toolbar, the words are also colored); all the major search sites do this. Lots of bold words often mean well-optimized pages.

✔ **Bold words in the links (page titles):** Bold words in each page result's link indicate that someone has been optimizing the pages; the links are the page titles, so the more bold text you see as you scan down, the more often site owners have been placing the keywords into the <TITLE> tags and the more competitive the search terms are likely to be.

✔ **Complete phrases on the page:** The more frequently you see the full phrase you searched for, the more competitive the terms are likely to be; if the search engine returns mostly pages with the words scattered around, it's not very competitive.

Figure 3-1: Searching for _personal injury attorney_ brings up lots of bold text.

Here's another example. Search Google for _rodent engineering_. What do you see? Something similar to Figure 3-2. First, notice there are no PPC ads. Next, notice very little bold or highlighted text on the page, and _none_ of the page titles (the links at the top of each search result) contain the full phrase, _rodent engineering._ You can see the difference between these two pages. The first search term, _personal injury attorney,_ is far more competitive than the second, _rodent engineering._

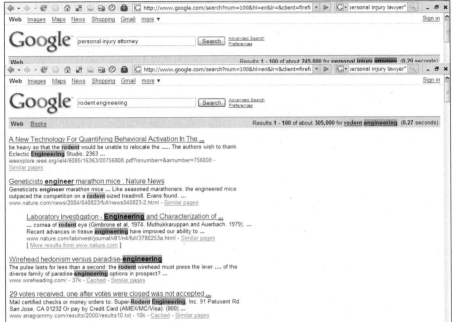

Figure 3-2:
Searching
for *rodent
engineering*
brings up
very little
bold or
highlighted
text.

How important is competitiveness? When targeting search terms that aren't very competitive, you may be able to create a few optimized pages and rank well. In very competitive areas, though, creating a few nicely optimized pages isn't enough. You *must* have links pointing to the site (perhaps many of them), and you may also need large numbers of pages. In some really competitive areas, it may take hundreds, if not thousands, of links.

Get your rodent running

Here's an example of how uncompetitive the phrase *rodent engineering* actually is. I created a page optimized for the term, and posted it to my Web site (`http://Rodent-Engineering.PeterKentConsulting.com`). Within a few days the page was ranked number one on Google for *rodent racing*. An example of how quickly things can happen for noncompetitive terms (in the real world, for competitive terms, things are far more complicated).

Going Beyond Getting to #1

Everyone wants to rank #1 for the top keywords. Lawyers want to rank #1 for *attorney* or *lawyer.* Real estate agents want to rank #1 for *real estate.* Shoe stores want to rank #1 for *shoes,* and so on.

But what does being #1 achieve? You're trying to get people to your Web site, not to get any particular position, right? Getting ranked in search engines is merely a way to generate that traffic to your site. People often assume that to generate traffic, they have to get the #1 position for the top keywords. That's not the case. You can generate plenty of traffic to your site without ever getting to #1 for the most popular phrases. And in many cases, the traffic arriving at your site will be better — the visitors will be more appropriate for your site. There are two things to understand: *highly targeted keyword phrases,* and the *search tail.*

Highly targeted keyword phrases

If your keywords are very competitive, look for keywords that aren't so sought after:

- ✔ **Go local.** One common strategy is, of course, to focus on local keywords. If you're a real estate agent, don't target *real estate.* Instead, target real estate in your area: *Denver realtor, Chicago real estate, Dallas homes for sale,* and so on.

- ✔ **Focus on more specialized search terms.** A realtor might target traffic on keywords related to commercial real estate, or condos, for instance.

- ✔ **Incorporate spelling mistakes.** Some realtors target the very common misspelling *realator.*

These specialized search terms are hidden away in the search *tail,* so I explain that concept.

Understanding the search tail

The *search tail* is an important concept to understand. Although the first few top keywords may get far more searches than any other search, when you look at the total number of searches, the top terms actually account for only a small percentage of the searches.

Look at Table 3-1 for search terms taken from Wordtracker, a great little tool that shows what search terms people are typing into search engines. I searched for *video games* and Wordtracker returned 300 results containing that term. I don't have room for 300, so I show the first few.

Table 3-1	Search Terms for *Video Games*		
		Searches/Day	*Cumulative Searches*
1	video games	9,132	9,132
2	music video games	859	9,991
3	adult video games	621	10,612
4	used video games	269	10,881
5	video games xbox	240	11,121
6	video games playstation 2	237	11,358
7	violent video games	230	11,588
8	online video games	229	11,817
9	sex video games	209	12,026
10	free video games	194	12,220
11	history of video games	186	12,406
12	xxx video games	151	12,557
13	video games game cube	145	12,702
14	trade video games	134	12,836
15	violence in video games	128	12,964
16	cheap video games	128	13,092
17	nude video games	103	13195
18	video poker games	101	13,296

Look at the Searches/Day column. It starts at 9,132 searches a day for *video games,* but immediately drops to 859 for *music video games.* By the time you get to the 18th search term, it's down to just 101 searches a day. Position 300 only gets 7 searches a day. This fact leads people to focus on the top phrases, where, it appears, most of the searching is going on.

However, look at the Cumulative Searches column. As you go down the list, you see the total of all searches from position one down to the current position. The first 18 keyword phrases account for 13,296 searches a day, of which 9,132 — 69 percent — are the top phrase *video games*. As you continue down, the cumulative number continues growing, of course. By the time you reach 300, the cumulative number has risen to 18,557, of which only 49 percent is the top phrase.

As you can see from the numbers in Table 3-1 and Figure 3-3, there's this long "tail"; the searches tail off. Wordtracker only gave me the first 300 search phrases; certainly thousands more contain the phrase *video games.*

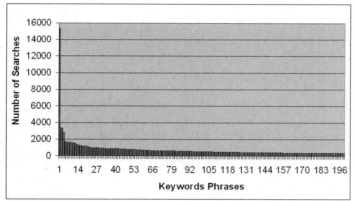

Figure 3-3:
Searches
tail off.

For each phrase, Wordtracker gave an estimate of how often the phrase is searched upon every day. And even in these first 300 searches, most are *not* for the term *video games,* but are for phrases *containing* the term *video games.*

There's more, of course. What if you look, for instance, for the term *computer games?* How about *online games?* How about searching for the term *online video games?* You get a completely different set of 300 keyword phrases from Wordtracker.

Thus, if you only get matched with the exact phrase *video games,* you're missing 49 percent of the first 300 phrases, many of which — perhaps most — would be useful to you. Add the thousands of other related phrases, and the primary term becomes less and less important.

It's essential that you understand that most of the action is not at the top; it's in the search tail! This means two things:

- ✔ Even if you can't rank well for a primary term, there's still plenty of room to play.
- ✔ If you focus *only* on a primary term, you're missing most of the action.

Controlling Search Engine Variables

You have control over five basic variables, and a sixth that waits for no man. Everything in this book fits somewhere into one of these six categories:

- ✔ Keywords
- ✔ Content
- ✔ Page optimization
- ✔ Submissions
- ✔ Links
- ✔ Time

Everything you do will be with the intention of affecting in some way one of the first five variables, and as you work the sixth, time will keep on ticking. Here's a quick summary of each.

Keywords

As you read in Chapter 5, and as I discuss earlier in this chapter, keywords are incredibly important. They're the very foundation of your search engine strategy. Keywords target searchers. You place keywords in your pages and in links pointing to your pages as bait to attract people to your site. Pick the wrong keywords, and you're targeting the wrong people.

Content

Content, from a search engine perspective, really means text, and as you read in Chapter 9, you need content, and a lot of it. Search engines index words, and you want them to index the keywords you're interested in. The more words you have on your site — the more pages of text content — the more times your keywords can appear.

Think of a page of content as a ticket in the lottery; the more pages you have, the more lottery tickets you have. One common SEO strategy is to build huge sites, hundreds of thousands of pages, with vast amounts of text with keywords scattered through. Because of the nature of the search tail explained earlier in this chapter, each page has a chance to match a search now and then. The site has hundreds of thousands of lottery tickets.

You can play the content game a couple of ways:

- ✔ Create thousands of pages and hope that some of the text matches searches now and then.
- ✔ Create pages optimized for specific phrases that you know are used frequently.

Page optimization

Content is just a start. Content has to be placed onto the pages in the correct way; the pages must be *optimized* to get the most out of the keywords. As you read in Chapters 2 and 6, you must place the words onto the pages in the correct places and formats.

If a search engine finds the relevant keywords on your page, that's good. If it finds the keywords in the right places on the page, that's a really powerful thing that differentiates your page from your competitors'.

Submissions

In some ways *submissions* — submitting information to the search engines; telling them where your pages can be found, and asking them, in effect, to come to your site and index it — isn't as important as many people imagine. This may be one of the biggest scams in the business (a business replete with scams!) — the idea that you have to *submit* your pages to thousands of search engines, when in fact, up until mid-2005, it really didn't matter much. You could submit, but the search engines would quite likely ignore the submission; links are what really counted.

However, in 2005, Google introduced a new concept, the *XML sitemap*, and was quickly followed by Yahoo!, and more recently MSN Live Search. This file is placed into your Web site's root directory containing a list of links to all your pages so the search engines can more easily find them. (In effect, now, there are two different types of submissions; one, the one many companies are still selling as a service, is still a scam, while the other is essential.)

Reading history

We don't know exactly how Google handles all this, of course, but you can be fairly sure that Google uses some kind of historical data to help rank pages. In fact, there's even a patent application submitted in the names of various Google employees (though strangely, without Google's name itself on the patent), that discusses the idea of using historical data. (A long complicated URL takes you to the patent, so I've provided the link at `www.searchengine bulletin.com`.) This document is wonderful bedtime reading if you're looking for a way to get to sleep without drugs. You won't find an explanation of how Google ranks Web pages, but you will find a lot of interesting possibilities.

These days I recommend that you assume that submitting to the search engines will not get you indexed — that the way to get indexed is by making sure that the search engines find links to your site — but that you also provide Google, Yahoo!, and MSN Live Search the XML sitemap they want, so those search engines can use them if they decide to (they may not). In addition, you'll add a line to your `robots.txt` file so that other search engines, such as Ask.com, can find the sitemap even though you don't submit it to them. You read more about this in Chapter 11.

Links

Links pointing to your Web site are incredibly important in a competitive keyword market. If you're targeting *rodent engineering,* you probably don't need to worry too much about links (though every site needs at least some incoming links — links pointing to your site from other sites). But if you have lots of competition vying for your keywords, you won't win without links.

Links are so important, in fact, that a page can rank in the first position in any of the three major search engines even if the page doesn't have the keywords that have been searched for — as long as links pointing to the page have the keywords. I explain this in Chapter 14. The more competitive your area, the more important links become.

Time and the Google sandbox

Finally, the one factor you have little control over. You only really have control over time in the sense that the sooner you get started, the older your search engine project becomes. Age is critical because the older the site, the more credibility the search engines give it.

There's something known as the *Google sandbox* or *aging delay.* (Some people will tell you that these are actually two different types of time-related effects.) The idea is that when Google first finds your site, it puts it into a sandbox; it may index it, but it won't necessarily rank it well to begin with. It may take months before the site comes out of the sandbox. (People talk about the *Google sandbox,* but it seems likely that other search engines have something similar.)

There's a lot of debate about the effect of age; some say it's critical, and that for about eight months your site hasn't a chance of ranking well (I'm not in that camp), and others say that while search engines may take into account age to some degree, it's by no means an overwhelming factor (that's where I sit).

It comes down to this: The longer your domain has been registered, the better, and the longer your site has been up, the better. So you have control over this essential factor in just one way; the sooner you get started, the better. Register your domain name as soon as possible. Get a site, even a few pages, posted as soon as possible, and get links pointing from other sites to your site as soon as you can. Get new content posted as soon as possible. The sooner you start, the sooner you'll start ranking well.

Determining Your Plan of Attack

Now you know what you're facing. As you read in Chapter 1, you can more or less forget those thousands of search sites and focus on no more than five search systems. And, as I explain in this chapter, you have six essential factors to play with: keywords, content, page optimization, links, submissions, and time.

Forget about time — all I'll say is, get started right away! As for the other factors, how do you proceed? It depends to some degree on your budget and the competitiveness of the area you're working in.

- ✔ **Do a keyword analysis.** Regardless of competition or budget, you have to do one. Would you study for an exam without knowing what the exam is about? Would you plan a big meal, and then send an assistant to the grocery store without explaining which supplies you need? If you don't do a keyword analysis, you're just guessing. In my experience, you'll almost certainly fail to pick all the right keywords. See Chapter 5 for the lowdown on how to do this analysis.

- ✔ **Create readable pages.** If you want your site to appear, you have to create pages that the search engine spiders or bots can read. (This isn't an issue for the search directories, but if you expect a bot to read your site, the pages have to be readable.) You may be surprised to hear that millions of pages on the Web cannot be read by search engines. For the lowdown on determining whether your pages are being read, see Chapter 2; to find out how to fix the problem if they're not, see Chapters 6 and 7.

✔ **Create keyworded pages.** Having readable pages is just a start. Next, you have to put the keywords into the pages — in the right places and in the right format. See Chapter 6 for details.

✔ **Register with the search systems.** When your pages are ready to be indexed, you need to do two things:

- Let the search systems know where those pages are.
- Get the search systems to include the pages in their indexes and directories.

Sometimes these tasks are harder than you might expect. You can get into the search systems in various ways, as described in detail in Chapters 11 and 12.

✔ **Get other sites to link to your site.** Check out Chapters 14 through 16 to find out how the number and type of links pointing to your site affect your rank.

The preceding strategies are the basics, but you may want to — or even need to — go farther. I cover these additional techniques in detail later:

✔ **Register with other places.** You may also want to register at specialized sites that are important for your particular business. See Chapter 13.

✔ **Register with the shopping indexes.** If you're selling a product, it's a good idea to register with the shopping indexes. Although these indexes don't match the big search systems in volume of searches, they're still important. This is covered in Chapter 17.

✔ **Use pay per click.** You can get noticed in search engines two ways. You can use *natural search* — that is, get ranked in search engines without paying — or you can use *pay per click*. Many companies go straight to pay per click, a system by which you get ranked well but pay each time someone clicks a link to your site. This is usually not a good idea (though sometimes it's a great way to push a product temporarily, such as a special offer), but at some point, you may want to use pay per click in addition to natural search; see Chapter 18.

But there's more. If you're in a very competitive market, you may want to really push two techniques:

✔ **Create large amounts of content.** Make hundreds, perhaps thousands, of pages of content.

✔ **Go after links in a big way.** You may need hundreds, perhaps thousands, of links to rank well if your competitors have done the same.

Two Things to Remember

Before we leave this chapter, I want to tell you about two things that are really worth remembering.

The first is that the ideal situation is to have a site that is so useful or cool or wonderful in some way that people naturally link to it. That's really what search engines are looking for, and much of what is done in the SEO field is intended to *simulate* this situation. People find ways to create links to their Web site to make the search engines *think* that the site is so useful or cool or wonderful in some way that thousands of people are linking to it. Of course, the real thing is better than the simulated thing, but quite frankly it's very difficult to pull off. If you're selling ball bearings, just how useful or cool or wonderful can you make your site? There's a limit to anyone's imagination, after all, so you may have to play the simulation game — but keep in mind what the search engines *really* want.

The other thing I want you to know is that things have a tendency to bounce around in the search engine field. Your site probably won't be on an arrowlike upward trajectory, constantly improving in its search engine position — rather, things go up, and things go down. Here's an example.

I have a client selling industrial equipment, who really wanted to rank well for two particular terms (among many others); we'll say phrase A and phrase B. Well, for a long time he was ranked pretty well, near the top of the search results, for both phrases. Then sometime in the summer of 2007, things got "all shook up." Not just his site, but thousands of sites. Google changed something, and continued changing that something over a period of weeks, and people found their search results dropping, and then rising, and then dropping again. Talk about a roller coaster. . . .

Phrase A dropped like a stone — once position #3, it disappeared — it wasn't in the first 100 search results. It was gone for several days, and then suddenly reappeared for a few days. Then it disappeared again — in fact, it did this several times, bouncing up and down, sometimes near the very top of the search results, and then completely unfindable. Meanwhile, through all this, phrase B remained rock solid, moving up and down, as search results tend to, among the first 5 results.

Then phrase B disappeared too, and played the same game for a while. Then both bounced around, and finally everything settled down and they ended up back where they were in the first place. Today, phrase A is in position #2 (right behind Wikipedia), and phrase B is in position #8; in both cases the site ranks ahead of *all* the competitors (in the second case the phrase has another meaning, and most of the sites ahead of him are government and education sites, which are often hard to beat).

Now, this sort of fluctuation is terribly frustrating, frightening even. If your business depends on a high rank, any day your rank drops is a bad day! (You can even out these fluctuations by getting traffic to your site in other ways, by the way; through PPC advertising, for instance, or affiliate marketing.)

It's tempting when these things happen to blame yourself (or your SEO consultant); whatever you did to the site last, that's what caused the problem. But it's very hard to correlate any particular action with a particular increase or decrease in search engine rank. Often when a rank drops, it's because of something that Google has done, not anything you've done. Perhaps they decide that a certain type of link — reciprocal or paid links (see Chapter 15) — should no longer be of much value. Or perhaps they give more weight to a particular page tag, or more weight to another form of link. You may have changed something completely different, see your site drop, assume it's because of the action you took, and be totally unaware of the real cause of the drop. In the example above, my client decided that he was being punished for creating links in Craigslist.com back to his site — then, later, being punished for *not* creating links in Craigslist.

Sometimes you just have to wait to let things settle down, and *keep on keeping on!* Keep on creating well-optimized content, and keep on creating links (and various, different types of links) back to your site. This stuff really does work; you just have to work at it.

This chapter provides an overview of the search engine battle you're about to join. Now it's time to jump in and make it all happen, so Chapter 4 explains what search engines really like to see: Web sites that people on the Internet believe are really useful.

Chapter 4

Making Your Site Useful and Visible

In This Chapter

▶ Understanding the basic rule of Web success

▶ Knowing why search engines like content

▶ Making your site work for visitors and search engines

*O*bviously, it's important to create Web pages that search engines will read and index, pages that you hope will rank well for important keywords. But if you're going to build a Web site, you need to step back and figure out what purpose the site should serve and how it can accomplish that purpose.

Creating a *useful* site is the key. Even if your sole aim is to sell a product online, the more useful the site is to visitors, the more successful it's likely to be. Take Amazon.com, for instance. It certainly wasn't the first online retailer of books and music, or any of the other products it offers. But one of Amazon's real strengths is that it doesn't just sell products; it's a really *useful* site, in many ways:

✔ It provides tons of information about the products it sells. The information is useful even if you don't buy from Amazon.

✔ You can save information for later. If you find a book you're interested in but don't want to buy right now, save a link to it and come back next month, next year, or five years from now.

✔ Other site owners can become partners and make money by promoting Amazon.

✔ Other businesses can easily sell their products through Amazon.

✔ You can read sample chapters, look at tables of contents, listen to snippets of music, and so on.

✔ You can read product reviews from both professional reviewers and consumers.

Would Amazon be so successful if it just provided lists of the products it sells, instead of offering visitors a veritable cornucopia of useful stuff? Absolutely not.

Having done a little consulting work for Amazon, I've spent some time looking at the site from an SEO perspective, and what interests me are the many ways in which Amazon drops keywords into their pages. As you discover elsewhere in this book, keywords on Web pages are a huge part of SEO — and Amazon's pages are scattered with keywords. Take a look at the books pages, for instance, and you'll find the following:

- ✓ **Editorial Reviews:** These are descriptions of the book by the publisher, stacked full of keywords related to the subject covered by the book.

- ✓ **Customer Reviews:** When someone reviews a book about, say, Search Engine Optimization, they tend to use words related to the subject, such as *websites*, *SEO*, *programming*, *PHP*, *sitemaps*, *link bait*, and so on.

- ✓ **Tags customers associate with this product:** Essentially a list of keywords other customers associate with the book.

- ✓ **Books on Related Topics:** Other books will often have titles containing relevant keywords, and the **Discusses** subsection is all keywords.

- ✓ **Capitalized Phrases (CAPs):** A list of capitalized phrases in the book (often very relevant keywords).

However, much of this (and the other useful features on Amazon product pages) was done *without* SEO in mind. Amazon added most of these things to make the site *useful* — SEO was an afterthought. Reviews, for instance, certainly do add keywords to the page, but they also help buyers make a decision (and can dramatically increase *conversion rates* — that is, converting shoppers to buyers). So creating a useful site often serves two purposes; it generates traffic through non–search engine channels, *and* it helps your site rank well in search engines.

Consider this: The more useful your site is, the greater the chance of success. The more people talk about your site, the more likely journalists are to write about it, the more likely it is to be mentioned on radio or TV, the more people will link to it from their Web sites. Search engine marketing and non–search engine marketing are both important because either form of Web site promotion can lead to more links pointing to your site. And, as you find out in Chapters 14 and 15, links to your site are critical to search engine success.

With that in mind, this chapter focuses on the basics about what you need to do to create a successful Web site.

Revealing the Secret but Essential Rule of Web Success

Here's a simple rule to success on the Web:

Make your site useful and then tell people about it.

That's not so complicated, really. Figure out how your site can be useful and then find as many ways as possible to let people know about it. You'll use search engines, of course, but you should be using other methods, too. Remember, search engines are not the only way to get people to your site. In fact, many Web sites have succeeded without using search engines as their primary method of attracting visitors.

Many successful companies have done little or nothing to promote themselves through search engines, yet they still turn up at the top when you search for their products or services. Why? Because their other promotions have helped push them higher in the search engines, by creating thousands (even tens or hundreds of thousands) of links to them around the Internet.

The evolving, incorrect "secret"

Over the last decade, a number of popular ideas about what makes a successful Web site have been bandied around, and all are wrong to some degree. Here are some of those dated secrets to successful Web sites:

- ✔ **Links:** When the Web began booming in 1994, it was all about *links*. You would hear in the press that the secret to a successful Web site was linking to other sites.

- ✔ **Cool:** Then people started saying that the secret of success was to make your site *cool*. Cool sites were more entertaining and more likely to attract repeat visitors.

- ✔ **Community:** Then people started talking about *community;* yeah, that's the ticket! The secret to a successful Web site was creating a community where people could meet and chat with each other.

- ✔ **Content:** Then around 2000, people discovered that the secret was *content*. By putting more stuff, particularly textual information, on your site, you could be more successful.

Specific one-size-fits-all secrets to success never make sense.

Amazon — Success sans search

It's unlikely that search engines were a large factor in Amazon's success — Amazon grew rapidly mainly because of the enormous press attention it received, beginning in 1994. Today, I'd bet that relatively few people arrive at Amazon.com through search engines. Rather, they already know the Amazon brand and go straight to the site, or they go through the hundreds of thousands of Amazon affiliate sites.

The most harmful of the preceding ideas was that your site had to be cool. This silly idea led to the expenditure of billions of dollars on useless but pretty Web sites, most of which (thankfully!) have since disappeared. Unfortunately, some of the *it's-all-about-cool* crowd is still in the Web business and still convincing businesses to spend money on ridiculous, wasteful things, such as Flash intros for their Web sites.

Uncovering the real secret

Ready to hear the real secret of site-creation success? Your Web site has to be *useful*. The problem with the secrets I just mentioned is that they're too specific, leading people to build sites that were in many cases inappropriate. Sure, links are important to Yahoo!, but they're much less important to the vast majority of Web sites. If you own an entertainment site, you may want to make it cool and entertaining. Certainly, community can be an effective tool, but not every site has to have it. Content is very important, too — especially from a search engine perspective — but many successful Web sites don't have much content. (I talk in more detail about content in the next section because it's a special case.)

I've been writing this since 1997: *Forget cool; think useful.*

When you're planning your Web site, think about what kinds of folks you want to attract to the site. Then try to come up with ideas about what features and information might be *useful* to them. Your site may end up with a lot of link pages, providing a directory of sorts for people in your industry. Or maybe you really need a cool and entertaining site. Or perhaps you decide to use discussion groups and chat rooms as a way to build community and pull the crowds into your site; that's fine. Or maybe you decide to create a huge repository of information to attract a particular type of customer. That's okay, too. Maybe you do *all* these things. But the important first step is to think about what you can do to make your site more useful.

Showing a bias for content

Content is a special case. Search engines are biased toward ranking content-heavy Web sites well for a couple of reasons:

- ✔ Search engines were originally academic research tools designed to find *text information*. Search engines mostly index text — *content*.
- ✔ Search engines need something to base their judgments on. When you type a term into a search engine, it looks for the words you provided. So a Web site built with few words is at a disadvantage right from the start.

As you discover elsewhere in this book — such as in the discussion of PageRank in Chapter 14 — search engines do have other criteria for deciding if a Web site matches a particular search (most notably the number and type of links pointing to the site). But search engines do have a huge bias toward textual content.

Unfortunately, this bias is often a real problem. The real world simply doesn't work the way search engines see it. Here's an example: Suppose your business rents very expensive, specialized photographic equipment. Your business has the best prices and the best service of any company renting this equipment. Your local customers love you, and few other companies match your prices, service, or product range. So you decide to build a Web site to reach customers elsewhere, and ship rentals by UPS and FedEx.

Search engines base your rank, to a great degree, on the number and type of keywords in your pages.

To rank well, a competitor has added a bunch of pages about photography and photographic equipment to its site. To compete, you have to do the same. Do your customers care? No, they just want to find a particular piece of equipment that fills their need, rent it, and move on quickly. All the additional information, the content that you've added, is irrelevant to them. It's simply clutter.

This is a common scenario. I once discussed the content issue with a client who was setting up a Web site at which people could quickly get a moving-service quote. The client wanted to build a clean, sparse site that allowed customers to get the quote within a couple minutes. "But we don't want all that stuff, that extra text, nor do our clients!" he told me, and he had a good point.

You can't ignore the fact that search engines like content. However, you can compete other ways. One of the most important ways is getting links from other sites, as you discover in Chapter 15. Search engines like to see links on other sites pointing to your site. Sites that have hundreds or thousands of other sites linking to them often rank well. But they still need at least *some* content for the search engines to index. And the best situation is lots of useful content with lots of incoming links.

Making Your Site Work Well

I've been writing about site design for almost seven years, and I'm happy to say that many of the rules of good site design just happen to match what search engines like. And many of the cool tricks that designers love cause problems with search engines. So I want to quickly review a few tips for good site design that will help both your site visitors and the search engines to work with your site.

Limiting multimedia

Much multimedia used on the Web is pointless because it rarely serves a useful purpose to the visitor. It's there because Web designers enjoy working with it and because many people are still stuck in the old "you've got to be cool" mindset.

Look at the world's most successful Web sites (with the exception of sites like YouTube.com, of course, which are all about multimedia), and you'll find that they rarely use multimedia — Flash animations and video, for example — for purely decorative purposes. Look at Amazon: Its design is simple, clean, black text on white background, with lots of text and very little in the way of animations, video, or sound (except, for instance, where it provides music samples in the site's CD area and, more recently, videos demonstrating products). Look at Yahoo!, Google, CNN, or eBay — they're not cool; they just get the job done.

You can employ multimedia on a Web site in some useful ways. I think it makes a lot of sense to use Flash, for instance, to create demos and presentations. However, Flash intros are almost *always* pointless, and search engines don't like them because Flash intros don't provide indexable content. Anytime you get the feeling it would be nice to have an animation, or when your Web designer says you should have some animation, slap yourself twice on the face and then ask yourself this: Who is going to benefit: the designer or the site visitor? If that doesn't dissuade you, have someone else slap you.

Using text, not graphics

A surprising number of Web sites use graphics to place text onto pages. Take a look at the Web site shown in Figure 4-1. Although this page appears to have a lot of text, every word is in an image file. Web designers often employ this technique so all browsers can view their carefully chosen fonts. But search engines don't read the text in the images they run across, so this page provides *no* text that can be indexed by search engines. Although this page may contain lots of useful keywords (you find out all about keywords in Chapter 5), the search engines read nothing. From a usability perspective, the design is bad, too, because all those images take much longer to download than the equivalent text would take.

Figure 4-1:
This looks like text, but it's actually images that slow the page load and provide search engines nothing to read.

Avoiding the urge to be too clever

I advise people to stay one step behind in Web technology and try not to be too clever. From a usability standpoint, the problem is that not all browser types work the same; they have different bugs and handle technical tricks differently.

If you're always working with the very latest Web-development technology, more of your visitors are likely to run into problems. Cool technology often confuses search engines, too. As an SEO friend likes to say, "Google likes black text on a white background." In other words, search engines like *simple*. The more complicated your Web pages are, the harder it is for search engines to read and categorize them.

You must strike a compromise between employing all the latest Web-design technology and tools and ensuring that search engines can read your pages. From a search engine perspective, in fact, one step behind probably isn't enough!

Don't be cute

Some sites do everything they can to be cute. The Coca-Cola site was a classic example of this a few years ago, though it finally got the message and changed. The site had icons labeled *Tour de Jour, Mind Candy, Curvy Canvas, Netalogue,* and so on. What do these things mean? Who knows? Certainly not the site visitor.

This sort of deranged Web design is far less common now than it used to be, but you still see it occasionally — particularly in sites designed by hip Web-design firms. One incredibly irritating technique is the hidden navigation structure. The main page contains a large image with hotspots on it. But it's unclear where the hotspots are, or what they link to, until you point at the image and move the mouse around. This strikes me as the Web-design equivalent of removing the numbers from the front of the homes in a neighborhood. You can still figure out where people live; you just have to knock on doors and ask.

Sweet and sickly cuteness doesn't help your site visitors find their way around and almost certainly hurts you with the search engines.

Making it easy to move around

Web design is constantly getting better, but it still surprises me that designers sometimes make it difficult for visitors to move around a Web site.

Think carefully about how your site is structured:

- ✔ Does it make sense from a visitor's standpoint?
- ✔ Can visitors find what they need quickly?
- ✔ Do you have *dangling* or *orphaned* pages — pages where a visitor can't find a link to get back into your main site?

  Search engines don't like dangling pages, and consider what happens if someone on another site links directly to the page: Visitors can get to the page but not to the rest of your site.

Providing different routes

People think differently from each other, so you need to provide them with numerous avenues for finding their way around your site. And by doing so, you're also giving more information to search engines and ensuring that search engines can navigate your site easily.

Here are some different navigational systems that you can add to your site:

- ✔ **Sitemap:** This page links to the different areas of your site, or even, in the case of small sites, to every page in the site. See `www.peterkent consulting.com/sitemap.htm` as an example.
- ✔ **Table of Contents or Index page:** You can sort the page thematically or alphabetically.
- ✔ **Navigation bars:** Most sites have navigation bars these days.
- ✔ **Navigation text links:** Little links at the bottom of your pages, or along the sides, that can help people find their way around — and help the search engines, too.

Using long link text

It's a proven fact that Web users like *long link text* — links that are more than just a single word and actually describe where the link takes you. Usability testing shows that long link text makes it much easier for visitors to find their way around a site. It's not surprising if you think about it; a long link provides more information to visitors about where a link will take them.

Unfortunately, many designers feel constrained by design considerations, forcing all navigation links, for instance, to conform to a particular size. You often see buttons that have only enough room for ten or so characters, forcing the designer to think about how to say complicated things in one or two words.

Long links that explain what the referenced page is about are a great thing, not only for visitors, but also for search engines. By using keywords in the links, you're telling the search engines what the referenced pages are about.

You also have a problem if all the links on your site are on image buttons — search engines can't read images, so image buttons provide no information about the referenced page. You can't beat a well-keyworded text link for passing information about the target page to the search engines.

Don't keep restructuring

Try to ensure that your site design is good before you get too far into the process. Sites that are constantly being restructured have numerous problems, including the following:

- Links from other Web sites into yours get broken, which is bad for potential visitors as well as for search engines (or, more precisely, bad for your position in the search engines because they won't be able to reach your site through the broken links).

- If you don't restructure carefully, all the pages you have indexed in the search engines may be lost, so you have to start over from the beginning — it may take weeks or months to get fully reindexed.

- Anyone who has bookmarked your page now has a broken bookmark.

It's a good idea to create a custom 404 error page, which is displayed in your browser if the server is unable to find a page you've requested. (Ask your Web server administrator how to do this; the process varies among servers.) Create an error page with links to other areas of the site, perhaps even a sitemap, so that if visitors and searchbots can't find the right page, at least they'll be able to reach some page on your site.

Editing and checking spelling

Check your pages for spelling and editing errors. Not only do error-free pages make your site appear more professional, they ensure that your valuable keywords are not wasted. If potential visitors are searching for *rodent racing,* for example, you don't want the term *rodint racing* in your Web pages. (Except, that is, if you are trying to catch traffic from oft-misspelled keywords, which I discuss in Chapter 5.)

Ugly doesn't sell

Before we move on, I really have to cover this, um, sensitive subject, because I've run into a lot of people wasting money on SEO that would be better spent on Web design.

You see, I often get e-mails from people saying that they've had their site up "for months now, and haven't sold a thing; can you take a look and tell me why?" I type the URL into my browser, wait for the page to load, and I'm then knocked out of my chair by the unadulterated grotesqueness of the page.

(I now keep a pair of very heavily shaded sunglasses — polarized, UV-filtered, glare-protected glacier glasses — for these very cases. If I get a feeling about the site I'm about to see, on go the glasses.)

I don't get it. I know some people are colorblind, but are some ugly blind? Can't they see?

Here's the fact: Ugly doesn't sell. By *ugly,* I mean a range of problems:

- ✔ Awful color combinations that just don't work.
- ✔ Terrible typeface choices that make the pages close to unreadable.
- ✔ Combinations of fonts and colors that make the text close to unreadable — such as white text on black backgrounds (no, it's *not* cool; ask yourself, why do virtually all the world's top Web sites use black text on a white background?).
- ✔ Cutesy backgrounds that look — cutesy, not professional.
- ✔ Incredibly clunky images that look like they were created by an amateur in front of the TV one evening.
- ✔ Messy page layouts that look amateurish.

I sometimes help clients build Web sites, but I know my limitations. I'm not a graphic designer, and I don't pretend to be one; I'll build sites, but find an expert to do the graphic design. Way too many people out there have decided to play graphic designer. If you're not one, don't try to act like one.

Having said that, be careful with graphic designers. Too many people in the Web business build beautiful pages that aren't particularly functional, and some of them like to use every graphic design tool in the box, making your site beautiful but unusable.

This is not merely a matter of esthetics. In fact, I'm not saying that you need a beautiful Web site, just a professional-looking site. The fact is, sites that look unprofessional, like they were built by a couple of guys who just learned HTML last week after they got home from work in the evenings, have trouble converting visitors to buyers. Would you buy from a site that looks like it was built by one-handed gnomes? Well, if you wouldn't, why would anyone else? They don't.

By the way, I do understand that many small businesses have money issues; they can't afford a top professional designer. But there is actually no direct correlation between good Web design and dollars. It's possible to pay very little and get a decent site or to pay a lot and get garbage.

If, thanks to budgetary considerations — you're stone cold broke and plan to pay the designer with food and beer — you have to use Cousin Joe, the fireman, to create your site, or perhaps your sophomore daughter, Jenny (I've seen both situations), and if Joe or Jenny has, let's say, less-than-adequate design skills, what do you do? Buy some templates! Search online for *web page templates* and then spend a few hours looking for something nice. Even if you've got the slimmest of budgets and have to use a non-designer to create your site, you still don't settle for bad design.

There's a level below which you must not go. Remember the phrase, "the kingdom was lost for the want of a nail"? Or, "penny smart, pound foolish"? Well, no amount of search engine optimization will make up for bad Web design. You might have the best SEO in the world, rank #1 for all your keywords — but if your visitors land on a dreadful site, all is for naught.

Part II

Building Search Engine–Friendly Sites

"Look, I've already launched a search for 'reanimated babe cadavers' three times and nothing came up!"

In this part . . .

*T*ime for the details. In this part, you discover things that help your site rank well in search engines — and things that almost guarantee that your site won't do well in search engines. Understand the information in this part, and you're way ahead of most Web site owners, designers, and developers.

You discover what search engines like to find in your Web pages that are likely to help your site rank well: simplicity, text content with the right keywords, keywords in heading tags and bold text, and so on. You also discover what things have the opposite effect, making search engines stumble when they reach your site or even leave the site without reading any pages. From frames to dynamically generated pages to session IDs, these things can be the kiss of death if you're not careful.

I also let you in on a few secrets that search engines hate, techniques that people often use to "trick" the search engines but that can also be dangerous. Many folks in the search engine optimization business shy away from these techniques for fear of having their pages penalized or entire sites banned from the search engines.

Finally, this part shows you how to quickly build the content on your site. Content is king as far as the search engines are concerned, but the problem is where to find enough text to satisfy them.

Chapter 5

Picking Powerful Keywords

1 was talking with a client some time ago who wanted to have his site rank well in the search engines. The client is a company with annual revenues in the millions of dollars, in the business of, oh, I don't know . . . staging rodent-racing events. (I've changed the details of this story a tad to protect the client's privacy.)

I did a little research and found that most people searching for rodent-racing events use the keywords *rodent racing.* (Big surprise, huh?) I took a look at the client's Web site and discovered that the words *rodent racing* didn't appear anywhere on the site's Web pages.

"You have a little problem," I said. "Your site doesn't use the words *rodent racing,* so it's unlikely that any search engine will find your site when people search for that."

"Oh, well," was the client's reply. "Our marketing department objects to the term. We have a company policy to use the term *furry friend events.* The term rodent is too demeaning, and if we say we're racing them, the animal rights people will get upset."

This is a true story; well, except for the bit about rodent racing and the furry friends thing. But, in principle, it happened. This company had a policy not to use the words that most of its potential clients were using to search for it.

You may be asking yourself how it's possible that a company can build a Web site only to discover later that the keywords its potential clients and visitors are using are not in the site. Well, I can think of a couple of reasons:

✔ Most sites are built without any regard for search engines. The site designers simply don't think about search engines or have little background knowledge about how search engines work.

✔ The site designers do think about search engines, but they guess, often incorrectly, what keywords they should be using.

I can't tell you how the client and I resolved this problem because, well, we didn't. (Sometimes company politics trump common sense.) But I am going to tell you how to pick keywords that make sense for your site, as well as how to discover what keywords your potential site visitors are using to search for your products and services.

Understanding the Importance of Keywords

When you use a search engine, you type in a word or words and click the Search button. The search engine then looks in its index for those words.

Suppose that you typed *rodent racing.* Generally speaking, the search engine looks for

✔ Pages that contain the exact phrase *rodent racing.*

✔ Pages that don't have the phrase *rodent racing,* but do have the words *rodent* and *racing* in close proximity.

✔ Pages that have the words *rodent* and *racing* somewhere, though not necessarily close together.

✔ Pages with word stems; for instance, pages with the word *rodent* and the word *race* somewhere in the page.

✔ Pages that have links pointing to them, in which the link text contains the phrase *rodent racing.*

✔ Pages with links pointing to them with the link text containing the words *rodent* and *racing,* although not together.

The process is actually a lot more complicated. The search engine doesn't necessarily show pages in the order I just listed — all the pages with the exact phrase, and then all the pages with the words in close proximity, and so on. When considering ranking order, the search engine considers (in addition to hundreds of secret criteria) whether the keyword or phrase is in

✔ Bold text

✔ Italicized text

✔ Bulleted lists

✔ Text larger than other text on the page

✔ Heading text (<H> tags)

Despite the various complications, however, one fact is of paramount importance: If a search engine can't relate your Web site to the words that someone searches for, it has no reason to return your Web site as part of the search results.

Picking the right keywords is critical. As Woody Allen once said, "Eighty percent of success is showing up." If you don't play the game, you can't win. And if you don't choose the right keywords, you're not even showing up to play the game. If a specific keyword or keyword phrase doesn't appear in your pages (or in links pointing to your pages), your site *will not* appear when someone enters those keywords into the search engines. For instance, say you're a technical writer in San Diego, and you have a site with the term *technical writer* scattered throughout. You will *not* appear in search results when someone searches for *technical writer san diego* if you don't have the words *San Diego* in your pages. You simply will not turn up.

Understanding how to search helps you understand the role of keywords. Check out the bonus chapter I've posted at www.SearchEngineBulletin.com to find the different ways you can search by using search engines in general and Google in particular.

Thinking Like Your Prey

It's an old concept: You should think like your prey. Companies often make mistakes with their keywords because they choose based on how they — rather than their customers — think about their products or services. You have to stop thinking that you know what customers call your products. Do some research to find out what consumers really do call your products.

Do a little keyword analysis. Check to see what people are actually searching for on the Web. You'll discover that the words you were positive people would use are rarely searched, and you'll also find that you've missed a lot of common terms. Sure, you may get some of the keywords right; however, if you're spending time and energy targeting particular keywords, you may as well get 'em all right.

The term *keyword analysis* has several meanings:

- ✔ When I use it, I'm referring to what I'm discussing in this chapter — analyzing the use of keywords by people searching for products, services, and information.

- ✔ Some people use the term to mean *keyword-density* analysis — finding out how often a keyword appears in a page. Some of the keyword analysis tools that you run across are actually keyword-density analysis tools.

- ✔ The term also refers to the process of analyzing keywords in your Web site's access logs.

Starting Your Keyword Analysis

Perform a *keyword analysis* — a check of what keywords people use to search on the Web — or you're wasting your time. Imagine spending hundreds of hours optimizing your site for a keyword you think is good, only to discover that another keyword or phrase gets two or three times the traffic. How would you feel? Sick? Stupid? Mad? Don't risk your mental health — do it right the first time.

Identifying the obvious keywords

Begin by typing the obvious keywords into a text editor or word processor. Type the words you've already thought of, or, if you haven't started yet, the ones that immediately come to mind. Then study the list for a few minutes. What else can you add? What similar terms come to mind? Add them, too.

When you perform your analysis, you'll find that some of the initial terms you think of aren't searched very often, but that's okay. This list is just the start.

Looking at your Web site's access logs

Take a quick look at your Web site's access logs (often called *hit logs*). You may not realize it, but most logs show you the keywords that people used when they clicked a link to your site at a search engine. (If your logs don't contain this information, you probably need another program.) Write down the terms that are bringing people to your site.

Examining competitors' keyword tags

You probably know who your competitors are — you should, anyway. Go to their sites and open the source code of a few pages.

1. **Choose View⇨Source from the browser's menu bar.**

2. **Look for the `<META NAME="keywords">` tag for any useful keywords.**

Often, the keywords are garbage, or simply not there; but, if you look at enough sites, you're likely to come up with some useful terms you hadn't thought of.

Brainstorming with colleagues

Talk to friends and colleagues to see if they can come up with some possible keywords. Ask them something like, "If you were looking for a site where you could find the latest scores for rodent races around the world, what terms would you search for?" Give everyone a copy of your current keyword list and ask if they can think of anything to add. Usually, reading the terms sparks an idea or two, and you end up with a few more terms.

Looking closely at your list

After you've put together your initial list, go through it looking for more obvious additions. Don't spend too much time on this; all you're doing here is creating a preliminary list to run through a keyword tool, which figures out some of these things for you.

Obvious spelling mistakes

Scan through your list and see if you can think of any obvious spelling mistakes. Some spelling mistakes are incredibly important, with 10, 15, or 20 percent (sometimes even more) of all searches containing the misspelled word. For example, about one-fifth of all Britney Spears–related searches are misspelled — spread out over a dozen misspellings.

The word *calendar* is also frequently misspelled. Look at the following estimate of how often *calendar* is searched for each day in its various permutations:

> *calendar:* 10,605 times
>
> *calender:* 2,721
>
> *calander:* 1,549
>
> *calandar:* 256

Thirty percent of all searches on the word *calendar* are misspelled. (Where do I get these estimates, you're wondering? You find out later in the "Using a Keyword Tool" section.)

If the traffic from a misspelling is significant, you may want to create a page on your site that uses that misspelling. Some sites contain what I call "Did You Mean" pages, such as the one shown in Figure 5-1. Some sites contain pages with misspellings in the `<TITLE>` tags, which can work very well. These don't have to be pages that many people see. After all, the only people who will see the misspelled titles in a search results page are those who misspelled the words in the first place.

One nice thing about misspellings is that competitors often miss them, so you can grab the traffic without much trouble.

Figure 5-1:
A page designed for the spelling challenged.

Synonyms

Sometimes similar words are easily missed. If your business is home related, for instance, have you thought about the term *house*? Americans may easily overlook this word, using *home* instead, but other English-speaking countries use the word often. Add it to the list because you may find quite a few searches related to it.

You might even use a thesaurus to find more synonyms. However, I show you some keyword tools that run these kinds of searches for you; see "Using a Keyword Tool," later in this chapter.

Split or merged words

You may find that although your product name is one word — *RodentRacing,* for instance — most people are searching for you by using two words, *rodent* and *racing.* Remember to consider your customer's point of view.

Also, some words are employed in two ways. Some people, for instance, use the term *knowledgebase,* while others use *knowledge base.* Which is more important? Both should be on your list, but *knowledge base* is used around four to five times more often than *knowledgebase.* If you optimize your pages for *knowledgebase* (I discuss page optimization in Chapter 6), you're missing out on around 80 percent of the traffic!

Singulars and plurals

Go through your list and add singulars and plurals. Search engines treat singulars and plurals differently. For example, searching on *rodent* and *rodents* provides different results; therefore, it's important to know which term is searched for most often. A great example is to do a search on *book* (1,635 searches per day, according to Wordtracker, which is discussed later in this chapter) and *books* (16,475 searches per day) in Google. A search on *book* returns Barnes and Noble as the number-one result, while *books* returns Amazon.com (and has for several years now).

Don't worry about upper- versus lowercase letters. You can use *rodent* or *Rodent* or *RODENT,* for example. Most search engines aren't case sensitive. If you search for *rodent* (probably 90 percent of all searches are in lowercase), virtually all search engines will find *Rodent* or *RODENT* — or *rODENT* or *ROdent,* for that matter.

Hyphens

Do you see any hyphenated words on your list that could be used without the hyphen, or vice versa? Some terms are commonly used both ways, so find out what your customers are using. Here are two examples:

- The terms *ecommerce* and *e-commerce* are fairly evenly split, with a little over 50 percent of searches using the latter term.
- The dash in *e-mail* is far less frequently used, with *email* being the most common term.

Find hyphenated words, add both forms to your list, and determine which is more common because search engines treat them as different searches.

Search engines generally treat a hyphen as a space. So searching for *rodent-racing* is the same as searching for *rodent racing*. However, there is a real difference between *e-commerce* and *ecommerce*, or *rodentracing* and *rodent-racing*.

Geo-specific terms

Is geography important to your business? Are you selling shoes in Seattle or rodents in Rochester? Don't forget to include terms that include your city, state, other nearby cities, and so on.

Your company name

If you have a well-known company name, add that to the list, in whatever permutations you can think of (for example, Microsoft, MS, MSFT, and so on).

Other companies' names and product names

If people are likely to search for companies and products similar to yours, add those companies and products to your list. That's not to say you should use these keywords in your pages (you can in some conditions, as I discuss in Chapter 6), but it's nice to know what people are looking for and how often they're looking.

Using a Keyword Tool

After you've put together a decent keyword list, the next step is to use a keyword tool. This tool enables you to discover additional terms you haven't thought of and helps you determine which terms are most important — which terms are used most often by people looking for your products and services.

Both free and paid versions of keyword tools are available. I discuss the freebies first, but I may as well cut to the chase and tell you that I recommend that you fork over the dough and use Wordtracker, probably the world's top search engine keyword tool. So you can skip to that section if you want, or read on.

Yahoo! used to provide a neat little keyword tool associated with their PPC (pay per click) service (see Chapter 18). However, this free tool is long gone; Yahoo! stopped providing it some time in 2006.

Today, to get to the Yahoo! keyword tool, you need to sign up for a PPC account (or at least begin the process). For instance, go to `http://search marketing.yahoo.com` and begin the sign up process for a "Self Serve sponsored search" account. (Don't worry, it says that you have to put down a deposit, but you don't until you get way past the keyword analysis tool).

You tell Yahoo! where you want to run your ads in the first step and then, in the second step, you pick your keywords. You'll see a page similar to that shown in Figure 5-2.

You enter some keywords and then click Next. A screen similar to Figure 5-3 appears.

This screen shows a list of suggested keywords with an estimate of the monthly searches (for some entries, a very broad estimate — I call a range of *40,757–381,544* pretty broad, for instance!).

You can go down the list clicking the Add button to add the keywords you want and then click the Get More Keywords button to select more.

Google used to hide its keyword tool inside the PPC signup process, but now provides direct access to it at `https://adwords.google.com/select/KeywordToolExternal`. The tool doesn't give numbers; rather, it shows bars that provide a general, relative idea of how often words are searched for. See Figure 5-4.

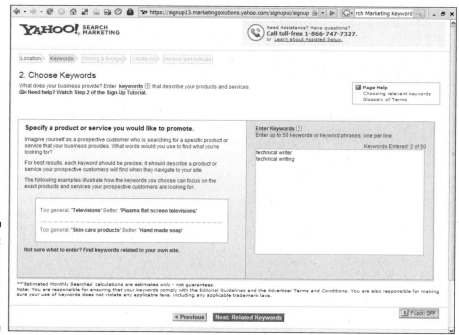

Figure 5-2:
The Yahoo!
PPC
Keyword
Analysis
tool.

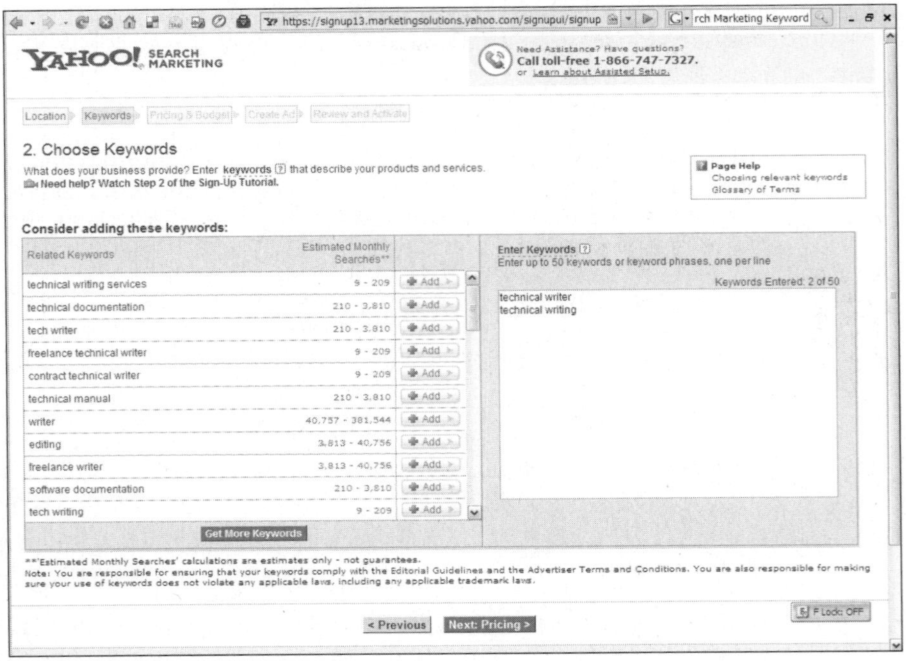

Figure 5-3:
Yahoo! PPC
Keyword
Analysis
tool results.

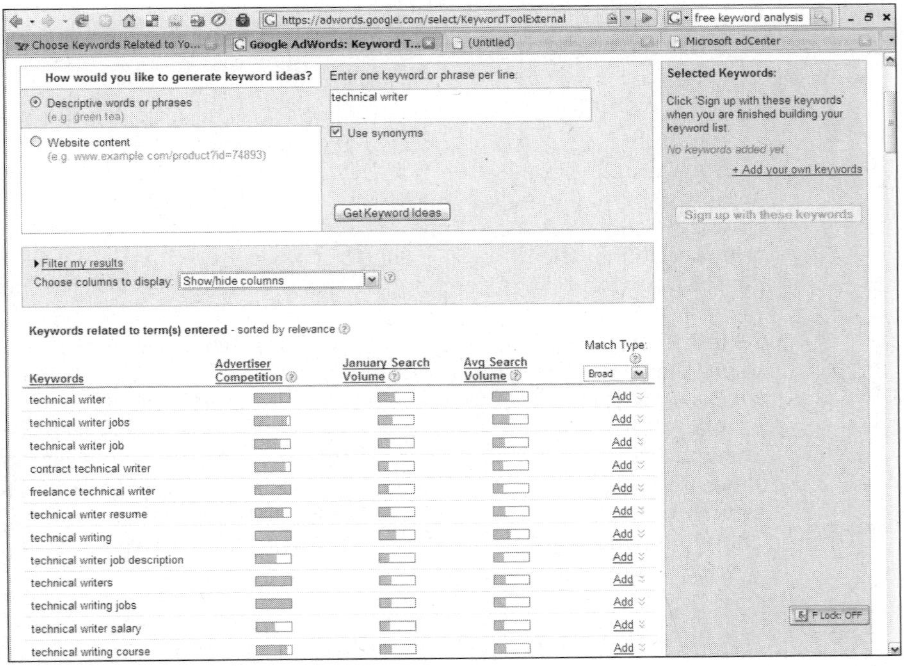

Figure 5-4:
Google's
free
keyword
analysis
tool.

Microsoft AdCenter (`https://adcenter.microsoft.com`) doesn't currently provide access to the keyword tool until you finish setting up your account, so I guess, strictly speaking, it's not free (you have to pay a $5 signup fee).

Using these tools isn't very convenient for SEO (rather than PPC) purposes and also takes what's referred to in the search engine optimization business as *a bloody long time*. (Well, the business in England, anyway.) This is why I suggest that you use Wordtracker.

To find some of the other software tools and Web-based services, do a search on *keyword* or *keyword analysis*. The top tool is Wordtracker, which is discussed in the next section.

Using Wordtracker

Wordtracker (`www.wordtracker.com`) is perhaps the most popular keyword tool among SEO professionals.

Wordtracker, owned by a company in London, England, has access to data from several very large metacrawlers. A *metacrawler* is a system that searches multiple search engines for you. For example, type a word into Dogpile's search box (`www.dogpile.com`), and the system searches at Google, Yahoo!, MSN, and Ask.com.

Wordtracker gets the information about what people are searching for from Metacrawler.com, Dogpile.com, and others — around 100 million searches each month. It stores 100 days of searches in its databases — somewhere around 312 million searches. Wordtracker combines the data for the last 100 days and then allows its customers to search this database. Ask Wordtracker how often someone searched for the term *rodent,* and it tells you that it was searched for (at the time of writing) 122 times over the last 100 days but that the term *rodents* is far more popular, with 355 searches over the last 100 days.

Certain searches are seasonal: *pools* in the summer, *heaters* in the winter, and so on. Because Wordtracker has only the last 100 days of information, it may not be representative for a full year for some terms. And some searches may be influenced by the media. While searches for *paris hilton* were very high in November and December 2003, when I wrote the first edition of this book — oh, bad example, they're still absurdly high, unfortunately. Okay, here's another example. While searches are currently very high for *mitt romney* (though nowhere near as high as *paris hilton),* they'll drop after the media interest wanes.

Endorsement disclaimer

I generally don't like endorsing a product; elsewhere in this book, I mention products and even state that they're good. Wordtracker is a special case. It's been around a long time, and is very popular among professionals. It's cheap to use, too, so I recommend that you do so. Disclaimer:

I've done a little work for this firm. In fact, you may find some of my writing on the Wordtracker site. However, I mentioned Wordtracker in glowing terms in the first edition of this book, *before* I ever did business with the company.

Here's what information Wordtracker can provide:

- ✔ The number of times in the last 100 days that the exact phrase you enter was searched for out of 400 million or so searches
- ✔ An estimate of how many times each day the phrase is used throughout all the Web's search engines
- ✔ Similar terms and synonyms, and the usage statistics about these terms
- ✔ Terms used in hundreds of competing sites' KEYWORDS meta tags, ranked according to frequency
- ✔ Common misspellings
- ✔ A comparison of how often a term is searched for with how many pages appear for that term — a nice way to find terms with relatively little competition

Do metacrawlers provide better results? Here's what Wordtracker claims:

- ✔ **Search results at the big search engines are skewed.** Many Web site owners use search engines to check their sites' rankings, sometimes several times a week. Thus, many searches are not true searches. Metacrawlers can't easily be used for this purpose, so they provide cleaner results.
- ✔ **Wordtracker analyzes searches to find what appear to be fake, automated searches.** Some companies carry out hundreds of searches an hour on particular keywords — company or product names, for instance — in an attempt to trick search engines into thinking these keywords generate a lot of interest.

Wordtracker is well worth the price. You can pay for access by the

- ✔ Week for $30
- ✔ Month for $59
- ✔ Year for $329

Many professionals in the SEO business have a regular account with Wordtracker, but for individual sites, it may be worth getting just a day or two of access. One strategy is to build your list first (as described in this chapter) and then sign up for a day and run Wordtracker for that day. You may get enough done in a couple of hours; if not, you can always sign up for another day. (Of course these prices may change, so check the Wordtracker site.)

Anyone heavily involved in the Web and search engines can easily get addicted to this tool. Sometimes you've just got to know how often people are searching for *paris hilton* (52,276 times a day), *barack obama* (5,643), or *super nanny* (189).

Some search numbers sound very low; only 189 people searching for *super nanny,* for example. *Primary* terms often are low because most searches are not for primary terms; many searches are for *the super nanny, super nanny show, super nanny on tv,* and other (sometimes bizarre) phrases. While individual phrases may seem to have low numbers, these combined phrases often add up to a very large number.

Creating a Wordtracker project

Wordtracker allows you to create projects so you can store different groups of terms — perhaps one for each Web site or, if you're a consultant, one for each client. The first thing you do — after plunking down your money and setting up the standard username and password stuff — is create a project. Here's how:

1. **Log in and click the Projects button on the main navigation page.**

   The Projects page appears, as shown in Figure 5-5.

2. **Give your project a name and then click the Change Project Name button to save the new name.**

   Wordtracker allows you to have seven projects, storing different keyword lists. You can empty old projects and rename them as you move on to new Web projects. This may be an important feature if you're an SEO professional or a Web designer working on multiple Web sites.

3. **Click the Import button and then copy and paste the words from the list of keywords you created earlier into the large text box.**

   You get one entry per line, as shown in Figure 5-6.

Click here to set the new name.

Type your new project name here.

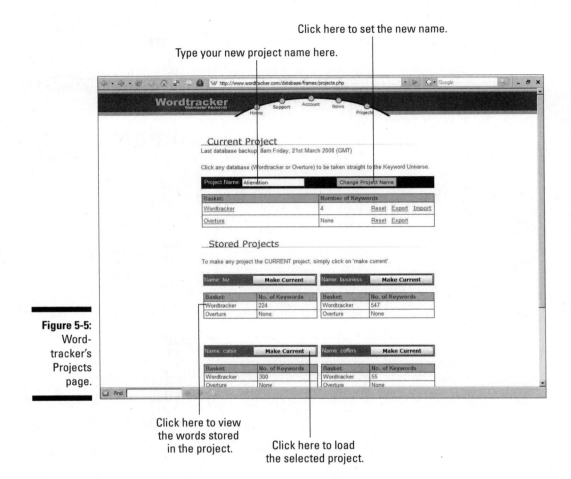

Figure 5-5:
Word-
tracker's
Projects
page.

Click here to view
the words stored
in the project.

Click here to load
the selected project.

4. Click the Submit button.

I recommend that you leave the Compressed Import button selected.
Doing so changes all the entries to lowercase regardless of how you
typed them.

Most search systems are not case sensitive, so *Rodent* is the same as
rodent.

After the list is imported, another page opens, showing your list with a
number in parentheses next to each keyword or keyword phrase; this is
the *count,* or the number of times the word or phrase appears in the
database.

Paste your keywords list here.

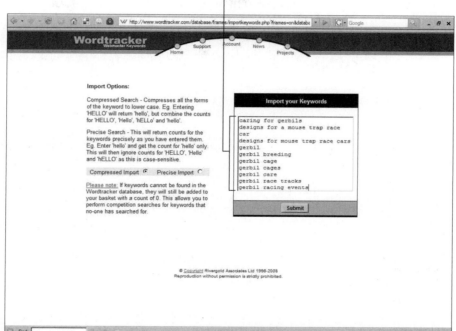

Figure 5-6:
The Import
page.

Adding keywords to your initial project list

To use Wordtracker to find more words that might be appropriate, follow
these steps:

1. **Click the Home button in the navigation bar at the top of any
   Wordtracker page.**

   You're taken to the Wordtracker home page.

2. **Click the Keyword Universe link.**

   You see the page shown in Figure 5-7.

3. **Type the first keyword in your list into the box on the left.**

4. **Click the Proceed button.**

Both the Lateral and Thesaurus check boxes are selected by default. Here's the lowdown on these options:

- *Lateral:* Wordtracker looks for 200 Web sites it thinks are related to the word you typed and grabs keywords from those site's KEYWORDS meta tags. (You find out more about KEYWORDS meta tags in Chapter 6.)

- *Thesaurus:* Wordtracker looks up the word in a thesaurus.

After clicking the Proceed button, wait a few minutes while Wordtracker builds a list. Scroll down the left frame to see the list.

5. **Click a word in the left frame to load the corresponding table in the right frame.**

The table shows you actual searches from the Wordtracker database containing the word you clicked, and other keyword phrases containing that word. So, for instance, if you click *rodent,* you see search terms such as *rodents, rodent control, rodents revenge, rodent, rodent repellent, rodent pictures,* and so on.

Type a word here and click Proceed.   Click here to add new words to your project.

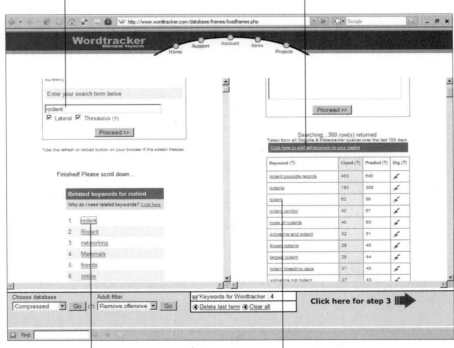

Figure 5-7:
The
Keyword
Universe
page.

Click a word to load the   Click a word to add it to your list.
list in the right frame.

Next to each term in the table are the following two numbers:

- ✔ **Count:** The number of times Wordtracker found the search term in its database. The database contains searches for 100 days — more than 400 million searches. So the Count value is the number of times the term was used in the last three months in the search engines from which Wordtracker builds its database.

- ✔ **Predict:** An estimate of how many times this term is likely to be used each day in all the Internet search engines combined.

Wordtracker assumes that the search engines it's working with account for a certain percentage of all searches, so it simply takes the Count number and multiplies accordingly.

I believe these numbers are too low. From what I've seen and heard, these terms may actually be searched 50 to 100 percent more often than the Predict number. However, what counts is the relative, rather than absolute, number. If one phrase has a Predict value of 12,000 times a day, and another one 6,000 times a day, the actual numbers may be 24,000 and 12,000, but what really matters is that one is much more than the other.

Here's what you can do with the list of search terms in the right frame:

- ✔ Click the Click Here to Add All Keywords to Your Basket link to add all the keyword phrases to your project. (The number next to the basket in the bottom frame increases as you add phrases to the project.)

- ✔ Click a term to add just that term to the project.

- ✔ Click the shovel icon in the Dig column to see similar terms. Click the shovel in the _rodents revenge_ row, for example, to see a smaller list containing _download rodents revenge, rodents revenge download, download rodents revenge game,_ and so on.

Should you add all the words in the list at once, or one by one? That depends. If the list contains mostly words that seem relevant, click the All link. You can remove the few that are no good later. If most of the list seems to be garbage, scroll down the list and add only the useful words.

After you've finished tweaking the list, here are a couple other things you can do:

- ✔ Click another phrase in the left frame, which loads a new list in the right frame with search terms related to that phrase.

- ✔ Type another word from your original list into the box at the top of the left frame. Wordtracker retrieves more terms related to it from the thesaurus and KEYWORDS meta tags.

> ✔ Type a term into the text box at the top of the right frame and click the Go button to create a list based on that term.

The left frame is handy because it runs your words through a thesaurus and grabs words from KEYWORDS meta tags. But I also like to use the text box at the top of the right frame: I grab a few keyword phrases from my list and copy them into the box. (Each one needs to be on a separate line.) This is a quick way to find matching phrases for the terms already in your list. Typing a word into the text box at the top of the right frame is the same as clicking a word in the left frame — Wordtracker looks for real search phrases that include the word. Type (or paste) multiple words into the text box and Wordtracker looks for matches for each of those words.

Cleaning up the list

After you work through your list, checking for relevant terms, click the Click Here for Step 3 link at the bottom of the page. On the Step 3 page, you see the first 100 words in your project with the most common appearing first; see Figure 5-8.

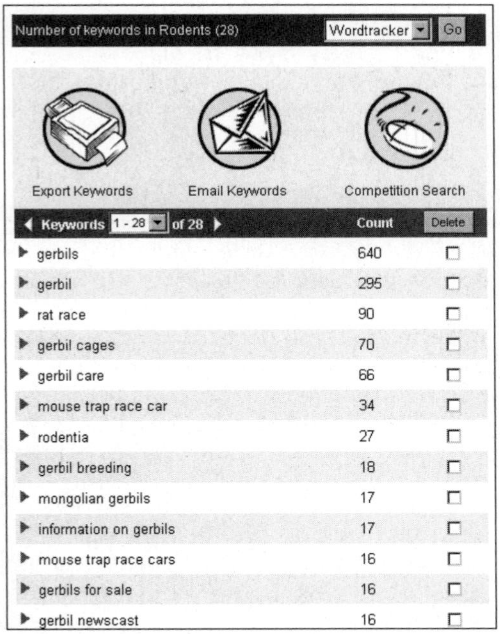

Figure 5-8: Clean your keyword phrase list here.

Scroll through this list carefully and look for any keywords that really aren't appropriate. It's possible you'll find some, especially if you clicked the All link on the previous page. To delete a term, select the check box to the right of the unwanted term and click the Delete button at the top. Then scroll to the bottom of the list and work your way up. If you delete 15 terms from the page, 15 more are pulled from the next page, so you need to check them also. Use the right-pointing triangle at the top of the list to move to the next page.

Remove only those terms that are totally inappropriate. Don't worry about terms that aren't used much or terms that may be too general. I get to that topic in a moment.

Exporting the list

When you're satisfied with your list, you can export it from Wordtracker. At the top of the Step 3 page, click the Export Keywords button to open a window that contains your compiled list. The window contains a list of keyword phrases — a simple list with no numbers. To display the list with the Count and Predict numbers, click the Click Here to Get a Tab Delimited List of Keywords link.

You can highlight the Wordtracker list and copy and paste it into a word processor or text editor. You can also click the Email Keywords button at the top of the Step 3 page to e-mail the list to yourself or a colleague.

Performing competitive analysis

By doing a competitive analysis, you can identify terms that are searched for frequently but yield few results. If you then use these keywords on your pages, your pages are more likely to rank high in the search engines because you face little competition from other sites.

To do a competitive analysis, follow these steps:

1. **Click the Click Here for Step 3 button at the bottom of the Keyword Universe page.**

   The Step 3 page appears.

2. **Click the Competition Search button at the top of the Step 3 page.**

   Another page appears, as shown in Figure 5-9.

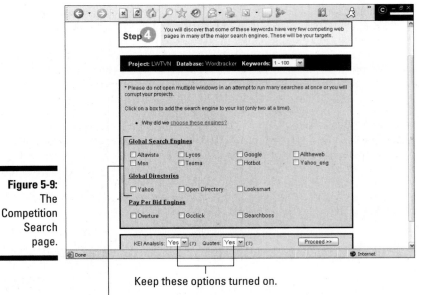

Figure 5-9:
The
Competition
Search
page.

Keep these options turned on.

Select two search systems in which Wordtracker checks for competing pages.

3. **Check various search engines and directories, two at a time.**

   Wordtracker tells you how often the term is searched for and how often the keyword phrase appears in Web pages in the indexes you selected.

At the bottom of the Competition Search page, you find the KEI Analysis and Quotes drop-down lists. You generally want to keep these options turned on.

- ✔ **Quotes:** Wordtracker encloses your search term in quotation marks when entering it into the selected search engines. For instance, if your phrase is *rodent racing,* Wordtracker searches for *"rodent racing".* The quotation marks tell the search engine that you want to find only those pages that contain the exact term *rodent racing,* providing a better idea of your true competition. If you search for the term without using quotation marks, you get all the pages with the word *rodent* or *racing* somewhere in the page, which returns far more results because the terms don't necessarily appear together or in order. You want to leave the Quotes option turned on because you're competing with sites that have the exact term in their pages.

- ✔ **KEI Analysis:** Wordtracker calculates the *KEI (Keyword Effectiveness Index),* which is a comparison of the number of people searching for a term and the number of Web pages returned by a search engine for that term. See Figure 5-10. The higher the KEI, the more powerful the term.

KEI is not always useful. A term that has few competing pages and is searched upon infrequently can generate a high KEI. This term would have little benefit to you because although the competition is low, the number of searches is also low. Also, it doesn't factor in how many people are actually optimizing their pages for the keyword; that's the real competition. See Chapter 3 for a discussion of this issue.

The Competition Search also provides information on *pay-per-click (PPC)* services, which allow you to buy a position in the search results, as discussed in Chapter 18. Wordtracker shows you the prices that you'd pay for these terms in a variety of PPC systems. Some people like to run a PPC check even if they're not doing a PPC campaign because it may give them an idea of what terms other people think are effective for sales. However, just because others are spending a lot of money on a particular term doesn't mean they're actually making money from it!

The KEI indicates a phrase with a very high Count : Competition ratio.

BEST SEARCH TERMS FOR GOOGLE

Google gets 35.1100% of all search engine traffic (approx. 112 million a day).

What do these headings mean? Click here

The KEI was invented by search engine positioning specialist Sumantra Roy of 1stSearchRanking.com.

0	10	100	400+
Poor Keyword	Good Keyword		Excellent Keyword

No.	Keyword (Why quotes? Click here)	KEI Analysis	Count	24Hrs	Competing ❓
1	"gerbil newscast"	256.000	16	6	1
2	"how to build a mouse trap race car"	64.000	8	3	0
3	"designs for a mouse trap race cars"	36.000	6	2	0
4	"human rat race greetings"	36.000	6	2	0
5	"designs for a mouse trap race car"	36.000	6	2	0
6	"mouse trap race car designs"	25.000	5	2	0
7	"mouse trap races"	24.000	12	4	6
8	"mouse trap race cars"	18.286	16	6	14
9	"how to make a mouse trap race car"	16.000	4	1	0
10	"gerbil cages"	10.938	70	25	448
11	"gerbil in a blender"	7.682	13	5	22
12	"mouse trap race car"	6.494	34	12	178

Figure 5-10: The Competition report.

Finding keywords more ways

Wordtracker has a number of other search tools available (although I use mainly those discussed earlier in the chapter):

- ✔ **Full Search:** Wordtracker returns similar terms in the same conceptual ballpark (a very large ballpark, though).

- ✔ **Simple Search:** You can place a bunch of keyword phrases into a text box to find actual search terms that include those keywords. For example, *rat* turns up *rat terrier, pet rats, naked mole rat,* and so on.

- ✔ **Exact/Precise Search:** This is a mixture of several tools, including the Exact Search, the Compressed Exact Search, and the Precise Search.

- ✔ **Compressed Search:** This is useful for finding plurals and singulars of words from a single list.

- ✔ **Comprehensive Search:** You can dig out a few useful related terms mixed in with a large number of unrelated terms.

- ✔ **Misspelling Search:** This is a good way to find common misspellings of your keywords.

Choosing Your Keywords

When you've finished working with a keyword tool, look at the final list to determine how popular a keyword phrase actually is. You may find that many of your original terms are not worth bothering with. My clients often have terms on their preliminary lists — the lists they put together without the use of a keyword tool — that are virtually never used. You also find other terms near the top of the final list that you hadn't thought about.

Removing unhelpful terms

To clean up your list, scan through it for keyword phrases that probably won't do you any good.

You missed the target

Take a look at your list to determine whether you have any words that may have different meanings to different people. Sometimes, you can immediately spot such terms.

Cam again?

One of my clients thought he should use the term *cam* on his site. To him, the term referred to *Complementary and Alternative Medicine.* But to the vast majority of searchers, *cam* means something different. Search Wordtracker on the term *cam,* and you come up with phrases such as *web cams, web cam, free web cams, live* *web cams, cam, cams, live cams, live web cams,* and so on. To most searchers, the term *cam* refers to *Web cams* — cameras used to place pictures and videos online. The phrases from this example generate a tremendous amount of competition, but few of them would be useful to my client.

Ambiguous terms

A client of mine wanted to promote a product designed for controlling fires. One common term he came up with was *fire control system.* However, he discovered that when he searched on that term, most sites that turned up don't promote products relating to stopping fires. Rather, they're sites related to fire control in the military sense — weapons fire control.

This kind of ambiguity is something you really can't determine from a system that tells you how often people search on a term, such as Wordtracker. In fact, it's often hard to spot such terms even by searching to see what turns up when you use the phrase. If a particular type of Web site turns up when you search for the phrase, does that mean people using the phrase are looking for that type of site? You can't say for sure. A detailed analysis of your Web site's access logs may give you an idea; see Chapter 20 for the details.

Very broad terms

Look at your list for terms that are incredibly broad. You may be tempted to go after high-ranking words, but make sure that people are really searching for your products when they type in the word.

Suppose that your site is promoting *degrees in information technology.* You discover that around 40 people search for this term each day, but approximately 1,500 people a day search on *information technology.* Do you think many people searching on *information technology* are really looking for a degree? Probably not. Although the term generates 40,000 to 50,000 searches a month, few of these will be your targets.

Here are a few reasons to forgo a term that's too broad:

✔ **Tough to rank.** It's probably a very competitive term, which means ranking well on it would be difficult.

> ✔ **Relevance is elsewhere.** You may be better off spending the time and effort focusing on another, more relevant term.
>
> ✔ **Maintaining focus.** It's difficult to optimize Web pages for a whole bunch of search terms (see Chapter 6). Therefore, if you optimize for one term, you won't be optimizing for another (perhaps more appropriate) term.

Picking combinations

Sometimes it's a good idea to target terms lower on your list rather than the ones up top because the lower terms *include* the higher terms.

Suppose that you're selling an e-commerce system and find the following list. The numbers are the *Predict* values — the number of times Wordtracker believes the term is used each day:

```
1828        e-commerce
1098        ecommerce
881         shopping cart
574         shopping cart software
428         shopping carts
260         ecommerce software
130         ecommerce solutions
109         e-commerce software
92          e-commerce solutions
58          shopping carts and accessories
26          ecommerce software solution
```

The term *e-commerce* is probably not a great term to target because it's very general and has a lot of competition. But lower on the list is the term *e-commerce solutions*. This term is a combination of two keyword phrases: *e-commerce* and *e-commerce solutions*. Thus, you can combine the Predict numbers — 1,828 searches a day plus 130 a day. If you target *e-commerce solutions* and optimize your Web pages for that term, you're also optimizing for *e-commerce*.

Notice also the term *ecommerce* (which search engines regard as different from *e-commerce*) and the term a little lower on the list, *ecommerce software*. A term even lower encompasses both of these terms — *ecommerce software solution*. Optimize your pages for *ecommerce software solution*, and you've just optimized for three terms at once.

The keyword analysis procedure I describe in this chapter provides you a much better picture of your keyword landscape. Unlike the majority of Web site owners, you'll have a good view of how people are searching for your products and services.

Yet More Keyword Tools

Though Wordtracker is probably the most popular keyword-analysis tool on the market, it's certainly not the only one.

There's KeywordSpy (http://www.keywordspy.com). This slick-looking system seems to focus primarily on keywords for pay-per-click campaigns though some of their tools could be useful for organic campaigns, too. It's also a useful competitive-analysis tool, because by tracking PPC ads being run on Google, the system can see what keywords your competitors are bidding on. The data it holds related to organic searches comes from "publicly available information from various sources such as ISPs log files" (Web site traffic logs contain keywords that visitors at the site used to find the site). KeywordSpy also has historical data, so you can see how keyword use may have changed over time.

Then there's Trellian's Keyword Discovery (http://www.keyword discovery.com). This tool gathers data by monitoring searches carried out by 4 million Web users, through the use of the Trellian toolbar (http://www.trellian.com/toolbar/), and some kind of "panel" that the site mentions without explaining what it is. One of the nice things about Keyword Discovery is that you can gather research keywords regionally; you can discover what keywords people are using in different areas of the world.

You may also want to check out Wordze (http://www.wordze.com/), an interesting service that provides historical keyword data, information on keywords in links pointing to many comparative sites, and so on.

Chapter 6

Creating Pages That Search Engines Love

*I*n this chapter, you find out how to create Web pages that search engines *really* like — pages that can be read and indexed and that put your best foot forward. Before you begin creating pages, I recommend that you read not only this chapter but also Chapter 7 to find out how to avoid things that search engines hate. There are a lot of ways to make a Web site work, and ways to break it, too. Before you get started creating your pages, you should be aware of the problems you may face and what you can do to avoid them.

I'm assuming that you or your Web designer understand HTML and can create Web pages. I focus on the most important search engine–related things you need to know while creating your pages. It's beyond the scope of this book to cover basic HTML and Cascading Style Sheets.

Preparing Your Site

When you're creating a Web site, the first thing to consider is *where* to put your site. By that, I mean the Web server and the domain name.

Finding a hosting company

Although many large companies place their Web sites on their own Web servers, most small companies don't. They shouldn't do this, in fact, because there's simply no way you can do it anywhere near as cheaply and reliably as a good hosting company can do it. Rather, a hosting company rents space on its servers to other businesses. Although you have to consider many factors when selecting a hosting company, I focus on the factors related to search engine optimization.

When looking for a hosting company, make sure that you can

- **Upload Web pages you created by yourself.** Some services provide simple tools you can use to create Web pages; it's fine if they provide these tools as long as you can also create pages yourself. You must have control over the HTML in your pages.

- **Use the company's traffic-analysis tool or, if you plan to use your own analysis tool, access the raw traffic logs.** A *log-analysis* tool shows you how many people visit your site and how they get there. See Chapter 21 for more information about traffic analysis.

- **Use your own domain name.** Don't get an account in which you have a subdirectory of the hosting company's domain name.

You need to consider many issues when selecting a hosting company, most of which aren't directly related to the search engine issue. If you want to find out more about what to look for in a hosting company, I've posted an article about selecting a host on my Web site, at www.SearchEngineBulletin.com.

Picking a domain name

Search engines read *uniform resource locators (URLs),* looking for keywords in them. For instance, if you have a Web site with the domain name rodent-racing.com and someone searches at Google for *rodent racing,* Google sees *rodent-racing* as a match; because a dash appears between the two words, Google recognizes the words in the domain name. (Google also interprets periods and slashes as word separators.) If, however, you run the words together (*rodentracing*), Google doesn't regard the individual words as individual words; it sees them as part of the same word. That's not to say that Google can't find text *within* words — it can, and you sometimes see words on the search results pages partially bolded when Google does just that — but when ranking the page, Google doesn't regard the word it found inside another word as the same as finding the word itself.

Read the fine print

Several years ago, I recommended that a non-profit client of mine register the *.com* version of their domain name. (They'd been using *.org* for years.) During the few hours that the *.com* domain was not yet pointing to their site, but was pointing to the domain registrar's site, the company received several calls from people trying to get to its Web site. These people wanted to let the company know that something was wrong with its server because its domain name was pointing to the wrong place. For years, the company printed all its materials using *.org*; they had never printed anything with *.com* because they didn't own it; however, people were still trying to get to *.com*.

To see this concept in action, use the *allinurl:* search syntax at Google. Type *allinurl:rodent,* for example, and Google finds URLs that contain the word *rodent* (including the directory names and filenames).

So, putting keywords into the domain name and separating keywords with dashes provides a small benefit. Another advantage to adding dashes between words is that you can relatively easily come up with a domain name that's not already taken. Although it may seem like most of the good names were taken long ago, you can often come up with some kind of keyword phrase, separated with dashes, that's still available. Furthermore, search engines don't care which first-level domain you use; you can use *.com*, *.net*, *.biz*, *.tv*, or whatever; it doesn't matter.

Now, having said all that, let me tell you my philosophy regarding domain names. In the search engine optimization field, it has become popular to use dashes and keywords in domain names, but in most cases the lift provided by keywords in domain names is relatively small, and you should consider other, more important factors when choosing a domain name:

- ✔ **A domain name should be short, easy to spell, and easy to remember.** And, it should pass the "radio test." Imagine you're being interviewed on the radio and want to tell listeners your URL. You want something that's instantly understandable, without having to be spelled. You don't want to have to say "rodent dash racing dash events dot com"; it's better to say "rodent racing events dot com."

- ✔ **In almost all cases, you should get the *.com* version of a domain name.** If the *.com* version is taken, do *not* try to use the *.net* or *.org* version for branding purposes! People remember *.com,* even if you say *.org* or *.net* or whatever. So, if you're planning to promote your Web site in print, on the radio, on TV, on billboards, and so on, you need the *.com* version.

A classic example is a situation involving Rent.com and Rent.net. These two different Web sites were owned by two different companies. Rent.net spent millions of dollars on advertising; every time I saw a Rent.net ad on a bus, I had to wonder how much of the traffic generated by these ads actually went to Rent.com! (Rent.net is now out of business — it was bought by Homestore.com — and Rent.com isn't. I don't know whether that's a coincidence!)

Are keyworded domain names worth the trouble? Because the lift provided by keywords in the domain name may be rather small — and, in fact, putting too many keywords into a name can *hurt* your placement. You should probably focus on a single brandable domain name (a *.com* version).

On the other hand, you might register both versions. For instance, register both Rodent-Racing-Events.com *and* RodentRacingEvents.com. Use Rodent-Racing-Events.com as the primary domain name, the one you want the search engines to see. Then do a 301 Redirect to point RodentRacingEvents.com to Rodent-Racing-Events.com. (See Chapter 21 for information on the 301 Redirect.) That way, you can tell people to go to "rodent racing events dot com" without having to mention the dashes, yet the search engine will regard all links to either domain as pointing to the same site and see the keywords *rodent* and *racing* in the domain name.

Don't use a domain-forwarding service for Web sites that you want to turn up in search engines. Many registrars now allow you to simply forward browsers to a particular site: A user types *www.domain1.com*, and the registrar forwards the browser to *www.domain2.com*, for instance. Such forwarding systems often use frames (discussed in Chapter 7), which means search engines don't index the site properly. Your site should be properly configured by using the name server settings, not a simple forward.

Seeing Through a Search Engine's Eyes

What a search engine sees when it loads one of your pages isn't the same as what your browser sees. To understand why, you need to understand how a Web page is created. See Figure 6-1 and read this quick explanation:

1. A user types a URL into his browser or clicks a link, causing the browser to send a message to the Web server asking for a particular page.

2. The Web server grabs the page and quickly reads it to see whether it needs to do anything to the page before sending it.

3. The Web server compiles the page, if necessary.

In some cases, the Web server may have to run ASP or PHP scripts, for instance, or it may have to find an *SSI (server-side include),* an instruction telling it to grab something from another page and insert it into the one it's about to send.

4. After the server has completed any instructions, it sends the page to the browser.

5. When the browser receives the page, it reads through the page looking for instructions and then, if necessary, further compiles the page.

6. When the browser is finished, it displays the page for the user to read.

Here are a few examples of instructions the browser may find inside the file:

- **`<SCRIPT>` tags containing JavaScript scripts or references to scripts stored in other files:** The browser then runs those scripts.

- **Cascading Style Sheets (CSS):** These instructions tell the browser how the page — in particular, the text on the page — should be formatted.

- **References to images or other forms of media:** After the browser finds these references, it pulls them into the page.

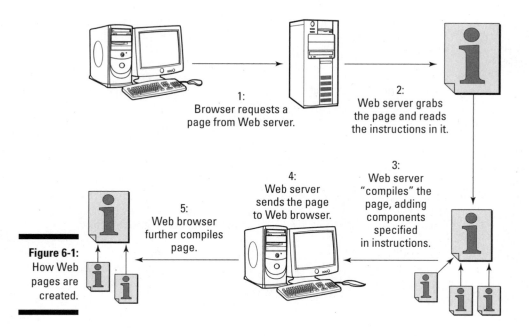

1:
Browser requests a
page from Web server.

2:
Web server grabs
the page and reads
the instructions in it.

3:
Web server
"compiles" the
page, adding
components
specified
in instructions.

4:
Web server
sends the page
to Web browser.

5:
Web browser
further compiles
page.

Figure 6-1:
How Web
pages are
created.

Scripting

ASP and *PHP* scripts are little programs that are written into Web pages. The scripts are read by a program working in association with the Web server when a page is requested. The search-bots see the results of the scripts because the scripts have been run by the time the Web server sends the page. *Server-side includes* *(SSIs)* are simple statements placed into the HTML pages that name another file and, in effect, say to the Web server, "Grab the information in this file and drop it into the Web page here." Again, the searchbots see the information in the SSI because the Web server inserts the information before sending the Web page.

So that's what happens normally when Web pages are created. But *searchbots,* used by search engines to index pages, work differently. When a searchbot requests a page, the server does what it normally does — constructs the page according to instructions and sends it to the searchbot. But the searchbot doesn't follow all the instructions in the page — it just reads the page. For example, it doesn't run scripts in the page, and it doesn't use the Cascading Style Sheet information to format the page.

Thus you can use two kinds of instructions to build Web pages:

- ✒ **Server-side instructions:** These instructions, such as ASP and PHP scripts and SSI instructions, are carried out by the server before sending the information to the searchbots.

- ✒ **Browser-side (or *client-side*) instructions:** These instructions are embedded into the Web page and generally ignored by searchbots. For instance, if you create a page with a navigation system built with JavaScript, the search engines don't see it. Some people even use browser-side instructions to *intentionally* hide things from search engines.

Of course, it's possible for an SSI to place browser-side instructions into a page. In this case, although the searchbot sees the instructions — because the server has placed them there — the searchbot ignores the instructions.

This concept is very important:

Server side = visible to searchbots

Browser side = not visible to searchbots

Understanding Keyword Concepts

Here's the basic concept of using keywords: You put keywords into your Web pages in such a manner that search engines can find them, read them, and regard them as significant.

Your keyword list is probably very long, perhaps hundreds of keywords, so you need to pick a few to work with. (If you haven't yet developed a keyword list, refer to Chapter 5 for details.) The keywords you pick should be either

✔ Words near the top of the list that have many searches.

✔ Words lower on the list that may be worth targeting because you have relatively few competitors. That is, when someone searches for a keyword phrase by using an exact search in quotes (*"rodent racing"* rather than *rodent racing*), the search engine finds relatively few pages.

It's often easy to create pages that rank well for the keywords at the bottom of your list because they're unusual terms that don't appear in many Web pages. However, they're at the bottom of your list because *people don't often search for them!* Therefore, you have to decide whether it's worthwhile to rank well on a search term that's searched for only once or twice a month.

Picking one or two phrases per page

You optimize each page for one or two keyword phrases. By *optimize,* I mean that you create the page in such a manner that it has a good chance of ranking well for the chosen keyword phrase or phrases when someone uses them in a search engine.

You can't optimize a page well for more than one keyword phrase at a time. The <TITLE> tag is one of the most important components on a Web page, and the best position for a keyword is at the beginning of that tag. Remember that only one phrase can be placed at the beginning of the tag. (However, sometimes, as you find out in Chapter 5, you can combine keyword phrases — for example, optimizing for *rodent racing scores* also, in effect, optimizes for *rodent racing.*)

Have primary and secondary keyword phrases in mind for each page you're creating, but also consider all the keywords you're interested in working into the pages. For instance, you might create a page that you plan to optimize for the phrase *rodent racing,* but you also have several other keywords that you want to scatter around your site: *rodent racing scores, handicap, gerbil, rodentia, furry friend events,* and so on. Typically, you pick one main phrase for each page and incorporate the other keyword phrases throughout the page, where appropriate.

Place your keyword list into a word processor, enlarge the font, and then print the list and tape it to the wall. Occasionally, while creating your pages, glance at the list to remind yourself which words you need to weave into your pages.

Checking prominence

The term *prominence* refers to where the keyword appears — how prominent it is within a page component (the body text, the `<TITLE>` tag, and so on). A word near the top of the page is more prominent than one near the bottom; a word at the beginning of a `<TITLE>` tag is more prominent than one at the end; a word at the beginning of the `DESCRIPTION` meta tag is more prominent than one at the end; and so on.

Prominence is good. If you're creating a page with a particular keyword or keyword phrase in mind, make that term prominent — in the body text, in the `<TITLE>` tag, in the `DESCRIPTION` meta tag, and elsewhere — to convey to search engines that the keyword phrase is important in this particular page. Consider this title tag:

```
<TITLE>Everything about Rodents - Looking after Them,
         Feeding Them, Rodent Racing, and more.</TITLE>
```

When you read this tag, you can see that *Rodent Racing* is just one of several terms the page is related to. The search engine comes to the same conclusion because the term is at the end of the title, meaning it's probably not the predominant term. But what about the following tag?

```
<TITLE>Rodent Racing - Looking after Your Rodents, Feeding
         them, Everything You Need to Know</TITLE>
```

Placing *Rodent Racing* at the beginning of the tag places the stress on that concept; search engines are likely to conclude that the page is mainly about rodent racing.

Watching density

Another important concept is *keyword density*. When a user searches for a keyword phrase, the search engine looks at all pages that contain the phrase and checks the *density* — the ratio of the search phrase to the total number of words in the page.

Suppose that you search for *rodent racing* and the search engine finds a page that contains 400 words, with the phrase *rodent racing* appearing 10 times — that's a total of 20 words. Because 20 is 5 percent of 400, the keyword density is 5 percent.

Keyword density is important, but you can overdo it. If the search engine finds that the search phrase makes up 50 percent of the words in the page, it may decide that the page was created purely to grab the search engine's attention for that phrase and thus decide to ignore it. On the other hand, if the density is too low, you risk having the search engines regard other pages as more relevant for the search.

You can get hung up on keyword density, and some people use special tools to check the density on every page. This strategy can be very time consuming, especially for large sites. You're probably better off "eyeballing" the density in most cases. If the phrase for which you're optimizing appears an awful lot, you've overdone it. If the text sounds clumsy because of the repetition, you've overdone it.

Placing keywords throughout your site

Suppose that someone searches for *rodent racing* and the search engine finds two sites that use the term. One site has a single page in which the term occurs, and the other site has dozens of pages containing the term. Which site does the search engine think is most relevant? The one that has many pages related to the subject, of course.

Some search engines — such as Google — often provide two results from a site, one indented below the other. So if your site has only one page related to the subject, this can't happen.

To see how this practice works in the real world of search engines, refer to Figure 6-2, which appears a little later in this chapter. You notice that Google provides two pages from the Britney Spears Guide to Semiconductor Physics. (Britney Spears's lectures — on semiconductor physics, radiative and nonradiative transitions, edge-emitting lasers, and VCSELs — are not what she is best known for and are probably of little interest to most of her fans, yet interesting nonetheless.)

In most cases, you're not likely to grab a top position by simply creating a single page optimized for the keyword phrase. You may need dozens, perhaps hundreds, of pages to grab the search engines' attention (with plenty of links between pages and from other sites back to yours — which you find out about in Chapters 14 through 16).

Creating Your Web Pages

When you're creating your Web pages, you need to focus on two essential elements:

✔ The underlying structure of the pages

✔ The text you plunk down on the pages

The next sections fill you in on what you need to look out for.

Naming files

Search engines get clues about the nature of a site from its domain name as well as from the site's directory and file structure. The added lift is probably not large, but every little bit counts, right? You might as well name directories, Web pages, and images by using keywords.

For example, rather than create a directory named */events/,* you could name it */rodent-racing-events/.* Rather than have a file named gb123.jpg, you can use a more descriptive name, such as rodent-racing-scores.jpg. Don't have too many dashes in the file and directory names, though, because overdoing it can cause the search engine to ignore the name.

You can separate keywords in a name with dashes, but *not* with underscores, despite what your Web designer may tell you. Try this test: Search Google for *rodent-racing* and then for *rodent racing,* and you'll notice that the results are almost the same (with perhaps just a slight difference). Now try searching for *rodent_racing.* When I tried, Google returned no results whatsoever — it couldn't find any page with the word *rodent_racing* in it. Don't let anyone tell you that you should be using underscores rather than dashes in file and directory names — it's simply not true! (There have been claims recently that Google plans to change this, and will treat underscores in the same way it treats dashes, but it certainly doesn't at the time of writing.)

Creating directory structure

It may be a good idea to keep a *flat* directory structure in your Web site. Keep your pages as close to the root domain as possible, rather than have a complicated multilevel directory tree. Create a directory for each navigation tab and keep all the files in that directory.

Many observers believe that search engines downgrade pages that are lower in the directory structure. This effect is probably relatively small, but in general you're better off using a structure with two or three sublevels rather than five or ten. For instance, the first page that follows would be weighted more highly than the second page:

```
http://www.domainname.com/dir1/page.html
```

```
http://www.domainname.com/dir1/dir2/dir3/dir4/page.html
```

Viewing TITLE tags

Most search engines use the site's <TITLE> tag as the link and main title of the site's listing on the search results page, as shown in Figure 6-2.

<TITLE> tags not only tell a browser what text to display in the browser's title bar, but they're also very important for search engines. Searchbots read page titles and use that information to determine what the pages are about. If your <TITLE> tags have a keyword between them that competing pages don't have, you have a good chance of getting at or near the top of the search results.

The <TITLE> tag is one of the most important components as far as search engines are concerned. However, these tags are usually wasted because few sites bother placing useful keywords in them. Titles are often generic: *Welcome to Acme, Inc.,* or *Acme Inc. – Home Page.* Such titles are not beneficial for search engine optimization.

I searched at Google for *intitle:welcome* to find out how many pages have the word *welcome* in their <TITLE> tags. The result? Around 89 million! Around 76 million have *welcome to* in the title (*allintitle:"welcome to"*). Having *Welcome to* as the first words in your title is a waste of space — only slightly more wasteful than your company name! Give the search engines a really strong clue about your site's content by using a keyword phrase in the <TITLE> tags. Here's how:

1. **Place your <TITLE> tags immediately below the <HEAD> tag.**

2. **Place 40 to 60 characters between the <TITLE> and </TITLE> tags, including spaces.**

3. **Put the keyword phrase you want to focus on for this page at the beginning of the <TITLE> tag.**

   If you want, you can repeat the primary keywords once. Limit the number of two-letter words and very common words (known as *stop words*), such as *as, the,* and *a,* because search engines ignore them.

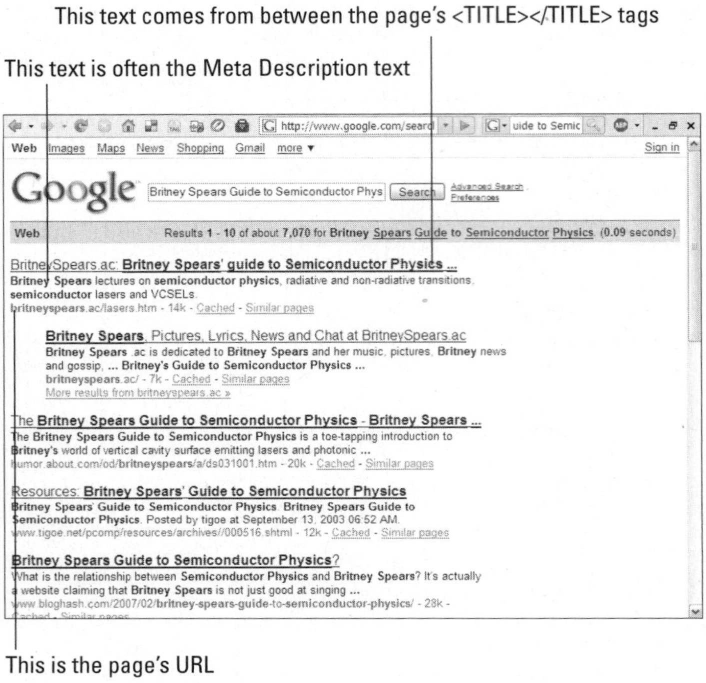

This text comes from between the page's <TITLE></TITLE> tags

This text is often the Meta Description text

Figure 6-2: Search results from Google, showing where components come from.

This is the page's URL

Here's a sample <TITLE> tag:

```
<TITLE>Rodent Racing Info. Rats, Mice, Gerbils, Stoats,
       all kinds of Rodent Racing</TITLE>
```

The <TITLE> tag and often the DESCRIPTION tag (explained in the next section) appear on the search results page, so they should encourage people to visit your site.

Using the DESCRIPTION meta tag

Meta tags are special HTML tags that can be used to carry information, which can then be read by browsers or other programs. When Internet search engines were first created, Webmasters included meta tags in their pages to make it easy for search engines to determine what the pages were about. Search engines also used these meta tags when deciding how to rank the page for different keywords.

The DESCRIPTION meta tag describes the Web page to the search engines. Search engines use this meta tag in two ways:

- ✔ They read and index the text in the tag.

- ✔ In many cases, they use the text verbatim in the search results page. That is, if your Web page is returned in the search results page, the search engine may grab the text from the DESCRIPTION tag and place it under the text from the <TITLE> tag so that the searcher can read your description.

Now, this process can vary between search engines, and over time for the same search engine. Until sometime in 2007, in most cases Google *didn't* use the text from the DESCRIPTION meta tag in its search results page. Rather, Google grabbed a *snippet* (a block) of text near where it found the search keywords on the page and then used that text in the results page. However, Google changed the manner in which it gathers the search-results description text. At the time of this writing, here's how it works:

- ✔ If Google finds all keywords you entered in the search query in the DESCRIPTION, it uses the DESCRIPTION text.

- ✔ If Google finds some of the keywords in the DESCRIPTION and some in the body of the Web page, it uses part of the DESCRIPTION and part of the body text.

- ✔ If Google finds none of the words in the DESCRIPTION, it grabs a snippet or two of text from the body of the page.

And, as I explain in Chapter 12, sometimes search engines use the site description from a Web directory in the index search results; Yahoo! does this, for instance.

Still, using the DESCRIPTION meta tag is important for the following reasons:

- ✔ Sometimes search engines *do* use the DESCRIPTION you provide; Google often uses it these days.

- ✔ Search engines index the DESCRIPTION.

- ✔ Many smaller search engines use the DESCRIPTION tag in their results.

The DESCRIPTION meta tag is pretty important, so you should use it. Place the DESCRIPTION tag immediately below the <TITLE> tags and then create a nice keyworded description of up to 250 characters (again, including spaces). Here's an example:

```
<META NAME="description" CONTENT="Rodent Racing - Scores,
        Schedules, everything Rodent Racing. Whether
        you're into mouse racing, stoat racing, rats,
        or gerbils, our site provides everything you'll
        ever need to know about Rodent Racing and
        caring for your racers.">
```

It's okay to duplicate your most important keywords once, but don't overdo it or you'll upset the search engines. Don't, for instance, do this:

```
<META NAME="description" CONTENT="Rodent Racing, Rodent
        Racing, Rodent Racing, Rodent Racing, Rodent
        Racing, Rodent Racing, Rodent Racing, Rodent
        Racing, Rodent Racing, Rodent Racing">
```

Overloading your DESCRIPTION (or any other page component) with the same keyword or keyword phrase is known as *spamming* (a term I hate, but hey, I don't make the rules), and trying such tricks may get your page penalized; rather than *help* your page's search engine position, it may cause search engines to omit it from their indexes.

Sometimes Web developers switch the attributes in the tag: <META CONTENT="your description goes here" NAME="description"> for instance, rather than <META NAME="description" CONTENT="your description goes here">. Make sure that your tags don't do the former because some search engines choke on such tags.

By the way, you should consider your DESCRIPTION tag as not only a search engine component but also a sales tool. Remember that much of the tag — perhaps the first 150 to 160 characters — will quite likely be seen in the search results (especially the Google search results), so you want to use something that encourages people to click the link — something that helps your links stand apart from the others on the page. An example is a compelling sales message or your phone number, which helps build credibility by ensuring that people recognize that it's a real site and not some search engine spam result!

Tapping into the KEYWORDS meta tag

The KEYWORDS meta tag was originally created as an indexing tool: a way for the page author to tell search engines what the page is about by listing (yep) keywords. Although quite important many years past, this meta tag isn't so important these days. Some search engines may use it, but many don't and even those that do, don't give it much value. Still, you might as well include the KEYWORDS meta tag. You do have a list of keywords, after all.

Don't worry too much about the tag — it's not worth spending a lot of time over. Here are a few points to consider, though:

- **Limit the tag to 10 to 12 words.** Originally, the KEYWORDS tag could be very large, up to 1,000 characters. These days many search engine observers are wary of appearing to be spamming search engines by stuffing keywords into any page component, and so recommend that you use short KEYWORDS tags.

✔ **You can separate each keyword with a comma and a space.** However, you don't have to use both — you can have a comma and no space, or a space and no comma.

✔ **Make sure that most of the keywords in the tag are also in the body text.** If they aren't, it probably won't do you any good either. Many people also use the KEYWORDS tag as a good place to stuff spelling mistakes that are commonly searched.

✔ **Don't use a lot of repetition.** You shouldn't do this, for instance: *Rodent Racing, Rodent Racing, Rodent Racing, Rodent Racing, Rodent Racing, Rodent Racing,* or even *Rodent Racing, Rodent Racing Scores, Rodent Racing, Gerbils, Rodent Racing Scores, Rodent Racing.* . . .

✔ **Don't use the same KEYWORD tag in all your pages.** You can create a primary tag to use in your first page and then copy it to other pages and move terms around in the tag.

Here's an example of a well-constructed KEYWORD tag:

```
<META NAME="keywords" CONTENT="rodent racing, racing
           rodents, gerbils, mice, mouse, raceing, mouse,
           rodent races, rat races, mouse races, stoat,
           stoat racing">
```

Using other meta tags

What about other meta tags? Sometimes if you look at the source of a page, you see all sorts of meta tags, as shown in Figure 6-3. Meta tags are useful for various reasons, but from a search engine perspective, you can forget almost all of them. (And most meta tags really aren't of much use for any purpose.)

You've heard about DESCRIPTION and KEYWORDS meta tags, but also of relevance to search engine optimization are the REVISIT-AFTER and ROBOTS meta tags:

✔ REVISIT-AFTER tells search engines how often to reindex the page. Save the electrons; don't expect search engines to follow your instructions. Search engines reindex pages on their own schedules.

✔ ROBOTS blocks search engines from indexing pages. (I discuss this topic in detail later in this chapter.) But many Web authors use it to *tell* search engines to index a page. Here's an example:

```
<META NAME="robots" CONTENT="ALL">
```

This tag is a waste of time. If a search engine finds your page and wants to index it, and hasn't been blocked from doing so, it will. And if the search engine doesn't want to index the page, it doesn't. Telling the search engine to do so doesn't make a difference.

```
<meta name="resource-type" content="document">
<meta http-equiv="pragma" content="no-cache">
<meta name="revisit-after" content="1">
<meta name="classification" content="Arts and Crafts">
<meta name="description"
content="New York Alive! Photographs is an online gallery containing dozens of signed, original, custom-
printed black and white photographs of New York City, its landmarks, buildings, neighborhoods, people,
and places. Buy original images for home or office direct from the photographers.">
<meta name="keywords"
content=" New York City, New York, New York NY, NYC, skyline, landmarks, buildings, Manhattan,
Brooklyn, neighborhood, neighbourhood, neighborhoods, neighbourhoods, photography, fine, fine art, art,
artist, artists, artistic, arts, photo, photographic, photographs, photograph, photographer, photographers,
pictures, black, black and white, white, images, imagery, image, gallery, galleries, virtual, online, on-line,
exhibits, exibits, exhibition, exhibitions, exhibit, contemporary, Central Park, Greenwich Village, Soho,
Wall Street, Statue of Liberty, Harlem, Washington Heights, Lower East Side, Ethnic, Empire State
Building, Flatiron, Flat Iron, Building, Chrysler, Brooklyn Bridge, Wall Street, New York Stock Exchange,
Chinatown, Little Italy, Yankees, people">
<meta name="robots" content="ALL">
<meta name="distribution" content="Global">
<meta name="rating" content="General">
<meta name="copyright" content="(c) Naomi Diamant, 2000. All rights reserved.">
<meta name="author" content="Abacus Consultants">
<meta http-equiv="reply-to" content="abacusconsultants@yahoo.com">
<meta name="language" content="English">
<meta name="doc-type" content="Public" ">
<meta name="doc-class" content="Completed">
<meta name="doc-rights" content="Copywritten Work">
```

Figure 6-3: An example of all sorts of meta tags you generally don't need. I've bolded the names to make them easier to see.

Here's a special Google meta tag that you can use in a couple of ways:

```
<META NAME="googlebot" CONTENT="nosnippet">
```

This meta tag tells Google not to use the description *snippet,* the piece of information it grabs from within a Web page to use as the description; instead, it uses the DESCRIPTION meta tag. However, this tag, at least at the time of writing, may be rather redundant because Google isn't usually using a snippet (as explained earlier in this chapter); also, this tag has the effect of removing the page from Google's cache.

Here's another example:

```
<META NAME="googlebot" CONTENT="noarchive">
```

This meta tag tells Google not to place a copy of the page into the cache. If you have an average corporate attorney on staff who doesn't like the idea of Google storing a copy of your company's information on its servers, you can tell Google not to.

These Google meta tags may work, but many users report that sometimes they don't.

Including image ALT text

You use the `<IMG>` tag to insert images into Web pages. This tag can include the `ALT=` attribute, which means *alt*ernative text. `ALT` text was originally displayed if the browser viewing the page couldn't display images. `ALT` text is also used by programs that "speak" the page (for individuals without sight). In many browsers, `ALT` text also appears in a little pop-up box when you hold your mouse over an image for a few moments. (If you use Firefox, you can install an add-on, Popup ALT Attribute, to make it happen.)

`ALT` tags are also read by search engines. Why? Because these tags offer another clue about the content of the Web page. How much do `ALT` tags help? Almost not at all these days because some Web designers have abused the technique by stuffing `ALT` attributes with tons of keywords. But using `ALT` tags can't hurt (assuming that you *don't* stuff them with tons of keywords, but rather simply drop in a few here and there) and may even help push your page up a little in the search engine rankings.

You can place keywords in your `ALT` attributes like this:

```
<IMG SRC="rodent-racing-1.jpg" ALT="Rodent Racing - Ratty
          winners of our latest Rodent Racing event">
```

Adding body text

You need text in your page. How much? More than a little, but not too much. Maybe 200 to 400 words is a good range. Don't get hung up on these numbers, though. If you put an article in a page and the article is 1,000 words, that's fine, and some pages may not have much text at all. But in general, when building a page that you want people to find in the search engines, a number in the 200–400 word range is good. That amount of content allows you to really define what the page is about and helps the search engine understand what the page is about.

Keep in mind that a Web site needs content in order to be noticed by search engines. (For more on this topic, see Chapter 9.) If the site doesn't have much content for the search engine to read, the search engine will have trouble determining what the page is about and may not properly rank it. In effect, the page loses points in the contest for search engine ranking. Certainly, placing keywords in content is not all there is to being ranked in search engines; as you find out in Chapters 14 through 16, for instance, linking to the pages is also very important. But keywords in content are very significant, so search engines have a natural bias toward Web sites with a large amount of content.

This bias toward content could be considered very unfair. After all, your site may be the perfect fit for a particular keyword search, even if you don't have much content in your site. In fact, inappropriate sites often appear in searches simply because they have a lot of pages, some of which have the right keywords.

Suppose that your rodent-racing Web site is the only site in the world at which you can buy tickets for rodent-racing events. Your site doesn't provide a lot of content because rodent-racing fans simply want to be able to buy tickets and nothing more. However, because your site has less content than other sites, it is at a disadvantage to sites that have lots of content related to rodent racing, even if these other sites aren't directly related to the subject. (On the other hand, if rodent-racing fans throughout the world decide that your site is *the* one on which to buy tickets, and enough of them link to you, you can still rank well regardless of how much page content you have.)

You can't do much to confront this problem, except to add more content (or create a lot of links)! You can find some ideas on where to get content in Chapter 9, and read all about links in Chapters 14 through 16.

Creating headers: CSS versus <H> tags

Back when the Web began, browsers defined what pages looked like. A designer could say, "I want body text here and a heading there and an address over there," but the designer had no way to define what the page actually looked like. The browser decided. The browser defined what a header looked like, what body text looked like, and so on. The page might appear one way in one browser program, and another way in a different program.

These days, designers have a useful new tool available to them: *Cascading Style Sheets (CSS)*. With CSS, designers can define exactly what each element should look like on a page.

Now, here's the problem. HTML has several tags that define headers: <H1>, <H2>, <H3>, and so on. These headers are useful in search engine optimization because when you put keywords into a heading, you're saying to a search engine, "These keywords are so important that they appear in my heading text." Search engines pay more attention to them, weighing them more heavily than keywords in body text.

But many designers have given up on using the <H> tags and rely solely on CSS to make headers look the way they want them to. The plain <H> tags are often rather ugly when displayed in browsers, so designers don't like to use them. <H> tags also cause spacing issues; for example, an <H1> tag always includes a space above and below the text contained in the tag.

However, there's no reason you can't use both <H> tags *and* CSS. You can use style sheets in two basic ways:

✔ Create a style class and then assign that class to the text you want to format.

✔ Define the style for a particular HTML tag.

Many designers do the former; they create a style class in the style sheet, like in the following example:

```
.headtext { font-family: Verdana, Arial, Helvetica, sans-
          serif; font-size: 16px; font-weight: bold;
          color: #3D3D3D }
```

Then they assign the style class to a piece of text, like this:

```
<DIV CLASS="headtext">Rodent Racing for the New
          Millennium!</div>
```

In this example, the `headtext` class makes the text appear the way the designer wants the headings to appear. But, as far as search engines are concerned, this is just normal body text.

A better way is to define the `<H>` tags in the style sheets, as in the following example:

```
H1 {
font-family: Verdana, Arial, Helvetica, sans-serif;
font-size: 16px;
font-weight: bold;
color: #3D3D3D
}
```

Now, whenever you add an `<H1>` tag to your pages, the browser reads the style sheet and knows exactly which font family, size, weight, and color you want. It's the best of both worlds — you get the appearance you want, and search engines know it's an `<H1>` tag.

Formatting text

You can also tell search engines that a particular word might be significant in several other ways. If the text is in some way different from most of the other text in the page, search engines may assume that it has been set off for some reason, that the Web designer has treated it differently because it *is* in some way different and more significant than the other words.

Here are a few things you can do to set your keywords apart from the other words on the page:

✔ Make the text **bold.**

✔ Make the text *italic.*

✔ Uppercase the First Letter in Each Word, and lowercase the other letters in the word.

✔ Put the keywords in bullet lists.

For each page, you have a particular keyword phrase in mind; this is the phrase for which you use the preceding techniques.

Another way to emphasize the text is to make a piece of text larger than the surrounding text. (Just make sure that you do this in a way that doesn't look tacky.) For example, you can use <H> tags for headers but also use slightly larger text at the beginning of a paragraph or for subheaders.

Creating links

Links in your pages serve several purposes:

✔ They help searchbots find other pages in your site.

✔ Keywords in links tell search engines about the pages that the links are pointing at.

✔ Keywords in links also tell search engines about the page containing the links.

You need links into — and out of — your pages. You don't want *dangling* or *orphan* pages — pages with links into them but no links out. All your pages should be part of the navigation structure. It's also a good idea to have links within the body text, too.

Search engines read link text for not just clues about the page being referred to, but also for hints about the page containing the link. I've seen situations in which links convinced a search engine that the page the links pointed to were relevant for the keywords used in the links, even though the page didn't contain those words. The classic example was an intentional manipulation of Google, late in 2003, to get it to display George Bush's bio (www.white house.gov/president/gwbbio.html) when people searched for the term *miserable failure.* This was done by a small group of people using links in blog pages. Despite the fact that this page contains neither the word *miser-able* nor the word *failure,* and certainly not the term *miserable failure,* a few dozen links with the words *miserable failure* in the link text were enough to trick Google. (After several years, Google put a stop to this practice, but the principle still applies. I discuss this Googlebomb in Chapter 14.)

So when you're creating pages, create links on the page to other pages, and make sure that other pages within your site link back to the page you're creating, using the keywords you placed in your <TITLE> tag.

Don't create simple Click Here links or You'll Find More Information Here links. These words don't help you. Instead, create links like these:

> For more information, see our *rodent-racing scores page*.

> Our *rodent-racing background page* provides you with the information you're looking for.

> Visit our *rat events* and *mouse events* pages for more info.

Links are critical. Web developers have played all sorts of tricks with key-words — overloading <TITLE> tags, DESCRIPTION tags, ALT attributes, and so on — and all these tricks are well known to search engines and don't do much harm any more. Search engines constantly look for new ways to analyze and index pages, and link text is a good way for them to do that.

In Chapters 14 through16, you find out about another aspect of links: getting links from other sites to point back to yours.

Using other company and product names

Here's a common scenario: Many of your prospective visitors and customers are searching online for other companies' names or for the names of products produced or sold by other companies. Can you use these names in your pages? Yes, but be careful how you use them.

Many large companies are aware of this practice, and a number of lawsuits have been filed that relate to the use of keywords by companies other than the trademark owners. Here are a few examples:

- A law firm that deals with Internet domain disputes sued Web-design and Web-hosting firms for using its name, Oppedahl & Larson, in their KEYWORDS meta tags. These firms thought that merely having the words in the tags could bring traffic to their sites. The law firm won. Duh! (Didn't anyone ever tell you not to upset large law firms?)

- Playboy Enterprises sued Web sites that were using the terms *playboy* and *playmates* throughout their pages, site names, domain names, and meta tags to successfully boost their positions. Not surprisingly, Playboy won.

- Insituform Technologies Inc., sued National Envirotech Group after discovering that Envirotech was using its name in its meta tags. Envirotech lost. The judge felt that using the name in the meta tag without having any relevant information in the body of the pages was clearly a strategy for misdirecting people to the Envirotech site.

So, yes, you can get sued. But then again, you can get sued for anything. In some instances, the plaintiff loses. Playboy won against a number of sites, but lost against former playmate Terri Welles. Playboy didn't want her to use the terms *playboy* and *playmate* on her Web site, but she believed she had the right to, as a former Playboy Playmate. A judge agreed with her. The real point of the Terri Welles case is that nobody owns a word, a product name, or a company name. They merely own the right to use it in certain contexts. Thus, Playboy doesn't own the word *playboy* — you can say "playboy," and you can use it in print. But Playboy owns the right to use the word in certain contexts and to stop other people from using it in those same contexts.

If you use product and company names to mislead or misrepresent, you could be in trouble. But you can use the terms in a valid, nonfraudulent manner. For instance, you can have a product page in which you compare your products to another, named competitor. That's perfectly legal. No, I'm not a lawyer, but I'm perfectly willing to play one on TV, given the opportunity. And I would bet that you won't be seeing the courts banning product comparisons on Web sites.

If you have information about competing products and companies on your pages, used in a valid manner, you can also include the keywords in the `<TITLE>`, `DESCRIPTION`, and `KEYWORDS` tags, as Terri Welles did:

```
<META NAME="keywords" CONTENT=" terri, welles, playmate,
          playboy, model, models, semi-nudity, naked,
          censored by editors, censored by editors,
          censored by editors, censored by editors,
          censored by editors, censored by editors,
          censored by editors, censored by editors">
```

And there's nuthin' Playboy can do about it.

What's ironic is that firms are being sued for putting other companies' names and brand names in their `KEYWORDS` tags, when it has very little influence on search engine rank these days.

Creating navigation structures that search engines can read

Your navigation structure needs to be visible to search engines. As I explain earlier in this chapter, some page components are simply invisible to search engines. For instance, a navigation structure created with JavaScript doesn't work for search engines. If the only way to navigate your Web site is with the JavaScript navigation, you have a problem. The only pages search engines will find are the ones with links pointing to them from other Web sites; search engines can't find their way around your site.

Here are a few tips for search engine–friendly navigation:

✔ If you use JavaScript navigation or another technique that's invisible (which is covered in more detail in Chapter 7), make sure that you have a plain HTML navigation system too, such as basic text links at the bottom of your pages.

✔ Even if your navigation structure is visible to the search engines, you may want to have these bottom-of-page links as well. They're convenient for site visitors and provide another chance for the search engines to find your other pages.

Yet another reason for bottom-of-page, basic text navigation: If you have some kind of image-button navigation, you don't have any keywords in the navigation for the search engines to read.

✔ Add a sitemap page and link to it from your main navigation. It provides another way for search engines to find all your pages.

✔ Whenever possible, provide keywords in text links as part of the navigation structure.

Blocking searchbots

You may want to block particular pages, or even entire areas of your Web site, from being indexed. Here are a few examples of pages or areas you may want to block:

✔ Pages that are under construction.

✔ Pages with information intended for internal use. (You should probably password-protect that area of the site, too.)

✔ Directories in which you store scripts and CSS style sheets.

Using the ROBOTS meta tag or the robots.txt file, you can tell search engines to stay away. The meta tag looks like this:

```
<META NAME="robots" CONTENT="noindex, nofollow">
```

This tag does two things: *noindex* means "Don't index this page," and *nofollow* means "Don't follow the links from this page."

To block entire directories on your Web site, create a text file called robots. txt and place it in your site's root directory — which is the same directory as your home page. When a search engine looks at a site, it generally requests the robots.txt file first; it requests http://www.domainame.com/robots.txt.

The robots.txt file allows you to block specific search engines and allow others, although this is rarely done. In the file, you specify which search engine (user agent) you want to block and from which directories or files. Here's how:

```
User-agent: *
Disallow: /includes/
Disallow: /scripts/
Disallow: /info/scripts/
Disallow: /staff.html
```

Because `User-agent` is set to *, all searchbots are blocked from `www.domainname.com/includes/`, `www.domainname.com/scripts/`, `www.domainname.com/info/scripts/` directories, and the `www.domainname.com/staff.html` file. (If you know the name of a particular searchbot that you want to block, replace the asterisk with that name.)

Be careful with your `robots.txt` file. If you make incomplete changes and end up with the following code, you've just blocked all search engines from your entire site:

```
User-agent: *
Disallow: /
```

In fact, this technique is sometimes used nefariously; I know of one case in which someone hacked into a site and placed the `Disallow: /` command into the `robots.txt` file — and Google dropped the site from its index!

Chapter 7

Avoiding Things That Search Engines Hate

*I*t is possible to look at your Web site in terms of its search engine friendliness. (Chapter 6 of this book does just that.) It is equally possible, however, to look at the flip side of the coin — the things people often do that hurt their Web site's chances with search engines, and in some cases even making their Web sites invisible to search engines.

This tendency on the part of Web site owners to shoot themselves in the foot is very common. In fact, as you read through this chapter, you're quite likely to find things you're doing that are hurting you. Paradoxically, serious problems are especially likely for sites created by mid- to large-size companies using sophisticated Web technologies.

Steering you clear of major design potholes is what this chapter is all about. Guided by the principle First Do No Harm, the following sections show you the major mistakes to avoid when setting up your Web site.

Dealing with Frames

Frames were very popular a few years ago, but they're much less so these days, I'm glad to say. A *framed* site is one in which the browser window is broken into two or more parts, each of which holds a Web page (as shown in Figure 7-1).

Frame 1 contains
navigational links.

Frame 2 contains
content pages.

Figure 7-1:
A framed
Web site;
each frame
has an
individual
page. The
scroll bar
moves only
the right
frame.

Frames cause a number of problems. Some browsers don't handle them
well — in fact, the first frame-enabled browsers weren't that enabled and
often crashed when loading frames. In addition, many designers created
framed sites without properly testing them. They built the sites on large,
high-resolution screens, so they didn't realize that the sites would be almost
unusable on small, low-resolution screens.

From a search engine perspective, frames create the following problems:

✔ **Search engines index individual pages, not framesets.** Each page is
indexed separately, so pages that make sense only as part of the frameset end up in the search engines as independent pages — *orphaned*
pages, as I like to call them. (Jump ahead to Figure 7-2 to see an example
of a page, indexed by Google, that belongs inside a frameset.)

✔ **You can't point to a particular page in your site.** This problem may
occur in the following situations:

• *Linking campaigns (see Chapters 14 through 16):* Other sites can link
only to the front of your site; they can't link to specific pages.

- *Pay-per-click campaigns (see Chapter 18):* If you're running a *pay-per-click (PPC)* campaign, you can't link directly to a page related to a particular product.

- *Indexing products by shopping directories (see Chapter 17):* In this case, you need to link to a particular product page.

Search engines index URLs — single pages, in other words. By definition, a framed site is a collection of URLs, and search engines therefore don't know how to properly index the pages.

The HTML Nitty-Gritty of Frames

Here's an example of a *frame-definition,* or *frameset,* document:

```
<HTML>
<HEAD>
</HEAD>
<FRAMESET ROWS="110,*">
<FRAME SRC="navbar.htm">
<FRAME SRC="main.htm">
</FRAMESET>
</HTML>
```

This document describes how the frames should be created. It tells the browser to create two rows, one 110 pixels high and the other * high — that is, it occupies whatever room is left over. The document also tells the browser to grab the navbar.htm document and place it in the first frame — the top row — and place main.htm into the bottom frame.

TECHNICAL STUFF

Refraining

Here's how Google responded to a question about frames from the technical editor of the first edition of this book, Micah Baldwin, of the blog Current Wisdom:

"Google does support frames to the extent that it can. Frames can cause problems for search engines because frames don't correspond to the conceptual model of the Web. In this model, one page displays only one URL. Pages that use frames display several URLs (one for each frame) within a single page. If Google determines that a user's query matches the page as a whole, it will return the entire frameset. However, if the user's query matches an individual frame within the larger frameset, Google returns only the relevant frame. In this case, the entire frameset of the page will not appear."

Google often does just that — return a page pulled out of its frame; the page is, in effect, "orphaned."

Most bigger search engines can find their way through the frameset to the `navbar.htm` and `main.htm` documents, so Google, for instance, indexes those documents. Some older systems may not, however, effectively making the site invisible to them.

But suppose the pages *are* indexed. Pages intended for use inside a frameset are individually indexed in the search engine. In Figure 7-2, you can see a page that I reached from Google — first (on the left) in the condition that I found it and then (on the right) in the frameset it was designed for.

This is not a pretty sight — or site, as it were. But you can work around this mess by doing the following:

✔ Provide information in the frame-definition document to help search engines index it.

✔ Ensure that all search engines can find their way through this page into the main site.

✔ Make sure that pages are open in the correct frameset (perhaps).

The next few sections give you the details for following these strategies.

I found this page indexed in Google . . .   . . . it really belongs in this frame.

Figure 7-2:
The document on the left, which I found through Google, belongs in the frameset shown on the right.

Providing search engines with the necessary information

The first thing you can do is provide information in the frame-definition document for the search engines to index. First, add a <TITLE> and your meta tags, like this:

```
<HTML>
<HEAD>
<TITLE>Rodent Racing - Scores, Mouse Events, Rat Events,
        Gerbil Events - Everything about Rodent
        Racing</TITLE>
<meta name="description" content="Rodent Racing - Scores,
        Schedules, everything Rodent Racing. Whether
        you're into mouse racing, stoat racing, rats,
        or gerbils, our site provides everything you'll
        ever need to know about Rodent Racing and
        caring for your racers.">
<META NAME="keywords" CONTENT="Rodent Racing, Racing
        Rodents, Gerbils, Mice, Mouse, Rodent Races,
        Rat Races, Mouse Races, Stoat, Stoat Racing,
        Rats, Gerbils">
</HEAD>
<FRAMESET ROWS="110,*">
<FRAME SRC="navbar.htm">
<FRAME SRC="main.htm">
</FRAMESET>
</HTML>
```

Then at the bottom of the <FRAMESET>, add <NOFRAMES> tags — <NOFRAMES> tags were originally designed to enclose text that would be displayed by a browser that couldn't handle frames — with <BODY> tags and information inside, like this:

```
<FRAMESET ROWS="110,*">
<FRAME SRC="navbar.htm">
<FRAME SRC="main.htm">
<NOFRAMES>
<BODY>
<H1>Rodent Racing - Everything You Ever Wanted to Know
        about Rodent Racing Events and the Rodent
        Racing Lifestyle</H1>
<P>[This site uses frames, so if you are reading this,
        your browser doesn't handle frames]</P>
<P>This is the world's top rodent-racing Web site. You
        won't find more information about the world's
        top rodent-racing events anywhere else ...[more
        info]
</BODY>
</NOFRAMES>
```

```
</FRAMESET>
</HTML>
```

Although few people still use browsers that can't work with frames, you can use the <NOFRAMES> tags to provide search engines with information that they can index. For example, you can place the information from main.htm into the NOFRAMES area. Provide 200 to 400 words of keyword-rich text to give the search engines something to work with. Make sure that the content between the <NOFRAMES> tags is about your site and is descriptive and useful to visitors.

Google suggests that the NOFRAMES area should be for alternate content (though, as every good editor knows, it probably means *alternative*) and says:

> *If you use wording such as 'This site requires the use of frames,' or 'Upgrade your browser,' instead of providing alternate content on your site, then you will exclude both search engines and people who have disabled frames on their browsers. For example, audio Web browsers, such as those used in automobiles and by the visually impaired, typically do not deal with such frames. You read more about the* <NOFRAMES> *tag in the HTML standard here at the following URL:* www.w3.org/TR/REC-html40/present/frames.html#h-16.4....

Unfortunately, many Web designers use the <NOFRAMES> tags as a convenient place to add keywords, even if the page isn't a frame-definition document. For this reason, search engines may treat the text within the tags in one of three ways: Ignore it if it's not within <FRAMESET> tags; downgrade it, awarding fewer points to text in a FRAMESET; or ignore it altogether. I believe that although in years past putting keywords within the <NOFRAMES> tags was effective, text placed here is no longer given much weight by the search engines.

Providing a navigation path

You can easily provide a navigation path in the NOFRAMES area: Simply add links in your text to other pages in the site. Include a simple text-link navigation system on the page and remember to link to your sitemap.

Remember also to do the following:

✔ Give *all* your pages unique <TITLE> tags and meta tags, as shown in Figure 7-3. Many designers don't bother to do this for pages in frames because browsers read only the TITLE in the frame-definition document. But search engines index these pages individually, not as part of a frameset, so they should all have this information.

✔ Give *all* your pages simple text-navigation systems so that a search engine can find its way through your site.

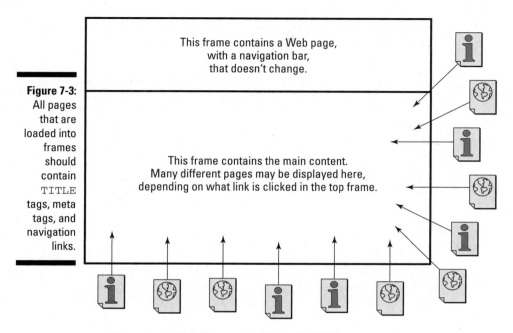

Figure 7-3:
All pages
that are
loaded into
frames
should
contain
TITLE
tags, meta
tags, and
navigation
links.

Pages loaded into frames should contain TITLEs, meta tags,
and simple text navigation links to help the search engines
index the pages and travel through the site.

You'll run into one problem with these links inside the pages. The links work
fine for people who arrive at the page directly through the search engines;
and any link that points at another page works fine in that situation or for
someone who arrives at your home page and sees the pages in the frames.
However, any link that points at a frame-definition documentinstead of at
another page doesn't work properly (unless you use the fix I'm about to
describe) if someone is viewing the page in a frame.

Suppose that you have a link back to the frame-definition document for your
home page. If someone is viewing one of your pages inside a frame, as you
intended it to be viewed, and clicks the link, the frame definition loads the
new frameset into the existing frameset. Now, rather than see, say, two
frames, the visitor sees three frames — the two new frames are loaded into
the current frame. To get around this problem, use the _top target, like this:

```
<a href="index.html" TARGET = "_top">Home</a>
```

This line "breaks" the frames, opening the index.html document alone in the
browser window.

Opening pages in a frameset

Given the way search engines work, pages in a Web site are indexed individually. (Refer to Figure 7-3.) If you create a site by using frames (hey, it takes all kinds!), presumably you want the site displayed in frames. You don't want individual pages pulled out of the frames and displayed, well, individually.

You can use JavaScript to force the browser to load the frameset. Of course, this technique won't work for the small percentage of users working with browsers that don't handle JavaScript — but those browsers probably don't handle frames, either. This technique also won't work for the small percentage of people who turn off JavaScript; but, hey, you can't have everything.

You have to place a small piece of JavaScript into each page so that when the browser loads the page, it reads the JavaScript and loads the frame-definition document. It's a simple little JavaScript that goes something like this:

```
<script language="javascript">
<!--
if (top == self) self.location.href = "index.html";
// -->
</script>
```

Admittedly, this JavaScript example causes two problems:

- ✔ The browser loads the frameset defined in `index.html`, which may not include the page that was indexed in the search engine. Visitors may have to dig around in the Web site to find the page that, presumably, had the content they were looking for.

- ✔ The Back button doesn't work correctly because each time the browser sees the JavaScript, it loads the `index.html` file again.

Another option is to have a programmer create a customized script that loads the frame-definition document and drops the specific page into the correct frame. If you work for a company with a Web-development department, this is a real possibility.

The only good fix is to not use frames in the first place! I've spent a lot of time on frames, for one purpose, really: so that you can quickly fix a site that's using frames. But you shouldn't build Web sites with frames. You may need to fix what someone else did or what you did in earlier, less knowledgeable, days. In general, though, frames are used far less today than they were used five years ago, for good reason: They're an unnecessary nuisance. Sure, frames may be appropriate in a few instances, but the general rule is this:

> If you think it's a good idea to build a Web site by using frames, you're almost certainly wrong!

Handling iframes

An *iframe* is an inline floating frame. This feature may now be more common than regular frames, as regular framing has fallen out of favor. You can use an iframe to grab content from one page and drop it into another, in the same way that you can grab an image and drop it into the page. The tag looks like this:

```
<iframe src ="page.html">
</iframe>
```

iframes have problems similar to the ones regular frames have. In particular, search engines index the main page and the content in an iframe separately, even though to a user they appear to be part of the same page.

First, you can add a link within the <IFRAME> tag so that older searchbots find the document (some may not), like this:

```
<iframe src="page.html"><a href="page.html"
        target="_blank">Click here for more Rodent
        Racing information if your browser doesn't
        display content in this internal
        frame.</a></iframe>
```

You can also use the JavaScript discussed in the preceding section to load your home page and to provide a link at the bottom of the iframe content that people can use to load your home page. And you may want to add links at the bottom of the iframe content, in case someone stumbles across it, orphaned, in a search result.

Fixing Invisible Navigation Systems

Navigation systems that never show up on search engine radar screens are a common problem, probably even more common than the frames problem I cover in the previous section. Fortunately, you can deal with a navigation-system problem very easily.

Many Web sites use navigation systems that are invisible to search engines. In Chapter 6, I explain the difference between *browser-side* and *server-side* processes, and this issue is related. A Web page is compiled in two places — on the server and in the browser. If the navigation system is created in the browser, it's probably not visible to a search engine.

Examples of such systems include those created by using

- ✔ Java applets
- ✔ JavaScripts
- ✔ Macromedia Flash

How can you tell whether your navigation is invisible to search engines? If you created the pages yourself, you probably know how you built the navigation system (although you may be using an authoring tool that did it all for you). If that's the case, or if you're examining a site built by someone else, here are a few ways to figure out how the navigation system is built:

- ✔ If navigation is created with a Java applet, when the page loads, you probably see a gray box where the navigation sits for a moment, with a message such as Loading Java Applet.
- ✔ Look in the page's source code.
- ✔ Turn off the display of JavaScript and other active scripting, and then reload the page to see whether the navigation is still there. (I explain how to do this in the section "Turning off scripting and Java," a little later in this chapter.)

Looking at the source code

Take a look at the source code of the document to see how it's created. Open the raw HTML file or choose View➪Source from the browser's main menu, and then look through the file for the navigation.

If the page is large and complex, or if your HTML skills are correspondingly small and simple, you may want to try the technique in the later section "Turning off scripting and Java."

Suppose that you find the following code where the navigation should be:

```
<applet code="MenuApplet" width="160" height="400"
          archive="http://www.yourdomain.com/menu.jar">
```

This navigation system was created with a Java applet. Search engines don't read applet files, so they won't see the navigation system.

Here's another example:

```
<script type="javascript" src="/menu/menu.js"></script>
```

This one is a navigation tool created with JavaScript. Search engines have difficulty reading JavaScript, so they won't see this navigation system either.

Here's an example of a Flash-based navigation system. Links in Flash navigation systems can't be read by many search engines:

```
<embed src="flash/rcbank_nav02.swf" quality=high
       pluginspage="http://www.macromedia.com/shockwav
       e/download/index.cgi?P1_Prod_Version=ShockwaveF
       lash" type="application/x-shockwave-flash"
       width="750" height="84"></embed>
```

The preceding examples are easy to identify. The script calls a Java applet or JavaScript, and you know that the searchbots don't read these, so they don't see the navigation.

Here's another form that can create a problem:

```
<a href="javascript:void(0)"
       onclick="Javascript:window.open('http://yourdom
       ain.com/rat-race/','Rat
       Race','width=550,height=600,left=20,
       top=20,screenX=0,screenY=100,resizable=yes,
       scrollbars=yes')"
       onMouseOut="MM_swapImgRestore()"onMouseOver="MM
       _swapImage('rat_race','','images/rat_race2.gif'
       ,1)"> <img src="images/rat_race1.gif"
       alt="Living and Shopping" name="rat_race"></a>
```

This link uses JavaScript *event handlers* to do several things when triggered by particular events:

- ✔ onclick runs when someone (guess!) clicks the link. This action opens a new window and places the referenced document in that window.

- ✔ onMouseOver runs when someone points at the link. In this case, it runs the MM_swapImage function, which changes the image file used for this navigation button.

- ✔ onMouseOut runs when the mouse is moved away from the link. In this case, it runs the MM_swapImgRestore function, presumably to display the original image.

The link in this example is real, but it doesn't work if JavaScript is turned off, because the URL normally goes in the href= attribute of the anchor tag (the <A> tag); href= is disabled in this link because it uses JavaScript to do all the work. Search engines don't follow a link like this.

Turning off scripting and Java

You can also turn off scripting and Java in the browser and then look at the pages. If the navigation system has simply disappeared or if it's there but doesn't work any more, you've got a problem.

How do you disable JavaScript and Java? Every browser's a little different, so I don't go into details here; check your browser's Help information.

Reload a page that you want to check after disabling JavaScript — use the Reload or Refresh button — and see whether the navigation system is still there. If it is, try to use it. Does it still work? If the navigation system has gone or if it's broken, the search engines will have a problem. (Figures 7-4 and 7-5 show you how effective this little trick can be. Navigation bar? Now you see it, now you don't.)

Disabling scripting and Java doesn't stop Flash from working, and, unfortunately, you have no simple, quick, and temporary way to stop Flash from working in Internet Explorer. Some other browsers have such a tool, though. Your best option for Internet Explorer is to install other blocking software, such as PopUpCop (`www.popupcop.com`) or jTFlashManager (`www.jtedley.com/jtflashmanager`) — or just look closely in your code for `.swf` files.

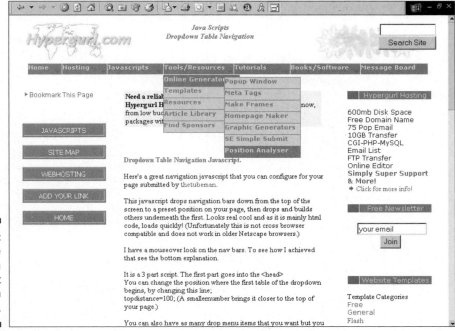

Figure 7-4:
This page has a JavaScript navigation menu bar.

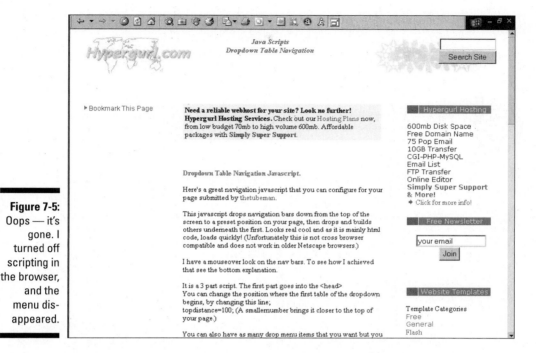

Figure 7-5:
Oops — it's
gone. I
turned off
scripting in
the browser,
and the
menu dis-
appeared.

Fixing the problem

If you want, you can continue to use invisible menus and navigation tools; they can be attractive and effective. Search engines don't see them, but that's okay because you can add a secondary form of navigation that duplicates the top navigation.

You can duplicate the navigation structure by using simple text links at the bottom of the page, for instance. If you have long pages or extremely cluttered HTML, you may want to place small text links near the top of the page, perhaps in the leftmost table column, to make sure that search engines get to them. (Table columns on the right are lower on the page, as far as the HTML is concerned, and search engines read the text in the HTML rather than view the page as people do.)

Flush the Flash animation

Using Flash animations sometimes makes sense, but usually it doesn't. Many Web designers place fancy Flash animations on their home pages just to make them look cool. But rarely do these animations serve any purpose beyond making site visitors wait a little longer to see the site. Some search engines can now read and index Flash content (albeit not well), but Flash animations generally don't contain any useful text for indexing. So, if you built your entire home page — the most important page on your site — by using Flash, the page is worthless from a search engine perspective.

Even if a page with Flash animation *does* appear in the search results — perhaps because you used the perfect <TITLE> tag — the search engine doesn't have much to work with. For example, in Figure 7-6, the search engine may find the following text:

> Skip Intro. The Celtic Bard is optimized for a 56k modem and above. If you are running a 28.8 modem please be advised you will have to wait for the Flash elements to download.

This bit of text is probably not what you want the search engine to index.

Most home-page Flash animations automatically forward the browser to the next page — the *real* home page — after they finish running. If you decide to include Flash, make sure that you include a clearly visible Skip Intro link somewhere on the page.

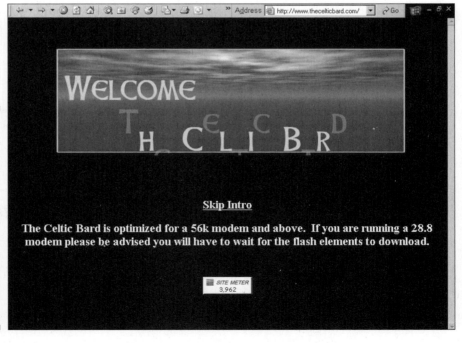

Figure 7-6:
Check out this classic example of a Flash animation. At least the site designer is honest in explaining that some site visitors will have to wait.

Search engines can index Flash files, but generally not well. If you create a page based on Flash, you can do a few things to help with indexing:

- ✔ Make sure to use your <TITLE> tags and DESCRIPTION and KEYWORDS meta tags.

- ✔ Put text between <NOSCRIPT> and </NOSCRIPT> tags. You can use the text displayed in the Flash within these tags, or if you're using audio, use a transcription of the text audio.

Avoiding Embedded Text in Images

Many sites use images heavily. The overuse of images is often the sign of an inexperienced Web designer — in particular, one who's quite familiar with graphic-design tools — perhaps a graphic artist who has accidentally encountered a Web business. Such designers often create entire pages, including the text, in a graphical-design program and then save images and insert them into the Web page.

The advantage of this approach is that it gives the designer much more control over the appearance of the page — and is often much faster than using HTML to lay out a few images and real text.

Putting text into graphics has significant drawbacks. Such pages transfer across the Internet much more slowly, and because the pages contain no real text, search engines don't have anything to index.

For example, the text shown in Figure 7-7 isn't real text; the text is part of one large image. This example may be the perfect text to get you ranked highly for your most important keyword phrase, but because it's a picture, it doesn't do you any good.

Reducing the Clutter in Your Web Pages

Simple is good; cluttered is bad. The more cluttered your pages, the more work it is for search engines to dig through them. What do I mean by *clutter?* I'm referring to everything in a Web page that is used to create the page but that is not actual page content.

For instance, one of my clients had a very cluttered site. The HTML source document for the home page had 21,414 characters, of which 19,418 were characters other than spaces. However, the home page didn't contain a lot of text: 1,196 characters, not including the spaces between the words.

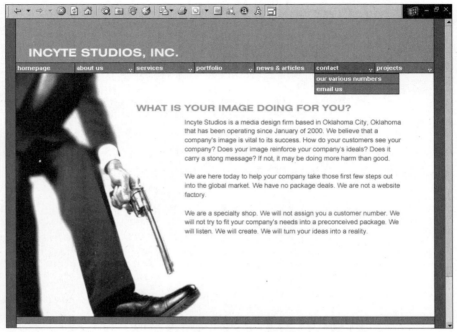

Figure 7-7:
This entire
page is
invisible to
search
engines. It's
made up of
one large
image and a
JavaScript
navigation
tool.

So, if 1,196 characters were used to create the words on the page, what were the other 18,222 characters used for? They were used for elements such as these:

- ✓ **JavaScripts:** 4,251 characters
- ✓ **JavaScript event handlers on links:** 1,822 characters
- ✓ **The top navigation bar:** 6,018 characters
- ✓ **Text used to embed a Flash animation near the top of the page:** 808 characters

The rest is the normal clutter that you always have in HTML: tags used to format text, create tables, and so on. The problem with this page was that a search engine had to read 18,701 characters (including spaces) *before it ever reached the page content*. Of course, the page didn't have much content, and what was there was hidden away below all that HTML.

This clutter above the page content means that some search engines may not reach it. Fortunately, you can use some simple methods to unclutter cluttered pages. (In my client's pages, we were able to remove around 11,000 text characters without much effort.)

Use external JavaScripts

You don't need to put JavaScripts inside a page. JavaScripts generally should be placed in an *external file* — a tag in the Web page "calls" a script that is pulled from another file on the Web server — for various reasons:

- **They're safer outside the HTML file.** That is, they're less likely to be damaged while making changes to the HTML.

- **They're easier to manage externally.** Why not have a nice library of all the scripts in your site in one directory?

- **The download time is slightly shorter.** If you use the same script in multiple pages, the browser downloads the script once and caches it.

- **They're easier to reuse.** You don't need to copy scripts from one page to another and fix all the pages when you have to make a change to the script. Just store the script externally and change the external file to automatically change the script in any number of pages.

- **Doing so removes clutter from your pages!**

Creating external JavaScript files is easy: Simply save the text between the `<SCRIPT></SCRIPT>` tags in a text editor, and copy that file to your Web server (as a `.js` file — `mouseover_script.js`, for instance).

Then add an `src=` attribute to your `<SCRIPT>` tag to refer to the external file, like this:

```
<script language="JavaScript" type="text/javascript"
        src="/scripts/mouseover_script.js"></script>
```

In this example, placing scripts in external files would have removed over 20 percent of the text characters from the file.

Use document.write to remove problem code

If you have a complicated top navigation bar — perhaps a navbar with text colors in the main bar that change when you point at options, or menus with drop-down lists — your code character counts can easily be up to 6,000 characters or so. That's a lot of characters, which can easily end up being a significant portion of the overall code for the page. You can easily remove all this clutter by using JavaScript to write the text into the page. Here's how:

1. **In an external text file, type this text:**

```
<!--
document.write("")
//-->
```

2. **Grab the entire chunk of code that you want to remove from the HTML page, and then paste it between the following quotation marks:**

```
document.write("place code here")
```

3. **Save this file and place it on your Web server.**

4. **Call the file from the HTML page by adding an `src=` attribute to your `<SCRIPT>` tag to refer to the external file, like this:**

```
<script language="JavaScript" src="/scripts/navbar.js"
        type="text/javascript"></script>
```

Of course, if you remove the navigation from the page — remember that the searchbots don't read these JavaScripts, so they don't see the navigation — you don't have navigation that the search engines can follow. Remember to add simple text navigation somewhere else on the page (maybe at the bottom, now that the page is much smaller). Simple text navigation takes up much less room than a complex navigation bar.

Use external CSS files

If you can stick JavaScript stuff into an external file, it shouldn't surprise you that you can do the same thing — drop stuff into a file that's then referred to in the HTML file proper — with Cascading Style Sheet (CSS) information. For reasons that are unclear to me, many designers place CSS information directly into the page, despite the fact that the ideal use of a style sheet is generally *external*. One of the basic ideas behind style sheets is to allow you to make formatting changes to an entire site very quickly. If you want to change the size of the body text or the color of the heading text, for example, you make one small change in the CSS file and it affects the whole site immediately. If you have CSS information in each page, though, you have to change each and every page. (Rather defeats the object of CSS, doesn't it?)

Here's how to remove CSS information from the main block of HTML code. Simply place the targeted text in an external file — everything between and including the `<STYLE></STYLE>` tags — and then call the file in your HTML pages by using the `<LINK>` tag, like this:

```
<link rel="stylesheet" href="site.css" type="text/css">
```

Move image maps to the bottom of the page

An image map (described in detail later in this chapter) is an image that contains multiple links. One way to clean up clutter in a page is to move the code that defines the links to the bottom of the Web page, right before the </BODY> tag. Doing so doesn't remove the clutter from the page — it moves the clutter to the end of the page, where it doesn't get placed between the top of the page and the page content. That makes it more likely that the search engines will reach the content.

Avoid the urge to copy and paste from MS Word

That's right. Don't copy text directly from Microsoft Word and drop it into a Web page. You'll end up with *all sorts* of formatting clutter in your page!

Here's one way to get around this problem:

1. **Save the file as an HTML file.**

   Word provides various options to do this, but you want to use the simplest: Web Page (Filtered).

2. **In your HTML-authoring program, look for a Word-cleaning tool.**

   Word has such a bad reputation that HTML programs are now starting to add tools to help you clean the text before you use it. Dreamweaver has such a tool, and even Microsoft's own HTML-authoring tool, FrontPage, has one. It's in the Optimize HTML dialog box, on the Options menu.

Managing Dynamic Web Pages

Chapter 6 explains how your standard, meat-and-potatoes Web page gets assembled in your browser so that you, the surfer, can see it. But you can assemble a Web page in more than one way. For example, the process can go like this:

1. The Web browser requests a Web page.

2. The Web server sends a message to a database program requesting the page.

3. The database program reads the URL to see exactly what is requested, compiles the page, and sends it to the server.

4. The server reads any instructions inside the page.

5. The server compiles the page, adding information specified in server-side includes (SSIs) or scripts.

6. The server sends the file to the browser.

Pages pulled from databases are known as *dynamic pages,* as opposed to normal *static pages*, which are individual files saved on the hard drive. The pages are dynamic because they're created on the fly, when requested. The page doesn't exist until a browser requests it, at which point the data is grabbed from a database by some kind of program — a CGI, ASP, or PHP script, for instance, or from some kind of content-management system — and dropped into a Web page template and then sent to the browser requesting the file.

Unfortunately, dynamic pages can create problems. Even the best search engines sometimes don't read them. Of course, a Web page is a Web page, whether it was created on the fly or days earlier. After the searchbot receives the page, the page is already complete, so the searchbots *can* read them if they want to. So why don't search engines always read dynamic pages? Because in some cases search engines don't want to read them (or their programmers don't want them to).

Search engine programmers have discovered that dynamic pages are often problem pages. Here are a few of the problems that searchbots can run into while reading dynamic pages:

✔ Dynamic pages often have only minor changes in them. A searchbot reading these pages may end up with hundreds of pages that are almost exactly the same, with nothing more than minor differences to distinguish one from each other.

✔ Search engines are concerned that databased pages might change frequently, making search results inaccurate.

✔ Searchbots sometimes get stuck in the dynamic system, going from page to page to page among tens of thousands of pages. On occasion, this happens when a Web programmer hasn't properly written the link code and the database continually feeds data to the search engine, even crashing your server.

✔ Hitting a database for thousands of pages can slow down the server, so searchbots often avoid getting into situations in which that is likely to happen.

✔ Sometimes URLs can change (I talk about session IDs a little later in this chapter), so even if the search engine indexes the page, the next time someone tries to get there, it's gone; and search engines don't want to index dead links.

All these problems were more common a few years ago, and in fact the major search engines are now far more likely to index databased pages than they were a few years ago. However, databased pages have another problem: The filenames are often complicated database queries instead of simple filenames containing useful keywords, as you see in the following section.

Determining whether your dynamic pages are scaring off search engines

You can often tell whether search engines are likely to omit your pages just by looking at the URL. Go deep into the site; if it's a product catalog, for instance, go to the farthest subcategory you can find. Then look at the URL. Suppose that you have a URL like this:

```
http://www.yourdomain.edu/march/rodent-racing-scores.php
```

This URL is a normal one that should have few problems. It's a static page — or at least it looks like a static page, which is what counts. Compare this URL with the next one:

```
http://www.yourdomain.edu/march/scores.php?prg=1
```

This filename ends with `?prg=1`. This page is almost certainly a databased dynamic page; `?prg=1` is a *parameter* that's being sent to the server to let it know which information is needed for the Web page. This URL is okay, especially for the major search engines, although a few smaller search engines may not like it; it almost certainly won't stop a searchbot from indexing it. It's still not very good from a search engine perspective, though, because it doesn't contain good keywords.

Now look at the following URL:

```
http://yourdomain.com/march/index.html?&DID=18&CATID=13&Ob
          jectGroup_ID=79
```

This URL is worse. It contains three parameters: `DID=18`, `CATID=13`, and `ObjectGroup_ID=79`. Three parameters may be too much. These days, Google may index this page; at one point it probably wouldn't have. Still, the more parameters, the less likely the pages are to be indexed.

If you have a *clean* URL with no parameters, search engines should be able to find it. If you have a single parameter, it's okay for the major search engines, though not necessarily for older systems. If you have two parameters, it's still probably okay for major search engines. If you have three parameters, you start to risk limiting your page indexing. And, it doesn't matter how many parameters you have, using good, clean URLs with nice keywords are always better than long, complicated URLs with no keywords.

You can also find out whether a page in your site is indexed by using the following techniques:

✔ If you have the Google Toolbar, open the page you want to check, click the i button, and select Cached Snapshot of Page. Or, go to Google and type **cache:** *YourURL*, where *YourURL* is the site you're interested in. If Google displays a cached page, it's there, of course. If Google doesn't display it, move to the next technique. (For more information on the Google Toolbar — including where to download it — see Chapter 1.)

✔ Go to Google and type the URL of the page into the text box, and then click Search. If the page is in the index, Google displays some information about it.

✔ Use similar techniques with other search engines if you want to check them for your page. Take a look at their Help pages for more information.

Fixing your dynamic Web page problem

So how do you make search engines take a look at your state-of-the-art dynamic Web site? Here are a few ideas:

✔ **Find out whether the database program has a built-in way to create static HTML.** Some e-commerce systems, for instance, spit out a static copy of their catalog pages, which is intended for search engines. When visitors click the Buy button, they're taken back into the dynamic system.

✔ **Modify URLs so that they don't look like they're pointing to dynamic pages.** You can often help fix the problem by removing characters such as ?, #, !, *, %, and & and reducing the number of parameters to one. For the specifics, talk with the programmer responsible for the database system.

✔ **Use a URL rewrite trick — a technique for changing the way URLs look.** Different servers have different tools available; the `mod_rewrite` tool, for instance, is used by the Apache Web server (a very popular system), and ISAPI Rewrite can be used on Windows servers, for instance. *Rewriting* is a process whereby the server can convert fake URLs into real URLs. The server might see, for instance, a request for a page at

```
http://yourdomain.com/march/rodent-racing-scores.html
```

The server knows that this page doesn't exist and that it really refers to, perhaps, the following URL:

```
http://yourdomain.com/
        showprod.cfm?&DID=7&User_ID=2382175&st=6642&st
        2=45931500&st3=-
        43564544&topcat_id=20018&catid=20071&objectgro
        up_id=20121.
```

In other words, this technique allows you to use what appear to be static URLs yet still grab pages from a database. This topic is complicated, so if your server administrator doesn't understand it, it may take him or her a few days to figure it all out; for someone who understands URL rewriting, however, it's fairly easy and can take just a few hours to set up.

✔ **Find out whether the programmer can create static pages from the database.** Rather than create a single Web page each time it's requested, the database could "spit out" the entire site periodically — each night for instance, or when the database is updated — creating static pages with normal URLs.

✔ **You can get your information into Yahoo! by using a data feed (often known as a *trusted feed*).** However, note that if you use a trusted feed, you're charged for every click to your site — and even then, it doesn't get you anywhere with Google (the world's most popular search engine) because it doesn't have this service, or with MSN Live Search or Ask.com. See Chapter 11 for more information.

If you want to find out more about URL rewriting, here are a couple of places to look:

✔ www.asp101.com/articles/wayne/extendingnames

✔ httpd.apache.org/docs/mod/mod_rewrite.html

Using Session IDs in URLs

Just as dynamic Web pages can throw a monkey wrench into the search engine machinery, session IDs can make search engine life equally interesting. A *session ID* identifies a particular person visiting the site at a particular time, which enables the server to track which pages the visitor looks at and which actions the visitor takes during the session.

If you request a page from a Web site — by clicking a link on a Web page, for instance — the Web server that has the page sends it to your browser. Then if you request another page, the server sends that page too, but the server doesn't know that you're the same person. If the server needs to know who you are, it needs a way to identify you each time you request a page. It does that by using session IDs.

Session IDs are used for a variety of reasons, but their main purpose is to allow Web developers to create various types of interactive sites. For instance, if developers have created a secure environment, they may want to force visitors to go through the home page first. Or, the developers may want a way to resume an unfinished session. By setting cookies containing the session ID on the visitor's computer, developers can see where the visitor was in the site at the end of the visitor's last session. (A *cookie* is a text file containing information that can be read only by the server that set the cookie.)

Session IDs are common when running software applications that have any kind of security procedure (such as requiring a login) or that need to store variables or that want to defeat the browser cache — that is, ensure that the browser always displays information from the server, never from its own cache. Shopping cart systems typically use session IDs — that's how the system can allow you to place an item in the shopping cart and then go away and continue shopping. It *recognizes* you based on your session ID.

A session ID can be created in two ways:

✔ Store it in a cookie.

✔ Display it in the URL itself.

Some systems are set up to store the session ID in a cookie but then use a URL session ID if the user's browser is set to not accept cookies. (Relatively few browsers, perhaps 1 or 2 percent, don't accept cookies.) Here's an example of a URL containing a session ID:

```
http://yourdomain.com/index.jsp;jsessionid=07D3CCD4D9A6A9F
        3CF9CAD4F9A728F44
```

The 07D3CCD4D9A6A9F3CF9CAD4F9A728F44 piece of the URL is the unique identifier assigned to the session.

If a search engine recognizes a URL as including a session ID, it probably doesn't read the referenced page because the server can handle a session ID in two different ways when the searchbot returns. Each time the searchbot returns to your site, the session ID will have expired, so the server can do either of the following:

✔ **Display an error page rather than the indexed page or perhaps display the site's default page (generally the home page).** In other words, the search engine has indexed a page that isn't there if someone clicks the link in the search results page. This behavior is admittedly less common than the one described in the following bullet.

✔ **Assign a new session ID.** The URL that the searchbot originally used has expired, so the server replaces the ID with another one and changes the URL. So, the spider could be fed multiple URLs for the same page.

Even if the searchbot reads the referenced page (and sometimes it does), it probably doesn't index it or doesn't index much of your site. Webmasters sometimes complain that a search engine entered their site, requested the same page over and over, and left without indexing most of the site. The searchbot simply got confused and left. Or, sometimes the search engine doesn't recognize a session ID in a URL. One of my clients had hundreds of URLs indexed by Google, but because they were all long-expired session IDs, they all pointed to the site's main page.

Fixing the session ID problem is like performing magic: Sites that were invisible to search engines suddenly become visible! One site owner in a search engine discussion group described how his site had never had more than 6 pages indexed by Google, yet within a week of removing session IDs, Google had indexed over 600 pages.

When sites are run through URLs with session IDs, you can do various things:

✔ **Rather than use session IDs in the URL, store session information in a cookie on the user's computer.** Each time a page is requested, the server can check the cookie to see whether session information is stored there. (Few people change their browser settings to block cookies.) However, the server shouldn't *require* cookies, or you may run into further problems (as you find out in a moment).

✔ **Get your programmer to omit session IDs if the device requesting a Web page from the server is a searchbot.** The server delivers the same page to the searchbot but doesn't assign a session ID, so the searchbot can travel throughout the site without using session IDs. (Every device requesting a page from a Web server identifies itself, so it's possible for a programmer to send different pages according to the requestor — a topic I talk more about in Chapter 8.) This process is known as *user agent delivery,* in which user agent refers to the device — browser, searchbot, or other program — that is requesting a page.

The user agent method has one potential problem: In the technique sometimes known as *cloaking,* a server sends one page to the search engines and another to real site visitors. Search engines generally don't like cloaking because some Web sites try to trick them by providing different content from the content that site visitors see. Of course, in the context of using this technique to avoid the session-ID problem, that's not the intent; it's a way to show the *same* content that the site visitor sees, so it isn't true cloaking. However, the (very slight) danger is that the search engines may view it as cloaking if they discover what is happening. (I don't believe that the risk is big, though some people in the SEO business will tell you that it is.) For more on cloaking, see Chapter 8.

Examining Cookie-Based Navigation

Cookies — the small text files that a Web server can store on a site visitor's hard drive — can often prove as indigestible to search engines as dynamic Web pages and session IDs. Imagine this scenario: You visit a site that's using cookies, and at some point the server decides to store a cookie. The server sends the information to your browser, and the browser duly creates a text file, which it then stores on your computer's hard drive. This text file might contain a session ID (as discussed in the preceding section) or something else. Cookies enable systems to remember who you are so that you don't have to log in each time you visit.

Cookies are sometimes used for navigation purposes. For instance, you may have seen *crumb trails,* a series of links showing where you have been as you travel through the site. Crumb trails look something like this:

```
Home->Rodents->Rats->Racing
```

This information is generally stored in a cookie and is read each time you load a new page. Or, the server may read the cookie to determine how many times you visited the site or what you did the last time you were on the site, and then direct you to a particular page based on that information.

If you're using Internet Explorer 7 in Microsoft Windows, follow these steps to see what these cookie files look like:

1. **Choose Tools⇨Internet Options from the main menu.**

   The Internet Options dialog box appears.

2. **In the Internet Options dialog box, make sure that the General tab is selected.**

3. **Click the Settings button in the Browsing History area.**

   The Temporary Internet Files and History Settings dialog box appears.

4. **In the Settings dialog box, click the View Files button.**

   A Windows Explorer window opens, displaying the directory containing your temporary files, including cookies. The files are named *Cookies: username@domainname.com.* For instance, when I visited the www.nokiausa.com Web site, the server created a cookie named *Cookie: peter kent@nokiausa.com.*

5. **Double-click any of these cookie files.**

   View the file's contents. When a warning message appears, ignore it.

6. **Click Yes.**

   The cookie opens in Notepad.

Here are the contents of the cookie that was set by www.nokiausa.com. This cookie contains a session ID:

```
session_idA_da6Bj6pwoLg=_nokiausa.com/_1536_1240627200_303
            94925_36557520_29597255_*
```

There's nothing wrong with using cookies, *unless* they're *required* in order to navigate through your site. A server can be set up to simply refuse to send a Web page to a site visitor if the visitor's browser doesn't accept cookies. That's a problem for several reasons:

- ✔ A few browsers simply don't accept cookies.

- ✔ A small number of people have changed their browser settings to refuse to accept cookies.

- ✔ Searchbots can't accept cookies.

If your Web site *demands* the use of cookies, it doesn't get indexed. That's all there is to it! The searchbot requests a page, your server tries to set a cookie, and the searchbot can't accept it. The server doesn't send the page, so the searchbot doesn't index it.

How can you check to see whether your site has this problem? Turn off cookies in your browser (see your browser's Help information), and then try navigating your site.

I recommend that you select Prompt rather than Block to make it easier to test your site. Now each time a server tries to set a cookie, you see a warning box and you can accept or block the cookie at will.

Clear your cookies, too, so that you can start fresh, and then go to your Web site and see what happens. Each time the site tries to set a cookie, you see a message box, similar to the one shown in Figure 7-8. Block the cookie and then see whether you can still travel around the site. If you can't, the searchbots can't navigate it either.

Figure 7-8:
The Privacy
Alert dialog
box.

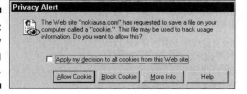

Follow these suggestions to fix this problem:

> ✔ **Don't require cookies.** Ask your site programmers to find some other way to handle what you're doing with cookies, or just do without the fancy navigation trick.
>
> ✔ **Use a user agent script (as you can with session IDs) that treats search-bots differently.** If the server sees a normal visitor, it requires cookies; if it's a searchbot, it doesn't.

Fixing Bits and Pieces

Forwarded pages, image maps, and special characters can also cause problems for search engines.

Forwarded pages

Search engines don't want to index pages that automatically forward to other pages. You've undoubtedly seen pages telling you that a page has moved to another location and that you can click a link or wait a few seconds for the page to automatically forward the browser to another page. This is often done with a REFRESH meta tag, like this:

```
<meta http-equiv="refresh" content="0;
          url=http://yourdomain.com">
```

This meta tag forwards the browser immediately to *yourdomain*.com. Quite reasonably, search engines don't like these pages. Why index a page that doesn't contain information but instead forwards visitors to the page *with* the information? Why not index the target page? That's just what search engines do.

If you use the REFRESH meta tag, you can expect search engines to ignore the page (unless it's a very slow refresh rate of over ten seconds, which is specified by the number immediately after content=). Don't listen to the nonsense that you'll hear about your site being penalized for using refresh pages: Search engines don't index the page, but they don't go so far as to penalize your entire site.

Image maps

An *image map* is an image that has multiple links. You might create the image like this:

```
<img name="main" src="images/main.gif" usemap="#m_main">
```

The `usemap=` parameter refers to the map instructions. You can create the information defining the *hotspots* on the image — the individual links — by using a `<MAP>` tag, like this:

```
<map name="m_main">
<area shape="rect" coords="238,159,350,183"
        href="page1.html">
<area shape="rect" coords="204,189,387,214" href="
        page2.html">
<area shape="rect" coords="207,245,387,343" href="
        page3.html">
<area shape="rect" coords="41,331,155,345" href="
        page4.html">
<area shape="rect" coords="40,190,115,202" href="
        page5.html">
<area shape="rect" coords="42,174,148,186" href="
        page6.html">
<area shape="rect" coords="40,154,172,169" href="
        page7.html">
<area shape="rect" coords="43,137,142,148" href="
        page8.html">
<area shape="rect" coords="45,122,165,131" href="
        page9.html">
<area shape="rect" coords="4,481,389,493" href="
        page10.html">
<area shape="rect" coords="408,329,588,342" href="
        page11.html">
        <area shape="rect" coords="410,354,584,391" href="
        page12.html">
    </map>
```

How do you know whether search engines will follow these links? Major search engines now read image maps, though some smaller ones may not. A larger problem these days is that links in images don't provide the benefit of keywords that search engines can read. The solution is simple: Use additional simple text links in the document.

Special characters

Don't use special characters, such as accents, in your text. To use unusual characters, you have to use special codes in HTML, and search engines often don't like these codes. If you want to write the word *rôle*, for example, you can do it in one of three ways:

```
R&ocirc;le
```

```
R&#244;le
```

```
rôle
```

Note that the last method is displayed correctly in Internet Explorer but not in a number of other browsers. You probably shouldn't use *any* of these forms, because search engines don't much like them, so they don't index these words. Stick to basic characters.

Chapter 8

Dirty Deeds, Done Dirt Cheap

· ·

· ·

*E*veryone wants to fool the search engines — and the search engines know it. That's why search engine optimization is such a strange business — a hybrid of technology and, oh, I dunno . . . industrial espionage, perhaps? Search engines don't want you to know exactly how they rank pages because if you did, you would know exactly how to trick them into giving you top positions.

Now for a bit of history. When this whole search engine business started out, search engines just wanted people to follow some basic guidelines — make the Web site readable, provide a <TITLE> tag, provide a few keywords related to the page's subject matter, and so on — and then the search engines would take it from there.

What happened, though, is that Web sites started jostling for position. For example, although the KEYWORDS meta tag seemed like a great idea, so many people misused it (by repeating words and using words that *weren't* related to the subject matter) that it eventually became irrelevant to search engines. Eventually, the major search engines stopped giving much weight to the tag or just ignored it.

Search engines try to hide their methods as much as they can, but it sometimes becomes apparent what the search engines want, and at that point, people start trying to give it to them in a manner the search engines regard as manipulative. This chapter discusses which things you should avoid doing because you risk upsetting the search engines and getting penalized — potentially even getting booted from a search engine for life!

Tricking Search Engines

Before getting down to the nitty-gritty details about tricking search engines, I focus on two topics: why you need to understand the dangers of using dirty tricks and what the overriding principles behind tricking the search engines are based on.

Deciding whether to trick

Should you use the tricks in this chapter, and if not, why not? You'll hear several reasons for not using tricks. The first I'm not going to belabor, because I'm not sure the argument behind this reason is very strong: ethics. You'll hear from many people that the tricks in this chapter are unethical, that those who use them are cheating and are one step on the evolutionary ladder above pond scum (or one step below pond scum, depending on the commentator).

Self-righteousness is in ample supply on the Internet. Maybe these people are right, maybe not. I do know that many people who try such tricks also have great reasons for doing so and are not the Internet's equivalent of Pol Pot or Attila the Hun. They're simply trying to put their best foot forward in a difficult technical environment.

Many people have tried search engine tricks because they invested a lot of money in Web sites that turn out to be invisible to search engines. These folks can't afford to abandon their sites and start again. (See Chapter 7 for a discussion of why search engines sometimes can't read Web pages.) You can, rightly so, point out that these folks can deal with the problem in other ways, but that just means the people involved are misinformed, not evil. The argument made by these tricksters might go something like this: Who gave search engines the right to set the rules, anyway?

One could argue that doing pretty much anything beyond the basics is cheating. Over the past few years I've heard from hundreds of people who have put into action many of the ideas in this book, with great results. So if smart Webmasters armed with a little knowledge can push their Web sites up in the ranks above sites that may be more appropriate for a particular keyword phrase, yet are owned by folks with less knowledge — is that fair?

Ethics aside, the really good reason for avoiding egregious trickery is that it may have the opposite effect and *harm* your search engine position. And a corollary to that reason is that other, legitimate ways exist to get a good search engine ranking. (Unfortunately, they're often more complicated and time consuming.)

Figuring out the tricks

The idea behind most search engine tricks is simple: to confuse the search engines into thinking that your site is more appropriate for certain keyword phrases than they would otherwise believe, generally by showing the search engine something that the site visitor doesn't see.

Search engines want to see what site visitors see, yet they know they can't. It will be a long, long time before search engines will be able to see and understand the images in a Web page, for instance. Right now, they can't even read text in the images, although that's something that could be possible soon. (Recent patents suggest that this is something Google is working on now — but I'll bet it will still be years before Google tries to read all the text it finds in the average Web site's images, if it ever does.) But to view and understand the images as a real person sees them? Michael Jackson could well be President of the United States before that happens.

The search engine designers have started with this basic principle:

> What the search engine sees — with the exception of certain things it's not interested in (images, JavaScript navigation systems, and so on) and of certain technical issues that are not important to the visitor (the DESCRIPTION meta tag, which <H> tag has been applied to a heading, and so on) — should be what the user sees.

For various reasons, searchbots aren't terribly sophisticated. They generally don't read JavaScript, Cascading Style Sheets (CSS), and so on because of the complexity of doing so. In theory, they could read these things, but it would greatly increase the time and hardware required. So by necessity, they ignore certain components.

Here's one other important principle: The text on the page should be there for the benefit of the site visitor, not the search engines.

Ideally, search engine designers want Web designers to act as though search engines don't exist. (Of course, this is *exactly* what many Web designers have done and the reason why so many sites rank poorly in search engines!) Search engine designers want their programs to determine which pages are the most relevant for a particular search query. They want you — the Web designer — to focus on creating a site that serves your visitors' needs and let search engines determine which site is most appropriate for which searcher.

What search engines definitely don't want is for you to show one version of a page to visitors and another version to search engines because you feel that version is what the search engine will like most.

Do these tricks work?

Tricks do work, at least in some circumstances for some search engines. Even some tricks that are very crude and have been known to search engines for a long time still work. On the other hand, over time, search engines get better and better at dropping the more obvious tricks; you don't find crudely keyword-stuffed pages and pages with hidden text ranking well very often these days, for instance, though only a couple of years ago you did.

Could you use every trick in the book and rank first for your keyword? Sure, but your rank may not last long, and the penalty it could incur can last for a long time. (Although in most cases, the pages will simply drop in rank as the search engines apply an algorithm that recognizes the trick, in some cases a search engine could decide to remove all pages from a particular site from the index, permanently.)

As Micah Baldwin, the technical editor for the first edition of this book, likes to point out, "If your competitors are ranking higher than you, it's not because of the tricks they played. It's because of the good, solid search engine optimization work you didn't do." These tricks can be dangerous. You may get caught in one of several ways:

- ✔ A search engine algorithm may discover your trickery, and your page or your entire site could be dropped from the search engine.

- ✔ A competitor might discover what you're doing and report you to the search engines. Google has stated that it prefers to let its algorithms track down cheaters and uses reports of search engine spamming to tune these algorithms, but Google will take direct action in some cases.

- ✔ Your trick may work well for a while, until a major search engine changes its algorithm to discover the trickery — at which point your site's ranking will drop like a rock.

If you follow the advice from the rest of this book, you'll surpass 80 percent of your competitors.

Concrete Shoes, Cyanide, TNT — An Arsenal for Dirty Deeds

The next few sections take a look at some search engine tricks employed on the Web.

Keyword stacking and stuffing

You may run across pages that contain the same word or term, or maybe several words or terms, repeated over and over again, often in hidden areas of the page (such as the `<KEYWORD>` tag), though sometimes visible to visitors. This is one of the earliest and crudest forms of a dirty deed, one that search engines have been aware of for years and are pretty good at finding these days. You'd think keyword stacking wouldn't work, but search engines aren't perfect, and sometimes keyword-stacked pages slip through.

Take a look at Figure 8-1. The Web designer has repeated the word *glucosamine* numerous times, each one in a hyperlink to give it a little extra oomph. I found this page in Google a few years ago by searching for the term *glucosamine glucosamine glucosamine*; more recently the same search phrase didn't pull up anything nearly as crude as this page.

Look at this tactic from the search engine's perspective. Repeating the word *glucosamine* over and over isn't of any use to a site visitor, so it's understandable why search engine designers don't appreciate this kind of thing. This sort of trick is working less frequently than it used to just a couple of years ago, and sites doing this are also becoming less abundant.

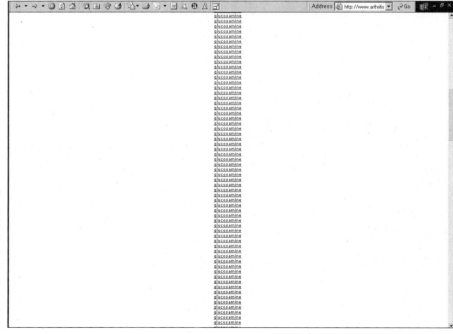

Figure 8-1:
The person creating this page stacked it with the word *glu-cosamine.*

The terms *keyword stacking* and *keyword stuffing* are often used interchangeably, though some people regard keyword stuffing as something a little different — placing inappropriate keywords inside image `ALT` attributes and in hidden layers.

Hiding (and shrinking) keywords

Another old (and very crude) trick is to hide text; that is, to hide it from the site visitor but make it visible to the search engine, allowing you to fill a simple page with keywords for the sake of search engine optimization. (Remember that search engines don't want you to show them content that isn't also visible to the site visitor.)

This trick, often combined with keyword stuffing, involves placing large amounts of text into a page and hiding it from view. For instance, take a look at Figure 8-2. I found this page in Google some time ago. It has hidden text at the bottom of the page.

If you suspect that someone has hidden text on a page, you can often make it visible by clicking inside text at the top of the page and dragging the mouse to the bottom of the page to highlight everything in between. You can also look in the page's source code.

There's a big space at the bottom of this page . . .

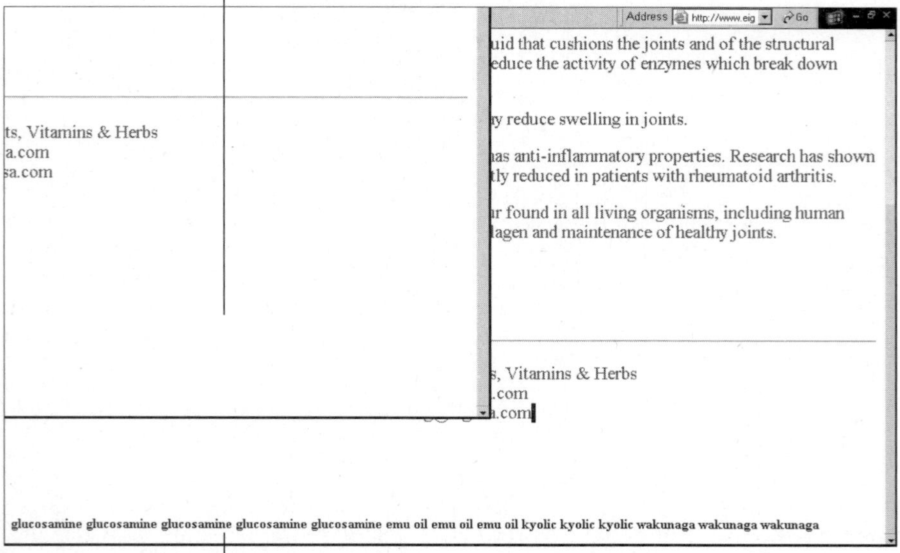

Address http://www.eig Go

uid that cushions the joints and of the structural educe the activity of enzymes which break down

ty reduce swelling in joints.

has anti-inflammatory properties. Research has shown tly reduced in patients with rheumatoid arthritis.

ur found in all living organisms, including human agen and maintenance of healthy joints.

ts, Vitamins & Herbs
a.com
sa.com

s, Vitamins & Herbs
.com
h.com

glucosamine glucosamine glucosamine glucosamine glucosamine emu oil emu oil emu oil kyolic kyolic kyolic wakunaga wakunaga wakunaga

Figure 8-2: This text is hidden at the bottom of the page.

. . . but if you drag the cursor down from the end of the text, you'll see the hidden text.

How did this designer make the text disappear? At the bottom of the source code (choose View⇨Source), I found this:

```
<FONT SIZE=7 COLOR="#ffffff"><H6>glucosamine glucosamine
    glucosamine glucosamine glucosamine emu oil emu
    oil emu oil kyolic kyolic kyolic wakunaga
    wakunaga wakunaga</H6></FONT>
```

Notice the `COLOR="#ffffff"` piece; `#ffffff` is hexadecimal color code for the color white. The page background is white, so — abracadabra — the text disappears.

I still see this trick employed now and then; just last week, when reviewing a client's site, I discovered a long link pointing back to my client's Web designer's site, hidden by making the text match the background color.

My opinion of this crude trick goes like this:

- ✔ **It probably doesn't help.** I doubt whether it helps anything any more.

- ✔ **It might not hurt.** You still find pages using this trick, so I suspect that in most cases, the search engines ignore it and it doesn't help or hurt.

- ✔ **. . . but it might.** Search engines *might* in *some* cases drop a page that has hidden text.

- ✔ **So why do it?** It doesn't help, but it might hurt, so don't do it!

Here are some other tricks used for hiding text from the visitor while still making it visible to the search engine:

- ✔ **Placing text inside** `<NOFRAMES>` **tags:** Some designers do this even if the page isn't a frame-definition document. I've seen this method work, too, but not in recent years.

- ✔ **Placing text inside** `<NOSCRIPT>` **tags:** `<NOSCRIPT></NOSCRIPT>` tags are used to put text on a page that can be read by browsers that don't work with JavaScript. Some site owners use them to give more text to the search engines to read, and from what I've seen, the major search engines often do read this text, or at least they did a year or two ago. However, the text inside these tags probably isn't given as much weight as other text on a page, and over time will probably be given less and less weight.

- ✔ **Using hidden fields:** Sometimes designers hide words in a form's hidden field (`<INPUT TYPE="HIDDEN">`).

- ✔ **Using hidden layers:** Style sheets can be used to position a text layer underneath the visible layer or outside the browser. This trick is quite common and probably hard for search engines to figure out.

Some Web designers still stuff keywords into page by using a very small font size. This trick is another one that search engines may look for and penalize.

Here's another variation: Some Web designers make the text color just a little different from the background color to make it hard for the browser to catch. However, the text remains invisible, especially if it's at the bottom of the page preceded by several blank lines. Search engines can look for ranges of colors to determine whether this trick is being employed.

Hiding links

A variation on the old hidden-text trick is to hide links. As you discover in Chapters 14 through 16, links provide important clues to search engines about the site's purpose. Some Web designers create links specifically for search engines to find, but not intended for site visitors. Links can be made to look exactly like all the other text on a page or may even be hidden on punctuation marks — visitors are unlikely to click a link on a period, so the link can be made "invisible." Links may be placed in transparent images or invisible layers, in small images, or in <NOFRAMES><NOSCRIPT> tags or may be hidden in any of the ways discussed earlier for hiding ordinary text.

Duplicating pages and sites

If content with keywords is good, then twice as much content is better, and three times as much is better still, right? Some site developers have duplicated pages and even entire sites, making virtual photocopies and adding the pages to the site or placing duplicated sites at different domain names.

Sometimes called *mirror pages* or *mirror sites,* these duplicate pages are intended to help a site gain more than one or two entries in the top positions. If you can create three or four Web sites that rank well, you can dominate the first page of the search results, with from four to eight entries out of the first ten. (Google, for instance, displays one or two pages from a site.)

Some people who use this trick try to modify each page just a little to make it harder for search engines to recognize duplicates. Search engines — in particular, Google — have designed tools to find duplication and often drop a page from their indexes if they find it's a duplicate of another page at the same site. Duplicate pages found across different sites are often okay, which is why content syndication can work well if done right (see the discussion of duplicate content in Chapter 15), but entire duplicate sites are something that search engines frown on.

Page swapping and page jacking

Here are a couple of variations on the duplication theme:

- **Page swapping:** In this now little-used technique, one page is placed at a site and then, after the page has attained a good position, it's removed and replaced with a less-optimized page. One serious problem with this technique is that major search engines often reindex pages very quickly, and it's impossible to know *when* the search engines will return.

- **Page jacking:** Some truly unethical search engine marketers have employed the technique of using other peoples' high-ranking Web pages, in effect stealing pages that perform well for a while. This is known as *page jacking*.

Doorway and Information Pages

A *doorway page* is created solely as an entrance from a search engine to your Web site. Doorway pages are sometimes known as *gateway pages* and *ghost pages*. The idea is to create highly optimized pages that are picked up and indexed by search engines and that, hopefully, rank well and thus channel traffic to the site.

Search engines hate doorway pages because they break one of the cardinal rules: They're intended for search engines, not for visitors. The sole purpose of a doorway page is to channel people from search engines to the real Web site.

One man's doorway page is another man's *information page* — or what some people call *affiliate pages, advertising pages,* or *marketing pages.* The difference between a doorway page and an information page is that the information page is designed for use by the visitor in such a manner that search engines will rank it well, whereas the doorway page is designed in such a manner that it's utterly useless to the visitor because it's intended purely for the search engine; in fact, originally doorway pages were stuffed full of keywords and duplicated hundreds of times.

Doorway pages typically don't look like the rest of the site, having been created very quickly or even by some kind of program. Doorway pages are part of other strategies. The pages used in redirects and cloaking (discussed in the next section) are, in effect, doorway pages.

Where do you draw the line between a doorway page and an information page? That's a question I don't answer here; it's for you to ponder and remains a matter of debate in the search engine optimization field. If a client asks me to help him in the search engine race and I create pages designed to rank well in search engines but in such a manner that they're still useful to the visitor, have I created information pages or doorway pages? Most people would say that I created legitimate information pages.

Suppose, however, that I create lots of pages designed for use by the site visitor — pages that, until my client started thinking about search engine optimization, would have been deemed unnecessary. Surely these pages are, by *intent,* doorway pages, aren't they, even if one could argue that they're useful in some way?

Varying degrees of utility exist, and I know people in the business of creating "information" pages that are useful to the visitor in the author's opinion only! Also, a number of search engine optimization companies create doorway pages that they simply *call* information pages.

Still, an important distinction exists between the two types of pages, and creating information pages is a widely used strategy. Search engines don't know your intent, so if you create pages that appear to be useful, are not duplicated dozens or hundreds of times, and don't break any other rules, they'll be fine.

Here's a good reality check. Be honest: Are the pages you just created truly of use to your site visitors? If you submitted these pages to Yahoo! or the Open Directory Project for review by a human, would the site be accepted? If the answer is no, the pages probably aren't informational. The "trick," then, is to find a way to convert the pages you created for search engine purposes into pages that are useful in their own right — or for which, at least, a valid argument for utility can be made.

Using Redirects and Cloaking

Redirecting and cloaking serve the same purpose. The intention is to show one page to the search engines but a completely different page to the site visitor. Why do people want to do this? Here are a few reasons:

- ✔ If a site has been built in a manner that makes it invisible to search engines, cloaking allows the site owner to deliver indexable pages to search engines while retaining the original site.

- ✔ The site may not have much textual content, making it a poor fit for the search engine algorithms. Although search engine designers might argue that this fact means that the site isn't a good fit for a search, this argument clearly doesn't stand up to analysis and debate.

✔ Each search engine prefers something slightly different. As long as search engines can't agree on what makes a good search match, why should they expect site owners and developers to accept good results in some search engines and bad results in others?

I've heard comments such as the following from site owners, and I can understand their frustration: "Search engines are defining how my site should work and what it should look like, and if the manner in which I want to design my site isn't what they like to see, that's not my fault! Who gave them the right to set the rules of commerce on the Internet?!"

What might frustrate and anger site owners more is if they realized that one major search engine *does* accept cloaking, as long as you pay for it. (See the information on trusted feeds in Chapter 11; a trusted feed is, in effect, a form of cloaking.) So cloaking is a crime, but one search engine says "Pay us, and we'll help you do it." (Is that a fee, a bribe, or a protection-racket payment?)

Understanding redirects

A *redirect* is the automatic loading of a page without user intervention. You click a link to load a Web page into your browser and, within seconds, the page you loaded disappears and a new one appears. Designers often create pages designed for search engines — optimized, keyword-rich pages — that redirect visitors to the real Web site, which is not so well optimized. Search engines read the page, but visitors never really see it.

Redirects can be carried out in various ways:

✔ By using the REFRESH meta tag. This is an old trick that search engines discovered long ago; most search engines don't index a page that has a REFRESH tag that quickly bounces the visitor to another page.

✔ By using JavaScript to automatically load another page within a split second.

✔ By using JavaScript that's tripped by a user action that is almost certain to occur. You can see an example of this method at work in Figure 8-3. The large button on this page has a JavaScript mouseover event associated with it; when users move their mice over the image — as they're almost certain to do — the mouseover event triggers, loading the next page.

You're unlikely to be penalized for using a redirect. But a search engine may ignore the redirect page. That is, if the search engine discovers that a page is redirecting to another page, it simply ignores the redirect page and indexes the destination page. Search engines reasonably assume that redirect pages are merely way stations on the route to the real content.

Figure 8-3:
The mouse
pointer
triggers a
JavaScript
mouseover
event on the
image and
loads
another
page.

Examining cloaking

Cloaking is a more sophisticated trick than using a redirect, and harder for search engines to uncover than a basic REFRESH meta tag redirect. When browsers or searchbots request a Web page, they send information about themselves to the site hosting the page — for example, "I'm Version 6.1 of Internet Explorer," or "I'm Googlebot." The cloaking program quickly looks in its list of searchbots for the device requesting the page. In addition, a cloaking program also has a list of IP numbers that it knows are used by searchbots; if the request comes from a matching IP number, it knows it's a searchbot.

So, if the device doesn't match, the cloaking program tells the Web server to send the regular Web page, the one intended for site visitors. But if the device name or IP number is listed in the searchbot list — as it would be for Googlebot, for instance — the cloaking program sends a *different* page, one that the designer feels is better optimized for that particular search engine. (The cloaking program may have a library of pages, each designed for a particular search engine or group of engines.)

Here's how the two page versions differ:

> ✔ **Pages provided to the search engine:** Often much simpler; created in a way to make them easy for search engines to read; have lots of heavily keyword-laden text that would sound clumsy to a real person.

✔ **Pages presented to visitors:** Often much more attractive, graphics-heavy pages, with less text and more complicated structures and navigation systems.

Search engines don't like cloaking. Conservative search engine marketers steer well clear of this technique. Here's how Google defines cloaking:

> *The term "cloaking" is used to describe a Web site that returns altered Web pages to search engines crawling the site.*

Well, that's pretty clear — cloaking is cloaking is cloaking. But, wait a minute:

> *In other words, the Web server is programmed to return different content to Google than it returns to regular users, usually in an attempt to distort search engine rankings.*

Hang on: These two definitions aren't describing the same concept. The phrase "in an attempt to distort" is critical. If I "return altered pages" without intending to distort rankings, am I cloaking? Here's more from Google:

> *This can mislead users about what they'll find when they click on a search result. To preserve the accuracy and quality of our search results, Google may permanently ban from our index any sites or site authors that engage in cloaking to distort their search rankings.*

Notice a few important qualifications: *altered pages . . . usually in an attempt to distort search engine rankings . . . cloaking to distort their search engine rankings.*

This verbiage is ambiguous and seems to indicate that Google doesn't totally outlaw the use of cloaking; it just doesn't like you to use cloaking to cheat. Some would say that using cloaking to present to Google dynamic pages that are otherwise invisible, for instance, or that are blocked from indexing perhaps by the use of session IDs (see Chapter 7), would be an acceptable practice. Indeed, however, as I've pointed out, many in the business disagree and advise that you never use cloaking in any circumstance.

Tricks versus Strategies

When is a trick not a trick but merely a legitimate strategy? I don't know, but I'll tell you that there are many ways to play the SEO game, and what to one man is a trick might be to another the obvious thing to do.

Here's an example: creating multiple Web sites. One client has *two* Web sites ranking in the top five on Google for his most important keyword. (No, I can't tell you what the keyword is!) Another client at one point had around seven of the top ten results for one of his critical keywords; several of the links pointed to his own Web sites, and several pointed to his products positioned on other people's Web sites.

Now, this is definitely a trick: Build a bunch of small Web sites that point links back to your "core" site, and then link all those sites from various places. The aim (and it can sometimes work if it's done correctly) is to boost the core site by creating many incoming links, but in many cases the "satellite" sites may also rank well. I've seen this technique work, and I've seen it fail miserably.

Is this a trick, though — building standalone sites with the intention of seeing which ones will rank best? And, not merely as a way to create links to a core site, but as a way to see what works best for search engines? I don't know. I'll leave it for you to decide.

Paying the Ultimate Penalty

Just how much trouble can you get into by breaking the rules? The most likely penalty isn't really a penalty. It's just that your pages won't work well with a search engine's algorithm, so they won't rank well.

You can receive the ultimate penalty: having your entire site booted from the index. Here's what Google has to say about it:

> *We investigate each report of deceptive practices thoroughly and take appropriate action when abuse is uncovered. At minimum, we will use the data from each spam report to improve our site ranking and filtering algorithms. The result of this should be visible over time as the quality of our searches gets even better.*

Google is describing what I just explained — that it tweaks its algorithm to downgrade pages that use certain techniques. But:

> *In especially egregious cases, we will remove spammers from our index immediately so they don't show up in search results at all. Other steps will be taken as necessary.*

One of the dangers of using tricks, then, is that someone might report you, and if the trick is bad enough, you get the boot. Where do they report you?

- ✔ Google at `http://ww.google.com/contact/spamreport.html`
- ✔ Yahoo! at `http://help.yahoo.com/l/us/yahoo/search/spam_abuse.html`
- ✔ MSN/Live Search at `https://support.live.com/eform.aspx?productKey=wlsearch`
- ✔ Ask.com at `http://asksupport.custhelp.com/cgi-bin/ask.cfg/php/enduser/ask.php`

People reporting spam may also be investigated, so don't throw stones in a glass house.

What do you do if you think you've been penalized? Suppose that your site is dropped from Google. It may not be a penalty — perhaps your site wasn't available at the point at which Google tried to reach it. But if the site doesn't return to the index after a few weeks (Google tries again later and reindexes if it finds it), you *may* have been penalized.

Sometimes sites get penalized due to unintentional mistakes. Perhaps you hired a Web-development team that implemented various tricks without your knowledge, or perhaps your company gave you a site to look after long after the tricks were used. Or, maybe you purchased a domain name that was penalized due to dirty tricks in the past. (Just changing owners isn't enough to automatically lift the penalty.) Stuff happens: Be truthful and explain the situation to the folks at Google.

If you think your site has been banned, follow these steps:

1. **Clean up any dirty tricks on your site.**

2. **E-mail** help@google.com **to explain that you fixed your site.**

   Don't expect a rapid reply.

3. **Wait a couple of weeks and then try again.**

4. **If you still receive no reply, try again after another couple of weeks.**

5. **If you still can't get a response, try calling 650-253-0000 and then pressing 0.**

6. **Ask the operator whom you can talk to about the problem.**

   You may be given another e-mail address to try, along with a password to put in the Subject line. (The password is changed each day.) By the way, I've heard from some site owners that if you have a *pay-per-click (PPC)* account with Google, you may be able to reach someone who can help by talking with your PPC account manager.

However, for all this talk of penalties, I want to reiterate that you have probably *not* been penalized. Just because your site has dropped in the search results doesn't mean that you're being punished. In most cases, it means that Google has changed the algorithm it's using and it no longer gives your pages, or the links pointing to your pages, the same weight it did in the past.

Also, by the way, in some cases Google just gets all messed up: Pages drop, pages rise, pages drop, and eventually, after a few weeks, things settle down. Just because you disappeared from the search engines today doesn't mean that you won't be number one tomorrow! And, if you find that situation confusing and frustrating — well, welcome to the world of SEO!

Chapter 9

Bulking Up Your Site — Competing with Content

Content is often an extremely important factor in getting a high ranking in the search engines. *Content* is a geeky Web term that means, in the broadest sense, "stuff on your Web site." A *content-rich* Web site is one that contains lots and lots of information for people to see, read, and use.

For search engines, content has a more narrow definition: words, and lots of 'em. So if you're interested in search engine optimization, you should concentrate on the *text* part of your Web site's content (the right text, of course, using the keywords you find out about in Chapter 5). You don't need to worry about pictures, video, or sound — at least as far as the search engines are concerned — because those forms of content don't help you get higher rankings. You don't need Flash animations, either, because although some search engines index them, they don't index well; how often do you find a Flash page ranking highly in the search results?

What you should be concerned about is text — words that the search engines can read. Now, it's not *always* necessary to bulk up your site by adding textual content — in some cases, it's possible to get high search engine rankings with a small number of keyword-laden pages. If that's your situation, congratulations. Sit back and enjoy the fruits of your rather minimal labors, and skip this chapter. But if you don't find yourself in this happy situation, you need this chapter.

You may find that your competitors have Web sites stacked full of content. They have scores of pages, perhaps even hundreds of pages — or hundreds of thousands — full of text that is nicely laden with all the juicy keywords you're interested in. That's tough to compete with.

Content is not a subject that's covered in many books, newsletters, or Web sites related to search engine optimization and ranking. Most publications say, "You need content, so create some." But I believe that this issue is critical and shouldn't be glossed over with such trite comments, especially when several simple ways exist to *find* content. If you know the shortcuts, creating content doesn't have to be difficult. This chapter describes a slew of shortcuts to free and low-cost content, such as government materials, marketing and technical documents from manufacturers, and even something new, called *copyleft*.

Creating Content Three Ways

You can compete in the search engines in several different ways: Create a few well-optimized pages, get lots of links into your site, target keywords that competitors have missed, and put masses of content on your site. (Chapter 3 has more on these "basic" strategies.) In some cases, when going up against a well-entrenched competitor, you may have no choice but to fight on several fronts. You may find that you *must* do something to stack your site with content.

Evaluate competing sites to help you determine at what point you should stop adding content. Compare your site to competitors that rank well in search engines. All major search engines now use some kind of link popularity to rate Web pages. If you're sure that your site has more well-optimized pages than those competing sites, it may be time to stop adding content. You may want to focus instead on getting links into your site. (For more on that subject, check out Chapters 14, 15, and 16.)

I've got some bad news and some good news about creating content:

✔ **The bad news:** The obvious way to create content — writing it yourself or getting someone else to write it for you — is a huge problem for many people. Most people find writing difficult, and even if they find it easy, the results are often less than appealing. Perhaps you know someone who can write well and you can convince this person to write a few paragraphs for you. But are your powers of persuasion sufficient to get you 10, 20, or 50 pages? What about 500 or 5,000? You can always pay someone for content, but the problem with paying is that it costs money.

✔ **The good news:** You can use some shortcuts to create content. Tricks of the trade can help you quickly bulk up your Web site (even if your writing skills match those of a dyslexic gerbil and your funds make the Queen of England's bikini budget look large in comparison). Note, though, that these tricks involve using *someone else's content*.

Here are three different ways to get content for your site:

✔ Write your own content.

✔ Convince (force, bribe) someone else to create your content.

✔ Find existing content from somewhere else.

Writing Your Own Stuff

The obvious way to create content, for many small-site owners anyway, is to start writing articles. That's not a terrible idea in many cases. Thousands of sites rank well using content from the sites' owners.

If you use the write-it-yourself approach, keep the following points in mind:

✔ **Writing content is time consuming, even for good writers.** You may want to evaluate whether you can devote the time to writing and maintaining your own content and then allocate time in your schedule to do so.

✔ **Many people are *not* good writers.** Not only is the writing process time consuming, but also the results are often rather pathetic (so I don't go into detail on this one).

✔ **If you *do* write your own stuff, pleeze spill chuck it.** Then have it edited by someone who has more than a third-grade education, and then spill chuck it again.

Do *not* rely on a word processor's grammar checker. This tool is worse than useless for most writers. Grammar checkers are of benefit only to those what already has a good grasp of grammar.

What will you write about? The obvious topic, of course, is your product or service (assuming that your site is selling something). The more you can say about each item you sell, the better. That should keep you busy for a while, but eventually most businesses find that they have written all they can about their products, and they still don't have a large site, so the next few sections present a few other ideas.

Summarizing online articles

Here's a quick way to get keywords onto your page:

1. **Use the search engines to track down articles related to your subject area.**

2. **Create a library area on your Web site in which you link to these articles.**

3. **For each link, write a short, keyword-laden summary of what the article is all about.**

The advantage to this kind of writing is that it's fairly quick and easy.

You may want to include the first few sentences of the article. This strategy comes under the gray area of copyright *fair use* (which you find out about in the appendix for this book). What really counts is what the article's owner thinks. In most cases, if you contact the article's owner (and you don't *have* to contact that person), the owner is happy to have you summarize the article, excerpt a small portion of it, and link to his or her site. Most people recognize that *this process is good for them!* However, occasionally you find someone who just doesn't get it and creates a fuss. Just remove the link and move on.

You may want to approach the owners of the sites you're linking to and ask them to add a link back to your site. See Chapter 15 for more information.

Reviewing Web sites

Similar to how you summarize, you can link to useful Web sites and write short (yes, keyword-laden) reviews of each one.

Reviewing products

Write short (um, keyword-laden) reviews of products related to the subject matter covered by your site. An additional benefit of such a program is that eventually people may start sending you free stuff to review.

Convincing Someone Else to Write It

You may find that having articles written (by others) specifically for your site is rather appealing, for two reasons. First, someone else does the work, not you. Second, if it doesn't turn out well, someone else (not you) gets blamed.

One approach, assuming that you can't force someone to write for you, is to pay someone. Luckily (for you), writers are cheap. For some reason, people often have a bizarre vision of a glamorous writing life that's awaiting them. (It has been 15 years since I wrote my first bestseller, and I'm still waiting for the groupies to turn up.) So you may be able to find someone to write for you for

$10 or $12 an hour, depending on where you live and how well you lie. Or, maybe you can find a high-school kid who can string together a few coherent words and is willing to work for less.

If you work for a large corporation, you may be able to convince a variety of people to write for you — people who may assume that it's actually part of their jobs (again, depending on how well you lie). Spread the work throughout various departments — marketing, technical support, sales, and so on — and it may turn into a decent amount of content. Still, you can use quicker and easier ways to get content, as described in the next section.

If you pay someone to write for you, draw up a simple contract saying that the work is a work for hire and that you're buying all rights to it. Otherwise, you don't own it and can use it for only limited purposes that are either stated in the contract or are more or less obvious. If you ask someone to write an article for your Web site and you don't get a contract giving you full rights, you can't later decide to syndicate the article on other sites or in newsletters. (Chapter 15 has more information on this syndication stuff.) If an employee writes the material for you on company time, the work is generally considered a work for hire and company property. However, if you have a very small company with an informal employment relationship and the writing is outside the scope of the employee's normal work duties, you should request that the employee sign a contract.

A huge (politically incorrect) business has grown up over the past few years: overseas outsourced SEO work, specifically (regarding this chapter's subject) the outsourcing of articles written for SEO purposes. If you hire an Indian writer or a Chinese writer, for example, you may find that the writing, um, doesn't sound quite *right*. On the other hand, you can find people in these countries (and in other, less obvious nations, such as South Africa), who can write very well and can produce articles for your site for around $15 or $20 apiece. If you want to try this method, you can find writers on sites such as Elance.com, Naukri.com, and Guru.com.

Using OPC — Other People's Content

Writing or hiring is the slow way to create content. Using someone else's content — that's the quick way. See the following list of quick content sources for your site (I explain the details later in this chapter):

- **Product information:** Contact the manufacturer or distributor of the products you sell on your site for marketing and sales materials, technical documentation, and so on.

- **Web sites and e-mail newsletters:** Contact the owners of other sites and e-mail newsletters and ask whether you can use their work.

- **Government sources:** Check U.S. government Web sites for free materials.

- **Content-syndication sites:** A number of sites provide free content for the asking.

- **Traditional syndication services:** Numerous companies sell materials you can use on your site.

- **RSS syndication feeds:** Check out this new, geeky technique for feeding syndicated content into Web sites.

- **Open content and copyleft:** This unusual new movement is probably based on the old Internet maxim "Information wants to be free."

- **Search pages:** You can search at a site to generate a search results page with your favorite keywords.

- **Press releases:** You may be able to find press releases related to your area of business. They're copyright free, and you can use them as you want. (Of course, you should make sure that they're not from competitors.)

- **A Q&A area on your site:** This is a way to serve your site visitors *and* get keywords onto the site.

- **Forums or message boards:** With forums and message boards on your site, your visitors create the keywords for you.

- **Blogs:** From the term *Weblogs,* these journals provide another way to let people create content for you.

This list gives you a good idea of the sources of content, and the "Hunting for Other People's Content" section, later in this chapter, explores how you find, evaluate, and procure content from these sources.

Before I show you how to help yourself to someone else's content, I need to warn you about a critical legal issue: copyright law. You must have a working knowledge of copyright restrictions so that you can properly evaluate whether (and how) it's appropriate to use the content you find. The next section gives you an overview of what you need to know, and the appendix in this book goes into excruciating detail, if you're curious.

Understanding Copyright —
It's Not Yours!

I'm continually amazed at how few people understand copyright — even people who should know better.

When I speak to clients about adding content to a Web site, I sometimes hear something like this: "How about that magazine article I read last week? Let's put that up there!" Or maybe, "Such and such a site has some great information — let's use some of that." That's called *copyright infringement.* It's against the law, and although serious harm is unlikely to befall you in most cases, you *can* get sued or prosecuted.

Let me quickly summarize copyright law so that you have a better idea of what you can and can't use on your site:

- As soon as someone creates a work — writes an article, writes a song, composes a tune, or whatever — copyright is automatic. There's no need to register copyright; the creator owns the copyright whether or not it has been registered. Most copyright works, in fact, aren't registered, which is a good thing. If they were, the Library of Congress, which houses the Copyright Office and stores copyright registrations, would be the size of Alabama.

- If you don't see a copyright notice attached, it doesn't mean that the work's copyright isn't owned by someone. Current copyright law doesn't require such notices.

- If someone owns the copyright, that person has the right to say what can be done with, um, copies. Therefore, you generally can't take an article you find in a newspaper, magazine, or Web site and use it without permission. (There are exceptions, which you find out about later in this chapter.)

- In the United States, certain kinds of copyright infringement are felonies. You may not only get sued but also prosecuted.

- If you don't know whether you have the right to use something, assume that you *don't.*

- You can't just rewrite an article. *Derivative works* are also protected. If the result is clearly derived from the original, you could be in trouble.

- Copyright has to be expressly assigned. If you hire me to write an article for your Web site and don't sign a contract saying that you own all rights or that the work was a work for hire, you only have the right to place it on your Web site. I still have the right to use the article elsewhere.

A number of exceptions can prove *very* important when you're gathering content, so listen closely:

- **If it's really old, you can use it.** Copyright eventually expires. Anything created before 1923, for instance, is free for the taking.

- **If the "guvmint" created it, you can use it.** The U.S. government spends millions of dollars creating *content.* This content is *almost* never copyright-protected.

✔ **If it's donated, you can use it.** Authors often *want* you to use their materials. If they have given the public permission to use it, you can use it.

✔ **It's only fair.** Copyright law has a *fair use* exception that allows you to use small parts of a work, without permission, under particular conditions.

I strongly suggest that you read the appendix in this book to get the details on copyright, and make sure that you beg or borrow, but not steal, other people's work.

Hunting for Other People's Content

In this chapter, I list different types of other people's content and warn you about copyright. Now it's time to get out there and grab tons of content. You're about to find some great places to look.

Keywords

When you're out on your content hunt, remember that the purpose is to find *keywords* to add keywords to your site. You can do that in several ways:

✔ **Find content with the keywords already in it.** You want content that has at least *some* of your keywords, though you'll often find that it's not enough.

✔ **Add keywords to the content you get.** In some cases, you shouldn't edit the content because you're expected to use the content without changes. In other cases, you may be allowed to modify the content. You can, for instance, modify *open content* (described later in this chapter), and some syndicators allow it. As syndicator Featurewell says, "Clients can make minor edits to stories and photos, provided they do not modify or change the meaning, tone or general context of the articles. . . ." Thus, you can replace a few words here and there with your keywords, as long as the article still makes sense and retains the same tone and context.

✔ **"Chunk up" the article.** Break it into smaller, Web-friendly pieces and separate each piece with a heading (containing keywords, of course).

Newspapers often modify content they buy. A syndicated column you read in New York may be different from the same column run in a paper in Los Angeles, because newspapers cut and modify for space reasons or because they don't like the way something is worded.

When adding content, you're generally interested in adding pages with a variety of keywords sprinkled throughout. Remember, if you have a rodent-racing site, you want lots of pages with the words *rodent, racing, race, event, mouse, rat,* and so on.

Product information

Does your Web site sell products that you buy from a wholesaler or manufacturer? If so, contact your source and find out what materials are available: brochures, spec sheets, technical documentation, or user manuals. Take a look at anything the manufacturer has available.

In many cases, the material may be available in Adobe Acrobat PDF files. You can post these files on your site within seconds, and they will be indexed by some search engines — Google, for instance. However, the ideal approach is to also convert the work to HTML files because you have more opportunities to insert keywords — in the TITLE, DESCRIPTION, and KEYWORDS tags, for example — and to stress keywords by putting them in bold, italic, and <H> tags, for example.

Web sites and e-mail newsletters

The Web is so full of content that it's about to sink (well, not your site obviously, or you wouldn't be reading this chapter). Why not grab a few articles you like from other sites or from the e-mail newsletters you subscribe to? In fact, you may want to go hunting to find articles for this very purpose.

If you ask nicely, many people are happy to let you use their content. In fact, as I explain in Chapter 15, many people use content-syndication as a strategy for site promotion. They *want* people to use their stuff, as long as the sites that are using the material provide *attribution* (clearly state where the material is from and who wrote it) and then provide a link back to the site of origin.

Asking for permission is quite easy: Simply contact the owner of the article you saw on a site or in a newsletter and ask whether you can use the article. I did this recently and, within *ten minutes,* received a positive response. Within 15 minutes, I had an article on my site that was loaded with keywords and that ranked very highly in the search engines in its own right. (I later realized that the author's page ranked number-three for one of my critical keywords. Thus, within minutes, I had a page that had the potential to rank very highly for some important keywords.)

When you talk to the article's owner, make sure that you praise the article. (After all, you do like it, or you wouldn't be asking. Too much good content is out there to be using garbage.) Also, clearly state that you will provide the owner's bio at the bottom of the article and a link back to the owner's site.

If you own your own site, you have it easy: You can simply save the e-mail response from the article's author as evidence of permission to use the article. If you're working for a large corporation with a legal department, however, you have a bigger problem: Your lawyers, working under the principle of "common sense is dead," will expect you to have the article's author sign a 32-page document providing permission, declaring that he or she has the right to give permission, and signing over exclusive and lifetime rights to the article and any spin-off toys or clothing derived from it. Sorry, I don't know how to help you here. (I would tell you to just remember what Shakespeare said — "First thing we do, let's kill all the lawyers" — except that I'm sure my publisher's legal department would complain.)

Where can you find these articles? For Web site articles, search for sites that are likely to have the type of information you need. I suggest that you avoid sites that are directly competing. Also keep your eyes open for newsletters while you're doing your Web search, or look for appropriate newsletters at some of these sites:

- ✔ **Coollist:** www.coollist.com
- ✔ **EzineHub:** www.ezinehub.com
- ✔ **Ezine-Universe:** http://new-list.com/
- ✔ **listTool:** www.listtool.com
- ✔ **NewJour:** gort.ucsd.edu/newjour
- ✔ **Newsletter Access:** www.newsletteraccess.com
- ✔ **Tile.Net:** http://tile.net

Try searching for a combination of one of your keyword phrases and the words *article* and *newsletter* — for instance, *rodent racing article* and *rodent racing newsletter.*

How do you know who owns the copyright to the article? Here's a quick rule of thumb: If the article has an attribution attached to it, contact that person. For instance, many e-mail newsletters are either written by a single person (in which case you contact him or her) or have a variety of articles, each one with an author bio and an e-mail address (in which case you contact the author, not the newsletter itself). In the majority of cases, the author has given the newsletter one-time rights and still owns the copyright.

Some mechanisms used for syndicating content ensure that search engines don't read the syndicated content! So, you need to make sure that you use the right technique. See "Content-syndication sites," later in this chapter, for more information.

Government sources

I love government sources because they're *huge,* with a surprising range of information. In general, documents created by the U.S. federal government are in the public domain. Under the terms of Title 17 United States Code section 105, works created by U.S. government departments do not have copyright protection.

However, you should be aware of some important exceptions:

- The government may still hold copyrights on works that have been given to the government — bequests or assignments of some kind.

- The law is a U.S. law, making U.S. government works copyright free. Most other governments hold copyrights on their works.

- In some cases, works that nongovernment agencies create on behalf of the government may or may not be protected by copyright — the law isn't clear.

- Works created by the National Technical Information Service (NTIS; www.ntis.gov) may have a limited, five-year copyright protection.

- The United States Postal Service is exempt from these regulations. The Postal Service can have copyright protection for its works. (It doesn't want people printing their own stamps!)

- In some cases, the government may publish works that were originally privately created works. Such documents are copyright protected.

Even with these exceptions, vast quantities of juicy government content are available. Now, don't think, "Oh, there probably aren't any government documents related to *my* area!" Maybe, maybe not. Where do you think all our tax billions go? The money can't *all* go to defense and schools. It has to be spent somehow, so some of it goes to creating vast amounts of Web content!

You can place this content directly on your Web site. You'll find the content in Web pages or Adobe Acrobat PDF files. You may want to convert PDF files to Web pages, for several reasons:

✔ Web pages load more quickly than PDF files.

✔ After a file is converted, you can link from the document into your site, whereas a PDF file itself becomes *orphaned* in the search result — a file with no indication of, or link to, the site it comes from.

✔ Although most major search engines index PDF files, PDF files usually don't rank well.

✔ You can do more keywording in Web pages.

And, just *how* do you convert PDF files? If you own Adobe Acrobat, you can try to use that program, though you may not like the results. Various other programs do it for you, such as PDF-to-HTML at `http://convert-in.com/pdf2html.htm` and PDF Online, a free system at `www.pdfonline.com`. Or, search for *pdf converter*.

You will find not only useful documents for your purposes (text-heavy documents that search engines can read) but also other materials that may be useful for your site, such as videos.

Here are a few good places to find government materials:

✔ **FedWorld:** `www.fedworld.gov`

✔ **Government Printing Office:**

- *Catalog of U.S. Government Publications:* `http://catalog.gpo.gov/F`

- *New Electronic Titles:* `www.access.gpo.gov/su_docs/locators/net`

✔ **Library of Congress — Government Web Resources:** `lcweb.loc.gov/rr/news/extgovd.html`

✔ **CIA's Electronic Reading Room:** `www.foia.cia.gov`

✔ **U.S. Department of State's Electronic Reading Room:** `http://www.state.gov/m/a/ips/`

✔ **FBI's Freedom of Information Web Site:** `foia.fbi.gov`

Or, just try this search syntax: *site:.gov your keywords*. For instance, typing *site:.gov rodent racing* tells the search engine to search within `.gov` domains only, for *rodent racing*.

Content-syndication sites

In the "Web sites and e-mail newsletters" section, earlier in this chapter, I discuss the idea of finding Web pages or e-mail newsletter articles you like and asking the owners for permission to use them. Well, here's a shortcut: Go to content-syndication sites.

Content-syndication sites are places where authors post their information so that site owners or newsletter editors can pick it up and use it for free. Why? Because you agree to place, in return, a short blurb at the bottom of the article, including a link back to the author's Web site.

Here are a few places to get you started in the wonderful world of content-syndication:

- ✔ **Article Dashboard:** www.articledashboard.com
- ✔ **EZineArticles.com:** ezinearticles.com
- ✔ **FreeSticky.com:** www.freesticky.com
- ✔ **GoArticles.com:** www.goarticles.com
- ✔ **IdeaMarketers.com:** www.ideamarketers.com
- ✔ **The Open Directory Project's List of Content Providers:** www. dmoz.org/Business/Publishing_and_Printing/Publishing/ Services/Free_Content
- ✔ **Purple Pages:** http://www.purplepages.ie/site/content/
- ✔ **World Wide Information Outlet:** certificate.net

Some Web sites have their own *syndication areas* — libraries from which you can pick articles you want to use. Also, see Chapter 15, where I talk about syndicating your own content and point you to other syndication sites.

Make sure that when you grab articles from a content-syndication site, you're not using a competitor's article! All these articles have links back to the author's site, so you don't want to be sending traffic to the enemy.

Geeky stuff you must understand

I have to get into a little technogeeky information now, I'm afraid. I hate to do it, but if you don't understand this topic, you're just wasting your time with content-syndication.

Many syndication systems use a simple piece of JavaScript to allow you to pull articles from their sites onto yours. For instance, take a look at this code I pulled from a site that syndicates news articles:

```
<script
        src="http://farmcentre.com/synd/synd.jsp?id=cfb
        mc"> </script>
```

This piece of code tells the Web browser to grab the synd.jsp file from the farmcentre.com Web site. That file uses JavaScript to insert the article into the Web page. Articles or other forms of content are automatically embedded in other ways, too. They may be inserted using Java applets, and sometimes with <iframe> tags.

None of these ways of embedding an article into your site does you any good with search engines. As I explain in Chapter 7, the search engine bots *don't read JavaScript!* Nor do they read Java applets. And, if they do read inside the `<iframe>` tags, it doesn't help because they follow the link that's used to pull the page into the frame and view that content as though it were on the origin Web site.

The `<iframe>` tag is used by Internet Explorer to place an internal frame inside a Web page. That frame contains information from another Web page — in this case, a page on another Web site. Depending on how the iframe is set up, it can appear as though the information inside the frame is part of the original page — readers can't tell the difference.

So the searchbot grabs the page and reads the source code. The searchbot sees the JavaScript (such as the preceding sample code) but ignores it, moving on to the next line. The syndicated article you wanted to place into the Web page *never gets placed into the page that the searchbot reads!* All the time and energy you spent placing content is wasted.

This whole geeky topic strikes me as quite humorous, really. Thousands of people are syndicating content or using syndicated content, mostly for search engine reasons. People syndicating the content want to place their links on as many Web pages as possible, for two reasons:

- ✔ Readers will see the links and click them.
- ✔ The search engines will see the links and rank the referenced site higher.

And, people using the syndicated content are doing so because they want content, stuffed with good keywords, for search engines to read.

In many cases, both the syndicators and the people using syndicated content are wasting their time because search engines aren't placing the content, seeing the keywords, or reading the links!

To avoid JavaScript, follow the suggestions in this list:

- ✔ **Don't use browser-side inclusion techniques.** That includes JavaScript, Java, and iframes.
- ✔ **Use server-side inclusion techniques.** That includes server includes, PHP, and ASP. If you're not sure whether a technique is server side or browser side, ask a knowledgeable geek — you want an inclusion technique that loads the content into the page *before* it's sent to the browser or searchbot.
- ✔ **Use manual inclusion techniques.** That is, copy and paste the content into your pages directly. Plenty of content relies on manual inclusion, and you may even get content owners who are using automatic-inclusion techniques to agree to let you manually copy their content.

As long as you're aware of syndicated content's pitfalls and how to avoid them, it's quite possible to find syndicated content and make it work so that you reap the search engine benefits of having that content on your site.

A *hosted-content service* hosts the content on its site along with a copy of your Web site template so that it looks like the content is on your site (unless you look in the browser's Location or Address bar, where you see the company's URL). The problem with these services is that search engines are unlikely to pick up the content because they see the same articles duplicated repeatedly on the same domain. Google, for instance, will probably keep one set and ignore duplicates. (Also, see the section "A Word about Duplicated Content," later in this chapter.)

The problem with automatic updates

Another problem with content-syndication sites involves *automatic updates,* which allow a content owner to change the content immediately. For example, sites that provide weekly or monthly newsletters use automatic updates. The content provider can use this technique to update the content on dozens or hundreds of sites by simply changing the source file. The next time a page is loaded on one of the sites with the syndicated content, the new information appears.

But if you're adding content for keyword purposes, automatic updating may not be such a good thing. If you find an article with lots of nice keywords, it could be gone tomorrow. Manual inclusion techniques ensure that the article you placed remains in place and also allow you to, for instance, break the article into chunks by adding keyword-laden headings. (Although it's hard to say whether a site owner who uses automatic updating is likely to let you use manual inclusion, plenty of content is out there.)

Traditional syndication services

Content-syndication is nothing new — it has been around for a hundred years. (I just made up that statement, but it's probably true.) Much of what you read in your local newspaper isn't written by the paper's staff; it comes from a syndication service.

Some syndication services sell content for your site. In general, this material should be better than free syndicated content. However, much of the free stuff is pretty good, too, so you may not want to pay for syndicated material until you exhaust your search for free content.

Here are a few places you can find commercial syndicated material:

- ✔ **AbleStable Syndication:** ablestable.com
- ✔ **Featurewell:** www.featurewell.com (Articles from $70)

- **Moreover:** www.moreover.com
- **The Open Directory Project list of content providers:** http://www.dmoz.org/News/Media/Services/Syndicates
- **OSKAR Consulting:** www.electroniccontent.com/conFinder.cfm?cat=beauty
- **United Media's uclick:** content.uclick.com
- **YellowBrix:** www.yellowbrix.com
- **Yahoo! News and Media Syndicates page:** dir.yahoo.com/Business_and_Economy/Business_to_Business/News_and_Media/Syndicates

Specialty syndication services provide content for particular industries. For example, Inman (www.inman.com) provides content for the real estate industry.

RSS syndication feeds

RSS is one of those geeky acronyms that nobody can define for certain. Some say it means *really simple syndication*; others believe that it means *rich site summary* or *RDF site summary*. What it stands for doesn't really matter. All you need to know is that RSS is the new big thing in content-syndication.

RSS systems comprise two components:

- An RSS *feed,* or a source of content of some kind
- An RSS *aggregator* or *news reader,* or a system that drops the information from the feed into a Web page

For example, all top search engines provide RSS feeds of their news headlines, at least for personal or noncommercial use. You can install an RSS aggregator on your site and point it to an RSS news feed. The page will then contain recent searches on news headlines.

The big advantage of RSS feeds is that you define the keywords you want to have sent to your site. Tell the feed that you want feeds related to rodent racing and, naturally, content is fed back to you with the keywords rodent racing in it, along with lots of other, related keywords.

What you need, then, is an aggregator that you can install into your Web site. Aggregators range from fairly simple to quite complicated — and that's assuming you have some technical abilities in the first place. (If you don't, there's no range; they're all quite complicated!)

Before you go to the trouble of getting an aggregator, decide whether you receive enough suitable content to make it worthwhile. Technical subjects predominate, so if your subject area is *macramé and knitting,* you *may* find a dearth of material. (On the other hand, search and you may be surprised). Also, often RSS feeds merely pass a link to material on another site, in which case you don't benefit much. Make sure that you're getting useful content passed to your site.

To find RSS feeds, keep your eyes open for RSS or XML symbols and other indicators showing that an RSS feed is available — many blogs, for instance, provide RSS feeds. You can see examples of these icons in Figure 9-1.

Figure 9-1:
Look for these sorts of icons and links to indicate that an RSS feed is available.

Check out these RSS feed sites:

- ✔ **NewsKnowledge:** www.newsknowledge.com
- ✔ **Syndic8:** syndic8.com

You can also find RSS feeds by searching for blogs. Google has a blog-search function at blogsearch.google.com.

However, you must remember that just because you find an RSS feed available doesn't mean that you can put it into your site without permission. In fact, many blog owners provide feeds so that their readers can view the blogs in a personal RSS reader; you can, for instance, subscribe to RSS feeds within Microsoft Outlook, Internet Explorer, and a Yahoo! or Google account. Before you use a feed, read the feed license agreement or, if you can't find it, contact the owner.

Unlike the automated syndication techniques I mention earlier in this chapter, which use JavaScript and other browser-side systems for inserting content, RSS aggregators for Web pages often use *server-side* techniques, so the content is inserted into the Web page *before* the search engines see it. That's what they call in the search engine business A Good Thing.

If you decide that you want to go ahead with RSS, you need an aggregator. Try searching for *news aggregator* or *rss aggregator,* and either check out the following software directories or ask your favorite geek to do so for you:

- ✔ **freshmeat:** freshmeat.net
- ✔ **SourceForge.net:** sourceforge.net

If your geek has never heard of freshmeat or SourceForge, it's just possible that he or she isn't quite geeky enough.

I have used the zFeeder aggregator (formerly zvonfeeds), which was fairly simple to work with. You can find it at zvonnews.sourceforge.net.

Open content and copyleft

Have you heard of *open-source software?* This type of software is created through the contributions of multiple individuals who agree to allow pretty much anyone to use the software, at no charge. Another movement that doesn't get quite the same attention as open-source software is the open-content movement. *Open content is*, as explained on the Open Content List Web site, free and available for your use.

Open content relies on the concept known as *copyleft.* Under copyleft, the owner of a copyrighted work doesn't release it into the public domain. Instead, he or she releases the work for public modification, with the understanding that anyone using the work must agree to not claim original authorship and to release all derivative works under the same conditions.

Stacks of information are released under copyleft. Start at these sites:

- ✔ **Creative Commons:** creativecommons.org
- ✔ **Open Content List:** www.opencontentlist.com
- ✔ **The Open Directory Project's open content page:** dmoz.org/Computers/Open_Source/Open_Content

You should check out open content — in particular, the open content encyclopedias, which have information on just about anything. You can find these encyclopedias on the Open Directory Project's open content page.

Watch for competitors' information. Some companies use open content as a way to get their links onto the Web.

Search results pages

The great thing about search results pages is that they have the exact keywords you define, liberally scattered throughout. When you conduct a search in a search engine — whether you're searching Web sites, a directory of magazine articles, or news headlines — what does the search engine return? Matches for your keywords.

RSS provides one way to insert searches — in particular, searches of news headlines — into your pages. Even though the page's content changes continually, you don't have to worry about the content changing to a page that doesn't contain your keywords, because the content is a reflection of the keywords you provide. You may also be able to find search pages that you can manually copy and paste. Sites that contain large numbers of articles and a search function may be good candidates. Run a search, and then copy the results and paste them into a Web page.

Make sure that the links in the search results still work and that they open the results in a new window. (You don't want to push people away from your site.) Also check with the site owner to make sure that this strategy is okay. In many cases, site owners are fine with it; again, it means more links to their sites!

Press releases

The nice thing about press releases is that you can use them without permission. The purpose of a press release is to send it out and see who picks it up. You don't need to contact the owner of the press release, because you already have an implied agreement that you can simply post the release wherever you want (unchanged and in its entirety, of course).

You may be able to find press releases that have the keywords you want, are relevant to your site in some way, and are not released by competitors. For instance, if you're in the business of running rodent-racing events, companies selling rodent-racing harnesses and other gear aren't direct competitors and may well have press releases you can use.

Where do you find these press releases? Try searching for *press releases* at a search engine. Combine the search term with some keywords, such as *rodent racing press release*. You can also find them at press release sites, such as these:

- ✔ **EmailWire:** www.emailwire.com
- ✔ **Free-Press-Release.com:** www.free-press-release.com
- ✔ **Hot Product News:** www.hotproductnews.com

- **I-Newswire.com:** i-newswire.com
- **Internet News Bureau:** www.internetnewsbureau.com
- **M2PressWIRE:** www.presswire.net
- **Online Press Releases:** www.onlinepressreleases.com
- **OpenPR.com:** www.openpr.com
- **PR Newswire:** prnewswire.com
- **PR Web:** www.prweb.com
- **PR.com:** www.pr.com
- **PR9.net:** www.pr9.net
- **PressBox.co.uk:** www.pressbox.co.uk
- **PR-GB.com:** www.pr-gb.com
- **PRLeap:** www.prleap.com
- **PRLog.org:** www.prlog.org
- **TransWorldNews.com:** www.prlog.org
- **USANews:** www.usanews.net

You might even subscribe to some of these press release services so that you get relevant press releases sent to you as soon as they're published.

Q&A areas

After you attract sufficient traffic to your site, you may want to set up a question-and-answer (Q&A) or Frequently Asked Questions (FAQ) area on your site. Visitors to your site can ask questions — providing you with keyword-laden questions in many cases — and you can answer them.

A number of free and low-cost software tools automate the creation and management of these Q&A areas. Search the utility sites, such as resource index.com, for these tools, and find a friendly geek if you need help installing a tool.

Make sure that search engines can read pages created by any tool you install on your site, such as the FAQ tool or the BBS and blog tools I tell you about next. Find a tool you like and then find out whether Google indexes the pages in the demo or sample sites. If not, ask the software author to point you to a demo that *does* have indexed pages.

Message boards

Message board areas can be quite powerful, in more than one way. Setting up a message board — also known as a forum or bulletin board system (BBS) — allows site visitors to place keywords in your site for you! A message board often draws traffic, bringing people in purely for the conversation.

Do you own a site about kayaks? As you sleep, visitors can leave messages with the word *kayak* in them over and over. Does your site sell rodent supplies? While you go about your daily business, your visitors can leave messages containing words such as *rodent, mouse,* and *rat.* Over time, this process can build up to hundreds of pages with many thousands of keywords.

BBS systems — even cool ones with lots of features, such as the ability to post photos — are cheap — and often free, in fact. They're relatively easy to set up, even for low-level geeks. Don't underestimate this technique: If you have a lot of traffic on your Web site, a BBS can be a great way to build huge amounts of content. Search for terms such as *bbs software* and *forum software.*

Blogs

Blogs are sort of like diaries. (The term is a derivation of we*blog.*) These systems allow people to write any kind of twaddle — er, musings — they want and then publish this nonsense — um, literature — directly to their Web sites. My cynicism aside, you *can* find some extremely interesting blogs out there.

In fact, over the past couple of years, blogs have become important SEO tools — search engines seem to like them, and visit frequently to index them. In fact, Google even owns one of the top blogging-tools companies, Blogger (`blogger.com`). (Would you bet that blogs hosted by Blogger are indexed by Google?!) In fact, there are plenty of blog-hosting sites, such as Blog.com, Blogster.com, and many more. Search for *blog hosting.*

Many blog-hosting services, such as Blogger, provide a way to integrate pages into your Web site, and blogs can be effective SEO tools, if you can find a way to create enough content. Although many people set up blogs, the number that *maintain* them is far lower!

If you use any tool that allows visitors to post messages on your site, you should monitor and delete inappropriate messages. Many search engine marketers use such tools to post messages (known as *blog spam*) with links pointing back to their sites.

Blogs can be quite useful for search engine optimization, but I don't think blogs are an SEO magic bullet, as some people have suggested. Blogs are a way to get more content onto your site, and they typically get reindexed frequently. They also have tools that interlink blogs, so if you run an active blog, you can get links back to your site. However, the big problem with blogs is that someone must have the time to write frequently, the inclination to write frequently, and the ability to write well and to write what people want to read. This is often a tall order!

A Word about Duplicated Content

Before you move on, a quick discussion about *duplicated content*. The idea is that search engines don't like the same content appearing in different places; after all, why would they want to provide people with lots of different ways to get to the same information? As a Google employee stated on the Google Webmaster Central blog (http://googlewebmastercentral.blogspot.com):

> *Our users typically want to see a diverse cross-section of unique content when they do searches. In contrast, they're understandably annoyed when they see substantially the same content within a set of search results.*

What does Google do about duplicated content? In general, it tries to eliminate copies. For instance:

> *. . . if your site has articles in "regular" and "printer" versions and neither set is blocked in robots.txt or via a noindex meta tag, we'll choose one version to list.*

A lot of paranoia exists about duplicated content, or talk about how sites can get themselves banned for using duplicated content. Most of this talk is gross exaggeration because sites often have good reasons to have duplicated content. Perhaps you're running news feeds from a popular central source or using press releases about events in your industry. It wouldn't make sense for search engines to penalize people for such innocent uses. Thus, as this employee stated,

> *In the rare cases in which we perceive that duplicate content may be shown with intent to manipulate our rankings and deceive our users, we'll also make appropriate adjustments in the indexing and ranking of the sites involved. However, we prefer to focus on filtering rather than ranking adjustments . . . so in the vast majority of cases, the worst thing that'll befall webmasters is to see the "less desired" version of a page shown in our index.*

(For more from this blog entry, search the blog for `deftly dealing with duplicate content`.)

In fact, there are various reasons why search engines can't penalize sites for republishing content. Whom will they punish — every site holding the content or all but the first one to publish it? And, how would they know who was first?

Here's another reason that the search engines can't "punish" sites for duplicated content. Say that I've noticed your rodent-racing site is coming up quickly in the search ranks and you've got a lot of excellent, unique content related to the exciting world of racing very small animals. If I were of a nefarious bent (which I'm not, but if I were. . . .), here's what I'd do: Build a bunch of Web sites on different servers, but build them anonymously. I'd then "scrape" data from your rodent site and republish it on these other sites, forcing the search engines to penalize you.

In general, then, the dire warnings about duplicated content are wrong. However, if Google *does* figure out that you have duplicated content, it may drop the duplicate pages.

So what can you do about duplicated content, with articles you get from syndication sites, for instance, or press releases you drop into your site? If you want to make it more likely that the content isn't ignored, mix it up a little: Add headings within the pieces, change a few words here and there, surround it with other information that's unique to your site, and so on. But don't worry about a penalty, because if every site that contains duplicate content were dropped from Google's index, the index would be empty.

Chapter 10

Finding Traffic via Geo-Targeting

*I*ncreasingly, the Internet is being used as a tool for finding local resources. You can find not only information or buy online, but you can also find homes for sale in your neighborhood, compare local independent insurance agents, and shop at stores close to you that sell the products you need. Thus, it's increasingly important to keep *geo-targeting* in mind when optimizing for search engines — that is, to target by not only a searcher's keyword but also by the searcher's geographic location.

Wait! Before you skip this chapter because you have a purely online business, you need to understand the *two* basic reasons you should consider geo-targeting:

✔ You have a local business.

✔ Your prospects — your target customers — search locally.

Say you are a local business. You sell insurance in your town or own a local health-food store or are a personal trainer with clients within a 5-mile radius. Clearly, you don't need to rank well on the terms *insurance, health food,* or *personal training.* You need to rank well on the terms *insurance denver, health food waco,* or *personal training paducah.* There's no point in competing for general terms against hundreds of thousands of other companies when you're interested in a fraction of the searches.

But, say you're not a local shop for local people. You sell to anyone, anywhere. You may find that the people you want to reach don't search for generic terms — they search for generic terms *in combination with local terms*. You may discover this concept if you do a good keyword analysis, which I describe in Chapter 5. Most people don't search for lawyers, for instance; they search for lawyers in a particular city. They don't search for insurance; they search for insurance in a particular state or city. They don't search for mortgages — they search for mortgages in a particular city.

You may find then, that if you want to reach the largest number of people, you *have* to consider the local aspect even if you sell nationally. Large online businesses targeting home buyers, for instance, often create *geo-targeted* pages designed to reach people in thousands of different locales.

Understanding Geo-Targeting's Importance

The local aspect of search is hugely important. For instance, research has uncovered these gems about Internet users:

- Most are *off-channel* or *Web-to-shop (W2S)* buyers.
- Almost half of Internet users spend extra dollars when in the brick-and-mortar stores on products they didn't research.
- More money is spent offline after online research than is spent online after online research.
- Forrester Research estimated, in 2007, that almost one-quarter of all retail sales are influenced in some way, directly or indirectly, by the Web.
- Forrester Research expects that by 2011, "online influenced offline sales" will reach $1 trillion. Thus, many businesses are trying to target people in their own areas, to get them to walk into their brick-and-mortar stores. Geo-targeting helps you find those people.

Looking Through Local Search

All four of the major search engines — Google, Yahoo!, MSN/Live Search, and Ask.com — now have local search features, sometimes incorporated into their map systems but still accessible from regular search. (Google Local became part of Google Maps, for instance). You can see an example of local-search results, from Google Maps, in Figure 10-1. In Figure 10-2, you can see the type of results that can be displayed for a particular business.

Click and mortified

Studies carried out by ShopLocal.com and reported in January 2008 show that

✔ The Web sees dramatic increases in traffic immediately before big retail shopping days, such as late in the evening on Thanksgiving Day (right before the "Black Friday" shopping mayhem).

✔ In particular, retail store Web sites see huge increases in traffic before big shopping days.

✔ Ninety-two percent of American consumers research products online; yet 95 percent of all purchases are, of course, made offline.

✔ A consumer who researches a product online and then goes to an offline retail store to purchase the product spends an average of $154 on additional, incremental, purchases.

A great deal of money and activity are involved in these "online-influenced offline sales!" One study in 2005 found that 25 percent of all Web searches made by people researching products are shoppers looking for local merchants.

Local search is the generic term given to the ability to search for information related to a particular location — a state, a city, or even a zip code. In some cases, there's a Local link immediately above the Search box; you click this link and then tell the search engine what you're looking for and where, and it finds the best matches it can. In other cases, a local search is carried out if you provide localization information (*pizza denver* or *tax attorney rhode island*, for example).

Thus, in some cases you have to specifically tell the search engine that you want a local search; at the time of writing, entering *pizza denver* into Yahoo! doesn't automatically start a local search, *unless* you click the Local link first. In other cases, the search engine figures out that you want a local search based on your search query.

Actually, Yahoo! is a bit of a hybrid. When you tell it that you want a local search, it then figures out where you are before you tell it. (I explain how in the next section in this chapter.) At the time of writing (and these things seem to change from month to month), clicking the Local link on Yahoo! displays two search boxes — one in which you enter your search terms and one that contains the city and state where Yahoo! thinks you're sitting.

Figure 10-1:
Google
Maps
provide
local-search
results,
including
business
details,
coupons,
and menus.

Figure 10-2:
Detailed
information
is provided
for each
business —
information
that the
business
owner can
add to.

How Does Local Search Work?

Local search is based on several different methodologies, including the science known as *geolocation,* the science of trying to figure out where the heck a computer *is,* geographically speaking. When a computer contacts a search engine and says, "Hi, I'm computer 67.176.77.58; can you search for information about *rodent racing* and send me the results?", how does the search engine figure out whether that computer is in Colorado and thus wants information about the famous Rocky Mountain prairie-dog racing, or is in Florida, and is interested in the famous African Gambian pouch rat races?

Local search generally works in a few basic ways. Different services use different combinations of these methods.

Search terms

If someone types *dentist new york,* the search engine can be pretty sure that the person is looking for a dentist in New York, not a dentist in Oklahoma City. Simple, eh?

Partner sites

Search services can guess at a location based on the Web site someone is using. If someone is searching at www.google.fr, it's a good bet that the person is in France; if someone searches at www.yahoo.co.uk, that person is probably in the United Kingdom. In other cases, partner sites can be even more specific, and related to a particular region or even city.

IP numbers

Internet Protocol (IP) numbers identify computers on the Internet. Every computer connected to the Internet at any moment has a unique IP number.

With information being sent to and fro — from your computer to Web sites and back — there has to be a way for the information to be "addressed" so that various servers on the Internet know where to deliver the information. Thus, every computer connected to the Internet has an *IP number,* or *IP address.*

From coast to coast

There are other cases in which geolocation doesn't work. To "mask" your location as an example, follow these directions:

1. Search for *anonymous browsing* at any major search engine.

2. Visit one of the anonymous Web-browsing sites.

3. Use one of these systems to visit an IP location site, such as `www.ip2location.com`.

4. See where it thinks you're coming from.

Quite likely, it thinks you're somewhere on the other side of the country or the world.

In some cases, two or more computers share an IP number, as in a situation in which a house or an apartment is using a cable or digital subscriber line (DSL) connection, with several computers connected through a single router; but for the purposes of figuring out location, this information isn't important, of course.

In some cases, computers "own" a particular IP number: Turn the computer off now and turn it on next week, and it has the same number. This is known as a *static IP number*. Often, however, computers share IP numbers. Log out of a dial-up account now and in five minutes dial back in, and your computer is assigned a different IP number (known as a *dynamic IP number*). That IP number is shared among many computers, but only one computer can use the number at any particular time.

Take a look at this IP number: `67.176.77.58`. This number uniquely identifies a particular computer in Colorado. If a server sends a page to that address, the page can go to only one place because at that moment only one computer on the Internet is using that number to identify itself. It's like a telephone number. Every telephone in the entire world has a unique number (when you include the country code). Pick up the phone and dial the full number, and there's only one telephone in the world that you can possibly be connected to.

An IP number is a *hierarchical* system. A block of numbers is assigned to a particular organization or company; that organization or company then assigns blocks of numbers to other organizations or companies, which can then assign their numbers to different organizations or companies, or divisions within a company, and so on.

Consider, again, 67.176.77.58. This number is "owned" by Comcast Cable Communications, a large American cable-TV company. In fact, Comcast has a large block of numbers: 67.160.0.0–67.191.255.255. Within that large block lies another block that Comcast uses in Colorado: 67.176.0.0–67.176.127.255. Clearly, 67.176.77.58 lies within this block.

If you want to see this process at work, a number of sites tell you where you are, or at least where they think you are. I just visited IP2Location (www.ip2location.com; you can also try www.whatismyip.com), and it identified my city — though not my zip code, and it got my latitude and longitude wrong.

Geo-targeting with IP numbers isn't perfect; it's definitely an imprecise science, for a few reasons:

✔ **You can't assume that a number assigned to a company in a particular area is being used in that area.** It's possible for two computers using two IP numbers just one digit apart — 67.176.77.58 and 67.176.77.59, for instance — to be thousands of miles apart. An IP number block assigned to an organization in one area can be used by many different computers in many different locations. For example, a computer in San Francisco assigned a block of IP numbers may use those numbers for computers in branch offices in San Diego, Oklahoma City, and Seattle.

✔ **Dynamic IP numbers are "here today, there tomorrow."** When you dial into a network and are assigned an IP number, you could be in California while the computer that assigned the number is in Virginia. When you log off and someone logs on and takes your number, the new computer might be in Wyoming. In particular, AOL messes up IP location because it assigns IP numbers to dial-up users all around the country.

Still, geolocation is getting better all the time. Although the authorities that assign blocks of IP numbers provide very basic geographic information, this information can then be combined with other clues, such as hostnames. For example, it's possible to trace the path from one computer to another and get the IP numbers and hostnames of the servers between the start and destination computers. The following path is from a computer in Australia to 67.176.77.58:

```
 1  FastEthernet6-0.civ-service1.Canberra.telstra.net (203.50.1.65)
 2  GigabitEthernet3-0.civ-core2.Canberra.telstra.net (203.50.10.129)
 3  GigabitEthernet2-2.dkn-core1.Canberra.telstra.net (203.50.6.126)
 4  Pos4-1.ken-core4.Sydney.telstra.net (203.50.6.69)
 5  10GigabitEthernet3-0.pad-core4.Sydney.telstra.net (203.50.6.86)
 6  10GigabitEthernet2-2.syd-core01.Sydney.net.reach.com (203.50.13.38)
 7  i-6-1.wil-core02.net.reach.com (202.84.249.201)
 8  sl-gw28-ana-10-0.sprintlink.net (144.223.58.221)
 9  sl-bb21-ana-11-0.sprintlink.net (144.232.1.29)
10  sl-bb22-ana-15-0.sprintlink.net (144.232.1.174)
11  sprint-gw.la2ca.ip.att.net (192.205.32.185)
```

```
12   tbr1-p014001.la2ca.ip.att.net (12.123.29.2)
13   12.122.10.25 (12.122.10.25)
14   12.122.9.138 (12.122.9.138)
15   12.122.12.134 (12.122.12.134)
16   gar1-p360.dvmco.ip.att.net (12.123.36.73)
17   12.125.159.90 (12.125.159.90)
18   68.86.103.141 (68.86.103.141)
19   68.86.103.2 (68.86.103.2)
20   * * *
21   c-67-176-77-58.hsd1.co.comcast.net (67.176.77.58)
```

The Internet uses IP numbers for addressing, but to make things easier for mere mortals, names (or *hostnames*) can be assigned to computers. Notice something about the hostnames in the preceding code? Some of them have geographic information embedded in them: Canberra, Sydney, co (Colorado), la2ca (Los Angeles, California), and so on. Another clue: Some major *Internet service providers (ISPs)* assign blocks of IP numbers geographically, so when you crack the code, you can figure out where people using that ISP actually live. Using clues such as these, geolocation engineers at various companies specializing in this science can fairly accurately locate IP numbers. The system isn't perfect, but it's close much of the time.

Reaching People Locally

Let me summarize:

- ✔ People often type location names with their keyword searches.

- ✔ Search engines are providing local search services, encouraging people to search locally.

- ✔ Local search services either require location information or guess where searchers are.

What, then, can you do to ensure that your site turns up when people search locally? Here are a few things you can do:

- ✔ **Include your full address in your Web pages.** Include your street, city, state, and zip code. Although you can put the address in the footer, you should put it near the top of the page somewhere. (If you don't know about prominence, see Chapter 6.)

- ✔ **Include in all your pages the names of all locations you're interested in.** Include a list of city names, for instance, in your footer or in a sidebar, ideally with links to pages with information about each of those cities.

✔ **Find other reasons to mention the city and zip code in the body of your text.** If possible, put them in <H> tags; use bold font on some of the references, too.

✔ **Include the full address in your TITLE and DESCRIPTION meta tags.**

✔ **Include city and state names in link text when linking from other sites to yours.** See Chapter 14 for more information.

✔ **If you use pay-per-click (PPC) campaigns, use geo-targeting.** I cover this topic in more detail in the magnificent tome *Pay Per Click Search Marketing For Dummies* (Wiley Publishing, Inc.).

✔ **Register for local search with the major search engines.** The next section in this chapter tells you how.

By adding location names in your pages, you increase the chance of being returned in the search results. For instance, your Chicago health-food store's Web site might have your address on the contact page. What happens when someone searches for *vitamins Chicago?* Your page probably isn't included in the search results, because the search engine is looking for a page containing the word *vitamins* on the same page as the word *Chicago*. If, however, every page on your site contains the address, you have a chance of being included in the search results.

Consider adding your address to product pages and adding product keywords to your contact page.

Registering for Local Search

In Chapter 11, you read about how to get your site listed in search engine indexes. Let me quickly cover *another* way here: how to get your business to turn up in the local-search results.

First note that your business may turn up in the results even if you take no action. The major search engines pull data from a lot of different sources, so your business information may find its way into the results from, for example, Yellow Pages data.

However, Google, Yahoo!, and MSN/Live Search let you submit information about your business directly to local search, increasing the likelihood of being found during a local search and increasing the amount of information that's seen when your information is viewed. (Ask.com doesn't have a way for you to provide data; it gets all its local data from partners.) Search engines search through the local search index *and* through the normal Web-page index.

The sort of information you provide depends on which system you're submitting to, of course. Typical information includes the elements in the following list (see Figure 10-3):

- ✔ Your street address
- ✔ Your phone and fax numbers
- ✔ A link to your Web site
- ✔ A business description
- ✔ The payment methods you accept
- ✔ Your operating hours
- ✔ The year your business was established
- ✔ The languages spoken by your staff
- ✔ The brands you sell

Table 10-1 summarizes the top four local-search systems.

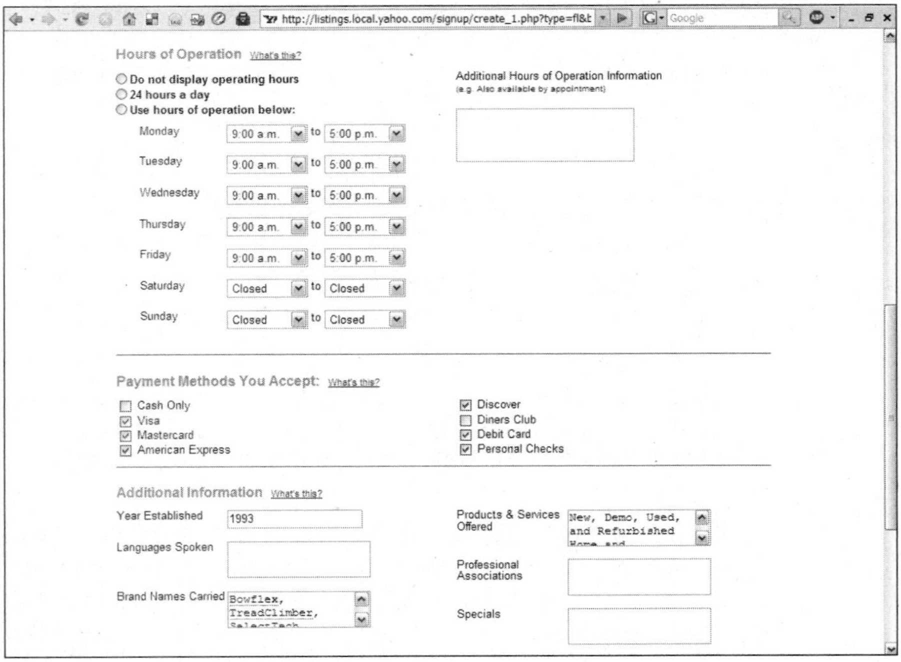

Figure 10-3: Provide as much information about your business to the search engines as you can.

Table 10-1:	The Big Four Go Local	
Site	*Description*	*URL*
Yahoo! Local Listings	Free or $9.95 per month and more for enhanced features. You get a free Web site either way.	`http://listings.local.yahoo.com/`
Google Local Search	Visit the Local Business Center to add your business. (It's free.) If you have more than ten locations, you can submit a data file.	`http://www.google.com/local/add/`
MSN Local Search	You can provide data to MSN Local Search at no charge.	`https://llc.local.live.com/BusinessSearch.aspx`
Ask Local	Ask.com doesn't provide a way to submit data directly to local search; however, if you submit to InsiderPages.com (see the following section for more information), your data is included in Ask.	`http://city.ask.com/`

In some search engines, when you enter information about your business, you're sent a letter or postcard with a verification code. Log back in to the system and enter the code, and your information is accepted. In others—well, there seems to be a degree of trust about who you are.

Finding More Local Systems

More local search systems are out there. For instance, if you want your business to appear in CitySearch search results (and why wouldn't you?), you want to register at www.InsiderPages.com, a local-search and review system recently purchased by CitySearch. It's free, so go ahead and do it: Go to www.insiderpages.com/advertiser, or look on the InsiderPages Web pages for links such as Update Your Business Information.

InsiderPages data is also distributed, so getting listed in InsiderPages can help your chances in Google, Yahoo!, MSN/Live Search, and Ask.com, too, and potentially in smaller systems, such as Excite.

In fact, the major search engines are developing partnerships with many different types of local-information companies, such as Yellow Page companies (YellowPages.com, SuperPages.com, and DexKnows.com, for example), review sites, menu and coupon services, and so on.

For instance, search for *japanese restaurant san francisco* in Google, and Google provides links to menus from Zagat and Menutopia; reviews from ViaMichelin, AOL, CitySearch, and local newspapers; coupons from Valpack, and so on.

Search for *personal injury attorney denver* in Yahoo!, and you may find information from eLocal Profiles, InfoUSA, WCities, and DiscoverYourTown.com.

Search for *shoe shop waco texas*, and you may find content provided by SuperPages (a large Yellow Pages Web site), CitySearch, JudysBook, and Yelp.

In other words, the major search engines are pulling local data from a large variety of sources, and those sources vary between search engines, locations, and subjects. Do a few searches for your particular phrases and locations, and figure out who's feeding data to whom. Then go to those sources and see how you get listed.

If I ran a restaurant, for instance, I would want to get my menus into Zagat, Menutopia, and MenuPix.com; submit a listing to CitySearch (by way of InsiderPages); and figure out how to get reviews into wCities.com, Zagat, 10Best.com, ViaMichelin, AOL, and the local papers. And, I would consider getting coupons into Valpack. Also, though of course I don't condone this type of behavior, let's be honest: Some of your competitors are dropping fake reviews into review sites, to prime the data pump, as it were.

By the way, don't forget local directories that perhaps don't feed data to the major search engines but that are still likely to be important in their own right. For instance, if I owned a restaurant in Denver, I would want to know how to get a review into *5280* magazine, which maintains a popular restaurant guide at www.5280.com. Sometimes it's not all about the major search engines, after all.

Part III

Adding Your Site to the Indexes and Directories

The 5th Wave   By Rich Tennant

"This is amazing. You can stop looking for Derek. According to an MSN search I did, he's hiding behind the dryer in the basement."

In this part . . .

Getting your Web site indexed by the search engines and directories should be easy. Let them know the URL and wait for them to add it, right? Wrong. Sure, you can submit information about your site to the search engines, but they probably won't index it.

In this part, I explain how to get your site into the major search engines, including the new Google, Yahoo!, and MSN sitemap systems. (Hint: You need to make it easy for the search engines to find your site on their own.) I also explain how to work with the two major search directories: Yahoo! (easy, just pay) and the Open Directory Project (easy to submit, and free, but you may never get in!).

This part also tells you how to find important but lesser-known systems and how they can help you. Sure, most searches are carried out through the major systems, but the specialized systems can often provide valuable, highly targeted traffic, and valuable links pointing back to your site.

Chapter 11

Getting Your Pages into the Search Engines

*Y*ou built your Web pages. Now, how do you get them into the search systems? That's what this chapter and Chapter 12 explain. In this chapter, I talk about how to get your pages into search engines, and in Chapter 12 I explain how to list your site with search directories.

Many site owners are confused about how to get their Web sites into search engines. They assume that in order to submit or register their sites, they go to a search engine's Web site, provide the URL to one (or all) of their pages, and wait for the search engine to come along and index the pages. The truth is that the process is more complicated.

Determining Why Your Pages Aren't Being Indexed

It's frustrating when you can't seem to get search engines to index your site. The top three search engines — Google, Yahoo!, and MSN/Live Search — provide a way for you to submit information about your site, but doing so often doesn't seem to make any difference. Your site may not be picked up. As Google says, "We do not add all submitted URLs to our index, and we cannot make any predictions or guarantees about when or if they will appear." MSN/Live Search is a little more positive, perhaps, but still offers no guarantee: "Submitting your site does not guarantee that your site will be indexed. But it does help us locate your site so that MSNBot can try to crawl it." Ask.com doesn't even provide a way for you to submit.

A search submission system that doesn't seem to work and a search engine that has no way for you to tell it about your site — what's going on here?

It's all about links. The search engines believe that they can maintain the quality of their indexes by focusing on Web pages that have links pointing to them. If nobody points to your site, the reasoning goes, why would the engines want to index it? If nobody else thinks your site is important, why should the search engines? They would rather find your pages themselves than have you submit the pages.

By the way, when I say that a page is in a search engine's index, it doesn't mean that the search engine has read and indexed the entire page. In many cases, the search engine has never even read the page but knows where the page is, based on links it has seen in pages that it *has* read. And, even if a search engine has read a page, it may not have read the entire page.

Linking Your Site for Inclusion

In Chapters 14 and 15, I talk about the importance of — and how to get — links pointing from other sites to yours. The more links you have pointing at your site, the more important the search engines will think your pages are.

Links are also important because they provide a way for search engines to find your site. Without links, you *might* get your site into search engine indexes, but chances are you won't. And, being included in the most important index — Google's — is much quicker through linking than through registration. I've had sites picked up and indexed by Google within two or three days of having put up a link on another site. If you simply submit your URL to Google, you may have to wait weeks for it to index your site (if it ever does).

But one or two links sometimes aren't enough for some search engines. They often are for Google: If it sees a link to your site on another site that it's already indexing, it will probably visit your site and index it, too. But other systems are far choosier and may not visit your site even if they do see a link to it. So the more links you have pointing to your site, the better. Eventually, search engines will get sick of tripping over links to your site and come see what the fuss is all about.

Don't think your work is done when you create a site and then submit a page or two to the search engines. Building links from other sites is an essential part of the process. It's frustrating and requires tremendous patience, but that's the way it works!

Submitting Directly to the Major Systems

To be honest, I don't bother submitting Web sites to search engines. (I *do*, however, submit sitemaps, a different subject that I cover in a moment.) Still, just in case you really want to submit your site, let's take a quick look at how to do it.

The process of submitting your site is quick and easy, so there's nothing to lose.

Why submitting is safe

Will submitting pages directly to search engines, or submitting many pages over and over, harm your search engine position? Will the search engines get annoyed and penalize your pages? Why am I even asking this question? Because there's a myth that registering a Web site can harm your chances of being indexed by search engines.

It's not true — and here's why: Imagine that your rodent-racing Web site is sitting at the top of page two for a popular search term in a particular search engine. You feel that this ranking isn't good enough, so you go to the search engine, run the search for that search term, and then grab the URLs of all pages that turn up on the first results page. You then submit those URLs to the search engine over and over and over again, perhaps using a submission program. You keep doing this for days, until the search engines get so annoyed that they remove all those pages, pushing your page to the top! Simple, eh? Too simple, in fact, which is why that tactic doesn't work.

However, you do need to be aware of some potential repercussions. Systems that repeat submissions to an egregious degree may be blocked. The search engine may identify your system's *IP address* (the unique number identifying your computer on the Internet) and then block you from submitting to, or even using, the search engine. If the IP address used by the program submitting URLs is the same as the IP address at which your Web site is hosted, your site can be penalized. These situations are rare, though, because the IP numbers used by such submission programs and the associated Web sites are usually different. It's far more common for search engines to simply block the submission program from submitting more than a certain number of URLs at a time.

Submitting for free

The following systems accept free URL submissions. Note that in some cases, they don't accept more than a specific number of submissions: one a day,

three a day, or whatever. Also, these systems do not want multiple URLs —
just one per Web site.

Submit your site for free at these sites:

- ✔ **Google:** www.google.com/addurl.html
- ✔ **Yahoo:** http://search.yahoo.com/info/submit.html
- ✔ **MSN/Live Search:** http://search.msn.com/docs/submit.aspx

How about Ask.com? It offers no way to submit your Web site. It relies on its
searchbots to find pages through links.

By the way, don't be bamboozled by Yahoo! into using its Search Submit
service. As I explain later in this chapter, you don't need to pay to get into
Yahoo!.

If a search engine doesn't provide a way for you to submit a URL, that doesn't
mean you can't get into the search engine. You need lots of links pointing to
your site so that the search engine will find it, and a fair amount of patience,
but it definitely can happen. And, just because the search engine *does* provide a way for you to submit a URL doesn't mean that you *will* get into the
search engine. You still need lots of links pointing to the site.

Submitting an XML Sitemap

I *do* recommend one form of site submission. It isn't a replacement for pointing links to your site, but it can, in some cases, improve indexing of your site.
I'm talking about creating and submitting XML sitemaps to the top three
search engines, and making it easy for other search engines, such as Ask.com,
to find the sitemap on their own.

In 2005 Google introduced a new submission system and was quickly followed
by Yahoo! and, more recently, MSN/Live Search. You read about sitemaps in
Chapter 7, of course. In that chapter, I recommend creating a sitemap page on
your site and linking to it from the home page. The sitemap is a page that visitors can see, and that any search engine can use to find its way through your
site.

But an XML sitemap is different: It's a special file, placed on your site, that
contains an index to help search engines find their way to your pages. You
create and place the file and then let the search engine know where it is.
This hidden file (visitors never see it) is in a format designed for those
search engines. I think it's worth your time to create these files because it's
not a huge task and it *may* help, particularly if your site is large.

In Google's words, "Using sitemaps to inform and direct our crawlers, we hope to expand our coverage of the web and speed up the discovery and addition of pages to our index." And if I can help Google by getting it to index my site more quickly, well, that's fine by me.

What does this sitemap file look like? Take a look at Figure 11-1.

Don't worry: XML sitemaps are easy to create; I show you how in a moment.

These sitemaps are typically named `sitemap.xml` (though different names can be used) and placed into the root directory of the Web site — in the same directory as the home page.

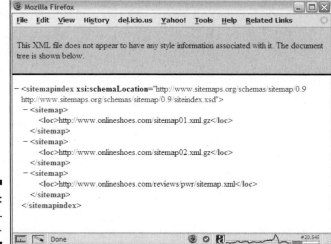

Figure 11-1:
A small XML sitemap.

Sitemap, schmitemap

Don't think that creating an XML sitemap is a magic trick guaranteed to get your site indexed. I've seen, for example, Yahoo! pick up the sitemap file, put it into the search results, come by and pick up 3 pages from the index, ignore the other 20, and leave a whole bunch of old, nonexistent pages in the index; I've also seen

MSN/Live Search apparently pay little attention to a sitemap. On the other hand, I've seen Yahoo! pick up hundreds of thousands of pages on a large site soon after finding multiple XML sitemaps. The sitemap may help, but there's no guarantee if or when the search engines will use it.

Creating your sitemap

You can create a sitemaps file in various ways. Google provides the Sitemap Generator program, which you can install on your Web server; it's a Python script, so if you don't know what that means, consider creating the file another way.

If you're the proud owner of a large, sophisticated, database-driven site, it's probably a job for your programmers; they should create a script that automatically builds the XML sitemap.

You can find technical details about the formatting of these sitemaps at www.sitemaps.org.

What if you own a small site, though, and have limited technical skills? No problem: Plenty of free and low-cost sitemap-creation tools are available.

Note that many of the tools call themselves *Google sitemap* creators, because Google was the first search engine to use sitemaps; but all you need is the basic Google XML sitemap format for all the other search engines, so if it creates a "Google" sitemap, it will work fine.

Some of these programs run on your computer, some require installing on your Web server, and some are services run from another Web site. Table 11-1 is by no means an exhaustive list of places to find third parties. (My favorite for small sites is XML-Sitemaps.com.)

Table 11-1	Third-Party Sitemap Creators	
Creator	*URL*	*Description*
Google	http://code.google.com/sm_thirdparty.html	Features a large list of sitemap tools
XML-Sitemaps.com	http://www.xml-sitemaps.com	Free up to 500 pages; $19.99 for a PHP script that creates sitemaps for larger Web sites
SitemapDoc	http://www.sitemapdoc.com	Indexes up to 500 pages
GSiteCrawler	http://gsitecrawler.com/	A free, Windows-based sitemap generator
AuditMyPC.com Sitemap Generator	www.auditmypc.com/free-sitemap-generator.asp	A free, Web-based generator that works on large Web sites

Creator	URL	Description
George Petrov's Google Sitemap Generator	`www.dmxzone.com/ShowDetail.asp?NewsId=10538`	A Dreamweaver extension that creates Google sitemaps
VIGOS Gsitemap	`www.vigos.com/products/gsitemap`	A free, Windows-based Google sitemap generator
Coffee Cup Google SiteMapper	`www.coffeecup.com/google-sitemapper`	Offers a $29 Windows program
Sitemaps Pal	`www.sitemapspal.com`	A free, Web-based generator for Google that offers extra features for a small fee
Google Sitemap Maker	`www.developsitemap.com`	A $20 Windows-based sitemap generator for Google

Sitemap files can be as large as 10MB and contain as many as 50,000 URLs. If you need to exceed either limit, you must create multiple sitemap files and a sitemap index file that refers to the individual sitemap files. Your XML Sitemaps can also be compressed in the `.gz` file format so they transfer more quickly to the search engine. For specifics of the sitemap protocol, see `www.sitemaps.org`.

Submitting your sitemaps

You can tell search engines about your sitemaps in three different ways:

- ✔ Submit a sitemap through the search engine's Webmaster account.
- ✔ Include a line in the `robots.txt` file telling a search engine where the file is.
- ✔ Ping the search engines.

You need a `robots.txt` file in the root directory of your Web site, with the following line inside it:

```
Sitemap: http://www.yourdomain.com/sitemap.xml
```

The URL should point to your sitemap, of course. The URL tells the search engines that don't provide a Webmaster account — such as Ask.com — where your sitemap is.

Another way to inform search engines of your sitemap's location is to ping them; I describe that process in the next section. But even if you use both a `robots.txt` file and pinging, you should probably also set up a Webmaster account and inform search engines by using the Web-based form you're provided with.

Submitting by using the Webmaster account

You should set up an account on all three major systems (Google, Yahoo! and MSN; Ask.com doesn't currently have Webmaster accounts), and submit your Web site's XML sitemap; then review the various tools that are available. Here's where you can find the Webmaster areas and sitemap-submission pages for the three top systems:

- ✔ **Google:** `http://www.google.com/webmasters/sitemaps`
- ✔ **Yahoo!:** `https://siteexplorer.search.yahoo.com/mysites`
- ✔ **MSN/Live Search:** `http://webmaster.live.com`

You don't need a separate account on each system for each Web site you own — you can submit multiple sites through each account, though MSN/ Live Search limits the number of sitemaps it accepts. (A total of 125 sitemaps is enough for most people, though!) However, in some cases Web site owners don't want search engines to know that their sites are associated; for instance, if a site owner has three sites, all of which rank on the first page for important keywords, he may not want it to be obvious that all sites are owned by the same person. In such a case, of course, he would set up separate accounts for submitting each sitemap.

Here's the basic process you use at all these services:

1. Set up an account.

   In each case, you have to set up a password-protected account.

2. Tell the search engine where the sitemap is.

   You provide the URL that points to your sitemap; the search engine checks to see whether it can find the file.

3. Create an authentication or verification file and place it in the root of your site.

   You're provided with an authentication or verification code, which is used to create a small text file that's stored on your server. Each system is slightly different, but Google, for instance, just requires an empty text file with the code used as the filename, whereas Yahoo! provides both a filename and a code that must be saved inside the file. (All three systems allow you to add a meta tag to your home page, if you prefer, rather than create a text file.)

4. Tell the search engine that the file has been placed and ask it to "verify" the file.

   After you create the file, the search engine checks to see whether the file is where it should be; if it is, the search engine assumes that you must own or have control over the specified site, and thus is willing to provide you with more information about the site.

Each system is different, so I don't go into detail beyond telling you how you can find (at the time of writing) the start of the submission process:

- ✔ **Google:** In the main Dashboard, add your site domain. Then click the Verify Your Site link to add the verification information, and click the Sitemaps button in the navbar to tell Google where your sitemap is.

- ✔ **Yahoo:** Start by adding your site; then click the Manage Your Site button to submit the sitemap, and use the Authenticate button to obtain the authentication code.

- ✔ **MSN/Live Search:** Click the Add a Site button to add your domain name and sitemap and receive your verification information.

Pinging search engines

Pinging a search engine means sending a message to the search engine telling it where a sitemap is. At the time this book was written, you could ping all four of the major systems — Google, Yahoo!, MSN/Live Search, and Ask.com — and some smaller systems, such as Moreover.com.

You can see this process in action for yourself. Create a sitemap, and then change the following URL to show the path to your sitemap:

```
http://www.google.com/ping?sitemap=http://www.yourdomain.
          com/sitemap.xml
```

Copy and paste this URL into a browser and press Enter, and you receive this response from Google:

   Sitemap Notification Received

Your Sitemap has been successfully added to our list of Sitemaps to crawl. If this is the first time you are notifying Google about this Sitemap, please add it via `http://www.google.com/webmasters/sitemaps` so you can track its status. Please note that we do not add all submitted URLs to our index, and we cannot make any predictions or guarantees about when or if they will appear.

These are the sitemap-submission URLS:

```
http://www.google.com/ping?sitemap=
http://www.google.com/webmasters/sitemaps/ping?sitemap=
http://search.yahooapis.com/SiteExplorerService/V1/ping?si
    temap=
http://webmaster.live.com/ping.aspx?sitemap=
http://submissions.ask.com/ping?sitemap=
http://www.moreover.com/ping?sitemap=
```

You can manually ping sites each time the search engine is updated. If you have a programmer build your sitemaps automatically, by pulling data from a database, the programmer should add a ping function to ping the search engines each time the sitemap is updated. And, some sitemap-creation programs that you can buy have built-in ping functions; the version of the XML-Sitemaps.com program that you install on your server can automatically ping for you.

Are sitemaps bad? I've heard the argument that sitemaps are bad because you might rely on the sitemap rather than create links to your site. This argument is similar to the one that airbags are bad because you might rely on them rather than drive safely. Sitemaps are *good*. But they're not a substitute for links pointing to your site. You still need links, and many of them.

Webmaster tools, too

As we've just seen, the three top search engines — Google, Yahoo!, and MSN — now provide Webmaster accounts through which you can submit your sitemap and provide various tools related to your sitemaps. Some of these tools are available even if you *don't* submit a sitemap, but if you do submit a sitemap and then prove that you are the owner of the site (through the authentication or verification process I mention earlier), you'll be provided with more information.

Right now, Google has the best tools and statistics associated with its Webmaster account; see Table 11-2 for a selection.

Table 11-2	Google's Webmaster Tools
Tool	*What It Does*
Web crawl	Corrects errors and problems encountered by Google's crawlers on your site.
Content analysis	Fixes potential problems with your pages: missing titles, duplicate titles, long or short title tags, duplicated or long meta tags, pages that can't be indexed, and so on.

Tool	What It Does
Top search queries	Indicates which search queries most often returned pages from your site and which ones were clicked.
Crawl stats	Displays PageRank information for your site. (See Chapter 14 for information on PageRank.)
What Googlebot sees	Displays Keywords found by Googlebot, in your site and in links pointing to the site.
Pages with external links	Shows links from other sites pointing to your site and indicates which page inside the site they point to (an excellent tool!).
Sitelinks	Indicates which pages on your site Google would use as sitelinks if it decided to present multiple links to your site in the search results. (See Chapter 21 for information about sitelinks.) You can block a particular page from appearing, if you want.
Pages with internal links	Shows links between pages within your site.
Analyze `robots.txt`	Checks to ensure that your `robots.txt` file works correctly.
Set geographic target	Lets you tell Google that you're interested in turning up in search results for a particular country only.
Enable enhanced image search	Improves the way Google indexes your images (see Chapter 21).
Set crawl rate	Slows the frequency of indexing, if you want.
Remove URLs	Removes pages that you don't want Google to index.

Using Paid Inclusion

Paid-inclusion programs provide you with the privilege of paying to have a search engine index your pages. Happily, such programs have fallen out of favor. Only one of the major systems, Yahoo!, now has a paid-inclusion program: Search Submit Basic at `http://searchmarketing.yahoo.com/srchsb/ssb.php`. Some smaller systems still have them, but they're rarely worthwhile.

Here's the concept: You pay Yahoo! a fee ($49 a year) for each page you want indexed, and Yahoo! guarantees to index your pages quickly, come back frequently to reindex (every seven business days), and keep your pages in the index for a full year. The system now accepts a maximum of only five URLs; if you want to submit more, you have to use Search Submit Pro, which is a cost-per-click system.

I don't like the idea of paid inclusion; it strikes me as a bit of a scam. The Federal Trade Commission doesn't like it much either, and consumer-advocate complaints have targeted paid inclusion based on federal law that "prohibits unfair or deceptive acts or practices in or affecting commerce [such as] a representation, omission, or practice that is likely to mislead the consumer acting reasonably in the circumstances, to the consumer's detriment."

The argument is over whether paid inclusions are, in effect, ads. Yahoo! says they're not; you're simply paying for an improved service in placing your URLs into the index, thereby improving the index.

But from the consumer's perspective, paid-inclusion ads are misleading. If a search engine has a complex algorithm designed to provide accurate, relevant search results, and if that algorithm includes links pointing to a site as a factor but then allows sites to partially bypass the algorithm — by being included in the index despite insufficient incoming links to attract the interest of the search engine — how is that not paying to be included in the search index and thus misleading searchers by mixing ads with organic search results? The pages you submit through Search Submit appear in the search results without any kind of indication that a payment has been made; they sit along with the rest of the "organic" or "free" results.

Yahoo! says that the paid-inclusion pages still have to compete on the same terms with all other pages in the index and aren't ranked any higher based on their payment status. That may be true, but paid-inclusion pages definitely rank higher than pages that are not in the index because their owners haven't paid! Note, by the way, that the founders of Google also consider paid inclusion to be misleading and have refused to allow their search engine to use such programs.

Excluding inclusion

If you're trying to decide whether to use paid inclusion, consider the following points:

- **You might pay never-ending fees.** You may get stuck paying fees year after year.

- **You can get indexed by using links.** If you have a good linking strategy, you should be able to get Yahoo! to index your site without having to pay. A large number of high-quality links into your site helps ensure that your site gets picked up.

Hasta la Vista, AltaVista, et. al.

The first edition of this book included information about four major paid-inclusion systems: Inktomi, AltaVista, FAST/AlltheWeb, and Ask.com. All these programs are gone now (the first three have been combined into the Yahoo! system).

✔ **You have to have links.** You can't pay to get into Google or MSN, so you have to get lots of links to your site anyway!

✔ **You pay for a no-show.** If you don't have a good linking strategy, your pages probably won't rank well anyway. Paid inclusion gets you into the index, but it doesn't affect your position in the index, so you may be paying to be on a search results page that few people read.

On the other hand, some people like paid inclusion because of the speedy updates. You can tweak pages and see the results in Yahoo! within a few days. On *another* hand, a site with lots of incoming links often gets reindexed every few days, even without paying.

Here's an interesting conundrum: Most pages are added to the Yahoo! index for free. Its searchbots add pages, and you can submit pages directly. If Yahoo!, with billions of pages in its index, limited its index to only paid inclusions, it would quickly go out of business. So, here are a few important questions about paid inclusion:

✔ **If you pay to have your pages indexed, what happens when the agreement period expires?** Presumably, Yahoo! should remove your pages; otherwise, the paid-inclusion program more or less collapses, doesn't it? That would mean that Yahoo!, in effect, holds you hostage, by removing pages that might otherwise have been indexed automatically by its searchbots!

✔ **What would stop you from indexing a single page by using paid inclusion — a page that contains lots of links to your other pages, to ensure that search engines find all your pages?** A sitemap page is a good example. Yahoo! wants you to submit multiple pages via the paid-inclusion program, so it would be against their interests to do this. Is Yahoo! disabling the normal algorithm for paid-inclusion pages to ensure that they aren't picked up for free?

✔ **If, in its normal course of travel, the Yahoo! searchbot runs across pages you have paid to have included, does it index those pages and flag them as no longer requiring payment?** Will Yahoo! refund your money for the rest of the submission period?

Using trusted feeds

Another form of paid inclusion is a *trusted feed* — a sort of *en masse* paid inclusion. As with paid inclusion, trusted-feed services used to be provided by several large search engines, but now Yahoo! is the only large system with this service. (It's known as Search Submit Pro:http://searchmarketing. yahoo.com/srchsb/ssp.php.) Trusted feeds are sometimes used by companies with dynamic Web sites (see Chapter 7 for more on what makes sites dynamic) and are generally intended for large numbers of pages — 1,000 or more. Yahoo! targets companies that are likely to spend $5,000 or more per month.

With Yahoo!'s trusted-feed program, you don't pay to have your pages included, but you do pay — $0.25 or more per click — every time a searcher clicks on a link in the search results pointing to your site. Your links appear in the organic search results along with the regular, free results, not in the sponsored results.

You provide information about your pages to Yahoo! You can get data into the search engines in a couple of ways: Provide an XML file containing all the information, or provide some other kind of data feed, such as an Excel spreadsheet. You provide this information:

- ✔ URL
- ✔ Page title
- ✔ DESCRIPTION meta tag
- ✔ KEYWORDS meta tag
- ✔ Page content

Providing the data in a trusted feed allows you to submit data to search engines so that they don't have to crawl your Web site to pick it up. It also allows you to submit the relevant data — ignoring irrelevant page content — which raises the question "Isn't this just a legal form of cloaking?"

Cloaking is a technique for showing a searchbot a different page from the one a site visitor would see, and it's frowned on by search engines. You can read about cloaking in Chapter 8.

Unlike basic paid inclusion, a trusted feed feeds data into the index; the searchbot doesn't have to index the page itself because you *tell* the searchbot what the page is about. A trusted feed is even closer to being an ad, therefore, than paid inclusion is.

Yahoo! argues that paid-inclusion programs don't help your site rank higher. But it's hard to make this argument for trusted feeds, especially when the Yahoo! sales staff is telling people that they can help *tweak* the data feed so that the pages rank better and when their online demo use phrases like "Search Submit Pro helps match your listings more effectively with relevant queries." Yahoo! even states in the online demo that the data feed "eliminates information that is irrelevant to your content and confusing to search engines." In other words, the trusted feed helps your site rank better. The demo — which you can view at `http://searchmarketing.yahoo.com/imgs/as/srchsbp.swf` — makes quite clear that the intention of the trusted feed is to manipulate the search results!

Submitting to Secondary Systems

You can also submit your site information to smaller systems with perhaps a few hundred million pages in their indexes — and sometimes far fewer. The disadvantage to these systems is that they're seldom used, compared to the big systems discussed earlier in this chapter. Many search engine professionals ignore the smaller systems altogether. So, if your site is ranked in these systems, you have less competition because they're so small.

These secondary systems may be worth submitting your site to:

- ✔ **ExactSeek:** `www.exactseek.com/add.html`
- ✔ **Gigablast:** `www.gigablast.com/addurl`

I provide a list of additional search engines at my site, `www.SearchEngineBulletin.com`, and you can find more, including regional sites, listed on the following pages:

- ✔ `www.searchenginewatch.com/links/article.php/2156161`
- ✔ `www.allsearchengines.com`
- ✔ `www.searchengines.com/generalKids.html`
- ✔ `www.searchengines.com/worldUSCan.html`
- ✔ `http://dmoz.org/Computers/Internet/Searching/Search_Engines/`
- ✔ `dir.yahoo.com/Computers_and_Internet/Internet/World_Wide_Web/Searching_the_Web/Search_Engines_and_Directories/`

Some smaller search engines encourage you to pay for a submission. Don't. Unless you know for sure otherwise, you can safely assume that the amount of traffic you're likely to get probably isn't worth the payment.

Little giant

Some secondary systems are still fairly popular sites. For instance, I've seen Alexa rank Exact-Seek as the 1,600th most popular Web site at one point, though recently it dropped to around 2,200.

Many smaller search sites don't have their own searchbots; they get their data from other systems, such as the Open Directory Project (which feeds around 350 different systems). So, sometimes you run across search sites to which you can't submit directly.

If you plan to submit your site to many search engines, you may want to use a programmable keyboard or a text-replacement utility or macro program, such as ShortKeys (www.shortkeys.com), which can make entering repetitive data much quicker:

- ✔ **Programmable keyboard:** You can assign a string of text — a URL, an e-mail address, and so on — to a single key. Then all you need to do is (for instance) press F11 to enter your e-mail address.

- ✔ **Text-replacement utility:** Replace a short string of text with something longer. To enter your e-mail address, for instance, you might type just *em*.

A few sites require that you submit your site with a username and password. Most sites require at least an e-mail address, and some also require that you respond to a confirmation e-mail before they add your site to the list. *Don't use your regular e-mail address!* Use a throwaway address because you'll receive a lot of spam.

Using Registration Services and Software Programs

You can also submit your pages to hundreds of search engines by using a submission service or program. Many free services are available, but some of them are outdated, running automatically for a few years now and not having kept up with changes on the search engine scene.

Many free services are definitely on the *lite* side. They're provided by companies that hope you'll spring for a fee-based full service.

Some free services also combine links and directory registrations, along with search engine registrations. (We discuss directory registrations in Chapter 12.) By providing links pointing to your site, they can guarantee that your site will be picked up by the major search engines; it's not the submissions to the search engines that are doing the work — it's the links!

Note also that some submission services increase their submission counts by including all services that are fed by the systems they submit to. For instance, if a service submits to Yahoo!, it counts it as multiple submissions because Yahoo! feeds AlltheWeb, Lycos, Terra.com, HotBot, Overture, InfoSpace, Excite, and more. Some submission services inflate their numbers by including search engines that don't even exist any more. In fact, I feel that some (many) submission services are little more than scams, charging in some cases very high monthly fees for what's really a service with relatively few benefits.

Still, if you want to try them, here are a couple of services (with more reasonable fees) that you might check out:

 ✔ **AdPro:** www.addpro.com
 ✔ **ineedhits:** www.ineedhits.com

There are many, many submission services; search for *search engine submission service,* and you'll find a gazillion of them.

A few submission software programs are available as well. Here are a few of the more popular ones:

 ✔ **Dynamic Submission,** which you can find at www.dynamicsubmission.com.
 ✔ **SubmitWolf** at http://www.trellian.com/swolf.
 ✔ **WebPosition Gold** at www.webposition.com. Okay, this program has some limited submission tools, but it's really more useful for checking search engine positions. See Chapter 21 for more on that score.

The big advantage of these software programs is that you pay only once rather than pay every time you use a service.

You actually have a couple of reasons to use these automated tools. You may get a little traffic out of these small search engines, though don't bank on getting much. But in many cases the systems being submitted to are not really search engines — they're search *directories,* and being listed in a directory may mean that major search engines pick up a link pointing to your site. (Several of the systems listed by AddPro, for instance, are directories rather than search engines.) I talk more about submitting your site to search directories in Chapter 12, and you discover the power of linking in Chapters 14 through 16.

Chapter 12

Submitting to the Directories

*I*n Chapter 11, you look at getting your site into the search engines. In this chapter, you look at getting your site into the directories. Submitting to directories is still a great way to get links. I also show you how to find a low-cost service to submit to hundreds of services at once — one service I use submits to 1,200 directories for $200. The major directories are very important to a search strategy, although they can be rather frustrating to work with. Compared to search engines, the overall process of working with directories is very different. In some ways, it's simpler; in other ways, it's not.

Pitting Search Directories Against Search Engines

Before you start working with directories, it's helpful to know a few basics about what directories are — and aren't:

- ✔ Directories don't send searchbots out onto the Web looking for sites to add (though they may send bots out to make sure that the sites are still live).

- ✔ Directories don't read and store information from Web pages within a site.

- ✔ Because directories don't read and store information, they don't base search results on the contents of the Web pages.

- ✔ Directories don't index Web pages; they index Web sites. Each site is assigned to a particular category. Within the categories, the directory's index contains just a little information about each site — not much more than a URL, a title, and a description. The result is a categorized list of Web sites — and that's really what the search directories are all about.

A few years ago, Yahoo! was based around its directory. In fact, Figure 12-1 shows an example of what Yahoo! looked like early in 1998 (courtesy of a wonderful service called the WayBackMachine at `www.archive.org`). The idea behind Yahoo! was a categorized directory of Web sites that people could browse. You could click links to drill down through the directory and find what you needed, similar to flipping through a Yellow Pages directory. Although you could use the Search box to peruse categories, site titles, and site descriptions, the tool was nothing like the Yahoo! search index of today, which can hunt for your term in billions of Web pages.

But Yahoo! made an enormous mistake. In fact, the image in Figure 12-1 is from a time when Yahoo! was at its peak, a time when most of the world's Web searches were carried out through its site — just a few months before Google began operations. Yahoo! evidently hadn't fully realized the weaknesses of the directory system until it was too late. These weaknesses include the following:

- **Directories provide no way for someone to search individual pages within a site.** The perfect fit for your information needs may be sitting somewhere on a site that is included in a directory, but you won't know it because the directory doesn't index individual pages.

- **Categorization is necessarily limited.** Sites are rarely about a single topic; even if they appear to be, single topics can be broken down into smaller subtopics. By forcing people to find a site by category and keyword in a very limited amount of text — a description and title — the directories are obviously very restrictive.

- **Hand-built directories are necessarily limited in size.** Hand-built directories, such as Yahoo! Directory and the Open Directory, add a site to their directories only after a real live human editor has reviewed the site. With hundreds of millions of Web sites, there's no way a human-powered system can keep up.

- **Hand-built directories get very dated.** Directories often contain some extremely old and out-of-date information that simply wouldn't be present in an index that is automatically reindexed every few days or weeks. (Yahoo! *spiders* the sites — that is, sends out searchbots to look through the sites — in its index for broken links and dead sites, but if the site's purpose has changed, Yahoo! may not realize that fact.)

The proof of directories' weaknesses is in the pudding: Google took over and now is the dominant search system on the Web. (To be fair, Yahoo! helped Google by integrating Google results into Yahoo! searches, although in the summer of 2004, it dropped Google and began using its own index.)

The old Yahoo! site directory is still there, but it's virtually hidden to many visitors. Just a couple years ago, the directory was still on the home page, but so low that you had to scroll to see it; now, the directory isn't even on the home page. You can find it by going to `dir.Yahoo.com` or by clicking the Directory link on the More menu at the top of the Yahoo! home page.

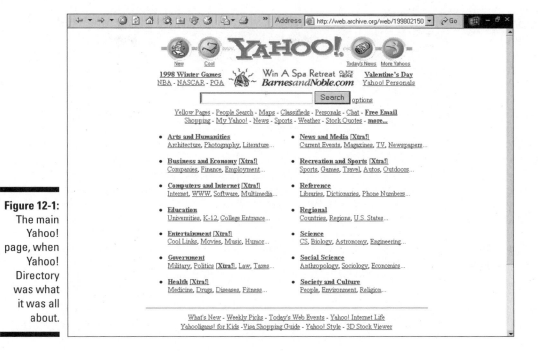

Figure 12-1:
The main
Yahoo!
page, when
Yahoo!
Directory
was what
it was all
about.

Why Are Directories So Significant?

If the Yahoo! Directory is hidden away, and if most people have never heard of the world's second most important directory (the Open Directory Project at `www.dmoz.org`), why do you care about them? They're still very significant for a number of reasons:

✔ Yahoo! Directory is part of the Yahoo! search system, one of the world's most popular search sites. As such, it still gets a lot of traffic. You can access it directly at `dir.yahoo.com`; some people do access it from the Yahoo! main page.

✔ The Open Directory Project feeds results to Google Directory, which is part of the world's *most popular* search site.

✔ The Open Directory Project feeds results to literally hundreds of other sites, large and small. Many of these sites are crawled by the major search engines (such as Google), so a link from the Open Directory Project can show up as links from many other sites, too.

✔ Yahoo! often uses directory entries for the blurb below a page title in Web search results — the search results page shown when someone searches their indexes. Google used to grab the site description from the

Open Directory Project (though doesn't seem to be doing so at the time of writing), and Yahoo! pulls the description from Yahoo! Directory, so having a directory entry sometimes allows you to control the text that appears on the search results pages for your site.

✔ Links in the major directories help provide context to search engines. If your site is in the Recreation: Pets: Rodents category in the Open Directory Project, for instance, the search engines know that the site is related to playing with rodents. The directory presence helps search engines index your site and may help your site rank higher for some search terms.

✔ Links, as you see in Chapters 14 through 16, are very important in convincing search engines that your site is of value. It's sometimes possible to get links from hundreds of search directories, on pages indexed by the major search engines.

By the way, don't underestimate the Open Directory Project just because you've never heard of it or because the submission forms are often broken or unreliable. Data from this system is widely spread across the Internet and has often been used to kick-start major search systems. Yahoo!, for instance, once used data from the Open Directory Project (which, incidentally, is owned by AOL/Netscape).

Submitting to the Search Directories

Chapter 11 has what some may find an unusual message: "Sure, you can submit to the search engines, but it may not do you any good." Search engines really like links to your site, and having links to your site is often the best way to get into the search engines.

However, the search directories won't find you unless you submit to them. And you can forget automated submission programs for the major directories — there's no way to use them. Submissions must be entered into Yahoo! and the Open Directory Project by hand.

Submitting to Yahoo! Directory

Submissions to Yahoo! Directory (once free) used to be very difficult. Surveys showed that people who had managed to get their sites listed in the directory had to try multiple times over a matter of months. Well, I've got good news and bad.

✔ The good news: You can get your site listed in Yahoo! Directory within about a week. Of all the major search systems, getting into Yahoo! Directory is easiest; Yahoo! guarantees to review your site within seven business days. They're not guaranteeing to include your site — only to review and add it if it's appropriate. In general, most people don't have many problems. Yahoo! will almost certainly accept your site if it is

- Functioning without a lot of broken links

- In the correct language for the particular Yahoo! Directory to which you are submitting (Yahoo! has directories in several languages.)

- Designed for multiple browser types; they expressly exclude Java-only sites

- In an appropriate category

✔ The bad news: It's probably going to cost you $299 per year for the privilege ($600 for adult sites). It's free if you have a noncommercial site — though it may take some time for your site to be accepted, if it is at all — but for any kind of commercial venture, you have to cough up the cash. (Note, however, that Yahoo! Directory still contains many sites that predate the paid-listing policy and do not require payment.)

Is listing in Yahoo! Directory worth $299? Hard to say, but here are some good reasons to do so:

✔ It seems likely that getting into its directory ensures that you get into the Yahoo! Web Search, and may even improve your indexing in Yahoo! Web Search. The company actually states that it "can increase the likelihood," but doesn't guarantee inclusion. I've seen a site get fully indexed fairly soon after submitting to the directory, though that could be coincidence.

✔ It's crawled by other search engines, such as Google, so having a link in the directory helps the search engines find your site and may encourage them to index it.

✔ Search engines use the directory to help them categorize your site.

✔ Many people, as I mention earlier, do use the directory.

✔ If your site is in the directory, you may be able to place a cheap ad at the top of your category. Some category sponsors are paying as little as $25 per month.

The 1-2-3s of getting listed

Here's how to get listed:

1. **Find a credit card.**

   Preferably the card is yours or that of someone who has given you permission to spend $299 (or is it $600?).

2. **Open your browser and go to** `dir.yahoo.com.`

   You're going to make sure that your site isn't already included.

3. **After the page has loaded, type your domain name into the Search box and click Search.**

   If you have total control over your site, this step isn't necessary. Of course, you'll know whether your site is already listed. But, for example, if you inherited it from another department in the company you work for, who knows, it may already be there. If it isn't, move to the next step.

4. **Return to the Yahoo! Directory main page and browse through the categories looking for the best match for your site.**

   You can find tips on choosing a category in the next section, "Picking a category."

5. **Look for a link that reads something like *Suggest a Site* or perhaps a promotional box of some kind.**

   The link is probably somewhere in the top right of the page.

6. **Click the link and follow the instructions.**

   You have to enter a site description, contact and billing information, and so on.

Picking a category

Because of the sheer volume of categories, picking a category is not as simple as it might seem. Yahoo! Directory has 14 major categories, and many thousands of subcategories. But understanding a few points about hunting for and submitting to a category can make the process a little smoother.

You need to choose a fairly specific category. You can't submit to a category or subcategory if it only holds other subcategories. For instance, you can't submit a site to the Business & Economy category; it's just too broad. Rather, you have to drill down farther into the subcategories and find a category that's specific enough to contain actual Web sites.

You'll probably find that your site could perhaps fit into several categories, so you're going to have to dig around for a while and pick the most appropriate. Although discouraged, you can put a single site into multiple categories, but of course you have to pay for each category. (And Yahoo! doesn't like doing this, anyway; it can take time and effort to persuade them.)

One good strategy is to look for your competitors: What categories are they assigned to? If you find a category with a whole bunch of companies similar to yours, you've probably found the right one.

While you move through Yahoo! Directory, you see that some category names have an @ sign at the end, such as Graduate Programs@, Booksellers@, Intranet@, and so on. These cross-references are to categories under different branches of the directory. For instance, if you browse down the directory to Recreation & Sports > Travel, you see a link to Tour Operators@; click this link, and you jump over to Business and Economy > Shopping and Services > Travel and Transportation > Tour Operators. In fact, virtually every Web site that sells or promotes a product ends up somewhere under Business and Economy, even if they're linked from other parts of the directory.

Also, you have to be inside an actual category before you can add a page. This is a little confusing, perhaps. When you first search in the directory, Yahoo! displays a page (see Figure 12-2) that contains a list of categories and a whole bunch of Web sites that match your search but from various different categories. Thus, you're not actually inside a category at this point, so you can't add a page here, but you will see links that take you into specific categories.

By the way, Yahoo! may not take your advice; it may put your site into a different category. If you're convinced your choice is best, ask them to change. I've successfully requested a change, by pointing out not that the category is best for my client, but that the placement was misleading to searchers because people visiting that category would not expect to see my client's type of Web site.

After searching, you see links to different categories within the index.

Figure 12-2:
After searching at Yahoo! Directory, you see links to directory categories.

After searching, you see links to
different catgories within the index

Submitting to the Open Directory Project

Yes, the Open Directory Project is free, and yes, you can submit much more quickly. But the problem is that there's no guarantee that your site will be listed. I've seen sites get into the Open Directory Project within a week or two of submission, and I've seen others that waited months — years! — without ever getting in. Additionally, the submission forms sometimes don't seem to work.

But don't give up. As I make abundantly clear, both earlier in this chapter and in Chapter 1, the Open Directory Project is very important. Here's how to submit:

1. **Read the editor's guidelines at** dmoz.org/guidelines/describing. html.

   If you know what guidelines the editors use, you may be able to avoid problems. It's hard to get into the directory, so you may as well give yourself the best chance of getting in.

2. **Go to** www.dmoz.org.

   The Open Directory Project home page appears.

3. **Find a suitable category for your site.**

   See "Picking a category," earlier in this chapter.

4. **Click the Suggest URL link at the top of the page.**

5. **Follow the (fairly simple) directions.**

Submitting to the Open Directory Project is much easier than doing so to Yahoo! Directory. You simply enter your home page's URL, a short title, a 25–30 word description for the site, and your e-mail address. That's it. Then you wait.

Nevertheless, understand that the editors at DMOZ don't care about your site, they care about the directory; in fact, read the DMOZ forums at www. resource-zone.com and you find that the attitude tends to be "tell us about your site, then go away and forget about it." All sorts of factors are working against you:

- 8,000 editors are managing more than 700,000 categories.

- Many small directories might only be reviewed by an editor every six months — or far less frequently.

- The editors regard a six-month wait, or longer, not particularly excessive.

- In some cases, editors may even ignore submissions. As one editor explained, "There is no obligation to review them in any order nor is there a requirement to review them as a priority. Some editors find it more productive to seek out sites on their own and rarely visit the suggested sites."

As another DMOZ editor succinctly explained it, DMOZ is "very much like a lottery." The fact is, as important as DMOZ is, you may never get into this directory!

Understanding different link types

A link from Yahoo! looks something like this:

```
http://rds.yahoo.com/_ylt=A9htfTeuNtRDAVsBGtyEzbkF;_ylu=X3
        oDMTB2bmc5YWltBGNvbG8DZQRwb3MDMQRzZWMDc3IEdnRpZ
        ANERlgwXzM-
        /SIG=1165et4rd/EXP=1138067502/**http%3a//abc.go
        .com/
```

A link from the Open Directory Project, and from many other search engines, looks like this:

```
http://abcnews.go.com/
```

In other words, links from the Open Directory Project, and many secondary directories, count as a link directly to your site for the purposes of PageRank (see Chapter 14). These links not only help search engines find your site and categorize it, but can also help ranking by acting as a "vote" for your site.

Submitting to Second-Tier Directories

Second-tier directories are smallish directories with nowhere near the significance of Yahoo! Directory or the Open Directory Project. They can help you a little if you're willing to spend a few hours registering your site with them.

Unlike search engines, directories can be *crawled* by a searchbot. Directories are categorized collections of sites that you can browse. If you can browse by clicking links to drill down through the directory, then so can a searchbot. In fact, the major search engines index many small directories. If you have a link in one of these directories and one of the major systems sees it, that can help your rank in that search engine, as explained in Chapter 14.

Finding second-tier directories

There are hundreds of directories, though you don't want to spend much time with most of them. Many of the directories you find are using data from the Open Directory Project, so you have, in effect, already submitted to them. (You did submit, didn't you?) Often these sites have a little Open Directory Project box near the bottom of the page, like the one shown in Figure 12-3.

This box will soon become familiar as you dig around looking for directories. However, sometimes, a site's relationship to the Open Directory Project isn't so clear.

Figure 12-3:
This box means the data comes from the Open Directory Project.

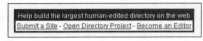

Here's the best way to deal with these directories; find a service that will submit for you. Realistically, these have to be done by hand — no automated programs can submit to a really large number of directories reliably — which is extremely time consuming and thus extremely expensive.

However, there are some firms that use Indian labor to make it affordable. I have worked with two of these firms so far; the first didn't work out so well, which is why I found another.

The firm I'm currently using charges $250 to submit to 1,000 Web directories, or $450 to submit to 2,000. Now, you won't get links in all 1,000, but you may get 400 or 800 over time, so that's a great price.

The firm I'm working with takes screenshots of each submission form, so you can be sure that the submission was completed properly (it uploads the snapshots to a file-sharing site). Now, for various reasons I don't want to pro- vide contact information for this firm in the book (it's a small firm, and hey, you know, these firms come and go!). However, I'll post information on my site (www.SearchEngineBulletin.com) so you can reach them and I can change the information if necessary.

Avoiding payment — most of the time

Don't bother paying registration fees to register with these second-tier sys- tems. As with search engines, the directory owners are also trying to get site owners to pay for indexing. For example, JoeAnt (www.joeant.com) wants a $39.99 one-time fee to take your information. In most cases, the listing simply isn't worth the fee. Regard being listed in these directories as cheap addi- tional links, not as something you need to spend a lot of money on.

On the other hand, you may run across directories that you feel really are of *value* — directories that provide good links back to your site (which helps with search engine rank) or that are likely to provide good traffic to your site.

However, before you buy, at least be sure you know what you're buying; sometimes a link is not a link. See Chapter 14 for information about links with *no value* — links that look to users like valid links, but that search engines either ignore or don't even see as a link to your site.

Chapter 13

Buried Treasure — More Great Places to Submit Your Site

In This Chapter

▶ Keeping track of what you find online
▶ Searching for specialized directories
▶ Browsing for specialized directories
▶ Getting listed in the Yellow Pages Web sites

*I*n Chapters 11 and 12, you find out about the places where you can register your site — the major search systems such as Google and the Open Directory Project, and secondary systems, such as hundreds of small directories.

Some of the sites you find out about in this chapter are more important than the secondary systems and, in some cases, even more important than the major search systems. That's right: Some companies do more business from the sites I discuss in this chapter than from the major search engines.

Don't forget the Yellow Pages sites, which handle billions of searches each year. Although most businesses probably won't want to pay for an ad on a Yellow Pages site (if you have a business phone line, you've already got a free listing), many businesses use these search systems very profitably. In general, if you've found the paper Yellow Pages to be worthwhile, you may find online Yellow Pages useful, too. In fact, if you're buying a Yellow Pages ad, your sales rep is probably trying to upsell you on Internet features these days, such as links to your Web site and additional information posted about your business on the Yellow Page search site.

Keeping a Landscape Log

I recommend keeping track of what you discover during your online research. You'll come across small directories related to your area of business, newsgroups, Web-based forums, mailing list discussion groups, and private sites created by interested individuals and competitors — all sorts of things that can help promote your site.

In effect, you're mapping the Internet *landscape* — the area of the Internet in which your business operates. You need to keep the information you gather so that you can use it after your research is complete. Maybe you find some directories that you want to register with. Or you discover some e-mail newsletters that you want to work with when you have the time. For instance, you may want to contact newsletters to see if they'll do a review of your site or your products. (There's more to promoting a site than just working with search engines!)

Your landscape log doesn't have to be complicated. It can be a Microsoft Word document or maybe an Excel spreadsheet. If you want to get really organized, you can use an ACT or Access database. I suggest that you keep the following information:

- Site name
- Company name, if different from the site name
- URL
- PageRank: I explain PageRank in Google in Chapter 14. It's a good indication of the value of any link you might get from the site. Generally, the higher the rank is, the more valuable the link.
- Alexa traffic rank: When you visit a site, look at the traffic ranking noted on the Alexa toolbar. (I suggest that you load this toolbar in Chapter 1.) This ranking provides a good indication of how much traffic the site gets so that you can decide if some kind of cooperative venture is worthwhile.
- Contact name: If you can find a contact name, it's useful to have.
- Contact e-mail address.
- Notes: Write a quick description of your impressions of the site and the help it may provide you.
- Actions: Keep track of your contacts with the site (to ask for a link, for example).

I'm not just talking about the research you do while looking for specialized directories. Whenever you work online and uncover competitors, potential partners, useful resources, and so on, you should store that information somewhere for later use.

Finding the Specialized Directories

For just about every subject you can imagine, someone is running a specialized search directory. Although specialized directories get very little traffic when compared to the big guys, the traffic they do get is highly targeted — just the people you want to attract. Such directories are often very popular with your target audience.

Here's an example of how to search for a specialized directory. Suppose that you're promoting your rodent racing Web site. Go to Google and type *rodent racing directory*. Hmmm, for some reason, Google doesn't find any directories related to rodent racing. Strange. Okay, try *rodent directory*. Now you're getting somewhere! I did this search and found several useful sites:

- ✔ **Pet Pedia:** I don't regard rodents as pets (racing rodents are working animals), but you could probably register the site here. Not a great PageRank, but still worth getting a link.

- ✔ **NetVet's Electronic Zoo:** This is a big list of links to rodent-related sites, though mostly related to research (the Digital Atlas of Mouse Embryology and the Cybermouse Project, for instance). It's got a good PageRank, too, PR6, so links from here would be valuable. Perhaps you can suggest that your site is related to research into cardiovascular performance of rodents under stress.

- ✔ **Rodent Resources at the National Center for Research Resources:** Hmmm, this is another rodent research site, but with an Alexa traffic rank of 497 and a PageRank of 8, getting listed in this directory would be very useful. (Maybe it's time to apply for a research grant.)

- ✔ **The Rodent Breeders List:** This directory strikes me as one of those "not very pleasant, but somebody's got to do it" things. (How do you breed rodents, anyway? Very carefully I assume.) Still, if you breed rodents for your races, you may want to get onto this list.

When you do a search for a specialty directory, your search results will include the specialty directories you need, but mixed in with them, you'll also find results from the Yahoo! Directory, Google Directory, and the Open Directory Project. If you want, you can clear out the clutter by searching like this:

```
rodent directory -inurl:yahoo.com -inurl:google.com -
      inurl:dmoz.org
```

This search phrase tells Google to look for pages with the words *rodent* and *directory,* but to ignore any pages that have `yahoo.com`, `google.com`, or `dmoz.org` (the Open Directory Project) in their URLs.

Note: Some of the specialty directories that you find actually *pull* data from the Open Directory Project. In order to get into one of these directories, you need to get into the Open Directory Project, as I explain in Chapter 12.

Hundreds of sites use the Open Directory Project information, so you're bound to run into them now and then. How can you tell when a site is pulling data from the Open Directory Project? Here are a few signs to look for:

- Although it's a little-known site, it seems to have a lot of data, covering a huge range of subjects.

- The directory seems to be structured in the familiar table of categories and subcategories.

- The real giveaway is usually at the bottom of the page, where you find a box with links to the Open Directory Project, along with a note crediting that organization. See Figure 13-1.

You may also want to search for these directories by using the term *index.* Although this term is not used as commonly as *directory,* some sites do use it. For instance, when I searched for *photography index,* I found the Nature Photo Index (`http://nature.photoarticles.com/`), which includes a directory of Web sites related to nature photography.

Finding directories other ways

You can use other methods to track down specialty directories. In fact, as you get to know the Internet landscape around your business, you eventually run into these directories. People mention them in discussion groups, for instance, or you find links to them on other Web sites.

I also like browsing for these directories in the major directories — Yahoo! and the Open Directory Project. Yahoo! Directory (`dir.yahoo.com`) has many subcategories for directories. It doesn't have one for rodent racing, which apparently gets no respect, but it certainly has directories for many other topics, such as the following:

- Snowboarding > Web Directories

- Photography > Web Directories

- Radio Stations > Web Directories

- Arts > Web Directories

- Comics and Animations > Web Directories

For some reason, Yahoo! Directory also has subcategories called Directories. (No, I don't know the difference between a Web Directories subcategory and a Directories subcategory.) Here's a sampling of the Directories subcategory:

With a traffic rank of almost 18,000, Directory.net is definitely not a top-level search system . . .

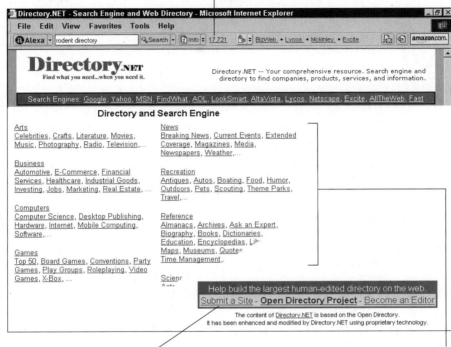

Figure 13-1:
Identifying
data pulled
from the
Open
Directory
Project.

Here's what gives it away — the
attribution to the Open Directory Project.

. . . but still, it has a huge
amount of information.

- ✔ Travel and Transportation > Directories
- ✔ Business and Economy > Directories
- ✔ Reference > Directories
- ✔ Haunted Houses > Directories
- ✔ Ethnic Studies > Directories

The best way to find the Web Directories or Directories subcategories is to go
to the Yahoo! Directory and browse for suitable categories for your Web site.
Each time you find a suitable category, search the page for the word *directory*
to see if the page includes a link to a Web Directory or Directories subcategory. (You can also use the Search box; search for *haunted houses directory*,
and one of the resulting links is *Haunted Houses > Directories*.)

The Open Directory Project also lists thousands of directories. Again, browse
through the directory (at www.dmoz.org) looking for appropriate categories,
and then search the page for the word *directories*. Or search for an appropriate

---

Unscientific subcategories

Yahoo! currently has around 1,400 directories subcategories, representing many thousands of directory Web sites. I found links to 13 directories of haunted houses (a number that one might almost imagine is intentional); 13 directories of humor sites; 7 directories of sites that provide electronic greeting cards; and 6 directories of fitness Web sites. This grossly unscientific survey suggests to me that probably almost 14,000 directory sites are listed in Yahoo!. Therefore, chances are good that several may be good candidates for listing your site.

---

directory, such as *golf directories, golf directory, rodent directories, rodent directory,* and so on. (Yes, searching on *directories* and *directory* provides different results.)

When you find a directory, see what's in it. Don't just ask for a link and move on. Dig around, see what you can find, and add information to your landscape log. The directory contains links to other sites that may also have their own directories.

Local directories

You can also find *local directories* — directories of businesses in your area. These local directories are often good places to get listed. They're easy to get into and can provide more site categorization clues for search engines, and they often have a high PageRank.

Here's how to find local directories easily:

✔ Search for a place name and the term *directory.* (For instance, look for *colorado directory* or *denver directory.*)

✔ Look in the regional categories of Yahoo! and the Open Directory Project.

Bothering with directories

Why should you care about these directories? Here are a few reasons:

✔ **They provide another channel to your site from the search engines.** When someone searches on, say, *fitness,* your Rodent Chasing for Cardiovascular Health site may not appear, but Buzzle.com and GymPost.com might. If you're listed in those directories, maybe the searcher will find you.

- ✓ **Some of the pages at these directory sites have a very good PageRank.** Links from pages with a high PageRank pass part of the PageRank to *your* site, helping you rise in the search engines. For instance, one of the directory pages I looked at on the GymPost.com site had a PageRank of 6, which is very good. (For the lowdown on PageRank, check out Chapter 14.)

- ✓ **Specialty directories provide context.** Specialty directories tell search engines what your site is about. If a search engine finds you in a fitness directory, it knows your site is related to fitness subjects.

- ✓ **As a general principle, links are good.** Almost all links help boost PageRank, but in addition, links increase the chances of search engines finding you. The more links to your site, the more often searchbots stumble across your site and index it.

- ✓ **Some of these directory sites get a lot of traffic.** Buzzle.com, for instance, is more or less the world's 9,000th most popular Web site. I know that sounds like a low rank, but with hundreds of millions of users online, and millions of Web sites, that's not bad. Some of these directories may be able to send you some really good traffic.

Getting the link

After you've found a directory, you need to get the link. In some cases, you have to e-mail someone at the directory and ask. Many of these little directories are run by individuals and are often pretty crudely built. The problem you may run into is that it may take some time for the owner to get around to adding the link — after all, the directory is just a hobby in many cases.

Some directories have automated systems. Look for a Submit Your Site link, or maybe Add URL, Add Your Site, or something similar. The site may provide a form in which you enter your information. Some directories review the information before adding it to the directory, and in other, less common, situations, your information may post directly to the site.

By the way, some of these directories may ask you to pay to be added to the directory or give you preferential treatment if you pay.

Should you pay?

Generally, no.

Why not?

Look, it sometimes seems like everyone's trying to get you to pay these days. Every time you try to get a link somewhere, someone's asking for money. For example, I recently ran across a portal with all sorts of directories that wanted me to pay $59 (*regularly* $99, though I'm not sure what or when *regular* is). That gets you into the index within seven days and gets you preferential placement.

Of course, that means this portal must have had listings over which I could have preferential placement; in other words, I *could* get in free. I scrolled down the page a little, and found the free Basic Submission.

The term *portal* is an Internet-geek term that, roughly translated, means "We've got all sorts of stuff on our site like news, and weather, and you know, *communities,* and, like, stuff, and we still have some of our dotcom cash left, which should keep us going a few more months while we try to figure out how to make money, and heck, if we don't, Uncle Joe still wants me to come work for him in his furniture store."

I recommend that you do *not* pay for these placements, at least to begin with. In most cases, they simply aren't worth spending $60, $100, or more for the link. It's worth spending a few moments getting a free link, though. If a site asks you to pay, dig around and see if you can find a free placement link. If not, just move on. (If the site can guarantee that you'll be on a page with a PageRank of 6 or 7 or better, the fee may be worth it. See Chapter 14 for more information about PageRank.)

At some point perhaps, it might be worthwhile to *consider* thinking about paying for such placements, but generally, only if you know that the site is capable of sending you valuable traffic or providing valuable links.

You don't have to pay

Luckily, you may find that some of the best directories are free. Take, for instance, the model rocket business. Hundreds of model rocket sites, often run by individuals or families, are on the Web. (See the site shown in Figure 13-2.) Many of these sites have link pages. Although these sites don't get huge numbers of visitors, they *do* get the right visitors (people interested in model rockets) and often have a pretty good PageRank. Most of these sites will give you a free listing, just for the asking. Look for a contact e-mail address somewhere.

Working with the Yellow Pages

The Yellow Pages companies are worried. Yellow Pages are incredibly profitable. The biggest Yellow Pages companies make billions of dollars each year, with profits of many hundreds of millions. They're real cash cows, but they're being steamrolled.

Figure 13-2: It's ugly and doesn't get much traffic, but it does have a reasonable PageRank, and if you ask nicely, the site may give you a link. (It probably won't give me a link now, but maybe you'll get one.)

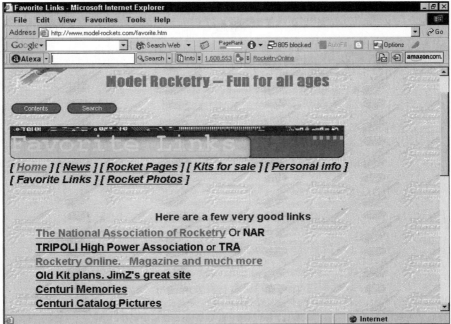

Millions of computer-literate, Internet-loving people no longer pick up a Yellow Pages book or, perhaps, pick one up once or twice a year, compared with several times a month in the pre-Internet days. The number of people who use the book is declining precipitously, as local searches move online.

As you see in Chapter 10, all the major search engines provide local search services, and the results are, in many cases, excellent. The Yellow Page companies are in trouble, but they do have one huge advantage: *feet on the street*. They have huge armies of salespeople talking to businesses every day.

The Yellow Page companies are fighting back, of course, and also entering into partnerships with the major search engines. It may make sense for you to list your Web site with the Yellow Pages sites — especially if your business already buys Yellow Pages ads.

You rarely hear much about the Yellow Pages sites in discussions about search engines, but they *are* search engines. Directories, anyway. And they're incredibly important ones, too. Billions of searches are carried out every year through the Yellow Pages sites, and these companies have billions of dollars in advertising budgets to push people to their Web sites.

Table 13-1 has the largest Yellow Pages sites and their Alexa traffic ranks, indicating the sites' overall popularity.

Table 13-1	Largest Yellow Pages Sites	
Site	*URL*	*Alexa Rank*
Yahoo! Yellow Pages (currently fed by from local Yellow Page companies through InfoUSA)	`yp.yahoo.com`	1
AT&T YellowPages.com	`www.yellowpages.com`	1,710
SuperPages	`http://superpages.com`	1,968
InfoSpace	`www.infospace.com`	2,816
Yell.com	`http://yell.com`	5,162
Yellowbook.com	`www.yellowbook.com`	10,427
Dex	`www.dexknows.com`	13,920
Yellow.com	`www.yellow.com`	38,103

The advantage to using Yellow Pages sites is that they generate lots of local searches. If you own a shoe shop, for example, potential customers may still be more likely to find you through a Yellow Pages site than through a search engine. And the data is being fed to the search engines, so you may be found there, too.

The disadvantage is that they're expensive. Basic listings are free because the basic listings come from the paper Yellow Pages and all business phone customers get a free basic listing. (You can also submit basic listings at some of the Yellow Page sites, such as YellowPages.com.) But these basic listings don't have links to your Web site, so however useful they are for generating phone calls, they won't generate clicks. For that, you have to pay. An ad like the one shown in Figure 13-3, for instance, will cost you $135 per year on YellowPages.com. On the real Yellow Pages sites, owned by the companies publishing Yellow Pages directories, ads often can be much more.

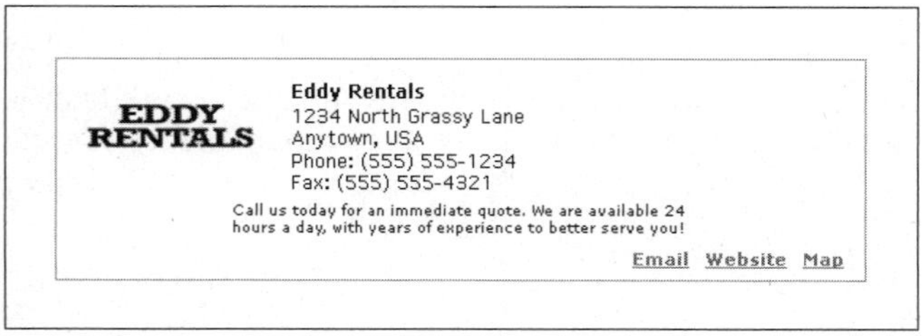

Figure 13-3:
Is it worth
$300 a year?
Sorry, I
really don't
know!

EDDY RENTALS
Eddy Rentals
1234 North Grassy Lane
Anytown, USA
Phone: (555) 555-1234
Fax: (555) 555-4321

Call us today for an immediate quote. We are available 24
hours a day, with years of experience to better serve you!

Email Website Map

Getting into the Yellow Pages

You can get your business into a Yellow Pages site three ways:

- ✔ **Get a business phone line.** You get your free listing in the local Yellow Pages book, which also gets your listing in the online Yellow Pages. As with the book, this is just a simple listing with no extras.

- ✔ **Buy a listing or ad through your local Yellow Pages rep.** This is the same guy selling you space in the paper book.

- ✔ **Sign up directly through the Web site.** Some Yellow Page sites allow businesses to buy an ad directly through their Web sites; look for an Advertise With Us link or similar.

The Yellow Pages companies share listings. If you have a business phone in Colorado, your listing is in a Dex paper book, on www.DexKnows.com, fed to Yahoo! Yellow Pages, and in other systems, such as the AT&T YellowPages.com site.

I recommend that if your company already buys Yellow Pages ads and your business is *geo-specific* — that is, you're trying to attract buyers in a particular area — you should look into using the Yellow Pages. Talk to your rep. The rep should be able to tell you how many searches are carried out in the company's online Yellow Pages, in a particular category and a particular region, each month. From that information, you may be able to decide if purchasing an ad makes sense.

The online Yellow Pages companies sell a variety of services, such as the following:

- ✔ A link from the listing in the online Yellow Pages to your Web site. Search engines probably will not recognize it as a link to your site; rather, you get a *servlet link* that forwards people to your site through the Yellow Page's server.

- ✔ An e-mail link.

- ✔ A page with detailed information, such as a map to your location, information about your products and services, payment options, and so on.

- ✔ A link to a picture of your ad that appears in the paper Yellow Pages.

- ✔ A pop-up promo box that appears when someone points at an icon and that can be modified through an online-management system.

- ✔ A link to a coupon that customers can print.

As I've already mentioned, these ads can be pricey. You pay by the month for each component — maybe $30 per month for a link to your Web site, $30 for a detailed information page, $20 for an e-mail link, and so on. (Rates vary among companies.) Such advertising probably makes sense if you're a dedicated advertiser in the paper Yellow Pages and you find that works for you. The online version may work, too. Dedicated users of the Yellow Pages are moving online, and the Yellow Pages companies are spending millions of dollars in an effort to encourage people to use their sites.

Part IV
After You've Submitted Your Site

The 5th Wave   By Rich Tennant

"I'm not sure I like a college whose home page has a link to The Party Zone!"

In this part . . .

Submitting your site to the search engines isn't enough. It doesn't guarantee that they'll include your site, and it doesn't guarantee that your site will rank well. So this part of the book is essential to your success. In particular, you must understand the value of links pointing to your Web site.

Search engines use links to find your site, to figure out what your site is about, and to estimate how valuable your site is. Search engine optimization without a link campaign is like looking for a job without a résumé: You may make contact, but you won't close the deal. In this part, you discover the different ways that search engines use links, and then you find out how to get those all-important incoming links.

But this part of the book has more. You find out about the shopping directories — specialized systems that index commercial products (and, in a few cases, services) — from Froogle and Google Catalogs to Shopping.com and Yahoo! Shopping. If you're selling online, you must know about these systems.

Finally, this part provides information that helps you make the most of a pay-per-click (PPC) advertising campaign. Billions of dollars are being spent on paid placement search results. Many companies use these ads very successfully, while others lose money. Read this part to find out how to be part of the right group!

Chapter 14

Using Link Popularity to Boost Your Position

*T*housands of site owners have experienced the frustration of being unable to get search engines to index their sites. You build a Web site, you do your best to optimize it for search engines, you register in the search engines, and then nothing much happens. Little or no traffic turns up at your site, your pages don't rank well in the search engines, and in some cases, you can't even find your pages in the search engines. What's going on?

Here's the opposite scenario: You have an existing site and find a few other sites to link to it. You make no changes to the pages themselves, yet all of a sudden, you notice your pages jump up in the search engines.

There's a lot of confusion about links and their relationship to Web sites. Most site owners don't even realize that links have a bearing on their search engine positions. Surely, all you need to do is register your page in a search engine and it will be indexed, right? Nope. This chapter takes the confusion out of links by showing you how they can help, and what you need to know to make them work.

Why Search Engines Like Links

A few years ago, pretty much all you had to do to get your site listed in a search engine — and maybe even ranked well — was register with the search engine. Then along came Google in 1998 and that all changed. Google decided to use the links from other Web sites as another factor in determining if the site was a good match for a search. Each link to a site was a vote for the site, and the more votes the site received, the better a site was regarded by Google.

Links pointing to a Web page do several things:

- ✔ **Links make it easier for search engines to find the page.** As the search-bots travel around the Web, they follow links. They index a page, follow the links on that page to other pages, index those pages, follow the links on those pages, and so on. The more links to a page, the more likely the page is picked up and indexed by search engines, and the more quickly it happens.

- ✔ **Search engines use the number of links pointing to a page as an indication of the page's value.** If lots of pages link to your page, search engines place a greater value on your page than pages with few links pointing to them. If you have lots of links from sites that are themselves linked to by many other sites, search engines conclude that your site must *really* be important. (Google calls this value the page's *PageRank,* but Google isn't the only search engine to use links as an indication of value; Yahoo!, for instance, has something called *Web Rank.*)

- ✔ **Links provide information to search engines about the page they're pointing to.** The link text often contains keywords that search engines can use to glean additional information about your page. The theme of the site pointing to your site may also give search engines an indication of your site's theme. For example, if you have links from hundreds of rodent-related Web sites, it's a good bet that your site has something to do with rodents.

- ✔ **Links not only bring searchbots to a page, but may also bring people to the page.** The whole purpose of your search engine campaign is to bring people to your site, right? Sometimes people will actually click the links and arrive at your site.

Links are very important. Sometimes they mean the difference between being indexed by a search engine and not being indexed, or between being ranked well in a search engine and barely being ranked at all. In this chapter, I delve into this subject, a topic broadly known as *link popularity,* to give you a good understanding of what links from other sites pointed to yours is all about. In Chapters 15, and 16 you discover how to get other sites to link to yours.

Backlinks are an integral part of the optimization of your Web site. A *backlink* — this may surprise you — is a link back to your site. Search engines look at backlinks to figure out what your site is about and how important it is. Links aren't something detached from your site; they're an integral part of your site.

Think of your Web site in terms of a regional map. Your site is the major city, and backlinks are the roads bringing traffic into the city. A geographer looking at the map wouldn't regard the city and roads as separate entities; they're all part of the same economic and social system. So don't think of the links pointing to your site as something "out there" — they're a critical part of your site. Here's an indication of just how important Google considers links to be: The original name of the Google search engine, before it was officially launched, was *BackRub,* so named for its ability to analyze backlinks. (Fortunately, the founders changed the name.)

Search engines are trying to figure out what site or page is the best match for a search. As you discover later in this chapter, search engines use links as one way to determine this. As with content though (discussed in Chapter 9), using the number of links to and from a site to measure significance is an imperfect method. A page can conceivably be the best page on a particular subject, yet have few links to it. Just because I publish a page today doesn't mean it's worse than a page that was published five years ago and now has many links to it. However, search engines have difficulty figuring out what the searcher needs, so they have to use what information is available to them. Using links is a way of recruiting Web site owners to help point out useful sites and pages. The strategy is imperfect, but that's the search engine world we're living in.

Understanding Page Value and PageRank

Search engines assign a value to your site based on the links pointing to it. The most popular term for this kind of ranking is *PageRank,* which Google uses. The *PageRank* is a value that Google gives to a page, based on the number and type of links into the page.

PageRank is mentioned frequently in the search engine optimization field for several reasons:

✔ Google is the world's most important search engine, and will remain so for the foreseeable future.

✔ You don't need a PhD to figure out a page's PageRank. The Google toolbar — the handy little tool I show you how to download in Chapter 1 — shows you the currently loaded page's PageRank. (Okay, strictly speaking that's not true, but it does provide an indication of the PageRank, more of which is discussed later in this chapter.)

> ✔ We also have a basic idea of how PageRank is calculated. Sergey Brin and Lawrence Page, founders of Google, published a paper about the algorithm while at Stanford University. It's almost certain that the algorithm used by Google now isn't the same as the one they published, but it's likely to be similar.

Although this section focuses on PageRank, other search engines use similar rankings, and the things you do with links that boost your PageRank also help boost your site with other search engines.

PageRank — One part of the equation

The PageRank value is just one part of how Google determines which pages to show you when you search for something. I want to stress that point because so many people get really hung up on PageRank. A low PageRank is often an indicator of problems, and a high PageRank is an indicator that you're doing something right, but PageRank itself is just a small part of how Google ranks your pages.

When you type a search term into Google and click Search, Google starts looking through its database for pages with the words you've typed. Then Google examines each page to decide which pages are most relevant to your search. Google considers many characteristics, such as what the `<TITLE>` tag says, how the keywords are treated (are they bold, italic, or in bulleted lists?), where the keywords sit on the page, and are keywords in links pointing to the page (in links both outside the site and within the site). Google also considers PageRank. Clearly, it's possible for a page with a low PageRank to rank higher than one with a high PageRank in some searches. When that happens, it simply means that the value provided by the high PageRank isn't enough to outweigh the value of all the other characteristics of the page that Google considers.

I like to think of PageRank as a tiebreaker. Imagine a situation in which you have a page that, using all other forms of measurement, ranks as well as a competitor's page. Google has looked at both pages, found the same number

---

Pulling rank

By the way, you can be forgiven for thinking that the term *PageRank* comes from the idea of, well, ranking pages. Google claims, however, that it comes from the name of one of the founders of Google and authors of the original PageRank document, Larry Page. (The other founder is Sergey Brin.) The truth is probably somewhere in between. Otherwise, why isn't it the Page-BrinRank?

of keywords in the same sorts of positions, and thinks both pages are equally good matches for a particular keyword search. However, your competitor's page has a higher PageRank than yours. Which page ranks higher in a Google search for that keyword? Your competitor's.

Many people claim that site owners often focus too much on PageRank (that may be true) and that PageRank isn't important. But, PageRank (or something similar) definitely is a factor. As Google has said:

> *"The heart of our software is PageRank(tm), a system for ranking web pages developed by our founders Larry Page and Sergey Brin at Stanford University. And while we have dozens of engineers working to improve every aspect of Google on a daily basis, PageRank continues to provide the basis for all of our web search tools."*

So, Google claims that PageRank *is* in use and *is* important. (It's likely that the current algorithm is not quite the same as the original, but it's probably similar.) But you need to keep its significance in perspective. It's still only part of the story.

It all comes down to what the searcher is searching for. A page that ranks well for one keyword or phrase may rank poorly for another. Thus, a page with a high PageRank can rank well for some keywords and badly for others.

The PageRank algorithm

I want to quickly show you the PageRank algorithm; but don't worry; I'm not going to get hung up on it. In fact, you really don't need to be able to read and follow it, as I explain in a moment. Here it is:

PR (A) = (1 – d) + d (PR (t1) / C (t1) + ... + PR (tn) / C (tn))

Where:

PR = PageRank
A = Web page A
d = A damping factor, usually set to 0.85
t1...tn = Pages linking to Web page A
C = The number of outbound links from page tn

I could explain all this to you, honestly I could. But I don't want to. Furthermore, I don't have to because you don't need to be able to read the algorithm. For instance, do you recognize this equation?

$$F_{ij} = G \frac{M_i M_j}{D_{ii}^2}$$

Don't think you can kid me. I know you don't know what this is. (Well, okay, maybe you do, but I'll bet over 95 percent of my readers don't.) It is the Law of Universal Gravitation, which explains how gravity works. I can't explain this equation to you, but I really don't care because I've been using gravity for some time now without the benefit of understanding the jumble of letters. The other day, for instance, while walking down the street, someone shoved a flyer into my hand. After walking on, glancing at the flyer, and realizing that I didn't want it, I held it over a trash can, opened my hand, and used gravity to remove it from my hand and deposit it into the trash can. Simple.

Rather than take you through the PageRank algorithm step by step, here are a few key points that explain more or less how it works:

- **As soon as a page enters the Google index, it has an intrinsic PageRank.** Admittedly, the PageRank is very small, but it's there.

- **A page has a PageRank only if it's indexed by Google.** Links to your site from pages that have not yet been indexed are effectively worthless, as far as PageRank goes.

- **When you place a link on a page, pointing to another page, the page with the link is voting for the page it's pointing to.** These votes are how PageRank increases. As a page gets more and more links into it, its PageRank grows.

- **Linking to another page doesn't reduce the PageRank of the origin page, but it does increase the PageRank of the receiving page.** It's sort of like a company's shareholders meeting, at which people with more shares have more votes. They don't lose their shares when they vote. But the more shares they have, the more votes they can place.

- **Pages with no links out of them are wasting PageRank; they don't get to vote for other pages.** Because a page's inherent PageRank is not terribly high, this isn't normally a problem. It becomes a problem if you have a large number of links to dangling pages of this kind. Or it can be a problem if you have a dangling page with a high PageRank. Though rare, this could happen if you have a page that many external sites link to that then links directly to an area of your site that won't benefit from PageRank, such as a complex e-commerce catalog system that Google can't index or an external e-commerce system hosted on another site. Unless the page links to other pages inside your Web site, it won't be voting for those pages and thus won't be able to raise their PageRank.

- **A single link from a dangling page can channel that PageRank back into your site.** Make sure that all your pages have at least one link back into the site. This usually isn't a problem because most sites are built with common navigation bars and often text links at the bottom of the page.

- **You can increase a site's overall PageRank two ways:**
  - Increase the number of pages in the site, although it's a small increase because the inherent PageRank of a new page is low.

Getting details

If you want all the nasty, complicated details about PageRank, you can find a number of sources of information online. One description of PageRank that I like is at the WebWorkshop site (www.webworkshop.net/pagerank.html). This site also provides a calculator that shows you the effect on PageRank of linking between pages in your site. Or you can get the lowdown on PageRank from the horse's mouth: Read *The PageRank Citation Ranking: Bringing Order to the Web* by Sergey Brin and Lawrence Page, the founders of Google. Search on the document's title at Google.

- Get links to the site from outside.

✔ **The page receiving the inbound link gets the greatest gain.** Thus, ideally, you want links into your most important pages — pages you want ranked in search engines. PageRank is then spread through links to other pages in the site, but these secondary pages get less boost.

It's important to understand that Web sites don't have a PageRank; Web pages have a PageRank. It's possible for a site's home page to have a high PageRank, although its internal pages rank very low.

Here are a couple of important implications from this:

✔ **You can vote large amounts of PageRank through your site with a single link.** A page with a PageRank of 5 can pass that to another page as long as it doesn't split the vote by linking to other pages.

When I use the term *pass,* I use it in the sense of passing on a virus, not passing a baton. You can pass PageRank from page to page. Linking from page A to page B passes PageRank from A to B in the same way that person A may pass a cold to person B. Person A doesn't get rid of the cold when he passes it to B; he's still got it. Moreover, page A still has its PageRank when it passes PageRank on to page B.

✔ **You can ensure that PageRank is well distributed around your Web site by including lots of links.** Linking every page to every other page is the most efficient way to ensure even PageRank around the site.

Huge sites equal greater PageRank

Because every page is born with a PageRank (as soon as Google finds it, anyway), the more pages in your site, the greater the site's intrinsic PageRank. If you create a linking structure that links all your pages well, you'll be providing your pages with a high PageRank simply because you have many pages.

However, don't think of creating pages as a search engine strategy. You'd need a huge number of pages to make a difference. If you own or manage a site that already has hundreds of thousands of pages, consider yourself lucky. But don't build hundreds of thousands of pages just to boost PageRank.

This fact provides another reason for Web sites to retain old pages, perhaps in archives. A news site, for instance, should probably keep all news articles, even very old ones. Of course, a massive repository of data often has a high PageRank for another reason — many other sites link to the data. Remove pages and you lose the links.

However, I also believe that in the last couple of years the PageRank algorithm has been adjusted from this original more-pages-means-higher-PageRank concept. I think that very large sites actually have a penalty of some kind. The new algorithm says, in effect, "if you're going to have hundreds of thousands of pages, well, you're going to have to work harder for your PageRank." While a small site might increase its PageRank rapidly with a few links from high PageRank sites, large sites may need many more links to have the same effect.

Measuring PageRank

How can you discover a page's PageRank? You can use the Google toolbar. (In a moment, I explain why you can never find out the *true* PageRank.) As I mention in Chapter 1, you should install the Google toolbar, which is available for download at www.toolbar.google.com. Each time you open a page in Internet Explorer or Firefox, you see the page's PageRank in a bar, as shown in Figure 14-1. If the bar is all white, the PageRank is 0. If it's all green, the PageRank is 10. You can estimate PageRank simply by looking at the position of the green bar, or you can mouseover the bar, and a pop-up appears with the PageRank.

If the PageRank component isn't on your toolbar, click the Settings button on the right of the bar and then the Options button to open the Toolbar Options dialog box. Click the More button at the top of the dialog box and then select the PageRank and Page Info check box, and click OK.

If you don't have the Google toolbar, you can still check PageRank. Search for the term *pagerank tool* to find various sites that allow you to enter a URL and get the PageRank. Mozilla's FireFox browser also has add-ons that display the PageRank in the status bar of every page.

Figure 14-1:
The
PageRank
bar on the
Google
toolbar
shows
PageRank.

Here are a few things to understand about this toolbar:

- ✔ **Sometimes the bar is gray.** Sometimes when you look at the bar, it's grayed out. Some people believe that this means Google is somehow penalizing the site by withholding PageRank. I've never seen this happen, though. I believe the bar is simply buggy, and that PageRank is just not being passed to the bar for some reason. Every time I've seen the bar grayed out, I've been able to open the Web page in another browser window (you may have to try two or three) and view the PageRank.

- ✔ **Sometimes the toolbar guesses.** Sometimes the toolbar guesses a PageRank. You may occasionally find it being reported for a page that isn't even in the Google index. It seems that Google may be coming up with a PageRank for a page on the fly, based on the PageRank of other pages in the site that have already been indexed.

  Also, note that Google has various data centers around the world. Because they're not all in sync and have data varying among them, it's possible for one person looking at a page's PageRank to see one number, while someone else sees another number.

- ✔ **A white bar is not a penalty.** Another common PageRank myth is that Google penalizes pages by giving them a PageRank of 0. That is, if you see a page with a PageRank of 0, something is wrong with the page, and if you link to the page, your Web page may be penalized, too. This is simply not true. Most of the world's Web pages show a PageRank of 0. That's not to say that Google won't take away PageRank if it wants to penalize a page or site for some reason. I'm just saying that you can't tell whether it's a penalty or simply a page with few valuable links pointing in.

- ✔ **Zero is not zero, and ten is not ten.** Although commonly referred to as *PageRank,* and even labeled as such, the number you see in the Google toolbar is not the page's actual PageRank. It's simply a number indicating the approximate position of the page on the PageRank range. Therefore, pages never have a PageRank of 0, even though most pages show 0 on the toolbar, and a page with a rank of, say, 2 might actually have a PageRank of 25 or 100.

The true PageRank scale is probably a logarithmic scale. Thus, the distance between PageRank 5 and 6 is much greater than the difference between 2 and 3. The consensus of opinion among people who like to discuss these things is that the PageRank shown on the toolbar is probably on a logarithmic scale with a base of around 5 or 6, or perhaps even lower.

Suppose, for a moment, that the base is actually 5. That means that a page with a PageRank of 0 shown on the toolbar may have an actual PageRank somewhere between a fraction of 1 and just under 5. If the PageRank shown is 1, the page may have a rank between 5 and just under 25; if 2 is shown, the number may be between 25 and just under 125, and so on. A page with a rank of 9 or 10 shown on the toolbar most likely has a true PageRank in the millions. With base 5, for instance, the toolbar PageRank would represent a true PageRank, as shown in Table 14-1.

Table 14-1	Pure Conjecture — What Toolbar PageRank Would Represent if PageRank Were a Logarithmic Scale Using Base 5
Toolbar PageRank	*True PageRank*
0	0–5
1	5–25
2	25–125
3	125–625
4	625–3,125
5	3,125–15,625
6	15,625–78,125
7	78,125–390,625
8	390,625–1,953,125
9	1,953,125–9,765,625
10	9,765,625–48,828,125

The maximum possible PageRank, and thus this scale, continually changes as Google recalculates PageRank. As pages are added to the index, the PageRank has to go up. Periodically, Google recalculates PageRank Web-wide, and, as we saw in the fall of 2007, PageRank drops for many sites, perhaps most.

How can you be sure that the numbers on the toolbar are not the true PageRank? The PageRank algorithm simply doesn't work on a scale of 1 to 10 on a Web that contains billions of Web pages. Perhaps more practically, it's not logical to assume that sites like Yahoo! and Google have a PageRank just slightly above small, privately owned sites. I have pages with ranks of 6 or 7, for instance, whereas the BBC Web site, one of the world's 50 most popular Web sites according to Alexa, has a PageRank of 9. It's not reasonable to assume that its true PageRank is just 50 percent greater than pages on one of my little sites.

Here are two important points to remember about the PageRank shown on the Google toolbar:

- ✔ Two pages with the same PageRank on the toolbar may actually have a very different true PageRank. One may have a PageRank that is a fifth, sixth, or maybe a quarter of the other.

- ✔ It gets progressively harder to push a page to the next PageRank on the toolbar. Getting a page to 1 or 2 is pretty easy, but to push it to 3 or 4 is much harder (though certainly possible). To push it to the higher levels is very difficult indeed — 8 or above is rare.

Leaking PageRank

It's possible for PageRank to *leak* out of a site, despite the fact that pages don't lose PageRank when they link to other pages. Here's how: Each time you link from one page to another, the origin page is voting for the recipient page. Thus, a link from one page in your site to another page in your site is a vote for that other page. If you link to a page on another site, you're voting for another site's page rather than your site's page.

Suppose that you have a page with a PageRank of 10,000 and it has 40 links on it. Each link is getting a PageRank vote of 250 ($250 \times 40 = 10,000$). Now suppose that half the links on the page are external. In that case, you're taking 5,000 votes and pointing to pages out of your site rather than inside your site. So PageRank leaks in the sense that your overall site PageRank is lower.

Generally, you should worry more about getting backlinks to your site from appropriate Web sites than about how much PageRank is leaking through your outgoing links. You can build PageRank quickly by using the techniques in Chapters 15 and 16, and in most cases, worrying about outgoing links won't save you much PageRank. Still, you can do two simple things to help reduce rank leak:

- ✔ If you have a page with lots of outgoing links, make sure that it also has links to the other pages in your site. You'll be splitting the vote that way between outgoing and internal links, rather than passing all of it on through outgoing links.

- ✔ Ideally, you want the page with the external links to be one with a low PageRank, reducing the outgoing votes. You can do that by minimizing the number of links from other pages on your site into the link page.

There are other theories on how Google figures out which pages rank above others. One is the PigeonRank system described by Google in a technical document that you can find in their technology area. Google suggests that "Low cost pigeon clusters (PCs) could be used to compute the relative value of Web pages faster than human editors or machine-based algorithms. By collecting flocks of pigeons in dense clusters, Google is able to process search queries at speeds superior to traditional search engines, which typically rely on birds of prey, brooding hens or slow-moving waterfowl to do their relevance rankings." Find details at `http://www.google.com/technology/pigeon rank.html`.

Page Relevance

Page relevance is harder to measure. The concept of page relevance is that a link from a page related in some way to your page is more valuable than a link from an entirely unrelated page. A link to your rodent-racing site from a Web site that is also related to rodent racing is more valuable than, say, a link from your Aunt Edna's personal Web site.

The problem with PageRank is that it's independent of keywords. The value is a number derived from links pointing at a page with no relation whatsoever to a specific keyword. Because a page has a high PageRank doesn't mean it's the type of page you're looking for when you search for a particular keyword.

Thus, search engines add something else to the mix: relevance or *context*. The major search engines are attempting to do this sort of analysis by matching keywords. In effect, search engines are trying to create a context-sensitive PageRank or *topic-sensitive* PageRank. A topic-sensitive PageRank is dependent on a particular topic. Instead of counting any and all links, only links from relevant Web sites are included.

One way search engines are probably trying to do this is by using Yahoo! and the Open Directory Project directory to provide some context. Because Web sites listed in the directory have been put into categories, it gives search engines a starting point to figure out what keywords and sites relate to what categories.

This discussion is getting complicated now, and you really don't need to know the details. However, if you want to read a little geek stuff related to relevance or context, search for a paper, "Topic-Sensitive PageRank," by Taher Haveliwala of Stanford University.

My feeling is that this sort of technology isn't as advanced as many believe or as advanced as search engines want you to believe. Still, people in the search engine business swear that links from related sites are more valuable than links from unrelated sites. To be more precise, links from sites that a search engine *thinks* are related are more valuable than those from sites that a search engine thinks are unrelated. Because the technology is imprecise, search engines don't always get it right. The fact is that no search engine really knows for sure if one site is related to another; it can only guess. As with everything else, relevance is just one ingredient in the mix.

Don't let anyone tell you that links from unrelated sites have no value. A link from an unrelated site helps search engines find your pages, boosts PageRank, can provide information about what your site is about (if you have good keywords in the links), and may even bring visitors to your site. These links just won't have the extra boost provided by relevance.

As I discuss in Chapters 15 and 16, the ideal link is one from a related Web site, not just any old Web site you can convince to link to you. The most powerful *link hubs* — networks of interlinked Web sites — are those that are tightly focused on a particular topic. Search engines respect that, want to uncover such situations and rank the target sites more highly, and are probably getting better every day at doing so.

Hubs and Neighborhoods

Search engines are also looking for what may be thought of as Web *neighborhoods, communities,* or *hubs* — groups of Web sites related to a particular subject, and the sites that appear to be most central to it. If you're positioned in the middle of a *cloud* — a web of Web sites related to a particular subject — that's a good thing.

Imagine a chart showing the world's rodent-racing Web sites and their connections. In this chart, little boxes represent the Web sites and lines show links between the sites. (Figure 14-2 gives an example of such a chart.) Some of the boxes seem to be sitting by themselves — very few links are going out, and very few are coming in. Other boxes have lots of links going out but few boxes linking back. Now imagine your rodent racing site. It's a hub with many links going out, and many links coming in. That would look pretty important on a chart. Don't you think search engines would find that interesting? In fact, search engines are trying to figure out this sort of thing all the time. Therefore, if you can build links to turn your site into a hub, that's a great thing! (That doesn't mean all you need to do is build lots of pages with outgoing links, by the way — far more important are the incoming links.)

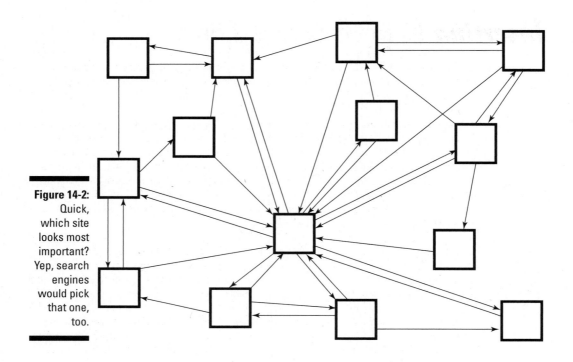

Figure 14-2:
Quick,
which site
looks most
important?
Yep, search
engines
would pick
that one,
too.

Trust in TrustRank

Yet another ranking concept: TrustRank. The idea, from a document written by Yahoo! search engine researchers, is that a small set of "seed pages" are selected manually; someone actually creates a list of Web sites and pages that are likely to be reputable pages that can be trusted.

Then computers measure how far each site is from the seed site, in the sense of how many links away. Sites linked to directly from the original list of trusted sites are assumed trustworthy, and sites they link to are probably reasonably trustworthy, and so on. The farther a site is from the trusted sites, the lower the site's TrustRank.

The basic principle, then? Links from reputable sites are likely to be more valuable than links from sites that are not clearly so reputable. A link from CNN.com, for instance, is likely to count for more than a link from TheKentFamilyNewsService.com.

But remember, this is just one more possible way to weight pages. It certainly doesn't mean that a site can't rank well without lots of trusted links.

Inserting Keywords into Links

As Chapter 5 makes abundantly clear, keywords in your pages are very important. But keywords *outside* your pages can also affect the page results. That is, the keywords in links pointing to your pages are very important.

If you have hundreds of links around the world pointing to your site, with the words *rodent racing* in the links, then search engines will get the idea that your pages are somehow related to rodent racing. It actually makes a lot of sense if you think about it. If hundreds of site owners create links pointing to your site, and, in effect, say, "This site I'm pointing to is about rodent racing," then Google is being given a darn good clue regarding what your site is about. In effect, Google has recruited site owners to tell it what other owners' sites are about.

Link text, in geek terminology, is known as *anchor text*. The link tag is an <A> tag, and *A* stands for *anchor*. Thus, if you hang around in geek company, you may hear links referred to as *anchors*. For more on anchors, see the "From the horses' mouths" sidebar.

In other words, Google and other search engines use links to get an idea of what the pages are about. Links can even help search engines figure out what a document is about if they can't read it for some reason (though that's not really the primary concern here).

Now, wait a second. This is important. If a link pointing to your site can describe to a search engine what your site is about, you'd better do all you can to make sure the link says what you want it to say! Even if you don't own the site pointing to the one you're trying to optimize (or are trying to get another site owner or site manager to link to your site), it's in your interest to get the right keywords into the link.

From the horses' mouths

Read this from the founders of Google, Sergey Brin and Lawrence Page:

"... anchors often provide more accurate descriptions of web pages than the pages them-selves ... This idea of propagating anchor text to the page it refers to was implemented in the World Wide Web Worm [a search engine that pre-dates Google] especially because it helps search non-text information, and expands the search coverage with fewer downloaded documents. We use anchor propagation mostly because anchor text can help provide better quality results."

The Anatomy of a Large-Scale Hypertextual Web Search Engine, 1998

While you browse the Web, take a close look at links on the sites you visit. Now that you know how critical it is to add keywords to links, you'll see that many links provide relatively little value to the sites they're pointing to. Sure, a link is better than no link, but a bad link could be better. Here are some of the problems you'll see:

✔ **Image links, including buttons or banners linking to sites:** Search engines can't read images, so they're not getting keywords from them. (You can add keywords to the ALT attributes onto the image, but search engines don't weight ALT text as highly as link text.)

✔ **One- or two-word links, such as company names:** In most cases, company names don't help you in search engines. Use the keywords your potential visitors and clients are using.

✔ **Combinations of descriptions and _click here_ links:** For instance: _For more information on rodent racing — rats, mice, gerbils, and any other kind of rodent racing — click here._ Wow, what a waste! All the keywords are there, they just have no link! Remember, _click here_ links are a total waste of hyperlink space.

The Googlebomb lives

Just how powerful is putting keywords in links? Well, let's discuss the _Googlebomb._

I'm going to show you a couple pages that rank very well for keywords that don't even appear in the pages. How could that be possible? It's all in the power of linking. First, search Yahoo! and MSN Live Search for the term _miserable failure._ The page that appears first (at least at the time of writing), in both cases, is www.whitehouse.gov/president/gwbbio.html, George Bush's bio page on the White House Web site.

This was done by a small group of people using links in blog pages. Despite the fact that this page contains neither _miserable,_ nor _failure,_ and certainly not _miserable failure,_ a few dozen links with the words _miserable failure_ in the link text were enough to trick the major search engines.

This is known as a _Googlebomb,_ and in fact, it used to work on Google, too, until Google bowed to criticism (after a couple of years) and changed _something_ to ensure that the President's page no longer appeared in the search results. But Yahoo! and MSN/Live Search did _not_ make this change — this particular Googlebomb, paradoxically, only works on Yahoo! and MSN/Live.

I'm not sure what Google did to remove the George Bush result. They say that they "came up with an algorithm that minimizes the impact of many Googlebombs." Nevertheless, they didn't completely throw out the concept of using keywords in links to tell them what the site is about. In fact, their statement suggests just that. They "minimized" the impact of "many Googlebombs;" they didn't completely stop them.

They most likely applied an algorithm that says something like, "If we see x number of links of type y pointing to the site using keywords that don't appear in the site, then ignore the links."

In any case, though, the fact is the basic principle behind Googlebombing remains valid: Putting keywords in links tells search engines what a referenced site is about, and the more links with keywords the better.

I often have clients ask me why a competitor ranks so well, also stating, "Their pages aren't better optimized than mine. We have more pages, and more pages with the right keywords. . . ." Without understanding all the variables, you can't tell for sure why a site ranks well. Is it because the site has been around much longer than yours? Is it because it has more content? Because the content is better optimized? Because the site has more incoming links? The last of these factors is often essential; when I do a link analysis (see Chapter 15) I often discover that the poorly optimized, yet highly ranked, site has a huge number of incoming links, with just the right keywords.

 Here's the ideal combination for links and the pages they point to: The keywords in the link match the keywords for which the referenced page is optimized.

Good Links and Bad

It seems likely that search engines — Google in particular — regard some links as more valuable than others. And it seems very likely to me that search engines — Google in particular — will, over time, tighten up how they regard links. Because search engines keep their techniques secret, the following practices may already be in use or could be soon:

- ✔ Links inside paragraphs of text are likely regarded as more valuable than links in large lists or links set apart from text.
- ✔ Search engines could compare incoming links with outgoing links, and downgrade a page or site if it appears to do a lot of reciprocal linking from link pages.
- ✔ Links pointing to a page inside a site might be valued more highly than links to the home page.
- ✔ Outgoing links concentrated on a few pages might be valued less than links spread around a site.

When site owners figured out that links were valuable, they started playing tricks to boost incoming links to their sites. Some tricks were so egregious that search engines decided they were unacceptable. The trick you hear about most often is the *link farm,* an automated system that allows site owners to very quickly create thousands of incoming links by joining with thousands of other site owners to exchange links. Another trick is to create multiple *shadow domains* or *satellite sites* — small, well-optimized Web sites that redirect traffic into a single site — and link them all into one site. Search engines don't like link farms and will exclude link-farm pages if they identify them.

However, as with much in the search engine optimization business, another myth has arisen. You may hear that if a link is found to your site from a link farm, you'll be penalized.

Let me set the record straight: Search engines do not penalize sites for incoming links. They can't, or it would encourage dirty tricks. Want to push a competitor's site down so your site can beat it? Then link to it from as many link farms as you can. Obviously, it wouldn't make sense for search engines to encourage this sort of thing, so links from such pages won't hurt your site — though they won't help it, either.

On the other hand, links *to* such sites may hurt you. Because you do have control over links from your site to others, if a search engine decides that you are linking to a bad neighborhood, it may penalize you.

The bottom line is that you should avoid working with link farms because they could potentially harm you, and they won't help you anyway.

Do search engines ever penalize? Sure. However, with billions of Web pages in the large indexes, these penalties have to be automated (though you can report cheating to search engines, and the offending site may be reviewed). In order to automate penalties, search engines have to create a very loose system that penalizes only the very worst offenses, or they risk penalizing innocent people. The proof is that if you spend time searching through the major search engines, you'll find many pages that clearly break the rules yet are still included in the indexes.

Recognizing Links with No Value

Some links have no value:

- If a page isn't in the search engines, the links from the page have no value. Search engines don't know about them, after all.

- If a page is regarded as a *link farm* (described in the preceding section) or some other kind of "bad neighborhood," as Google calls it, the search engine may know about the page but decide to exclude it from the index.

Identifying links that aren't links

I've seen this happen many times. Someone gets a link to his site from another site with a high PageRank, perhaps a perfectly related site, and is excited. That's a great vote for his site, isn't it? Then some jerk, perhaps me, has to burst his bubble and point out that, actually, no, it's not going to have the slightest effect on his site because it turns out the link is not a link.

When is a link not a link? In cases such as these:

- ✔ The link has been created in such a way that search engines can't read it or will intentionally ignore it.

- ✔ The link points somewhere else, perhaps to a program on someone else's Web site, which then forwards the browser to your site.

Here's an example:

```
http://ad.doubleclick.net/clk;6523085;7971444;q?http://www
        .yoursite.com
```

This link passes through an ad server hosted by an advertising company called DoubleClick. When someone clicks this link, which may be placed on a banner ad, for instance, a message goes to a program on the `ad.double click.net` ad server, which logs the click and then forwards the browser to `www.yourdomain.com`. You may think this is a link to `www.yourdomain.com`, and it may work like one, but as far as the search engine is concerned, it's really a link to `ad.doubleclick.net`.

Here's another example: Suppose the person creating a link to your site doesn't want the search engine to be able to read the link. This person may be trying to get as many incoming links as possible while avoiding outgoing links, so he does something like this:

```
<SCRIPT LANGUAGE="JavaScript">
<!--
document.write("Visit <A
        HREF='http://www.yourdomain.com/'>
Joe's Rodent Racing site here</A>.")
//-->
</SCRIPT>
```

The author is using JavaScript to write the link onto the page. You can see the link, other visitors can see it, and the link works when clicked, but search engines won't read the JavaScript, so they won't know there's a link there. What appears to be a perfectly normal link on a Web page is invisible to search engines; therefore, it does your site no good as far as PageRank or any other link-popularity algorithm goes.

Here's another form of link that search engines can't read:

```
<A HREF="#" class=results
        onclick="window.open('searchresult-
temp1.php?CS=cddzdzdrzfzpzpdc&SRCH=134893378&YD=0.88&RK=
3&PID=16&URL=yourdomain.com','merch','Height=' +
screen.availHeight + ',Width=' + screen.availWidth +
',left=0,top=0,scrollbars=yes,status=yes,toolbar=yes,
directories=yes,menubar=yes,location=yes,resizable=yes',
false)";>Everything About Rodent Racing!</A>
```

This is a real `<A>` link tag. However, it doesn't use the `HREF=` attribute to point to a Web page. Rather, it uses a JavaScript `onClick` event handler to make it work. The JavaScript runs a program that, in this case, loads the page into another window. Again, the link works in most browsers, but search engines won't see it.

Incidentally, it's also possible to do the reverse: make links appear to search engines to be links to your site when actually they're links to another site. For instance, look at the following link, created by a system called Links4Trade.com, which you find out about in Chapter 15:

```
<A HREF="http://www.yourdomain.com?cid=33003&refid=
139782&link=www%2Eyourdomain%2Ecom" onClick="return
rewrite(this);" class="">Joe's Rodent Racing</A>
```

This link starts off well, showing `yourdomain.com` as the page being linked to. In fact, if you took the URL from the `HREF=` and pasted it into a browser, it would work properly. However, when someone clicks the link, the JavaScript `onClick` event handler runs, taking the domain and passing it to a JavaScript function called `rewrite`. Because search engines don't read JavaScript, they don't see what really happens when someone clicks the link. (In this example, the click runs through a program on the Links4Trade.com site, which tracks how many people use the link.) Search engines think it's a link to your site, and I guess it is in a sense, but it has to pass through a program on a different site first.

Identifying nofollow links

There's a simple way to tell search engines to ignore links; use the `rel` attribute, like this:

```
<a href="http://www.domainname.com/page.html"
        rel="nofollow">Link Text</a>
```

You can also block all links on a page by using the `robots` meta tag, like this:

```
<meta name="robots" content="nofollow">
```

Tell the search engines not to follow the link — *nofollow* — and what exactly will they do? They ignore the link. It will be as if the link were never there. They won't bother following the link to the referenced page, and they won't use the information to index the page. That is, you get no PageRank, Web Rank, or equivalent benefit, and no benefit from the keywords in the link. (Actually it's possible that Yahoo! may at least follow the links, but won't provide any link benefit to the referenced site.)

More and more sites are using `nofollow` attributes to stop people placing links purely to help their search engine rank. Here's a classic example: Craigslist. The hugely popular Craigslist.com classified ad site used to be a great place to put links; businesses would drop ads into the system and include links back to their sites to help boost their search position. So, in the fall of 2007, Craigslist decided to put a `nofollow` attribute into all links placed on the site in order to discourage this behavior.

Recalling a Few Basic Rules about Links

You know that links are valuable and can help boost your position in the search engines. But, what sorts of links? Let me quickly summarize:

- Links from sites related to yours are often more valuable than links from unrelated sites. (Because the relevancy software is almost certainly imprecise, this isn't always the case.)

- Links from pages with a high PageRank are much more valuable than from pages with a low PageRank.

- Virtually all incoming links to your site have some kind of value, even if the pages have a very low PageRank or are not contextual. It may not be much of a value, but it's there.

- The more outgoing links on a page that has a link pointing to your site, the lower the value of the link to your site. This is because the vote is being shared. Thus, in some cases, a link from a low-PageRank page with no other links may actually be more valuable than a link from a high-PageRank page with many links.

- Links are even more valuable when they include keywords because keywords tell search engines what the referenced site is about.

- A link strategy that positions your site as an authority, or a *hub,* in a Web community or neighborhood can be a powerful way to get the attention of the search engines.

- Even *internal links* — links from page to page within your site — are valuable because the keywords in the links tell the search engine what the referenced page is about.

Chapter 15

Finding Sites to Link to Yours

*I*n Chapter 14, I explain the value of linking — why your site needs to have *backlinks* (links from other sites pointing to it). Now you have the problem of finding those sites.

Chapter 14 gives you some basic criteria. You need links from pages that are already indexed by the search engines. Pages with high PageRanks are more valuable than those with low PageRanks. Links from related sites may be more valuable, and so on. However, when searching for links, you probably don't want to be too fussy to start with. A link is a link. Contrary to popular opinion, links bring value — even links from unrelated sites.

It's common in the SEO business to say that only links from "relevant" sites have value, but I don't believe that's true. How do search engines know which sites are relevant, and which aren't? They don't. Sure, they can guess to some degree. But they can't be quite sure. Therefore, my philosophy is that every link from a page that's indexed by search engines has some kind of value. Some will have a higher value than others, but don't get too hung up on relevance. And don't worry too much about PageRank; sure, if you can go after sites with high PageRanks first, do it, but often it makes sense to simply *go get links* and not worry too much about the rank of the linking page.

Use this chapter to get links, and things will start happening. Your site will get more traffic, the search engines will pick it up, and you should find your pages rising in the search engine ranks.

Controlling Your Links

Before you run off to look for links, think about what you want those links to say. In Chapter 14, I talk about how keywords in links are tremendously important. The position of a page in the search engines depends not only on the text within that page, but also on text on other pages that refer to that page — that is, the text in the links. In fact, even a link from a low-PageRank page can bring real value, if it has good keywords in it.

For instance, suppose your rodent-racing company is called Robertson Ellington. (These were the names of your first two racing rats, and they still have a special place in your heart. And you've always felt that the name has a distinguished ring to it.) You could ask people to give you links like this:

Robertson Ellington
Everything you ever wanted to know about rodent racing — rodent-racing schedules, directions to rodent-racing tracks, rodent-racing clubs, and anything else you can imagine related to rodent racing

You got a few useful keywords into the description, but the link — Robertson Ellington — is the problem. The link text contains no keywords that count. Are people searching for *Robertson Ellington*, or are they searching for *rodent racing*?

A better strategy is to change the link to include keywords. Keep the blurb below the link, but change the link to something like this:

Rodent Racing — rats, stoats, mice, and all sorts of other rodent racing

Here are some strategies for creating link text:

- ✔ Start the link with the primary keyword or keyword phrase.

- ✔ Add a few other keywords if you want.

- ✔ Try to repeat the primary keyword or keyword phrase once in the link.

- ✔ Mix in a few other words.

You need to control the links as much as possible. You can do this a number of ways, but you won't always be successful:

- ✔ Provide a Link to Us page in your Web site. On this page, provide suggested links to your site — include the entire HTML tag so people can grab the information and drop it into their sites.

  Remember that although links on logos and image buttons may be pretty, they don't help you in the search engines as much as text links do. You can add ALT text to the image, but ALT text is not as valuable as link text.

Some site owners now distribute HTML code that creates not only image links but also small text links right below the images.

✔ When you contact people and ask them for links, provide them with the actual link you'd like to use.

✔ As soon as someone tells you he or she has placed a link, check it to see if the link says what you want. Immediately contact that person if it doesn't. He or she is more likely to change the link at that point than weeks or months later.

✔ Use a link-checking tool occasionally to find out who is linking to you and to see how the link appears. If necessary, contact the other party and ask if the link can be changed. (I mention some link-checking tools later in this chapter.)

Whenever possible, you should define what a link pointing to your site looks like, rather than leave it up to the person who owns the other site. Of course, you can't force someone to create links the way you want, but sometimes if you ask nicely. . . .

Always use the www. portion of your URL when creating links to your site: http://www.yourdomain.com and not just http://yourdomain.com. Search engines regard the two addresses as different, even though in most cases they are actually pointing to the same page. So if you use both URLs, you are, in effect, splitting the vote for your Web site. Search engines will see a lower link popularity. (See Chapter 14 for a discussion of how links are votes.)

Many sites use a 301 Redirect to point domain.com to the www.domain.com form. For instance, type **google.com** into your browser's Location bar and press Enter. Where do you go? You go to www.google.com because Google's server admins have "301'd" google.com to www.google.com. If you want to do this on your site, search for the term *301 redirect* for instructions.

Generating Links, Step by Step

Here is a quick summary of additional ways to get links; I describe them in detail next:

✔ **Register with search directories.** The Open Directory Project and the specialty directories aren't only important in their own right but often also provide links that other search engines read.

✔ **Ask friends and family.** Get everyone you know to add a link.

✔ **Ask employees.** Ask employees to mention you.

✔ **Contact association sites.** Contact any professional or business association of which you're a member and ask for a link.

✔ **Contact manufacturers' Web sites.** Ask the manufacturers of any products you sell to place a link on their sites.

✔ **Contact companies you do business with.** Get on their client lists.

✔ **Ask to be a featured client.** I've seen sites get high PageRanks by being linked to from sites that feature them.

✔ **Submit to announcement sites and newsletters.** This includes sites such as URLwire (www.urlwire.com).

✔ **Send out press releases.** Sending out press releases, even if distributed through the free systems, can sometimes get you links.

✔ **Promote something on your site.** If you have something really useful, let people know about it!

✔ **Find sites linking to your competition.** If other sites link to your competition, they may link to you, too.

✔ **Ask other sites for links.** During your online travels, you may stumble across sites that really should mention your site, as a benefit to their visitors.

✔ **Make reciprocal link requests.** Ask other site owners to link to you, in exchange for a link to them.

✔ **Respond to reciprocal link requests.** Eventually, other people will start asking you to link swap.

✔ **Search for** *keyword add url.* You can find sites with links pages this way.

✔ **Use link-building software and services.** Try using a link-exchange program or service to speed up the process.

✔ **Contact e-mail newsletters.** Find appropriate e-mail newsletters and send them information about your site.

✔ **Mention your site in discussion groups.** Leave messages about your site in appropriate forums, with links to the site.

✔ **Respond to blogs.** Blog sites are often well indexed by search engines.

✔ **Pursue offline PR.** Getting mentioned in print often translates into being mentioned on the Web.

✔ **Give away content.** If you have lots of content, syndicate it.

✔ **Apply for online awards.** Sign up for site awards.

✔ **Advertise.** Sometimes ads provide useful links.

✔ **Use a service or buy links.** Some services sell links from high-PageRank sites.

✔ **Just wait.** Eventually links will appear, but you must prime the pump first.

These link-building strategies are ranked by priority in a very general way. One of the first things you should do is to ask friends and family for links and one of the last is to wait. However, in between these strategies, the priority varies from business to business, or person to person. You may feel that a strategy lower on this list is important to do right away.

The next sections look at each of these link-generation methods.

Register with search directories

In Chapter 12, I discuss getting links from directories, the Yahoo! Directory, and the Open Directory Project. And in Chapter 13, I tell you about getting links from specialty directories. Links from directories are important not only because people can find you when searching at the various directories, but also because search engines often spider these directories.

Google, for instance, spiders both Yahoo! and the Open Directory Project. And the Open Directory Project results are syndicated to hundreds of smaller search engines, many of which Google reads. These links are also highly relevant because they're categorized within the directories; as you find out in Chapter 14, the search engines like relevant links. Therefore, if you haven't registered with the directories, consider that the first step in your link campaign.

Ask friends and family

Ask everyone you know to give you a link. Many people now have their own Web sites or blogs — *Weblogs* (which I discuss in more detail in Chapter 9 and later in this chapter). Ask everyone you can think of to mention your site. Send them a short e-mail detailing what you'd like them to say. You may want to create a little bit of HTML that they can paste straight into their pages, perhaps with a link to a logo stored on your Web site so the logo appears in their pages. If you do this, you get to control the link text to ensure that it has keywords in it: *The best darn rodent racing site on the Web,* for instance, rather than *Click here to visit my friend's site.*

Ask employees

Employees often provide, by accident, a significant number of links back to their employer's Web site. In particular, employees often mention their employer in discussion groups that get picked up by the search engines. So why not send an e-mail to all your employees, asking them to link to the company's site from their Web sites and blogs and to mention you in discussion groups? Again, you might give them a piece of HTML that includes an embedded logo.

You can also ask them to include a link to your site in the signature of their e-mails. The signature is the blurb that you see at the bottom of an e-mail message containing contact information. (Ask them to add a full link — not just www.domainname.com, but http://www.domainname.com.) That way, whenever they post messages via e-mail to discussion groups, search engines may pick up the link. And, you can ask them to always use a signature with the link when posting via non–e-mail methods, such as posting to Web-based discussion groups.

Of course, some employers don't want their employees talking about them in discussion groups because they're scared what the employees will say. If that's your situation, I can't do much to help you, except suggest that you read *Figuring Out Why Your Employees Hate You For Dummies* by I. M. N. Ogre.

Contact association sites

Association sites are a much-overlooked source of free and useful links. Contact any professional or business association of which you're a member and ask for a link. Are you in the local Better Business Bureau, the Lions Club, or Rotary Club? How about the Rodent Lovers Association of America, or the Association for Professional Rodent Competitions? Many such sites have member directories and may even have special links pages for their members' Web sites.

Contact manufacturers' Web sites

Another overlooked source of links is manufacturers' Web sites. If you sell products, ask the manufacturer to place a link from its site to yours. I know one business that sells several million dollar's worth of a particular toy that it gets from a single retailer. The link from the retailer, which doesn't sell directly to consumers, brings the company *most* of its business. This is a valuable link, but because the manufacturer is a well-known national company that gets plenty of traffic, the manufacturer's Web site has a PageRank of 6 on its main page. (See Chapter 14 to see why that's impressive.) The link to the retailer is on the manufacturer's home page, so not only does the link bring plenty of business, but it also gets plenty of attention from the search engines.

Contact companies you do business with

Many companies maintain client lists. Check with all the firms you do business with and make sure that you're on their lists.

Ask to be a featured client

While looking at a competitor's Web site for a client, I noticed that the competing site had a surprisingly high PageRank even though it was a small site that appeared to be linked to from only one place, www.inman.com, which is a site that syndicates content to real estate sites. It turned out that the competitor was linked to directly from one of Inman's highest PageRanked pages. Inman was using the client as an example of one of its customers.

If you're using someone's services — for Web hosting, e-mail services, syndication services, or whatever — you may want to contact the site and ask if *you* can be the featured client. Hey, someone's going to be, so it may as well be you.

Submit to announcement sites and newsletters

You may be able to find a way to get into one of the few site-announcement Web sites and e-mail newsletters still in existence. (The newsletters usually end up published on the Web, too.)

Check out URLwire (www.urlwire.com), for instance. This service claims to have over 125,000 readers, of whom 6,500 are journalists and site reviewers who get the e-mail newsletter. You have to pay from $300 to $1,000 to get into one of the announcements, but other announcement services are generally free.

Unfortunately, getting your site into the announcements can be difficult because of stiff competition. In fact, some announcement sites don't accept submissions — Yahoo! Picks, for instance, doesn't take suggestions. Sometimes to get picked up by these sites, you need to be mentioned in another influential announcement service, such as URLwire. However, if you *can* get in, the effect can be huge. Not only do you get a link from a site that is undoubtedly well indexed, but you probably also get picked up by many other sites and newsletters. URLwire in particular (no, I'm not getting a kickback!) is incredibly influential.

Here are a couple of announcement services still in business:

- ✔ **URLwire:** www.urlwire.com
- ✔ **Yahoo! Picks:** picks.yahoo.com/picks

These announcement services used to be abundant, but unfortunately, most have died off.

Send out press releases

Does your company publish press releases? You should distribute these as widely as possible. Even if you submit press releases through a large service, such as PR Newswire (prnewswire.com), you should also distribute them through the free and low-cost distribution services, which will quite likely get them placed onto other Web sites. You may want to write a few quick press releases and send them through the free-distribution services, just to see if you can generate some links.

This is the list of services I'm currently using when I send releases, with the cost:

- **Premier Web Design:** www.preweb.com, $200 ($180 if you buy ten at a time)
- **EmailWire:** www.emailwire.com, $20.75 (assumes two releases per month on a $299, six-month subscription)
- **PR Leap:** www.prleap.com, $20
- **Free Press Release:** www.Free-Press-Release.com, $0.60
- **PressBox:** www.pressbox.co.uk, Free
- **I-Newswire.com:** www.I-Newswire.com, Free
- **PRLog:** www.prlog.org, Free
- **PR.com:** www.pr.com, $39.95
- **PR-GB.com:** www.pr-gb.com, Free
- **PR9.NET:** www.pr9.net, Free
- **openPR:** www.openpr.com, Free
- **TransWorldNews:** www.transworldnews.com, $41.67 (based on two releases per month on an annual, $1,000 subscription)

Distribute to this list, and you get very wide distribution — you *will* end up in Google News, Yahoo! News, MSN News, and many, many other sites.

You may also want to create your own list of press-release distribution e-mail addresses and Web pages. For instance, look for industry journals in your field that accept press releases.

Of course, you need to get links into your press releases. All the above services allow you to add at least one link in the "About" area of the press release; many of them allow multiple links throughout the release. Some also allow you to create keyworded links. Therefore, you can create a link that says *Rodent Racing Scores* instead of just putting your URL in the release.

So, go to each site and find how to create press releases, including how to code links inside them. This varies from service to service. For instance, on Premier Web Design you'd create a link like this:

```
Robertson Ellington's http://www.RobertsonEllington.com/
         [rodent racing__title__ Rodent Racing] Web site
         ...
```

On PR Leap, on the other hand, you create the same link like this:

```
Robertson Ellington's
         [url=http://www.RobertsonEllington.com/]Rodent
         Racing[/url] Web site ...
```

In addition, some services use regular http URLs. So you have to know how links are created on each service. But it's worth it. I've done it; I've seen it work. Press releases are a very powerful way to create links back to your site. I'll help you out a little; at `http://www.SearchEngineBulletin.com`, you can find a document explaining how to create press releases.

Create a little "linkbait"

One of the most powerful link-building techniques is to place something very useful on your site and then make sure that everyone knows about it. I've included a little story in the "How links build links" sidebar at the end of this chapter. It shows how links can *accumulate* — how, in the right conditions, one link leads to another, which leads to another, and so on. In this true story, the site had something that many people really liked — a directory of glossaries and technical dictionaries. Over 2,000 sites link to this site, all because the site owner provided something people really wanted and appreciated.

This, by the way, is something known these days as *linkbait* — something so valuable to others that they link to it. It can be something fun, something useful, something weird, something exciting, something cool, or something important. Just something that provides so much value to other people that they link to it from their blogs and Web sites, and within discussion forums; something they want to tell others about. Matt Cutts, well-known blogger and Google employee (see Chapter 19), defines link bait as anything "interesting enough to catch people's attention."

Find sites linking to your competition

If a site links to your competition, it may be willing to link to you, too. Find out who links to competing sites and then ask them if they can link to yours. In some cases, the links are link-exchange links (which I look at in the later section, "Respond to reciprocal link requests"), but in many cases, they're just sites that provide useful information to their readers. If your competitors' sites are useful, and (I'm assuming) yours is too, you've got a good chance of being listed.

So how do you find who is linking to your competitors? You can do this a number of ways, as described in the next few sections. I list the methods in order of the number of links that you're likely to find, from the least to the most.

Google Toolbar

The Google Toolbar has a Backward Links command. (I show you how to download the toolbar in Chapter 1.) . Open your competitor's home page, click the little blue *i* button on the toolbar, and then choose Backward Links from the drop-down menu. This feature generally shows pages with a PageRank of 4 or more; it doesn't show all the links in Google's index. (Sometimes lower-ranked pages seem to sneak through.) It also shows links to that page, not links to all the pages on the site.

If you don't see the *i* button on the toolbar, click the Options button. Select the Page Info Menu check box on the Options tab of the Toolbar Options dialog box.

Google Search

Search for `link:domainname.com` in Google or in the search box in the Google Toolbar. (Searching for `link:domainname.com` and `link:www.domainname.com` returns the same number.)

However, I'm really mentioning these Google methods so that I can tell you they're not worth the trouble; I hear all the time from people who use these mechanisms, but the fact is they don't work! They do *not* show you the links pointing to a site; they show only a small (often very small) subset of those links. I rarely use them because the information is pretty much useless.

Yahoo! Search

Yahoo! has recently added more link information to its search results. Point your browser to `http://siteexplorer.search.yahoo.com`. Search for your domain name by using the full URL, `http://` included, like this: `http://www.yourdomain.com`. Click the Inlinks (xx,xxx) link and then, from the Show Inlinks drop-down box, choose Except from This Domain. In the To: drop-down box, choose Entire Site.

Here's an example. I searched Google for *link:www.cnn.com* and got 375,000 results. I searched Yahoo! for *http://www.cnn.com* and got 15,300,000— a much more likely number!

Link popularity sites

Online tools, such as LinkPopularity.com, can help you find links. Enter the competitor's URL and click the search button; LinkPopularity.com searches Google, AltaVista, and HotBot for you.

Another service I like is the tool at Marketleap (`www.marketleap.com/publinkpop`), which searches for links at AlltheWeb, Google, AltaVista, HotBot, and MSN.

Many such tools are available. Search for *link popularity tools*, and you'll find them.

Link popularity software

A number of link popularity software tools are available to run on your computer. My current favorite is SEO Elite (`www.SEOElite.com`, see Figure 15-1), a $167 program that looks for links to a site in various search engines, visits each of the pages containing the links, and then returns with the following information:

- ✔ The URL of the page linking to the site
- ✔ The Internet protocol (IP) number of the site on which the page is held
- ✔ Whether the link that the search engine *thinks* is on the page is still there
- ✔ The PageRank of the page
- ✔ The Alexa rank of the page
- ✔ The `<title>` tag text from the page
- ✔ The *anchor* text — that is, the link text
- ✔ The number of outbound links on the page
- ✔ The total number of links on the page (outbound plus internal site links)
- ✔ *Whois* information — data about who owns the site on which the page sits
- ✔ The link value — an estimate of the value of the link, based on the PageRank divided by the number of links on the page
- ✔ A contact e-mail address pulled from the page

This is a great little program, with nifty tools, such as the ability to find potential link partners and e-mail them, and a way to search for potential link-submission pages and quickly submit information to them. You can export your results to an Excel spreadsheet.

There are many link popularity programs out there; search and you'll find them. Be aware, though, that link popularity analysis is difficult, and there's no perfect tool.

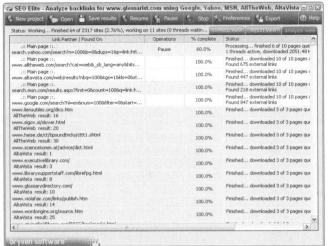

Figure 15-1:
The SEO
Elite link
popularity
tool in
action.

Asking for the link

When you find sites linking to your competitors, you discover that some of them may be appropriate for a link to yours; directories of products or sites, for instance, may want to include you. So how do you ask for the link? Nicely. Send an informal, chatty message. Don't make it sound like some kind of form letter that half a billion other people have received. This should be a personal contact between a real person (you) and another real person (the other site's owner or manager). Give this person a reason to link to your site. Explain what your site does and why it would be of use to the other site's visitors.

Ask other sites for links

During your travels online, you'll run across sites that provide lists of links for visitors — maybe your site should be listed, too. For instance, while working for a client that had a site related to a particular disease, I found sites that had short lists of links to sites about that disease; obviously, my client should also have been in those lists.

Approach these sites the same way you approach the sites linking to your competitors: Send an informal note asking for a link.

Make reciprocal link requests

A *reciprocal link* is one that you obtain in exchange for another. (It's often also referred to as a *link exchange*.) You ask site owners and managers to link to your site, and you in turn promise to link to theirs.

Reciprocal linking, if done right, can help you in two ways:

- ✔ The search engines see nice, keyworded links coming into your site from appropriate, relevant sites.

- ✔ You link to appropriate, relevant sites too. (In Chapter 14, I discuss the concept of hubs or value networks.)

Reciprocal linking is different from asking to be added to a list, although plenty of overlap exists. With the latter, you don't need to offer a link in exchange because the link list is a service to the other site's visitors. However, sometimes site owners respond with, "Sure, but will you link to us, too?" In this case, you've just found yourself in a reciprocal linking position.

Before I go farther, though, I need to address a couple issues. First, you may hear that reciprocal linking doesn't work, and even that reciprocal linking can get your site penalized; I don't think either is true.

First, will you be penalized for using reciprocal linking? If using these links gets you penalized, why does Google index so many reciprocally linked pages? Why do sites that use reciprocal linking rank so high? In addition, why would search engines penalize people for using a technique that they have in effect encouraged over the years — a technique so common that, for good or bad, it's part of the "landscape" of the Web?

Now, I'll admit there's been some talk about MSN penalizing sites for using reciprocal linking — specifically when they link to nonrelated sites. (You can read the story at `http://www.seroundtable.com/archives/006742.html`.) But there's a little unsubstantiated talk here and there, and a lot of conjecture. Again, regardless of the talk, I come back to my questions; if reciprocal linking gets you banned, then why . . .

Far more likely is that when search engines decide they don't like reciprocal linking, they'll start downgrading the links, just as, in fact, Google has done over the last few years.

Which brings us to the next major question: Does reciprocal linking actually work? I do think that there may still be some value in reciprocal linking — it can be a very fast way to create many links with lots of good keywords pointing to your site — but reciprocal linking is nowhere near as powerful as it once was. It truly was very powerful a few years ago; I've seen sites rank first on Google in very competitive markets, based almost entirely on reciprocal linking (and, by the way, at a time when many in the SEO business were saying that reciprocal linking didn't work!).

Today, however, reciprocal links carry much less weight, I don't use them so much these days, and I certainly wouldn't base a search engine campaign on reciprocal linking alone. Nevertheless, here's a quick look at what it's all about.

Relevant or contextual links are more valuable than irrelevant, noncontextual links. Links to your rodent-racing sites from other rodent-racing sites are more valuable than links from sites about Satan worship or *Star Trek*. If you get links from any site you can, without regard to whether the sites are of use to your visitors or whether your site is of use to theirs, search engines won't regard them as relevant links. However, I'm not saying, as many in the business would, that irrelevant links have no value; they clearly do, though perhaps not as much value as relevant links. Because search engines really don't know for sure what link is relevant and what isn't, even irrelevant links have some value.

Reciprocal linking is a popular method for obtaining links to your site. Find a site that appears to be in an area similar to yours — that is, attracts the same sort of people you want to attract and involves a related subject area — and then contact the owner and ask for a link.

Making the contact

Before you contact others to ask for reciprocal links, link from your site to their sites. Find a page from which it would make sense to link. If possible, avoid the use of links pages (which I discuss next). Rather, find a spot on your site where a link to the other site would *fit* — a position in which it would make sense from a visitor's point of view. Keyword the link nicely. (Do unto others as you would have them do unto you.)

Then contact the site owner. Let the site owner know that you've added the link *and* that you've keyworded it. In fact, why not explain keyworded links and their purpose? Doing so will probably make it easier to persuade the site owner to give you the type of keyworded link you want. Provide the URL to the page on which the link sits. You might even explain why you try to avoid the use of links pages.

Then ask for a reciprocal link and suggest a page on which it would make sense. You're better off *not* being on a links page if you can avoid it.

Should you use links pages?

You undoubtedly see *links pages* all over the place — pages with titles such as *Useful Links, Useful Resources, Visit Our Friends,* and so on. To be honest (I say that when I'm about to upset people), these pages don't generate much traffic to your Web site. How often do you find useful links useful or useful resources particularly, er, resourceful? Not very often, I bet. People simply don't use them. And having tested link-exchange software that measures the amount of traffic going through the links pages, I can tell you that they don't generate much traffic to Web sites. (I discuss link-exchange software later in this chapter.)

You may hear the term *link exchange.* In many quarters, this practice is frowned upon because it implies that the site owners simply want to accumulate as many links as possible and don't really care about the type of sites they're working with. It also implies the use of a links page. On the other hand, *reciprocal linking* implies a more circumspect methodology, in which links are carefully considered and placed throughout the site.

However, as I explain in Chapter 14, you have four reasons to get links to a Web site. One is to get traffic through the links, and I've pretty much killed that idea for the typical links page. The other reasons are to help search engines find your site; to tell search engines, through the use of keywords, what the site is about; and to push up your PageRank. And link pages *can* do that.

You're far better off *not* using links pages because of the following problems:

- ✔ **Search engines may already downgrade links from such pages.** A link from an ordinary page is likely to be more valuable than a link from a links page.

- ✔ **Links pages often have dozens or even hundreds of links on them.** Remember that the more links on a page, the lower the vote for each outgoing link.

- ✔ **Links pages may be further downgraded in the future.** If someone at Google or Yahoo! decides that removing the effect of links pages from their algorithms will improve search results — and there's good reason to think that it would have this effect — you could one day wake up and discover that links to your site from links pages no longer have any value.

I'm not saying that you should never use links pages. Life is an exercise in compromise, and, to be honest, a really good reciprocal-link campaign can be incredibly time consuming. However, the ideal situation would be to

- ✔ Scatter links to other sites around your site in locations that make sense.

- ✔ Encourage site owners linking back to you to do the same. Start educating the other sites you work with! (In fact, tell them to run out and buy this book; better still, tell them to buy ten copies of this book for colleagues, friends, and family.)

- ✔ Avoid having large numbers of links on one page.

- ✔ Avoid calling a page a *links* page. You might try using *resource* page, although I suspect this title is also overused.

Some people claim that search engines don't index these links pages. This simply isn't true. They often do, and the proof is in the pudding:

- Go to Google and search for these terms, making sure to include the quotation marks:

  - *"visit our friends"* (*I found 2,280,000 pages*)

  - *"link exchange"* (*over 64 million*)

  - *"links page"* (*over 23 million*)

  Sure, not all the pages you find are links pages, but many are.

- Go to some links pages and check to see if they're in the Google cache, or go to Google and search for the URLs of the pages to see if they're in the Google index. They often are.

- When you visit links pages, look at the Google Toolbar. You often see that they have a PageRank. However, I should reiterate: Links from links pages probably do not have the value of links from normal pages.

Finding links with high PageRanks

Ideally, you want links from pages with high PageRanks. Now, you may hear that you should focus on links from sites that are related to you, not from sites with high PageRanks. That's partially true. Although relatively little traffic goes through link exchanges, remember that links from related sites are more valuable than links from unrelated sites. Links to your rodent-racing site from other rodent-related sites will probably be more valuable, in terms of PageRank, than links from unrelated sites about music or Viagra. (On the other hand, I wouldn't be surprised if links from sites about horse racing or car racing are more valuable.)

The best strategy is to get related links from pages with high PageRanks! Them's the facts, ma'am, and it doesn't matter how many politically correct statements people want to make about not worrying about PageRank. The fact is, PageRank *does* matter.

I'm not implying that you should turn down links from pages with low PageRanks, but what if you could search for pages with a high PageRank, and then go after them? If you're looking for reciprocal-link partners anyway, you may as well use a search technique that uncovers sites with high PageRanks, for several reasons:

- If a page has a high PageRank, it has many links to it, or a small number of links from other pages with high PageRanks, or both. This means that search engines are more likely to find and reindex the page, thus are more likely to find and follow the link to *your* page.

- For obvious reasons, people are more likely to follow the links to your page, too.

✔ The vote from a page with a high PageRank counts for more than the vote from a page with a low PageRank.

Here are some ways to find pages with high PageRanks:

✔ **Use the Backward Links command on the Google Toolbar or the `links:domainname.com` search syntax.** (Both techniques are discussed in the "Find sites linking to your competition" section earlier in this chapter.) These techniques find only pages with a high PageRank — 4 or above — so you can look for pages linking to a competitor and know that the pages have a decent PageRank.

✔ **Use a link-analysis tool, such as SEO Elite.** This program, and some others, reports the PageRank of the linking pages; therefore, you can target pages with high PageRanks first.

✔ **Look in the Google Directory.** Go to `directory.google.com` and browse through the directory until you find an appropriate category. Each entry near the top of the category is shown with a green and gray bar in the left column. The longer the green part of the bar, the higher the PageRank.

3-way and 4-way linking

A more complicated form of reciprocal linking is one that many people are using these days. The idea is that instead of linking from site A to site B, and back from site B to site A, you create a three- or four-way link, as shown in Figure 15-2. (You may actually see this described as a *one-way link exchange,* but it's the same concept; the person you link to doesn't link back.)

It's easy for the search engines to recognize reciprocal linking, which is why I, and many others in the business, believe that the value of such linking has been downgraded.

Figure 15-2:
Traditional reciprocal linking (top left). Three- and four-way linking is probably more beneficial.

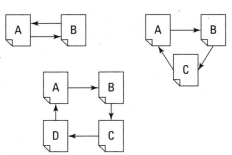

If a search engine sees a link from one site to another, and then sees a link coming back, there's a good chance it's a reciprocal link. (I'm sure it's more complicated than this but the basic principle remains. For instance, does the site have lots of outgoing links, to sites that link back, on the same page?) So it's pretty easy for search engines to recognize reciprocal linking, and because they're aware that such linking is used as an artificial way to boost ranking, they can lower the value of these links.

Say, however, you have a large collection of sites that want to trade links. Rather than have every site link to every other, you might try a more complicated structure where site A links to B, B links to C, and C links back to A; refer to Figure 15-2. Instead of getting two incoming links, each site only gets one, but it's probably of more value because it's not so obviously a reciprocal link. Or maybe you link site A to B, B to C, C to D, and D to A; in this case each site gets one link instead of three, but again, the links are likely to be more valuable than simple A-to-B-to-A reciprocal links. Some companies that perform SEO work for large numbers of clients use this technique, or even combine traditional reciprocal links with three-way or four-way linking.

I've seen a few services that purport to provide a 3-way linking service. However, when you start figuring the technical details of how 3-way linking works, it really gets quite complicated. How do you know who is linking to whom and how many links they're providing? How do you decide which sites are linking to which other sites? The two 3-way linking services I've examined closely were really a mess (and seem to be out of business now). That's not to say someone won't do a good job at some point, but (thus far) I haven't seen a good, automated 3-way linking service.

Use link-building software and services

Link-building campaigns are LTT: laborious, tedious, and time consuming. (I love making up acronyms; I'm just hoping this one takes off.) You have to find sites, add links on your site to the sites you want to exchange with, contact the owners, wait to see if they respond, try again when they don't, check to see if they actually add the links, and so on. It's a lot of work.

Some programs and online services can help you automate the process. They usually help you search for appropriate sites to work with, assist you in contacting the owners, and even create your links pages for you. A number of computer programs are available; perhaps the best known are Zeus (www.cyber-robotics.com) and ARELIS (www.axandra.com). Some people find the online services easier to work with, but you have to pay a monthly fee to use them (in some cases a few hundred bucks a year).

Link-building programs and services can be used or misused. You can easily use these systems to amass a large number of links in a hurry, without regard to relevance or context. Or you can use them to assist you in a careful campaign to garner links from sites that really make sense.

One free service is LinkPartners (`www.linkpartners.com`), a huge directory of people who want to exchange links. This service is associated with a pay service called LinksManager (`www.linksmanager.com`), which automates the process of contacting the site owners and verifying that the link-exchange partners have actually placed links on their pages. If you get a request for a link through LinksManager and accept the exchange, LinksManager does the work for you, adding the links to both your pages and the link-exchange partner's pages. It even automatically uploads the links pages to your Web site.

Another service I've used is Links4Trade (`links4trade.com`), which is similar to LinksManager, but it currently creates only a single page. (LinksManager creates a series of categorized pages.)

Some purists feel that using link-exchange programs is cheating, and indeed these services are walking a fine line between valid linking that the search engines accept and automated link-generation systems that the search engines hate. I've spoken with the owners of both LinksManager and Links4Trade, and they both tell me they've spoken with Google and they both were told that how they manage their programs is acceptable. Because the programs aren't totally automated and require some manual oversight and management, they're okay. Again, the proof is that these pages *are* indexed by Google.

Respond to reciprocal link requests

Eventually, other sites will start asking *you* to link swap. Remember, ideally, you should treat your outgoing links like gold and link only to relevant sites that will be of use to your visitors — but also remember that all links have *some* value.

Search for keyword add url

Go to Google and search for something like this:

```
"rodent racing" + "add url"
```

Google searches for all the pages with the term *rodent racing* and the term *add url.* You find sites that are related to your subject and have pages on which you can add links, as shown in Figure 15-3. (For some inexplicable reason, you don't find much with *"rodent racing" +"add url"*, but you find plenty with, for instance, *"boating" +"add url"* or *"psychology" +"add url"*.)

You can also try these searches:

```
"rodent racing" + "add a url"
"rodent racing" + "add link"
"rodent racing" + "add a link"
"rodent racing" + "add site"
"rodent racing" + "add a site"
"rodent racing" + "suggest url"
"rodent racing" + "suggest a url"
"rodent racing" + "suggest link"
"rodent racing" + "suggest a link"
"rodent racing" + "suggest site"
"rodent racing" + "suggest a site"
```

However, these aren't always high-quality links. Generally, the search engines don't really like this sort of linking, and the word on the street is that links from such pages probably don't have the same value that you get from links that are personally placed. On the other hand, they may be easy to get; it's a trade-off.

Incidentally, SEO Elite, which I mention earlier, includes a tool to carry out one of these types of link campaigns, searching for pages with submission forms related to whatever keywords you define, and then helping you submit these forms; see Figure 15-4.

Figure 15-3:
Searching for a keyword or keyword phrase along with +*"add url"* uncovers sites that are just waiting for you to add a link to your site.

Contact e-mail newsletters

E-mail newsletters can be an incredibly powerful method for getting the word out. The first step is to find all the appropriate e-mail newsletters — newsletters that write about the area in which you operate. After you've identified some newsletters, here are some ways you can work with them:

- **Send the newsletters a short announcement introducing your site.** I like to send informal messages to the editors to ask if they can mention the site and then give them a reason to do so. What makes your site interesting or useful to the newsletter readers?

- **Consider buying small ads in the newsletters.** Some ads are cheap, and if the newsletter is highly targeted, buying an ad may be worthwhile. Make sure that you know how many people subscribe to the newsletter. Lots of little newsletters with very few subscribers may charge pricey ad rates!

- **Offer some kind of cooperative campaign.** For example, provide a special offer for newsletter readers or put together a contest to give away your products.

- **Write articles for the newsletters.** I cover this topic in more detail in Chapter 16.

Mention your site in discussion groups

Search engines index many discussion groups. You need to find a discussion group that publishes messages on the Web, so an e-mail-based discussion group that doesn't archive the messages in Web pages can't help you.

Whenever you leave a message in the discussion group, make sure that you use a message signature that has a link to your site and also include the link in the message itself.

Sometimes URLs in messages and signatures are read as links, and sometimes they aren't. If you type **http://www.yourdomain.com** in a message, the software processing the message can handle the URL in one of two ways:

- ✔ It can enter the URL into the page as simple text.
- ✔ It can convert the URL to a true HTML link (`<A HREF=" http://www. yourdomain.com"> http://www.yourdomain.com/ </A>`).

If the URL is *not* converted to a true link, it won't be regarded as a link by the search engines.

Respond to blogs

Literally billions of blog pages are around the Internet, and some of them have to be related to the subject served by your Web site. Many blogs allow visitors to respond; you may want to respond to messages and include a link to your site. However, two things to consider:

- ✔ **Avoid blog spamming:** If you have nothing valid to say in response to a blog, don't bother. Responses placed on blogs for the sole purpose of garnering links are *blog spam* — an obnoxious vandalism of the blogosphere.
- ✔ **Links in blogs are dropping in value:** As a response to blog spam, search engines introduced a new link-tag attribute, `rel="nofollow"`. For instance, look at this link: `<a href="http://www.domain.com/" rel="nofollow">Visit My Cool Site</a>`. When a search engine sees the `nofollow` attribute, it ignores the link. As more blogging systems begin coding all links in responses in this manner, the less valuable responding to blogs becomes.

Pursue offline PR

Getting mentioned in print often translates into being mentioned on the Web. If you can get publications to write about and review your site, not only do many people see the link in print — and perhaps visit your site — but often your link ends up online in a Web version of the article.

Give away content

Many companies have vast quantities of content on their Web sites. It's just sitting there, available to anyone who visits. So why not take the content *to* the visitors before they reach your site? Placing the content on other Web sites is a powerful way not only to build links back to your site but also to get your name out there — to "brand" yourself or your company.

In Chapter 16, I cover this topic in more detail because you need to be aware of several technical issues.

Advertise

You may want to consider advertising in order to get links to your site. However, you need to consider a couple of issues first:

 ✔ Advertising is often grossly overpriced. It may be much too expensive to justify just for a link.

 ✔ Advertising links often don't count as links to your site. Rather, they're links to the advertising company, which runs a program that forwards the visitor's browser to your site. Search engines won't see the link as a link to your site. (See Chapter 14 for more information.)

In some cases, buying ads on a site to get a link does make sense. For instance, if many of your clients visit a particular Web site and it's possible to get a low-cost ad on that site, it may be worthwhile to buy an ad to both brand your company and to get a link that the search engines can read. And remember, it's a very relevant link, coming from a site important to your business.

Use a service or buy links

I can't stress enough that link campaigns can be very laborious, tedious, and time consuming. You may be better off paying someone to perform the work. Some of these services simply run the link-acquisition campaign for you. Others already have an inventory of ad space on thousands of sites and charge you to place a link on a set number.

OneWay TextLinks sells 100 links for $18.95 per month. Another company I've seen claims it can put links on 250 sites for $99. Some companies sell links from pages of specific PageRank, too. One company, for instance, claims to be able to sell you a link on a PageRank 8 site for $799. (A PageRank 4 page is just $29.) I have no idea how legitimate such services are.

The vote from a page is shared among all the pages it links to, so the more ads that are sold, the less the value of each ad. You should know exactly what page the link will be placed on, and you should be able to view the page. Consider buying links as a form of advertising that should be evaluated as such. How much of an impact will the ad have on bringing more visitors to your site?

Many companies do this sort of work, such as these:

- ✔ **Web Link Alliance:** www.weblinkalliance.com
- ✔ **Linking Matters:** www.linkingmatters.com
- ✔ **Text Link Ads:** www.text-link-ads.com
- ✔ **TextLinkBrokers.com:** www.textlinkbrokers.com
- ✔ **OneWay TextLinks:** www.onewaytextlinks.com

You can also find link-building services at outsourcing sites, such as Guru.com, Naukri.com, and Elance.com.

I'm not endorsing any of the companies I'm mentioning here. I'm just providing them as examples of the types of services available.

If you're interested in such a service, search for *buy links*, *purchase links*, *link popularity*, and *link building* at a major search engine. Make sure that you understand what you're getting into. As you've seen, you can use many methods to get links to a site, but they don't all provide the same value. Are you working with a company that can find good links from popular sites that are relevant to yours or a company that uses an automated link-exchange tool to gather links from anywhere it can? There's a real difference!

When you buy links, make sure that you buy the right type. You don't want links dropped onto a page using JavaScript, or ads served through an ad server. In the first case, the search engine probably won't read the link at all; in the second case, the link probably points at the ad server, not at your Web site. For instance, AdBrite (www.adbrite.com) sells text ads on a wide range of Web sites, but the link points to AdBrite, not to your site.

Here's an example showing you how to figure whether the link points to your site; an ad I found on one of their advertising sites:

```
Gastric Bypass Pill
Approved! FREE Samples
```

Now, pointing to a link displays one of two things in the browser's status bar:

✔ The URL the link points to

✔ A fake URL, which is placed there using JavaScript in the Web page

In this case, when I point at the link and look at the status bar in my browser, I see this URL:

```
http://www.zetacap.com
```

However, when I right-click the link, I see the real URL in the status bar:

```
http://click.adbrite.com/mb/click.php?sid=19822&banner_id=
        10235529&cpc=302e3030303030303030&ssc=08862a24b
        01e87aa1498dbcafcda01de
```

When I click the link, that's also the URL I see (for a second or two) before the ad server forwards me to the Zetacap.com Web site. As you can see, the link doesn't point to the advertiser's site — `www.zetacap.com` — it points to the `click.adbrite.com` ad server. I'm not suggesting that AdBrite is misleading people, by the way; they don't claim their links can help you with search engines; they're simply selling ads. But when you go looking for pages on which to place links, you must be aware of this issue.

Remember, a link campaign can be incredibly LTT — you know, laborious, tedious, and time consuming — so don't be surprised if a firm quotes, say, $2,000 to get you 30 links. It may be a reasonable price, assuming that the firm is doing it the right way. On the other hand, many firms, particularly in India, are doing link work for as little as $0.25 per link. (This is generally through reciprocal linking programs.)

Caution! Google doesn't like purchased links!

It's important to understand, though, that Google doesn't like purchased links. In fact, none of the major search engines are going to be pleased if you buy links pointing to your site. You can find an interesting discussion of this issue at `http://news.stepforth.com/blog/2007/06/google-cracks-down-on-link-buying.php`.

However, it's hard for search engines to deal with this problem for a couple of reasons. First, how do search engines know the link is purchased? Yes, there are highly automated systems that place purchased links, and the search engines may be able to find a *signature* — some kind of characteristic that identifies the link as purchased. However, how will a search engine know whether you ask Fred over at ReallyFastRodents.com, "Fred, if I give you $20 a month, will you link to my site?"

Additionally, if they penalize site owners for purchasing links pointing to their sites — well, how much is it worth to you to push your competitor out of the search engines? Sure, *you* may be too ethical to play this game, but plenty of people aren't. So, say you're tired of seeing ReallyRapidRodents.com ranking above your rodent-racing site month after month. Perhaps you could buy a bunch of links pointing to his site, report him to Google, and see Google drop him from the search engine. Therefore, search engines have to be very careful about penalizing sites for buying links. What's more likely is that when search engines identify the links as purchased, they'll downgrade or ignore them, not penalize the referenced site.

Just wait

I'm not really recommending that you sit and wait as a way to build links, but the fact is that if you're doing lots of other things — sending out press releases, getting mentioned in papers and magazines, contacting e-mail newsletters to do product giveaways, and so on — you'll gather links anyway. You've got to prime the pump first; then things seem to just take off.

Consider having a Link to Us page on your site to provide logos and suggest HTML text that people can drop onto their sites.

Fuggetaboutit

Don't bother getting links in guest books, Free for All pages, and link farms, for the following reasons:

- ✔ Many Web sites contain guest book pages, and one early link-building technique was to add a link to your Web site in every guest book you could find. The search engines know all about this technique, so although many guest books are indexed, links from them probably have very little value in most search engines.

- ✔ *Free for All (FFA)* pages are automated directories that you can add a link to. They bring virtually no traffic to your site, are a great way to generate a lot of spam (when you register, you have to provide an e-mail address), and don't help you in the search engines.

- ✔ *Link farms* are highly automated link-exchange systems designed to generate thousands of links very quickly. Don't get involved with link farms. Not only can they not help you, but also, if you link to one or host one on your site, you may be penalized in the search engines.

Search engines don't like these kinds of things, so save your time, energy, and money.

TECHNICAL STUFF

How links build links

I want to share a story that provides a wonderful illustration of how a link campaign can work. It shows how you can build links, PageRank, and traffic, all at the same time, the old-fashioned way. I found this story in one of Webmaster-World's discussion groups. As the author of the story puts it, you should remember how the "Internet started and what it was supposed to be all about: sharing information." The search engines want you to remember this, too.

The story is about an Aussie called Woz. Once upon a time, Woz had a site called Glossarist (www.glossarist.com), a directory of glossaries and topical dictionaries. This was a hobby for Woz, and he had done little to promote the site. However, one sunny day — July 26, 2003 — he noticed a 4,000 percent increase in traffic. (For the math challenged among you, traffic on that day was 40 times greater than the day before!) The site had been mentioned in the ResearchBuzz e-mail newsletter and Web site (www.researchbuzz.com), by the fairy godmother, Tara Calishain. Not surprisingly, ResearchBuzz is a resource for people interested in research. It's the sort of site that would be interested in a directory of glossaries and topical dictionaries.

The very next day, a wonderfully bright and sunny day, Glossarist was picked up by The Scout Report (scout.wisc.edu/Reports/ScoutReport/2001/scout-010727.html) which, perhaps a little more surprisingly, is a "weekly publication offering a selection of new and newly discovered Internet resources of interest to researchers and educators."

Then on August 9, a *really* sunny day, the site was mentioned in USAToday.com's Hot Sites (www.usatoday.com/tech/2001-08-09-hotsites.htm). I've had one of my sites mentioned in *USA Today,* and believe me, your traffic really spikes when that happens!

By the middle of August, Woz wuz able to identify links from over 200 sites — "libraries and student-resource pages from schools and universities, translation sites, business reference sites, writers sites, information architecture sites, and so on." He also got a lot of traffic from newsletters that had been forwarded from subscribers to friends and colleagues. (Both *ResearchBuzz* and *The Scout Report* are very popular e-mail newsletters.) Not only did site owners find out about him through these e-mails, but many visitors also came to his site through the e-mail links.

All this publicity was great, providing his site with a lot of traffic through those links and making it more likely that his site would be found and indexed by search engines. It also boosted his site's PageRank. By mid-August, the Glossarist PageRank had reached 3; by the end of August, it was 8, which is an excellent PageRank for a hobby site created by a single person without a marketing budget! (I just checked, and it's currently showing a PageRank of 6, which is still very good. It's also likely that Google has adjusted PageRank in the intervening years so that higher PageRanks are now harder to attain.)

By the end of August, Woz had around 300 links. And, as Woz claims, he didn't request a single one of these links. (I recently checked and found 31,900 links to this site!)

Don't underestimate the power of this kind of grass-roots promotion. It can be tremendously powerful. One link can set off a chain reaction, in the way that a single link in ResearchBuzz did.

Chapter 16

Even More Great Places to Get Links

*L*inking is incredibly important. The more great, keyworded links pointing to your site, the better. You can never have too many links, and for many sites, in particularly competitive areas, linking is a continual process that never ends.

So, let's get started discussing more great places to get links to your site.

Got Content? Syndicate It!

I discuss one aspect of syndication in Chapter 9 — using syndicated content to bulk up your Web site. Now, it's time to look at the flip side — syndicating your content to other Web sites and e-mail newsletters.

E-mail newsletters don't help your search engine position because search engines don't read them (although that could change at any time). However, most e-mail newsletters are placed into Web archives — that is, they become Web pages — that often *are* indexed by search engines. Furthermore, newsletter readers sometimes post articles from the newsletters on their sites or come directly to your site.

I recently searched Google for the term *load vs. no load,* and found the search results shown in Figure 16-1. The four entries I've pointed to in the figure are actually the same article — written by the same man and promoting the same Web site but appearing on *different* Web sites (none of them his, by the way). He also turns up several times for the term *load vs. no load mutual fund.*

What has this man, Ulli Niemann, done? He hasn't managed to get his Web site onto the first page for this search, but he has managed to get his work onto the first page. Searchers clicking on one of the entries have a very good chance of seeing his name, his work, and a link to his site (`www.successful-investment.com`). See how well this campaign has worked? Now he has a link in a book, too.

At the end of the day, it's not all about search engines; it's about getting out the word about your Web site through whatever method that works.

Some site owners use this form of syndication as the *only* type of promotion they do — and it can work incredibly well. They write articles and distribute them as widely as possible. But many sites already have a lot of content. Why not give it away and use it as a technique to grab more search engine positions, generate links to your site, and brand your site and company?

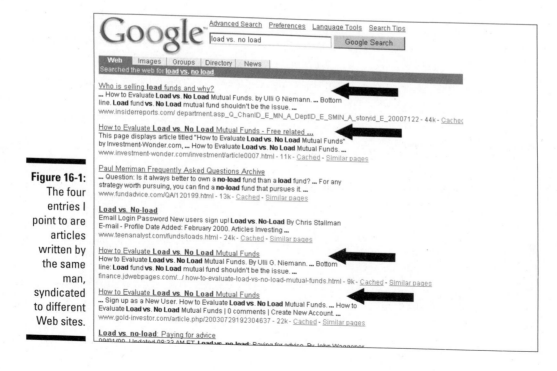

Figure 16-1:
The four entries I point to are articles written by the same man, syndicated to different Web sites.

Another huge advantage to using syndication is that the links you get back to your site are from relevant sites. Remember, the search engines like *relevant.* Ulli Niemann is an investment advisor, so what sort of sites do you think carry his articles? Finance and investment sites!

Four ways to syndicate

You can syndicate content four ways. You must understand, however, that some of the methods don't help you with search engines. In some cases, it's possible to syndicate content and *not* benefit from links pointing to your site, depending on how the content is distributed. The following list details the four main syndication categories:

✔ **Browser-side inclusion:** Many syndicators employ browser-side content inclusion through the use of JavaScripts; a *JavaScript* in a Web page pulls the article off the syndicating site. The problem is that the Web browser runs the JavaScripts when the page loads. Searchbots, however, don't run JavaScripts. Googlebot, when indexing the page, ignores the JavaScript and thus doesn't see the content or the link to your site in the content. Although site visitors will see the links (and click some), you won't get the benefit of the link popularity in the search engines.

✔ **Hosted content:** Some content syndicators, generally those *selling* content, host the content on their own servers, and the sites using the content link to it. The problem with this method is that if you host content for, say, 50 sites, you don't get the benefit of 50 links in the search engines. Google sees that you have the same article 50 times and ignores 49 of them.

✔ **Manual inclusion:** This method works well for search engines; they see the content and the links to your site. The problem, however, is that you're relying on the other site's owner to manually place the content into the page.

✔ **Server-side inclusion:** You can do server-side inclusions a number of ways, such as by using INCLUDE commands, running PHP or ASP scripts (server-side scripts), or by using a relatively new method, RSS feeds. The advantage is that the search engines *will* see your content and the links back to your site. The disadvantage is that the methods are more complicated to use than either manual or browser-side inclusion.

To ensure that search engines see links to your Web site, you simply can't use the first or second methods. That leaves the last two, of which the third, manual inclusion, is easiest and by far the most common.

If you want to syndicate your content, prepare the articles carefully. I suggest that you produce each article in two forms: plain text for text newsletters and HTML for HTML newsletters and Web sites. Make the HTML version simple so that it can be taken and dropped into any other Web page.

It's possible to make a JavaScript-style syndication give you at least one link that is readable by the search engines. Typically, syndicators ask users to drop a piece of JavaScript into their pages. Of course, you can ask them to drop a piece of HTML that includes a JavaScript inside. For instance, instead of using

```
<SCRIPT LANGUAGE="JavaScript" src="http://www.
       ronaldsrodents.com/content/article.js"></SCRIPT
       >
```

you can use

```
<SCRIPT LANGUAGE="JavaScript" src="http://www.
       ronaldsrodents.com/content/article.js"></SCRIPT
       ><P><STRONG>Article provided by <A
       HREF="http://ronaldsrodents.com>Ronald's
       Rodents</A>. Visit us for more great articles
       on rodent racing.</P>
```

Getting the most out of syndication

If you're going to syndicate your work, consider the following points when creating your articles:

- ✔ Every article should contain your site name near the top of the article. Put a site logo near the top and include a link on the logo back to your site.

- ✔ If you can find a way to work a link to your site into the article, all the better. You can do it a couple times maybe, but don't overdo it. Perhaps link to another article on your site for more information. Make sure that the link text has useful keywords. (Note, however, that most syndication services don't allow links in the body; we look at syndication services in a moment.)

- ✔ At the bottom of the article, include an attribution or bio box, including a keyworded link back to your site and a logo with a link on it. (Don't forget to use ALT text in the <IMG> tag.)

Set up a library on your Web site where people can access the articles. In the library, you should post certain conditions:

✔ Consider putting limits on the number of articles that can be used without contacting you first. For example, site owners can use up to five articles, and if they want more, they must get permission.

✔ State clearly that you retain copyright of the article and make clear the following conditions:

- *The user cannot change the content.*

- *All logos, attributions, copyright notices, and links must remain.*

- *Links must remain standard HTML <A> tags and cannot be converted to another form of link.*

Getting the word out

When you have your articles ready, you need to get them into the hands of people who can use them. First, you need to register with as many syndication directories as possible. Here's a large list, partially compiled with the help of Ulli Niemann:

✔ www.allnetarticles.com

✔ www.amazines.com

✔ www.articlecity.com

✔ www.authorconnection.com

✔ www.boazepublishing.biz

✔ www.certificate.net

✔ www.connectionteam.com/sources.htm

✔ www.content-wire.com/Online/Syndication.cfm?ccs=111&cs=1696

✔ www.ezinearticles.com

✔ www.ezine-writer.com.au

✔ www.freesticky.com/stickyweb

✔ www.freesticky.com/stickyweb/submitselfsyndicate.asp

✔ www.goarticles.com

✔ www.gold-investor.com

✔ www.greekshares.com

✔ www.ideamarketers.com

- www.investnewz.com
- www.jogena.com
- www.magportal.com
- www.marketing-seek.com
- www.netterweb.com
- www.shoppingwithwomen.com
- www.teenanalyst.com
- www.top7business.com/submit
- www.vectorcentral.com
- www.webpronews.com
- www.web-source.net/syndicator.htm
- www.windstormcomputing.com/pubs/free-ezine-content
- www.writers-and-publishers.com

This is actually a small list; there are hundreds of syndication libraries. Ideally, you'll get your articles into as many as possible (probably using a syndication service, as discussed in the "Syndication services" section). You'll get links from the article libraries themselves — most are indexed by the major search engines — and may be picked up by people looking for content for their sites, too.

Syndication services

A number of syndication services and software programs can help you distribute your articles. For example:

www.submityourarticle.com (service)

www.articlemarketer.com (service)

www.articlesender.com (free service)

www.articlesubmitterpro.com (software)

www.rypmarketing.com (service)

These services and programs distribute your articles to hundreds of different syndication libraries. You may even want to use several of these services. Follow this general procedure:

1. Write an article, putting keyworded links in the "resource" box at the bottom of the article (but not in the article itself).

2. Modify the article slightly so that you have a different version for each service.

3. Submit the article through each service — when using SubmitYOURArticle, use their ArticleLeverage system, which modifies each article slightly so each one it submits to an article library is slightly different.

4. If using the Article Submitter Pro software, add keyworded links within the article, then submit to only the article directories that allow keyworded links inside the articles.

Syndicating utilities

A number of companies do a tremendous job at building truly huge numbers of incoming links by giving away Web site utilities. One that comes to mind is the Atomz Express Search free search component from Atomz (`www.atomz.com`; now owned by WebSideStory). Every site using this program has at least one link, probably several, back to the Atomz.com site. I used a link analysis tool some time ago, and found about 6,000 links to Atomz.com. Another company with a huge number of incoming links is MapQuest (`www.mapquest.com`). Because it distributes maps, both paid and free, and because all those maps include links back to the home site, thousands of links around the Web point to MapQuest.

This technique has worked incredibly well for many technology companies but can also work for others with a little imagination. Whatever you give away — clip art, videos, flash animations, or PDF documents — make sure you include links back to your site. For instance, your rodent-racing site could distribute a utility for handicapping mice and rats. (I don't mean to damage them physically; I mean to calculate the race handicap.) The utility would have a link back to your site — nicely keyworded — providing you with lots of great backlinks for search engines to read.

Social Networking

The last couple of years have seen an explosion of what are termed *Web 2.0 sites* — Web sites that allow ordinary people to interact in communities. In particular, from an SEO perspective, we're interested in social networking and social bookmarking sites.

Social networking sites include Facebook and MySpace, in which users set up, in effect, their own mini Web sites with commentary, pictures, embedded programs, discussions, and so on.

Social bookmarking sites are simpler in many ways; they're essentially public collections of bookmarks. Del.icio.us, for instance, one of the most popular, currently has more than 3 million members, 100 million links, and 1.5 million pages indexed by Google. Google has indexed over 3.5 million pages at another popular bookmarking site, Digg.com.

These sites are indexed by the major search engines; Google currently has 143 million pages indexed from MySpace, and 399 million indexed from Facebook. Yet, it's quite rare for a MySpace, Facebook, or Del.icio.us page to turn up in search results. So why bother indexing them?

Indexing links from social networking and social bookmarking sites is really an extension of Google's original PageRank idea — Google used links between Web sites to help rank sites, and now they're using links from social networking sites to provide more popularity information. In the pre-Web 2.0 days, Google recruited a relatively small number of site owners to tell them which sites were important; that is, Google used the links created by Web site owners to tell them which sites were important.

Now, with the barriers to entry being much, much lower for social networking and social bookmarking — it's much easier to set up a MySpace or Digg account than to build a Web site — Google has a much larger army of site reviewers to help it figure how to rank Web sites. Facebook has around 100 million members, MySpace has perhaps 110 million, LinkedIn has almost 20 million, and even some of the small services you've never heard of have millions (Bedo has 20 million, and TravBuddy.com has almost a million). As of February 2008, there were around 160 million Web sites and more than a billion social networking accounts.

Therefore, rather than a relatively small number of Web site owners pointing links to your site, Google and the other major search engines are watching thousands of people creating bookmarks pointing to your site. So, the more links you can get in these social networking and social bookmarking accounts, the better!

A few important concepts:

- ✔ The more traffic to your site, the more bookmarks you get.
- ✔ The more interesting or more useful your site, the more bookmarks you get.
- ✔ Make it easy! Encourage people to link by using services like AddThis and link buttons.
- ✔ PR (public relations) campaigns can be used to generate links from social networking sites.

✔ Some people are creating fake social networking/bookmarking accounts to place links to their sites.

✔ Services can place links in social networking/bookmarking accounts.

If you want to check more, see these pages to find social networking and social bookmarking sites:

✔ http://en.wikipedia.org/wiki/List_of_social_software#Social_bookmarking

✔ http://en.wikipedia.org/wiki/List_of_social_networking_websites

Video sites

Many site owners have tried using video upload sites to create links pointing back to their Web sites; in general, it's not very effective, though.

If you have videos, post them on the video upload sites and create a link back to your site whenever you can. (I also recommend that any company creating videos for their sites make sure that they include the site's domain name in the video itself.) This way, whoever sees your video (and from wherever they see it) can always find you. You may get traffic from the links, but in most cases, you won't get search engine credit for the links because most of these services now convert links to nofollow links.

Here's an example of a link I found on YouTube, pointing back to a video-poster's site:

```
<a rel="nofollow"
        href="http://www.black20.com">http://www.black2
        0.com</a>
```

The rel="nofollow" piece tells the search engines to ignore the link.

At the time of writing, most video upload sites either do not allow linking or add the nofollow tag to links. If you still want to investigate for yourself or simply need to post your videos somewhere to generate traffic to your site (even if you don't get search engine credit), check out some of these directories of upload sites:

✔ http://www.xeep.net/top-25-most-popular-video-sharing-sites-on-the-web

✔ http://www.dvguru.com/2006/04/07/ten-video-sharing-services-compared

✔ `http://web2.econsultant.com/videos-hosting-sharing-searching-services.html`

✔ `http://en.wikipedia.org/wiki/List_of_video_sharing_websites`

And More . . .

A few more ideas for building links:

✔ Submit articles to genuine article sites, such as Suite101.com and Buzzle.com. Such sites solicit real articles from real writers (this is not the same as the article-syndication strategy I discuss earlier, which allows anyone to submit anything). These sites are often difficult to join, but if you can join and submit articles, the links can be very effective.

✔ It's not unusual for eBay merchants to include links back to their Web sites from their eBay listings. Of course, eBay listings only last a few days, but Google has, at the time of writing, 335 million indexed pages on eBay. If you do sell on eBay, create links back to your site wherever possible. (At the time of writing, eBay doesn't add the `nofollow` tag to links.) eBay *does* allow links pointing out from the site, as long as they are "links to pages that provide information about a member's store or service, provided the link and pages are not promotional in nature of items not offered for sale on eBay." Thus, as long as you link to a page with more information about the product, that's fine.

✔ Carry out traditional PR (public relations) campaigns, targeting blogs and newsletters, to promote your site. You need a good "story," but if you contact enough sites, you can get people to talk about you.

The nofollow Curse

A quick note about the `nofollow` tag mentioned earlier. This tag — `rel="nofollow"` — tells search engines to ignore a link. Strictly speaking, it tells them not to follow the link, but more important, it tells them not to give any credit to the referenced Web site. That is, a link to your site, with `rel="nofollow"` in the link, is as good as no link at all from a search engine perspective.

This tag was created to stop *blog spam*. When blogs first became popular, many people, trying to push their sites up in the search engines, were visiting blogs and posting messages in the blog with links back to their sites, solely in order to boost their sites in the search engines. Thus, blogs became inundated with absolute garbage. You could even hire Indian companies to place links in blogs for you or buy programs that hit thousands of blogs in a few hours.

So, the major search engines came together to figure a way to put a stop to it. They figured that if there were no real benefit to blog spam, it would stop. Therefore, nofollow was born.

What's happened over the last few years though is that, gradually, other sites have started using the `nofollow` tag. Wikipedia used to be a great place to put links back to your site until it started coding every link with `nofollow`. Craigslist, too, was a very popular place to post ads with links back until it too began using nofollow.

So, if you discover a good place to put links to your site, first check to see whether the links are genuine links; that is, make sure they don't have `nofollow` in the link itself, or `nofollow` in a meta tag at the top of the page. Secondly, check periodically. A site that currently allows "clean" links without `nofollow` tags may not always.

The best kind of link is a link with keywords in it that points to a page that is optimized for those same keywords. If your link reads *Rodent Racing Schedules,* the best page it can link to is one that has been optimized for the phrase *Rodent Racing Schedules.*

Who's Going to Do All This Work?!

Wow, finding sites to link to yours is a lot of work. It's very LTT (laborious, tedious, and time consuming). It's also not, shall we say, high-rent work. How do you get all this done? Assuming you're not using a link-acquisition firm, here are some options:

- ✔ Do you have kids? If not, get some. It's a little drastic, but after you've spent a week or two doing this stuff, it may not seem so bad.
- ✔ Do your neighbors or employees have kids?
- ✔ Do your siblings have kids?
- ✔ Local schools and colleges definitely have kids, so you may want to find one or two who will do a few hours of work each evening.

Chapter 17

Using Shopping Directories and Retailers

In This Chapter

▶ Finding the shopping directories

▶ Selling directly from third-party merchant sites

▶ Creating your datafeed files

*I*f your Web site is an e-commerce site, you have more places at which you can register. There's a whole 'nother category of search engines — shopping directories. These are giant catalogs of products. Search for *digital camera,* for instance, and you see a page with pictures of cameras, their prices, links to the appropriate Web sites, and so on. (A few of these services, such as NexTag, list services as well as products.)

Most of these directories expect you to pay, though not all do. Google Product Search is completely free, for example. In general, the ones that *do* expect you to pay charge only when someone clicks a link to visit your site, so these directories may be worth experimenting with.

I begin this chapter by talking about the different systems that are available and end by providing you with a little help on preparing your data for the directories.

Finding the Shopping Directories

The following directories are probably the most important shopping directories to research. Go to each one and try to find information about signing up and uploading your data. In some cases, that process is simple — the directory wants you to join, so you find a link that reads something like <u>Sell on Our Site</u> or <u>Merchant Info</u>. Sometimes, you have to dig a little deeper because the information is not clearly visible; you may need to use the Contact Us link and ask someone about signing up.

✔ **Google Product Search (formerly Froogle):** www.google.com/products

✔ **Yahoo! Shopping:** http://shopping.yahoo.com

✔ **Shopping.com:** www.shopping.com

✔ **BizRate & Shopzilla:** www.shopzilla.com

✔ **PriceGrabber.com:** www.pricegrabber.com

✔ **NexTag:** www.nextag.com

✔ **Pricewatch:** www.pricewatch.com

✔ **PriceSCAN:** www.pricescan.com

Most of these systems expect you to pay if you want to play — generally, you pay each time someone clicks a link to your site. Some let you list your products, and receive traffic, at no cost. Here is a rundown of the three types of systems:

✔ **Free:** You have no direct control over your position, but you don't have to pay for any traffic you get from the site. Google Product Search is the classic example.

✔ **Pay per click; fixed fee:** Yahoo! Shopping is of this type. You don't have any control over position because there's no bidding (as there is with the following type); you pay a fixed fee per click.

✔ **Pay per click; bidding:** Most of the other systems charge per click, but have bidding systems that help determine your position on search results pages. (As you may expect, merchants with the highest bids are listed first on the page.)

What will you pay for the *pay-per-click (PPC)* systems?

✔ In most cases, PPC systems don't charge a listing fee.

✔ You have to begin by funding your account — typically $50 to $250, which goes toward paying for your clicks.

✔ You pay each time someone clicks your link. Clicks vary in price, generally, from 10 or 15 cents up.

✔ In systems that accept bids, there's a minimum click rate, but the actual rate is dependent on how many people are bidding and their pain threshold; in some cases, clicks could even cost several dollars.

✔ You may be charged other fees, such as a fee to place a store logo next to your listing. (Some of the PPC systems give these logos to the highest bidders free.)

Google Product Search

Google Product Search — formerly Froogle (www.google.com/products) —
is Google's product directory. It's been incorporated into the main Google site
for years now, and has hundreds of millions of products in the index (Google
still labels the service as a beta service, though it's been running at least five
years). I'm sure you've seen Google Product Search, even if you don't realize
it. Search, for instance, for *lcd screen* at Google, and you see something similar
to that shown in Figure 17-1.

The first link, <u>Product search results for lcd screen,</u> takes you to the full
Google Product Search directory. The next three links are products that
have been pulled from the directory (the links point directly to the associated site). The final link, See **lcd screen** <u>results available through Google
Checkout</u>, takes you to a subset of entries (just those Google Product
Search entries that come from sites using Google Checkout, the Google
payment-processing system).

Click the first or last links, and you enter the directory and see something
similar to that shown in Figure 17-2.

Getting into Google Product Search is easy. Look for the Information for
Sellers link at the bottom of one of the Google Product Search results pages
for instructions. Google Product Search is actually integrated with Google
Base, another, less popular, Google product directory (see http://Base.
Google.com); you'll be adding your products to both Google Base and
Google Product Search.

You can submit information about your products one by one, in a Web form
on the Google Base site, or you can submit a *datafeed* file — a simple text file
containing the product data (which I discuss later in this chapter). In addition, if you have programmers working on your site, they can use a Google
API (Application Programming Interface) to feed data to Google.

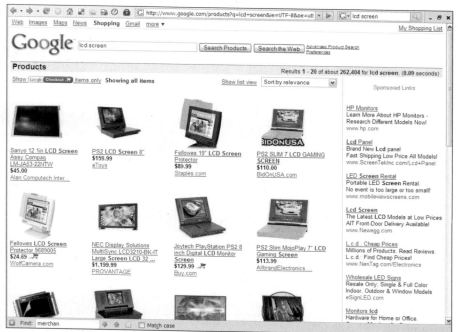

Figure 17-2:
Google
Product
Search.

Google Product Search doesn't display a lot of information about each product, so it doesn't require much information from you. You provide a link to the information page on your site, a link to an image of the product, the name and description, a price, and a category. Additionally, you can fill various optional fields, such as author name, model number, size, style, weight, and so on.

How, then, do you capture one of the top three positions we see in Figure 17-1? Feed Google with as much data as possible about all of your products, with links pointing to pages on your site that are well optimized for those products.

Yahoo! Shopping

Yahoo! Shopping (`http://shopping.yahoo.com`) charges you each time someone clicks a link to your site. Yahoo! finds the product you're looking for (see Figure 17-3) and then, when you click the link to the product page, finds merchants that sell the product; see Figure 17-4.

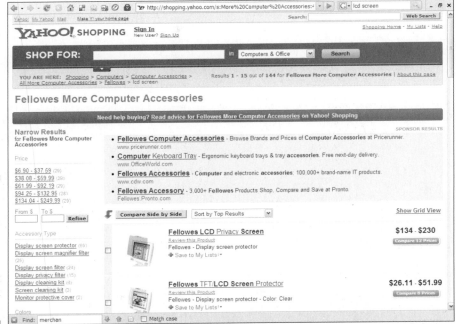

Figure 17-3:
Yahoo!
Shopping is
product-
centric,
taking you
to product
pages, not
merchants.

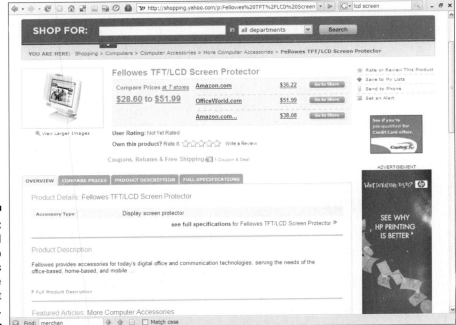

Figure 17-4:
You can find
links to
merchants
on the
product
page.

Mergers

Shopping.com was formed by a merger of DealTime and Epinions, the most popular product-comparison sites on the Web. Two separate sites, Shopping.com and Epinions.com, now exist; getting into Shopping.com gets you into both sites. It's worth noting that Epinions listings often rank well in search engines.

So how much is all this going to cost? That depends on the product category. Unlike some systems, Yahoo! charges a fixed fee per click that varies among categories; other systems charge a fee that is dependent on bidding, like the PPC systems. (See Chapter 18 for more on PPC systems.)

For instance, here are a few click prices:

Apparel	$0.25
Beauty	$0.30
Books	$0.15
Computers and Software	$0.50
Computers and Software > Desktop	$0.50
Computers and Software > Software	$0.50
DVD and Video	$0.20
Electronics	$0.50
Electronics > Digital Cameras	$0.60
Office Goods	$0.25
Religious and Spiritual	$0.15
Toys and Baby Equipment	$0.25
Video Games	$0.20

Shopping.com

Shopping.com (found on the Web at www.shopping.com, of all places) is also a pretty important (that is, popular) shopping directory. It also charges by the click, and each category has a minimum rate. For instance, the following list shows a few minimum *cost per clicks (CPCs):*

Books	$0.05
Cables and Connectors	$0.70
Computers	$0.70
Drive Cases	$0.70
Furniture	$0.25
Travel	$0.05
Kitchen Appliances	$0.30

Figure 17-5 shows the Digital Cameras page, a subcategory of Electronics.

Remember, these are *minimums;* your mileage may vary (and almost certainly will). Unlike with Google Product Search and Yahoo! Shopping, the higher your bid in a system like Shopping.com, the higher you'll initially appear on the product page. However, at Shopping.com, a site visitor can sort the product page by price, store name, and store rating, so as soon as a visitor sorts the page, most of the benefit of the higher bid price is lost. Bids are placed per category, by the way, not per product.

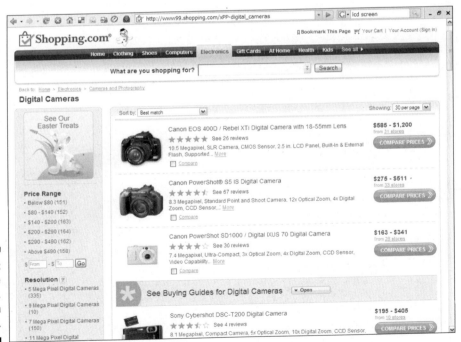

Figure 17-5:
The
Shopping.
com
directory.

As with most shopping directories, you can provide a datafeed file to Shopping.com. However, Shopping.com has another service, by which it grabs the information from your Web site for you. This costs $75 to set up and $50 per month, but the directory crawls your Web site every day.

PriceGrabber and PrecioMania

PriceGrabber (www.pricegrabber.com) and its Spanish-language *hermano* PrecioMania (www.preciomania.com) claim to send over a billion dollars in customer referrals each month, whatever that means. True or not (how do you measure a referral, anyway?), PriceGrabber is a significant shopping directory because it feeds data to various other shopping directories.

This system works two ways. You can pay per click for traffic sent to your Web site, as with most other shopping directories, or you can use the PriceGrabber Storefronts system and let PriceGrabber take the order and send the information to you to ship the product. (It charges 7.5 percent.)

BizRate & Shopzilla

BizRate & Shopzilla (www.shopzilla.com) are two popular per-click sites with common ownership. As with Shopping.com, these services charge a minimum fee per category, typically ranging from $0.35 to around a dollar, an extra $0.10 if you have a logo with the product, and the final rate dependent on bidding. Again, merchants with the highest bid are listed first, until the visitor re-sorts the list. Figure 17-6 gives the Shopzilla take on digital cameras — and, no, I'm not necessarily dropping any hints here, although my birthday *is* coming up.

NexTag

NexTag (www.nextag.com), yet another popular site, is also a PPC site with a category minimum and bidding for position. You don't pay a setup fee, but you do have to fund your account before you can get started. That's the norm with all these PPC shopping directories, but NexTag's $300 minimum to start is a little high.

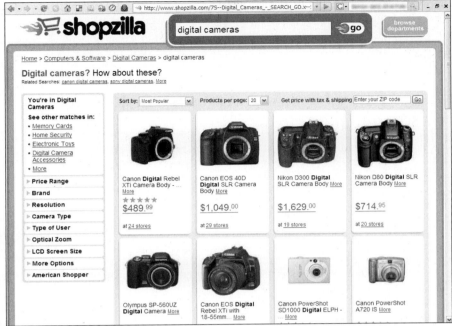

Figure 17-6:
The
Shopzilla
shopping
directory.

NexTag is one of the few shopping systems that lists not only tangible products but also services. If your business sells mortgages or travel services, for instance, you can be listed at NexTag.

You can load data into a Web-form system if you have only a few products. If you have more, you'll want to use a datafeed file. NexTag will take any datafeed file; if you create one for Yahoo! Shopping, for instance, you can use the same one for NexTag. Just send the Yahoo! one to your NexTag account manager, and he or she will handle it.

Pricewatch

Pricewatch (www.pricewatch.com) isn't well known outside of geek circles. Many people in the computer business use Pricewatch to buy their hardware after checking pricing at the site; the site is limited to computers, peripherals, and accessories. This crude system (shown in Figure 17-7) appeals to UNIX geeks in particular. It's fast and has no graphics on the search page (or even on the results pages in most cases).

Figure 17-7:
Pricewatch, a UNIX geek's dream shopping directory.

The Pricewatch folks claim to serve over 200 million pages each month, so if you have products in their categories, you may want to look into working with them. However, they don't necessarily make that easy. Contact them (you can find a contact page somewhere in the About area) and see if they get back to you!

PriceSCAN

PriceSCAN (www.pricescan.com) got off to a good start — it was one of the earliest shopping or price-comparison directories — but it seems to have been superseded by the other systems I've mentioned. However, PriceSCAN has one great advantage over most of them: As with Google Product Search, you can list your products for free. The directory does sell advertising, but the price comparisons are intended to be unbiased by fees or PPCs. E-mail the site at vendors@pricescan.com, and who knows, someone might even respond.

More Shopping Services

Yep, there's more, plenty more. Table 17-1 offers a quick rundown of some other places where you can list your products.

Table 17-1		Shopping Services
Service Name	*URL*	*Description*
Shop.com	`www.shop.com`	Originally CatalogCity.com; designed for catalog companies to sell their wares online, this site is looking for merchants with over 100 consumer-oriented products.
StreetPrices.com	`www.street prices.com`	A PPC site that claims to get 400,000 visitors each month, generating $325 million per month in "sales leads" (whatever that means). It charges from $0.50–$1.00 per click.
iBuyernet.com	`www.ibuyernet. com`	Is there anyone home? Who knows? This site doesn't seem very interested in signing up new merchants. In theory, though, they'll charge for sales, clicks, a monthly flat rate, or for ad impressions.
Dogpile, and PricingCentral.com	`ask.price grabber.com`, `dogpile.price grabber.com`, `pricingcentral. com`	These systems use PriceGrabber; get in there, and you're in these, too.
Pronto.com	`www.pronto.com`	A new "community" shopping site. You pay for clicks with minimum bids ranging from $0.15–$1.00.
Lycos Shopping	`shop.lycos.com`	Uses Pronto.com.

(continued)

Table 17-1 *(continued)*

Service Name	URL	Description
mySimon and Shopper.com	`www.mysimon.com`, `www.Shopper.com`	Combined, these are very important sites, but they don't make it easy for the average storeowner to work with them, so I've put them in the "more stuff" category. Owned by CNET, these systems don't have automated feeds set up for merchants. Contact them directly about how you can work with them; they may take a couple of months to get back to you. They have a variety of programs, from simple PPC text links (generally from $0.15–$0.50 per click) to featured advertising positions.
AOL Shopping	`webcenter.shop.aol.com`	A very exclusive property; if you want to work with AOL Shopping, you have to negotiate directly.
MSN Shopping	`eshop.msn.com`	Not quite as exclusive as AOL, but if you want to be in MSN Shopping, you still have to negotiate directly.
Kelkoo	`www.kelkoo.com`	Don't forget about shopping directories outside the United States. Kelkoo is one of the better-known systems in Europe.

There's also Google Catalogs (`http://Catalogs.Google.com`), which almost nobody knows exists, and which seems to be dead; you can visit and search the scanned mail-order catalogs, but most are several years old. Google doesn't seem to be doing much with Google Catalogs, but hasn't yet decided to actually kill it, so I'm not sure what the plans are; maybe it will be revived at some point.

Third-Party Merchant Sites

I want to quickly mention another type of listing you can get for your products — third-party merchant sites. I don't go into detail here because this is one step over the line between being in a search directory and being sold on another Web site.

You may want to consider selling your products on the major e-commerce sites, which consist of both auction and retail sites:

✔ With the auction sites, you sell your products, yep, at an auction and handle the transactions yourself.

✔ With the retail sites, the product is placed into a directory, and if anyone buys it, the retail site handles the transaction, sends you the information so you can ship the product, and then, a little while later, sends you the money (bar its commission, of course).

Many merchants use the auction sites as a way to generate traffic to their Web sites. By placing links in the ads, you can bring new customers directly to your site, and by carefully using price reserves, you can ensure that any sales you make through an auction aren't at a loss.

Check out the following sites to find out more about working with third-party retail sites:

✔ **Amazon.com WebStores:** Set up your own e-commerce site, running on Amazon, for $60 a month and 7 percent sales commission paid to Amazon. See `http://webstore.amazon.com`.

✔ **Amazon "Sell Your Stuff" and Pro Merchant Programs:** If you sell the same products Amazon sells, you can place links to your products from the same pages on which Amazon sells its products. (You've probably seen the This Item Also Available to Buy box on Amazon product pages.) See `http://www.amazon.com/gp/seller/sell-your-stuff.html`.

✔ **eBay:** This is the world's most popular e-commerce site, with billions of dollars of products being sold here. It's not just an auction site; it hosts thousands of stores, many of which sell fixed-price goods. See `www.ebay.com`.

✔ **Half.com:** Owned by eBay, this is a huge retail products site. See `http://www.half.ebay.com`.

Creating Data Files

Before you sign up with the shopping directories, you probably need a data file (often called a *datafeed*) containing information about your products. This is a simple text file carefully formatted, using the correct layout. A datafeed allows you to quickly upload hundreds, even thousands, of products into the directories within minutes.

Although the datafeed file can be a simple text file, creating it is a little difficult for some people. Of course, if you have geeks on your staff, they can handle it for you. The ideal situation is one in which all your product data is stored in a database that is managed by capable, knowledgeable people who know how to export to a text file in the correct format. All you do is give them the data file specification from the shopping directory, and they know exactly what to do. If that's your situation, be happy. If not, I'll help you.

I'm going to explain how to format your data in a spreadsheet program, which is probably the simplest method. If you have a large number of products, you may already have your data in some kind of database format. Unfortunately, you may need to *manipulate* your data — clean it up — before you can use it. I've noticed over the last couple of decades that, for some reason, data is usually a mess — whether the data files were created by small companies or large. The files are often badly formatted — for example, the text files contain the data, but the fields are improperly *delimited* (separated).

I suggest that you use a spreadsheet program to create your data file. Creating the file in a text editor is difficult and error prone, especially if you have a lot of products. Also, remember that each shopping directory is a little different, requiring different information. The spreadsheet file is your source file, from which you can create the various text files as needed.

You may already have a spreadsheet program; Microsoft Excel is hiding on millions of computers around the world, unknown to their owners. (It's part of Microsoft Office.) Or you may have Microsoft Works, which also includes a spreadsheet program. Various other database programs are available — StarOffice and AppleWorks contain spreadsheets, too. You don't need a terribly complicated program because the work you do with the file is pretty simple. However, you want to use a program that can have multiple sheets open and will allow you to link from a cell in one sheet to a cell in another.

You can also use a database program to manage all this data. It's just simpler in some ways to use a spreadsheet. Of course, you may already have your data in a database, especially if you have a lot of products.

The data you need

Take a look at the type of data you're going to need for your data file. Google Product Search, Google's shopping directory, requires the following data:

- ✔ **product_url:** A link to the product page on your Web site.
- ✔ **name:** The name of the product.
- ✔ **description:** A description of the product.
- ✔ **image_url:** A link to the image file containing a picture of the product.
- ✔ **price:** The cost of the product.
- ✔ **category:** The category in which you want to place the product.
- ✔ **offer_id:** Some kind of product number, such as a *stock keeping unit (SKU)* or *international standard book number (ISBN)*.

Those are the basic fields, but there are others you can include, such as instock, shipping, brand, UPC, manufacturer_id, and so on.

Each service is different, of course. Here's the data that can be included in Yahoo! Shopping:

- ✔ **code:** A SKU or other kind of identifier.
- ✔ **product_url:** A link to the product page on your Web site.
- ✔ **name:** The name of the product.
- ✔ **price:** The cost of the product.
- ✔ **merchant-category:** Your own product category, based on how you categorize products on your site — for instance, Electronics and Camera > Television and Video > VCR.
- ✔ **shopping-category:** The Yahoo! Store category under which the product will be placed.
- ✔ **description:** A description of the product.
- ✔ **image_url:** A link to the image file containing a picture of the product.
- ✔ **isbn:** If the product is a book, the ISBN.
- ✔ **medium:** If your products are music or videos, the medium (CD, DVD, VHS, 8mm, and so on).
- ✔ **condition:** The product's condition (new, like new, very good, good, and so on).
- ✔ **classification:** A product type, such as new, overstock, damaged, returned, refurbished, and so on.

- **availability:** Information about the product's availability.

- **ean:** The *European Article Number (EAN);* a number used for barcoding products.

- **weight:** The weight of the product.

- **upc:** The *Universal Product Code (UPC)* number; another bar code system.

- **manufacturer:** The manufacturer's name.

- **manufacturer-part-no:** The manufacturer's part number.

- **model-no:** The product's model number.

Don't worry — only five of these fields are absolutely required. As you can see, some fields are the same in both the Google Product Search and Yahoo! systems. (For details, you need to check the particular systems into which you want to load the data.)

Here's my suggestion. Begin by creating a spreadsheet file containing *all* the data you have about your products. At the very least, include this information:

- Product name

- Product description

- Product price

- Product category

- A URL pointing to the product's page on your Web site

- A URL pointing to the image file that contains a picture of the product on your site

You also want to include any other information you have — ISBNs, SKUs, EANs, media types, and so on. And, keep the file clean of all HTML coding; you just want plain text, with no carriage returns or special characters in any field.

Formatting guidelines

Some of you may have problems with the product URL. If your site is a framed site, as I discuss in Chapter 7, you've got a problem because you can't link directly to a product page. Even if you don't have a framed site, you might have a problem or two. I discuss that in a minute.

Each shopping directory varies slightly, but datafeed files typically conform to the following criteria:

✔ They are plain text files. That is, don't save them in a spreadsheet or database format; save them in an ASCII text format. Virtually all spreadsheet programs have a way to save data in such a format (typically as a `.csv` file).

✔ The first line in each file contains the header, with each field name — product_url, name, description, price, and so on — generally separated by tabs.

✔ Each subsequent line contains information about a single product; the fields match the headers on the first line.

✔ The last line of the file may require some kind of marker, such as END.

✔ In most cases, you can't include HTML tags, tabs within fields (tabs usually separate fields), carriage returns, new line characters within fields, and so on. Just plain text.

Creating your spreadsheet

Take a look at Figure 17-8. This is a simple spreadsheet file containing a number of data fields; it's an example data file from Google Product Search. Each row in the spreadsheet is a product, and each cell in the row — each field — is a different piece of information about the product.

Although the final product will be a text file, you want to save the spreadsheet file in a normal spreadsheet file format. When you're ready to upload data to a shopping directory, *then* you save it as a text file.

Figure 17-8:
A sample datafeed spreadsheet.

	File Edit View Insert Format Tools Data Window Help			
	A	B	C	D	E
1	code	product-url	name	price	shopping-category
2	p12-x	http://www.yourstore123.com/1.html	American Pride Polo Shirt	25	Apparel
3	w345	http://www.yourstore123.com/2.html	Women's Overalls	39.95	Apparel
4	f45	http://www.yourstore123.com/3.html	Carrot Cake	29.95	Flowers, Gifts and Registry > Gourmet and F
5	f46	http://www.yourstore123.com/4.html	Apple Pie	19.99	Flowers, Gifts and Registry > Gourmet and F
6	hg202	http://www.yourstore123.com/5.html	Replacement Blade of Cof	12.95	Home, Garden and Garage > Appliances
7	12kn	http://www.yourstore123.com/6.html	PowerMax Juicer	129.95	Home, Garden and Garage > Appliances > S
8	f235	http://www.yourstore123.com/7.html	Soft Recliner	399.99	Home, Garden and Garage
9	p3002-x12	http://www.yourstore123.com/8.html	Litter box - Gray	14.95	Home, Garden and Garage
10	3exe345	http://www.yourstore123.com/9.html	Handheld power drill	89.95	Home, Garden and Garage
11					

Getting those product URLs

To do this spreadsheet business right, you need the URL for each product's Web page. If you don't have many products, this is easy — just copy and paste from your browser into the spreadsheet. If you have thousands of products, though, it might be a bit of a problem! If you're lucky and you have a big IT budget or some very capable but cheap geeks working for you, you don't need to worry about this. Otherwise, here's a quick tip that might help.

Many companies have a source data file that they use to import into an e-commerce program. For this to be useful to you, figure out what page number the e-commerce program is assigning to each product. For instance, one e-commerce system creates its URLs like this:

```
http://www.yourdomain.com/customer/product.php?productid=18507
```

Notice that the `productid` number is included in this URL. Every product page uses more or less the same URL — all that changes is the `productid` number. So here's one simple way to deal with this situation. Suppose you have a data file that looks similar to the one in Figure 17-9, in which you have a product ID or code in one column, and an empty column waiting for the URL pointing to the product page.

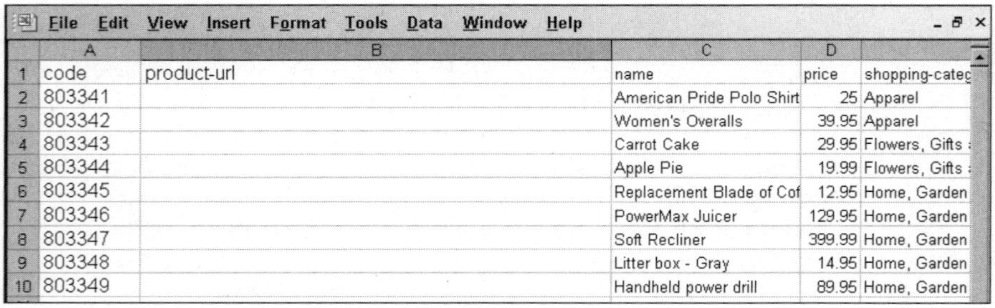

Figure 17-9:
Where do
you get the
URL from?

	A	B	C	D	
1	code	product-url	name	price	shopping-categ
2	803341		American Pride Polo Shirt	25	Apparel
3	803342		Women's Overalls	39.95	Apparel
4	803343		Carrot Cake	29.95	Flowers, Gifts
5	803344		Apple Pie	19.99	Flowers, Gifts
6	803345		Replacement Blade of Cof	12.95	Home, Garden
7	803346		PowerMax Juicer	129.95	Home, Garden
8	803347		Soft Recliner	399.99	Home, Garden
9	803348		Litter box - Gray	14.95	Home, Garden
10	803349		Handheld power drill	89.95	Home, Garden

Here's how to get these URLs into your product listing:

1. **Copy the blank URL into all the URL fields.**

   Copy the URL without the product ID in it, as shown in Figure 17-10. Some spreadsheet programs try to convert the URL to an active link, one you can click to launch a browser. You may want to leave the URL in that format so that later you can test each link. (*Note:* Working with these active links is often a nuisance because it may be hard to select a link without launching the browser.)

2. **Do one of the following to copy the number in the code field and paste it onto the end of the matching URL with a single keystroke:**

   • *Create a macro.*

   • *Use a programmable keyboard.*

   I love my programmable keyboard! It has saved me hundreds of hours. I use an old Gateway AnyKey programmable keyboard, which you can buy at eBay.

Figure 17-10:
Place a
blank URL in
the column
and then
copy the
product
code from
the code
column to
the end of
the URL.

	File Edit View Insert Format Tools Data Window Help			
	A	B	C	D
1	code	product-url	name	price	shopping-categ
2	803341	http://www.yourdomain.com/customer/product.php?productid=	American Pride Polo Shirt	25	Apparel
3	803342	http://www.yourdomain.com/customer/product.php?productid=	Women's Overalls	39.95	Apparel
4	803343	http://www.yourdomain.com/customer/product.php?productid=	Carrot Cake	29.95	Flowers, Gifts
5	803344	http://www.yourdomain.com/customer/product.php?productid=	Apple Pie	19.99	Flowers, Gifts
6	803345	http://www.yourdomain.com/customer/product.php?productid=	Replacement Blade of Cof	12.95	Home, Garden
7	803346	http://www.yourdomain.com/customer/product.php?productid=	PowerMax Juicer	129.95	Home, Garden
8	803347	http://www.yourdomain.com/customer/product.php?productid=	Soft Recliner	399.99	Home, Garden
9	803348	http://www.yourdomain.com/customer/product.php?productid=	Litter box - Gray	14.95	Home, Garden
10	803349	http://www.yourdomain.com/customer/product.php?productid=	Handheld power drill	89.95	Home, Garden

If you don't have a programmable keyboard (and you should have one!), the spreadsheet you're using may have a built-in macro program that allows you to program actions onto a single keystroke. (MS Excel does, for instance.) Another option is to use a macro program that you download from a shareware site. If you have only 20 or 30 products, programmable keyboards and macros don't matter too much. If you have a few thousand products, it's worth figuring out how to automate keystrokes!

Creating individual sheets

After you have all of your data in one sheet of the spreadsheet file, you can create a single sheet for each system to which you plan to upload data: one for Google Product Search, one for Yahoo! Shopping, and so on. (A *sheet* is a spreadsheet page, and all good spreadsheet programs allow you to have multiple sheets.)

Remember, each system requires different information, under different headings, and in a different order. So you need to link information from the original sheet to each individual sheet. You don't want to actually copy this information.

Say that you have five shopping directories you're working with and, after you've finished everything, you discover that you made a few mistakes. If you *copied* the data, you have to go into each sheet and correct the cells. If you *linked* between cells, you can just make the change in the original sheet, and the other five update automatically.

Here's how this works in Excel. I will assume you have two sheets, one named Yahoo! (which contains data for Yahoo! Shopping) and one named Original (containing all your product data). You want to place the information from the *productid* column in the Original sheet into the Yahoo! sheet, under the column named *code*. Here's how you do it in Microsoft Excel:

1. **Click the Yahoo! tab at the bottom of the window to open the Yahoo! sheet.**

2. **Click cell 2 in the *code* column.**

   In this example, this cell is A2, as shown in Figure 17-11.

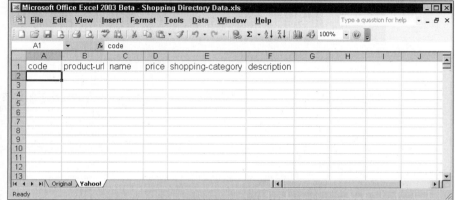

Figure 17-11:
The cursor on cell A2 in the Yahoo! sheet.

3. **Press the = (equal) key to begin placing a formula into the cell.**

4. **Click the Original tab at the bottom of the page to open the Original sheet.**

5. **Click cell 2 in the *productid* column.**

   In this example, this cell is A2, as shown in Figure 17-12.

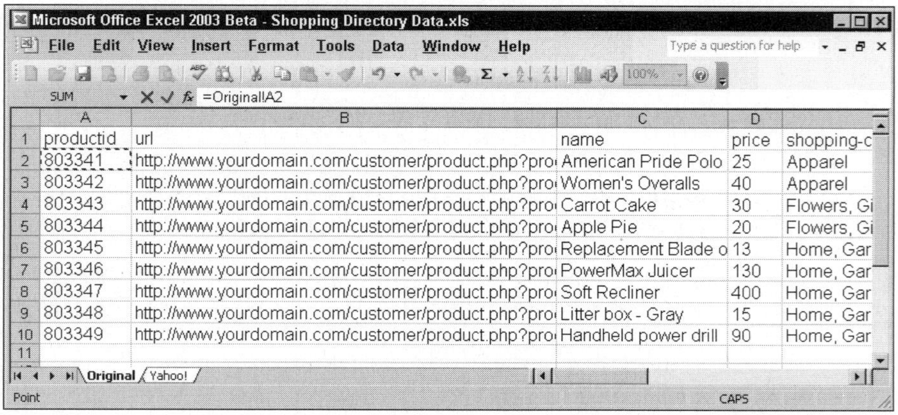

Figure 17-12:
The cursor on cell A2 in the Original sheet.

6. **Press Enter.**

   The program jumps back to cell 2 in the *code* column of the Yahoo!
   sheet, places the data from the Original sheet into that cell, and then
   moves down to the cell below.

7. **Click cell 2 and then look in the formula box at the top of the window.**

   You see this formula (or something similar): =Original!A2, as shown
   in Figure 17-13.

   This means, "Use the data from cell A2 in the sheet named Original." You
   haven't copied the data; rather you're linking to the data, so that if the
   data in A2 changes, so will the data in this cell.

Here's the formula pulling data from Cell A2 in the Original sheet.

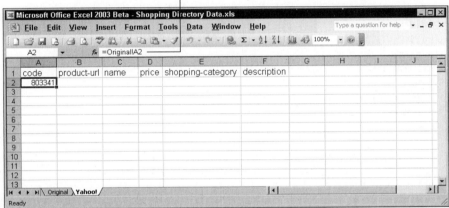

Figure 17-13:
Cell A2 in
the Yahoo!
sheet
contains
=Origin
al!A2.

8. **With cell 2 in the *code* column of the Yahoo! sheet selected, choose
   one of the following:**

   • *Press Ctrl+C.*

   • *Choose Edit⇨Copy from the main menu.*

   You've copied this data into the Clipboard.

9. **Press the down arrow (↓) to select the cell below.**

10. **Hold the Shift key and press PgDn multiple times, until the cursor has
    selected as many cells as there are products.**

    For instance, if you have 1,000 products, you want the last selected cell
    to be cell 1001. (Remember, the first cell contains the header, *code*.)

11. **Choose one of the following:**

    • *Press Ctrl+V.*

    • *Choose Edit⇨Paste from the main menu.*

The cursor jumps to cell 2 again, and data from the Original sheet — from the appropriate cells — now appears in the cells below cell 2.

12. **Press the Esc key to stop copy mode.**

The cells are now linked. If you change data in a *productid* cell in the Original sheet, it changes in the appropriate *code* cell, too.

Repeat this process for all the columns you need and for all the different sheets you need, and you're ready to export your text files.

Creating and uploading your data files

After you've created your sheets, you can export the text files you need to give to the shopping directories. Each spreadsheet program works a little differently. With some programs, you may find an Export command; in Microsoft Excel, you use the Save As command. Here's how to export the text files from Excel:

1. **Save the spreadsheet file in its original spreadsheet file format.**

   This ensures that any changes you've made are stored in the original file.

2. **Click the tab for the sheet you want to export to a text file.**

   That sheet is selected.

3. **Choose File⇨Save As from the main menu to open the Save As dialog box.**

4. **In the Save As dialog box, choose the appropriate file type from the Save As Type drop-down menu.**

   You generally need to select a text format, such as *CSV (Comma delimited; * .csv)* or *Text (Tab delimited; * .txt)*. Check the shopping-directory specifications, as some may accept other formats.

5. **Provide a filename in the Name field.**

   For example, use Yahoo! if you're submitting to Yahoo!, and so on.

6. **Click OK.**

   You see a message box saying that you can't save the entire file; that's okay; all you want to do is save the selected sheet.

7. **Click Yes.**

   Now you see a message box telling you that some features can't be saved as text. That's okay; you don't want to save anything fancy, just text.

8. **Click Yes.**

That's it; you've saved the file. It's still open in Excel, with the other sheets, so I suggest that you close the file. (Excel will ask again if you want to save the file — you can just say No.)

If you want to export another text file, reopen the original spreadsheet file and repeat these steps.

If you want, you can open the file in a text editor like Notepad to see what it really looks like.

After you've created the text file, you're ready to upload it to the shopping directory. Each directory works a little differently, so refer to the directory's instructions.

These data files expire. They last only one month at Google Product Search, for example. Check each system carefully and remember to upload the latest data file before it expires or when you have any important changes.

Chapter 18

Paying Per Click

· ·

· ·

Here's a quick way to generate traffic through the search engines: Pay for it. *Pay-per-click (PPC)* campaigns provide a shortcut to search engine traffic, and many companies, particularly large companies with large marketing budgets, are going directly to PPC and bypassing the search engine optimization stage totally.

In this chapter, you examine these PPC programs, discover their advantages and disadvantages, and find out how and where to employ them. It's an overview, of course. If you decide to spend money on this form of advertising, I recommend that you read the quite splendid *Pay Per Click Search Engine Marketing For Dummies* (Wiley Publishing, Inc.) by, um, me.

Defining PPC

If you use PPC advertising, you pay each time someone clicks on one of your ads. Figure 18-1 shows search results at Google, and Figure 18-2 shows results for the same search at Yahoo! You can see that many of the search results on these pages are actually ads. They're placed mainly based on pricing. (*Google AdWords,* as their PPC ads are known, is a special case, as I explain in a moment.) In other words, instead of going through all the trouble of optimizing your site and getting links from other sites into your site — the things that are explained in most of the rest of this book — you can simply buy your way to the top of the search engines! Maybe.

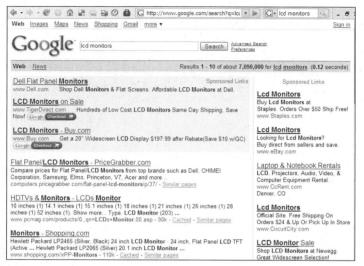

Figure 18-1:
Pay-per-
click
placements
in Google.

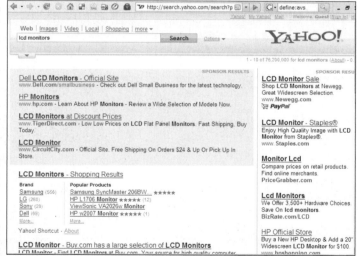

Figure 18-2:
Pay-per-
click
placements
in Yahoo!.

Here's how it all works:

1. You register with a PPC system, provide a credit card number, and then load your account.

2. You create one or more ads — providing a title, body text, and link to the page to which you want to direct visitors.

3. You associate keywords with each ad.

4. You bid on each keyword.

PPC advertising was simpler a couple of years ago. When you bid on a keyword, you were bidding on a position. Figure 18-3 shows how this used to work in Yahoo!; it's a list of keywords in the Yahoo! Search Marketing PPC system. The very first entry shows how much you are willing to bid on the keywords *web strategy*. In other words, if someone searched for *web strategy*, you were willing to pay $1.51 if that person clicked your ad. In this case, because the other people bidding on the term aren't willing to pay that much, Yahoo! lists your ad at the top. You can see how much others are willing to bid in the Top 5 Max Bids column.

This is how it used to work; you'd bid on a keyword, and if your bid was higher than the next guy, your ad would be placed higher. The highest bid got the top position; the second bid got the second position, and so on.

But over the years, PPC has evolved into something slightly different. Google began by modifying the bidding system. When Google has to position your ad for a particular search result, it chooses the ad position partly based on your bid price, but also partly on the *click rate* or *click-through rate* — the frequency with which people have clicked on your ad in the past. You may bid more than someone else may, but it might still be placed below the lower bidder if your ad has had a low click-through rate in the past. As Google puts it, "The most relevant ads rise to the top . . . Your ad can rise above someone paying more if it is highly relevant for a specific keyword."

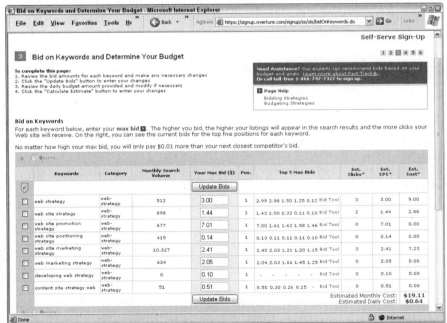

Figure 18-3: Bidding on keywords at Yahoo!

Over the years, both Yahoo! and MSN have also moved toward this process, so now your bid price is not the only factor that determines where your ad is positioned. The *quality* of the ad — how well it convinces people to click it — also affects the position.

The big question, of course, is how much should you bid? Here are a few things to consider:

✔ You must understand how much a click is really worth to you; most companies don't know this. I discuss this issue a little later in this chapter.

✔ The higher your position, the more traffic you are likely to get.

✔ In general, if you're not in the first three positions, there's a good chance your ad won't be seen often and will get *dramatically* lower click-throughs. Google, for instance, syndicates their top three AdWords to sites like AOL. Yahoo! displays the top three (sometimes four) results at the top of their search results.

✔ Sometimes, you may want to take position 3 because you want to be in the top three, yet position 1 is just too expensive. Many PPC marketers like positions 5 and 6; they still get a lot of clicks, but at a much lower price than higher positions.

✔ Other times, you may notice that position 1 is just $0.01 more than you're already paying; it may be worth paying the extra $0.02 to leapfrog the current bidder, just to boost your click-through.

The two types of ads

Most Tier 1 and Tier 2 PPC systems (see "The three PPC tiers," later in this chapter) now have two types of ads:

✔ **Search engine ads.** The search engine placements you saw earlier in this chapter.

✔ **Contextual or content match ads.** Ads placed on Web sites other than search engines. Figure 18-4, for instance, shows Google PPC ads — Google AdWords, distributed through the Google AdSense program — on a vitamin supplements Web site (see the *Ads by Google* tags).

In fact, you can sign up to run these ads on your Web site through Google's AdSense program (`adsense.google.com`) if you'd like to make money by running ads on your site. Sign up for this program, and Google examines your pages to see what ads are most appropriate for your page content. You place a little bit of code in your pages that pulls ads from the AdWords program, and Google automatically places ads into your page each time the page is loaded into a browser. If someone clicks the ad, you earn a little bit of the click price.

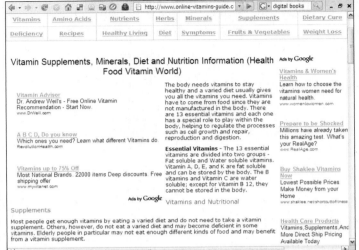

From the PPC advertiser's perspective, though, you should understand that these ads are probably not as effective as the ads placed on the search engines. Some advertisers claim that people who click these content ads are less likely to buy your product, for instance, than those who click the same ad at the search engine. You can turn off content ads if you want, as many advertisers do. I recommend that you begin your campaign with the content ads turned off; when you get rolling, you can experiment with content ads. Either way, make sure that you track the content ads carefully to ensure that they're really working for you.

Pros and cons

What's good about a PPC campaign?

- ✔ **It's faster.** It's a much quicker way to begin generating traffic to your Web site — hours or days, compared to weeks or months through *natural search,* as unpaid search results are often known in the business.

- ✔ **It's much more reliable.** With a natural search, you may exert huge effort (read, expense) and not do well. With PPC, you get what you pay for. If you're willing to bid high enough, you'll get the traffic.

- ✔ **It's more stable.** A site can do well in natural search results on one day, and then disappear on the next. With PPC, as long as you're willing to pay, your site is there.

- ✔ **Some people click PPC ads rather than the organic search results.**

What's bad about PPC?

- ✔ **You pay.** You have to pay for every click, which can add up to a great deal of money.

- ✔ **It's getting pricier.** Sticker shock is likely to get worse over the next year or two. Most people still don't even know what PPC is; wait and see what happens to pricing when PPC is as well known as other forms of advertising.

- ✔ **It's a crapshoot.** PPC doesn't always work, as you see later in this chapter — it's not possible for every company to buy clicks at a price that is low enough to be profitable.

- ✔ **It's not organic.** Many people prefer the free, natural search results — from 30 percent to 70 percent of all searchers (according to some research), depending on the search engine and type of search — so you're missing part of the market if you focus on PPC alone.

Ideally, PPC should be one part of an overall marketing campaign — it should be combined with the other techniques in this book. Many companies spend huge sums on PPC, yet totally ignore natural search, which can often be managed for a fraction of the sum.

The three PPC tiers

The PPC companies are *networks;* that is, they place ads on multiple search sites. Yahoo!, for instance, places ads not only on the Yahoo! Web site, but also on AltaVista, CNN, InfoSpace, Juno, NetZero, Dogpile, ESPN, and many others.

The other major service, Google's AdWords, appears on Google, of course, but also on AOL, Ask.com, EarthLink, CompuServe, Netscape, Excite — even on Amazon.com. In fact, Google has a service called AdSense, which allows virtually any Web site to carry Google PPC ads.

I think of the PPC market as being split into the following three tiers:

Tier 1

Tier 1 comprises three companies:

- ✔ Yahoo! Search Marketing at `SearchMarketing.Yahoo.com`
- ✔ Google AdWords at `www.AdWords.com`
- ✔ Microsoft AdCenter at `AdCenter.Microsoft.com`

These three systems are responsible for more PPC placements than all the rest of the networks combined. They're also the most expensive. A click that costs $0.05 on a Tier 2 or Tier 3 network may cost $2.00 on the major systems.

Tier 2

Tier 2 comprises a handful of smaller networks that may still channel decent traffic to you at much lower prices:

- **Ask.com:** SponsoredListings.Ask.com
- **Miva:** www.miva.com
- **Enhance Interactive:** www.enhance.com
- **ePilot:** www.epilot.com
- **7Search:** www.7search.com
- **ABC Search:** www.ABCSearch.com
- **Searchfeed:** www.searchfeed.com

Tier 2 networks can't channel as much traffic as you would get by bidding for first position on Yahoo! or AdWords. However, in some cases, they can send as much traffic as you're getting on those two behemoths, simply because you can't afford the big guys' top price per click.

ePilot, for instance, places ads on YellowPages.com, Locate.com, Search Bug, and so on. They may be small, little-known sites, but according to ePilot, the 100 or so systems they work with amount to almost 700 million searches a month. Enhance claims 1 billion searches throughout its network each month, on sites such as EarthLink and InfoSpace.

Tier 3

Finally, Tier 3. There are many other PPC networks — hundreds, in fact. Some are little more than a scam, encouraging the unwary to pay a setup fee with little real hope of ever getting any traffic.

On the other hand, many can generate a little traffic for you each month; the problem, however, is that you'll spend a huge amount of time managing these Tier 3 companies. In general, it's not worth working with the Tier 3 company directly; rather, it's possible to work with a company that will sell you clicks at a fixed rate, and then gather these clicks from a wide array of Tier 3 PPC systems. (You can find a huge list of PPC systems, over 200 at the time of writing, at payperclicksearchengines.com.)

Where do these ads go?

Refer to Figures 18-1 and 18-2, which show examples of ad placements. Ad placement can vary quite a bit from site to site. Typically, on Google, the first three ads are placed at the top of the search results, and then other ads are run down the right side of the page.

Do the same search at AOL, though, and you find the first three PPC ads are at the top of the page, followed by a whole bunch of natural search results — that is, results that were not paid for — followed by another four or five Google AdWords PPC ads at the bottom of the page. At Ask.com, you find that three PPC ads are at the top, and five are on the bottom. Again, ads run in different positions on different sites, and of course, all this varies periodically. The general trend over the last year has been to stuff more and more ads into search results pages. Some small sites run nothing but paid ads in their search results.

Generally, it's obvious that these placements are paid ads. In most cases, the ads are preceded by the words *Sponsored Links, Sponsored Web Results,* or something similar. In fact, the Federal Trade Commission mandates some kind of indication that a placement is paid. Despite that, there's a definite movement afoot to make it less and less obvious that more and more ads are appearing. AOL, for instance, currently hides all indication of sponsorship unless you actually point at the ad, which causes the ad background to turn gray and the words *Sponsored Link* to appear to the right of the link.

On some small systems, PPC ads run without *any* notification that they're ads. You probably won't see that happen on the large search sites, or with ads being fed by Google AdWords and Yahoo!, but some of the smaller ad networks evidently have lower standards.

By the way, the ads I've shown so far are simple text ads, but PPC companies are starting to allow advertisers to include logos, for instance.

It may not work!

"Half the money I spend on advertising is wasted; the trouble is, I don't know which half."

—*John Wanamaker, 1838–1922*

John Wanamaker's store in Philadelphia — imaginatively named *Wanamaker's* — was probably the world's first department store. He later opened one in New York, and was eventually the Postmaster General, but he's probably best remembered for the preceding quote. (Come on, be honest. Isn't that why you remember him?)

Wanamaker was almost certainly correct. Half (at least) of the money spent on advertising doesn't work, in the sense that the monetary value derived from the advertising is less — often considerably less — than the cost of the advertising. Back in Wanamaker's day, there was very little way to track advertising success. Even today, it's hard to know for sure if advertising works — except for direct mail and online ads. Because it is possible to track viewers' reactions to ads online in various ways, it's possible to track results very carefully, which is how we know that billions of dollars were wasted on banner ads in the last few years of the last century!

And those days are being repeated, thanks to the latest online ad fad, PPC search engine advertising. The boom in banner advertising in the years 1997 or so to 2000 was based on a simple principle: There's always some other idiot who's willing to pay ridiculous advertising rates because he doesn't know any better. The same thing is happening with PPC ads.

Now, I'm not suggesting that you shouldn't use PPC advertising, or that some people aren't using it successfully — some definitely are. I'm just suggesting that you should be careful. In the days of the banner-ad boom, companies were paying excessively for ads, often with little regard (it seemed) for the *metrics* (that is, the measurements; the payoff). And today, many people are paying too much for their clicks, and prices are on the way up.

If someone is paying $1.50 per click for the keywords in which you're also interested, do not assume that you should pay $1.51. A few things to remember:

- ✔ As weird as it may seem, many companies are losing money on their clicks. One company I spoke with was spending almost $300,000 a month on PPC advertising, realizing that they were losing money on the clicks; but, the VP of Marketing told me, they "have to keep the leads coming in." (I'm sure many of you who spend your days working in corporate America will find this easy to believe.)

- ✔ Some companies don't care if they make money on a click; they regard it as merely part of their branding campaign — if a company is used to spending hundreds of millions of dollars on TV ads, for instance, it may not care too much about tracking the direct benefits of a few million spent on PPC ads.

- ✔ Even if the company is making money on the clicks (I know another company spending $150,000 per month on very successful PPC ads), that doesn't mean *you* can make money based on the same click payment.

The last point is essential to understand. Say Company A sells books about rodent racing, making $10 per book after paying production costs. Company B sells racing rodents, and it makes $200 for every racer it sells. The book company is out of luck; there's no way it can compete for clicks against Company B. Company B could pay $50, $100, or more on clicks for every sale it makes; clearly, Company A couldn't.

Here's a quick rule: If your average profit per sale is $10 or $20, then a PPC campaign probably won't work for you. (Probably. It just might, but it's unlikely.)

Ideally, before you begin a PPC advertising campaign, you really should know what a click is worth to your company (realistically, however, this isn't always possible). In the next section, I discuss the value of clicks.

Valuing Your Clicks

In order to calculate a *click value* — the maximum amount it's worth spending for a click — you have to work your way backward from the end result, or the action taken by a visitor to your site.

The value of the action

Every commercial site has some kind of action that the site owner wants the site visitor to carry out: buy a product, pick up the phone and call the company, enter information into a form and request a quote, sign up to receive more information, and so on. You have to understand the value of this action.

Say you're selling a product. How much would you pay me if I brought you a sale? Perhaps you have a product that sells for $50, and it costs $25 to create (or buy) and ship to a customer. Your gross profit, then, is $25, so you could afford to spend up to $25 to get the sale without losing money.

However, the value of the click may actually be higher than this. Imagine, for a moment, that if you sell a product for $50, you have a one-third chance of turning the buyer into a regular customer, and you know that regular customers spend $50 with you every 3 months for 18 months on average. Thus, the lifetime value of your new customer is actually $150, not $25 ($25 per month for 18 months, divided by 3).

Don't let some Internet geek convince you that you should take into consideration lifetime value. If you know you truly do have a lifetime customer value, that's fine, but many millions of dollars have been spent on online advertising based on the concept of an assumed lifetime value, when in fact there was little lifetime value beyond the first sale.

Of course, you may not be selling a product online. You may be gathering leads for your sales staff, or getting people to sign up for a catalog, or taking some other action that isn't the end of the sales process, but in some sense, the beginning. This is more difficult to project; although, if you're working in an established company, it's information you (or someone in your organization) may know. How much does your company pay for sales leads? Most medium-to-large companies know this number.

Your online conversion rate

You have to know your online conversion rate, which you may not know when you begin your PPC campaign. If you have an established Web site that has been in business for a few months or years, then this is useful information that someone in the company should have. For every 1,000 people visiting your site, how many carry out the action you want (buy, call, sign up for more information, and so on)? How many visitors do you convert to customers or sales leads or subscribers (or whatever)?

I said, "For every 1,000 people," not "For every 100 people," for good reason. It may be a number below 1 percent. It may only be 7 or 8 out of every 1,000, for instance. I mention this because many people new to e-commerce do not realize that this is very much a numbers game, and that very low conversion rates are common. Sure, some businesses convert a much higher proportion of their visitors; but many businesses convert 1 percent or less. One would expect that businesses wanting people to fill in a form (to get a quote for insurance or mortgage rates, for instance) would have much higher conversion rates than companies selling products. (One company in this business told me its conversion rate is around 30 percent, for instance.)

Remember that e-commerce is in many ways much closer to the direct mail business than the retail store business. Although people often talk about online stores, commerce sites really are much more like online catalogs. In particular, they share the characteristic of low conversions. The success of direct mail campaigns is often measured in fractions of a percent because it often is online, too.

Figuring the click price

For a company selling a $50 product and making $25 per sale, you can assume that this company doesn't care about the customer's lifetime value, as indeed many small companies don't. (Most of their sales are one-off with little repeat business, or they can't afford to invest in lifetime-value customers anyway; they have to make money on every sale.)

You can also assume that this company has figured its conversion rate is around 2 percent; 1 out of 50 visitors buys the product. You know that each customer is worth a maximum of $25; therefore, a visitor is worth $0.50 ($25 divided by 50).

That is, $0.50 is the most the company could spend for each site visitor without losing money. (The company isn't actually *making* money, of course, and I've left out consideration of the cost of running the Web operation and other company overhead.) If this company discovers that it can buy clicks for $0.75 cents or a dollar, clearly it's going to lose money. If clicks are $0.25, and if these numbers hold true, then it stands to make a gross profit of $12.50 for every sale.

Different clicks equals different values

The preceding is a simplification, of course. In fact, different visitors to your site may be more or less valuable to your company. If Visitor A goes to your site after being told by a friend that your site "sells the best rodent-racing handicap software on the Web," Visitor A is likely to be pretty valuable because he might buy several of your company's products or become a repeat customer. *Much* more valuable than Visitor B, who clicked a link or banner ad that reads something like, "Ever Thought about Rodent Racing?" Visitor A went out of his way on the recommendation of a friend, presumably because he's interested in rodent-racing handicap software. Comparatively, Visitor B may simply be wondering what these idiots are talking about.

It's likely that search engine traffic is actually more valuable than the average value of a visit to your site. Whether a click on a PPC ad or a natural search result, people who come to your site after searching for a particular keyword are likely to be more interested in your products and services than someone who simply stumbles across your site.

Some large companies spend huge amounts of money trying to analyze their traffic carefully — they want to know where every visitor comes from and exactly what each does. Unfortunately, it's difficult for small companies to do this, but at least you need to be aware of this issue when selecting keywords for your PPC campaigns. Note also that the major PPC systems provide additional services that allow you to track results — systems that will help you see what people do when they arrive at your site. You can see how many PPC visitors actually buy your products, for instance, which gives you a solid idea of your site's click value.

They Won't Take My Ad!

One of the most frustrating things to deal with when working with a PPC network is having your ads dropped because they don't match the network's standard. Or, as often happens, because one of the company's editors *thinks* the ad doesn't match the network's standards, or even because your Web site isn't acceptable.

While some of the Tier 2 networks are much less fussy, Google, Yahoo!, and MSN have very strict guidelines about what sort of Web page or Web site your ads can link to. Each network is different, but the following are the type of things that can kill your ad campaign on one of the top PPC networks:

✔ Your site requires a password. Personally, I think if you're stupid enough to point an ad to a password-protected Web site, the PPC network should take your money and run.

✔ Your site's content doesn't match the ad. Perhaps you have a very weak ad that simply doesn't provide much information about the subject area you're advertising.

✔ Your ad contains abusive, objectionable, or threatening language.

✔ Your site appears to facilitate the use or distribution of illegal drugs. Yahoo!, for instance, won't take ads for sites that sell kits intended to help people cheat on drug tests.

✔ The landing page specified in your ad doesn't contain content related to the ad or have an obvious path to the related content.

✔ You used a trademarked term in your ad, but there's no content related to that product on your Web site.

✔ Your ad doesn't explain that the product you're selling on your site can only be shipped to a very limited area.

✔ Your site includes multilevel marketing. Such sites aren't allowed to use the terms *job* and *employment* on some PPC systems, but may use the terms *business opportunity* and *work*.

✔ You don't own the page you are linking to. Rules vary between systems; if you're an affiliate, you may have to link to your own page and then direct visitors to the retailer's site, for instance.

✔ The ad promises information that isn't on your site, but that will be delivered in some manner — by e-mail or snail mail, for instance — and the ad doesn't state that fact.

✔ Your site doesn't function in Internet Explorer.

✔ You're using a term that isn't allowed for your business. For instance, a finance company may not bid on the word *car* at Yahoo!

✔ Your auction site bids on terms related to products not currently on sale at the site.

- ✔ Your site contains content that may not be legal, is in some other way objectionable, or links to such a site.

- ✔ Your ad contains *superlatives* (biggest; best; greatest), ALL CAPS, or exclamation points!

- ✔ Your Web site disables the browser's Back button.

- ✔ Your Web site contains many broken links or malfunctions in some other way.

- ✔ Your ad's language doesn't match the language of the target Web site. If your ad is written in Spanish, it can't direct people to an English-language Web site.

- ✔ Your ad contains contact information, such as phone numbers and e-mail addresses.

- ✔ Your site spawns a pop-up window when the visitor arrives.

Phew! This isn't all of it, either.

Check your ads carefully after they've been accepted. Editors may change things without telling you, sometimes turning your finely tuned prose into something significantly different.

Why are the PPC networks so fussy? Surely, if you're paying, who cares if your site is broken or if your ad isn't relevant to the keywords you chose? It's your money, after all. Well, the networks are trying to achieve the following:

- ✔ They want as many of the ads as possible to be clicked; they don't want to clutter that valuable advertising space with irrelevant ads that nobody clicks because the networks are paid only when a searcher clicks.

- ✔ They want to protect the relevance of the search results. PPC ads now make up a significant proportion of search results. (In many cases, in particular with the smaller PPC networks, 100 percent of the first screen of results seen by the searcher is paid ads.) So, it's as important for paid results to be relevant as it is for natural search results.

Automating the Task

Working with PPC campaigns can be rather tedious. Ideally, you've got to keep your eye on the rankings each day or your ad could slip. In very competitive markets, it may be necessary to check several times a day. You may be using half a dozen systems, too. If you're working with thousands of keywords (one client has 4,000–5,000 keywords to manage), that's a huge job.

Super-lative

What makes following the rules all the more difficult is that the editors enforcing the rules often don't have a full understanding of the rules themselves. One Yahoo! editor may tell you that *all* superlatives are banned; another might tell you that they're okay in some contexts. An ad I ran for a client used the term *largest warehouse,* which I was told was okay by one editor after having the ad killed by another. (It was okay, I was told, because it was a "secondary superlative" that didn't directly relate to the search term. That's one of the unwritten rules you just have to stumble across.) And in another ad, the term *our latest discounts* became a problem. "Other companies may have more recent discounts," I was told. After pointing out that the superlative referred to my clients' discounts, not everyone else's, they let it through. And when advertising a product in the city of Superior, Colorado, the ad was killed because the word *superior* is a superlative! PPC editors are a huge frustration for many PPC marketers; it seems that everyone managing large PPC campaigns has their own "stupid PPC editor" story!

How do you handle all this without it getting totally out of control? Here are a few ideas:

- ✔ Many companies hire a full-time person, even two or three people, just to manage their PPC campaigns.

- ✔ Programs are available that help automate PPC management across multiple systems. Atlas Search (www.atlassolutions.com) and BidRank (www.bidrank.com) are a couple of well-known systems, but various other products are available.

- ✔ Some companies hire a third party to manage their PPC campaigns.

There's no easy answer. Automation software may be a good idea if you have a significant PPC campaign — tens or hundreds of thousands of dollars a month, with thousands of keywords over multiple PPC networks. Having used one of the major automation systems, I have to say it was complicated, buggy, and expensive — not something you would want to use for a simple PPC campaign. (That was some time ago. I'm hopeful that PPC management software is better now.)

Sometimes, it's actually cheaper to hire someone to manage the PPC campaign. One client, spending $150,000 per month on PPC, switched from having another company manage its PPC campaign to doing it itself. I estimated that the employee in charge of the PPC program probably spent two to three hours a day managing the program, and after my client realized that it could hire a full-time person to manage the program for 25 percent of what it was paying for another company to manage the PPC campaign, switching was easy!

Some companies use this strategy: They manage Google, Yahoo!, and perhaps two or three of the other, more-productive Tier 2 systems in-house, perhaps using software if they have a very big keyword list. Then they use a PPC management company, or software, such as Atlas Search or BidRank, to buy keywords from the smaller Tier 2 and Tier 3 PPC companies at a fixed price per click. For instance, you may agree to pay $0.35 per click. The management company then uses dozens, maybe hundreds, of smaller systems to get those clicks for you, keeping the difference between what they actually pay for the clicks (perhaps $0.05) and your $0.35.

Part V
The Part of Tens

"So far our web presence has been pretty good.
We've gotten some orders, a few inquiries,
and nine guys who want to date our logo."

In this part . . .

After you've got the basics of search engine optimization under your belt, this final part of the book gives you one last push in the right direction.

I talk about a number of myths and mistakes that are common in the search engine business. (No, you're *not* getting a #1 position on Google for $25; and yes, you should start thinking about search engines before you build your site.)

This part also points you in the direction of some great information resources, places where you can find out more about search engine optimization or get info on a particular search engine technique. I also tell you about useful tools to help you in your endeavors, from programs that help you analyze the traffic coming to your Web site to link checkers and search-rank tools.

Chapter 19

Ten-Plus Ways to Stay Updated

In This Chapter

▶ Staying updated with search engine technology
▶ Finding detailed information for particular projects
▶ Getting information directly from search engines
▶ Discovering what people are searching for
▶ Finding people to help you

*T*he naysayers said it couldn't be done, that a book about search engine optimization couldn't be written because the technology is changing so quickly. That's not entirely true — the basics really don't change, such as creating pages that search engines can read, picking good keywords, getting lots of links into your site, and so on.

But some details do change. Which are the most important search engines? What tricks are search engines really clamping down on? Why did your site suddenly drop out of Google (as many thousands did in the fall/winter of 2003, in the fall of 2007, and on various occasions in between)?

You may also need more detailed information than I can provide in this book. Perhaps you have a problem with dynamic pages, and you need to know the details of URL rewriting for a particular Web server, for instance. You need to know where to go to find more information. In this chapter, I provide you resources that you can use to keep up-to-date and track down the details.

Let Me Help Some More

Visit my Web site at www.SearchEngineBulletin.com. I point you to important resources, provide links to all the Web pages listed in this book (so you can just click instead of typing them), and provide important updates.

I also provide consulting services, including phone consultations. I can examine a company's online strategy not just from the perspective of search engines, but also from a wider view; I've been working online for 20 years now, and have experience in Web design, e-commerce and online transactions, traffic conversion, non–search engine traffic generation, and so on. An hour or two of advice can often save a company from the huge expense of going down the wrong path!

The Search Engines Themselves

One of the best ways to find information about search engines is by using carefully crafted search terms at the search engines themselves. Say you want to find detailed information about dealing with session IDs (see Chapter 7). You can go to Google and search for *search engine session id*. Or perhaps you have a problem with dynamic URLs, and know that you need to use something called *mod_rewrite*. Go to a search engine and search for *mod_rewrite* or *mod rewrite*. (The former is the correct term, while many people talk of *mod rewrite* in the vernacular.)

It's amazing what you can find if you dig around for a little while. A few minutes' research through the search engines can save you many hours of time wasted through inefficient or ineffective SEO techniques. I suggest you read the bonus chapter posted at `www.dummies.com/go/seofd3e`, which explains various techniques for searching at Google. A good understanding of how to use search engines will pay dividends.

Google's Webmaster Pages

Google is happy to tell you what it wants from you and what it doesn't like. No, it won't tell you exactly how it figures out search result rankings, but good information is there nonetheless. It's a good idea to review the advice pages Google provides for Webmasters. You can find them at the following URLs:

✔ **Google Webmaster Guidelines:**
`www.google.com/webmasters/guidelines.html`

✔ **Google Webmaster Help Center:** `www.google.com/support/webmasters/`

Yahoo!'s Search Help

Yahoo!'s search engine is the world's second most important, so perusing the Yahoo! Search Help area may be a good use of your time. You'll find information about how to use the system and how to work with it to get your pages indexed. See `http://help.yahoo.com/l/us/yahoo/search/`.

The bonus chapter I mention earlier covers Google, not Yahoo!, so if you want to know more about how to use Yahoo!'s search engine, take a look at the Search Tips, Advanced Search, and Yahoo! Shortcuts pages. (The shortcuts allow you to search for airport information, exchange rates, gas prices, patents, U.S. Post Office, FedEx, UPS packages, and more.)

MSN/Live Search's SEO Tips

You can find information about optimizing pages for submission to MSN/Live Search at `http://search.msn.com/docs`. You'll find a wide range of information, from how the MSNbot works to how to handle a site move.

Ask.com FAQ

One more for you. Ask.com has a limited amount of information for Webmasters at `http://about.ask.com/en/docs/about/webmasters.shtml`.

Search Engine Watch

The Search Engine Watch site gives you a great way to keep up with what's going on in the search engine world. This site provides a ton of information about a very wide range of subjects related not only to search engine optimization, but also the flip side of the coin — subjects related to searching online. In fact, perhaps its greatest weakness is that it provides *so much* information; it's really intended for search engine optimization experts rather than the average Webmaster or site manager. The site is divided into a free area and a paid-subscription area.

Visit the site at `www.searchenginewatch.com`.

The Official Google Webmaster Help Group

Google Groups hosts a very useful resource, the *Official Google Webmaster Help Group,* which has tens of thousands of members and hundreds of thousands of archived messages. It's a great way to find out what people in the business are saying about, well, just about anything.

`http://groups.google.com/group/Google_Webmaster_Help`

Google's Inside Scoop

Here are a couple of great ways to peep into the mind of Google:

- ✔ **Google Webmaster Central Blog:** A very useful site; a blog with information from actual employees of Google providing the Google view of search engine optimization. Visit `http://googlewebmastercentral.blogspot.com`.

- ✔ **MattCutts.com:** Matt Cutts is a well-known employee of Google (well known in SEO circles, that is). He's currently head of Google's "Webspam team," and writes in his blog about a wide range of issues, including many SEO issues. Go to `http://www.mattcutts.com/blog` to see what he has to say.

WebMaster World

WebMaster World (`www.webmasterworld.com`) is a very good discussion group, with many knowledgeable people. It'll cost ya, though: $89 for six months, or $150 for a year.

HighRankings.com

Hosted by a search engine optimization consultant, HighRankings.com is a pretty busy forum (free at this time) with discussions covering a wide range of subjects. Check it out at `www.highrankings.com/forum`.

Yahoo!'s Search Engine Optimization Resources Category

This is a good place to find a variety of resources related to search engine optimization: companies, online services, information resources, and so on. Check it out at `dir.yahoo.com/Computers_and_Internet/Internet/World_Wide_Web/Site_Announcement_and_Promotion/Search_Engine_Optimization__SEO_`.

The Open Directory Project Search Categories

Of course, the Open Directory Project also has a number of useful search categories:

- dmoz.org/Computers/Internet/Searching
- dmoz.org/Computers/Internet/Searching/Search_Engines
- dmoz.org/Computers/Internet/Searching/Directories
- dmoz.org/Computers/Internet/Searching/Search_Engines/ Specialized

You might also visit www.resource-zone.com, where you can find forums hosted by Open Directory Project editors who may be able to help you with DMOZ-related issues.

Get the Search Engine Buzz

If you want to find out what people are doing with search engines — popular searches, for instance — then check out some of these services.

Google Zeitgeist is an analysis of what people are searching for, when, and where. You can find the most popular brand-name searches, charts showing how searches peak for particular keywords during news events or in response to TV shows, the most popular searches for particular men, women, and fictional characters, the most popular movie searches in Australia, the most popular brands in Italy, and so on. Google provides weekly, monthly, and annual reports. Check it out at www.google.com/press/zeitgeist.html.

Other, similar tools are

- **Google Trends:** This is a very cool tool; enter a list of search terms, separated by commas, and Google displays a chart showing how often the terms have been searched over a particular time range, along with news stories correlated with particular peaks. You can even select a particular country.

- **Wordtracker:** Wordtracker periodically sends you a free report of the top 500 searches — with or without sexually explicit terms (www.word tracker.com).

- **Ask.com IQ (Interesting Queries):** A service showing you the top search terms and the top *advancing* search terms — the ones that are growing most quickly (`http://sp.ask.com/en/docs/iq/iq.shtml`).

- **Yahoo! Buzz:** "What the world is searching for," says Yahoo!. Information categorized in many ways (`buzz.yahoo.com`).

- **The Lycos 50:** More good information (`50.lycos.com`).

What I find depressing about these lists is just how obsessed people are with celebrities! Why do people care so much about who is marrying Jenna Bush, what act of stupidity Britney Spears has just committed, or who Paris Hilton is, um, dating?

Chapter 20

Ten Myths and Mistakes

In This Chapter

▶ Common mistakes made by site developers

▶ Harmful myths

▶ Problems that hurt your search engine rank

A lot of confusion exists in the search engine world; a lot of myths and a lot of mistakes. In this chapter, I quickly run through a few of the ideas and omissions that can hurt your search engine positions.

Myth: It's All about Meta Tags and Submissions

This is the most pervasive and harmful myth of all, held by many Web designers and developers. All you need, many believe, is to code your pages with the right meta tags — KEYWORDS and DESCRIPTION, and things like REVISIT-AFTER and CLASSIFICATION — and then submit your site to the search engines. I know Web designers who tell their clients that they'll "handle" search engine optimization, and then follow nothing more than this procedure.

It's completely wrong for various reasons. Most meta tags aren't particularly important (see Chapter 6), if used by search engines at all. Without keywords in the page content, search engines won't index what you need them to index. (See Chapters 6 and 7.) Submitting to search engines doesn't mean they'll index your pages. (See Chapter 11.) Moreover, what about links? (See Chapters 14 through 16.)

Myth: Web Designers and Developers Understand Search Engines

I'm a geek. I've worked in software development for more than 25 years. I still work closely with software developers (these days mostly Web-software developers) and Web designers; I build Web sites for my clients (so I work with developers and designers on these sites); my friends are developers and designers, and I'm telling you now that most developers and designers do *not* understand search engines to any great degree.

Most Web-development companies these days tell their clients that they know how to handle search engines, and even that they're experts. In most cases, that's simply not true; no more than it's true that I'm an expert in neurosurgery. This makes it very hard for business owners when they hire a Web-development team, of course, though perhaps this book will help. It will give you an idea of the sorts of questions you should ask your developers so you can figure out if they really *do* understand search engine requirements.

In addition, many Web developers don't enjoy working with search marketing experts. They think that all search engine experts want is to make the site ugly or remove the dynamism. This is farthest from the truth, and a Web developer who refuses to work with an SEO expert may just be worried for his or her job.

Myth: Multiple Submissions Improve Your Search Position

As far as the major search engines go, multiple submissions, even automated submissions, don't help. Someone recently told me that he was sure it did help because his position improved in, for instance, the Open Directory Project when he frequently resubmitted. This is completely wrong — in the case of the Open Directory Project, there's no way it could possibly help, as all entries have to be reviewed by a human editor and submitting multiple times is more likely to annoy the editor instead of convince him to let you in!

As you just read, *submitting* to search engines — requesting that they index your pages — often doesn't get your page indexed anyway. Far more important is a link campaign to get plenty of links to your site; see Chapters 14 through 16. And you should definitely be working with XML sitemaps (see Chapter 11). Multiple submissions to smaller search engines may help. But it won't help with the major systems. Some of these multiple-submission services are little more than a scam; in fact, on a number of occasions, I've reviewed the "here's where we submit your site to" lists for some of these services, and found out-of-business search engines included.

Mistake: You Don't Know Your Keywords

This is also a major problem — the vast majority of Web sites are created without the site owners or developers really knowing what keywords are important. (That's okay, perhaps, because most sites are built without any idea of using keywords in the content anyway.) At best, the keywords have been guessed. At worst — the majority of the cases — nobody's thought of the keywords at all.

Don't guess at your keywords. Do a proper keyword analysis. (See Chapter 5.) I can almost guarantee two things will happen. You'll find that some of your guesses were wrong — people aren't often using some of the phrases you thought would be common. You'll also discover very important phrases you had no idea about.

Mistake: Too Many Pages with Database Parameters and Session IDs

This is a surprisingly common problem. Many, many sites (in particular, sites built by big companies with large development teams) are created these days in such a manner that search engines won't read them. Search engines don't like database parameters or session IDs in a URL. (See Chapter 7.)

My favorite example used to be CarToys.com, a large chain of electronics stores. This site had thousands of products, but fewer than 100 pages indexed by Google, and most of those were Adobe Acrobat files, pop-up ads ("Free Shipping!"), or links to dynamic pages that wouldn't appear when a searcher clicked a link in the search results. Luckily for CarToys.com, someone at the company figured it all out, fixed the problem, and Google then picked up tens of thousands of pages.

Mistake: Building the Site and Then Bringing in the SEO Expert

Most companies approach search engine optimization as an afterthought. They build their Web site, and then think, "Right, time to get people to the site." You really shouldn't begin a site until you have considered all the different ways you're going to create traffic to the site. That's like starting to build a road without knowing where it needs to go; if you're not careful, you'll get halfway there and realize "there" is in another direction.

In particular, though, you shouldn't start building a Web site without an understanding of search engines. Most major Web sites these days are built by teams of developers who have little understanding of search engine issues. These sites are launched, and then someone decides to hire a search engine consultant. And the search engine consultant discovers all sorts of unnecessary problems. Good business for the consultant; expensive fixes for the site owner.

Myth: $25 Can Get Your Site a #1 Position

You hear a lot of background noise in the search engine business from companies claiming to be able to get your site into thousands of search engines and rank your site well for $25 a month. . . . Or a $50 flat fee . . . or $75 a month . . . or whatever.

The truth is that it's more complicated than that, and most people I've spoken to who have used such services have been very disappointed. They often don't get into the major search engines at all, and even if they get included in the index, they don't rank well. Search engine ranking is sometimes very easy — but other times it's complicated, time consuming, and tedious. Most of the offers streaming into your Inbox in spam e-mail messages or displayed in banner ads on the Web aren't going to work.

Myth: Google Partners Get You #1 Positions

If you receive a spam e-mail telling you that the sender has a "special arrangement" with Google and can get you a #1 position within hours or days, delete it; it's nonsense — a scam. It's true that you can buy a top position on Google through its AdWords PPC program (see Chapter 18), though you'll be bidding against your competitors. However, this scam refers to something different — to Google having a special program that allows certain privileged companies to sell top positions in the organic-search results.

Don't believe it; it's nonsense.

Mistake: You Don't Have Pages Optimized for Specific Keywords

Have you built pages optimized for your most important keywords? I spoke recently with a firm that ranked pretty well — #5 in the search results — for his most desired keyword phrase, but not well enough (obviously, the site owner wanted #1).

The funny thing was that he was doing very well considering the fact that he didn't have a single page optimized for the keyword phrase he desired. Sure, he had pages close, pages that had the individual words in the keyword phrase scattered throughout the page, but not a single page that was fully optimized for the phrase.

Therefore, think about your most important phrases. Do you have pages *fully optimized* — the phrase at the beginning of the `<TITLE>` tag, at the beginning of the `<DESCRIPTION>` tag, in `<H1>` tags, scattered throughout the page, and so on — for all these phrases? If not, maybe you don't *deserve* the #1 spot!

Mistake: Your Pages Are Empty

This one is a huge problem for many companies; the pages have nothing much for search engines to index. In some cases, the pages have little or no text that a search engine can read because the words on the page are embedded into images. In other cases, the words may be real text but are very few and aren't the right keywords.

Remember, search engines like — need — content. To a search engine, *content* means text that it can read and index. Whenever you provide text to a search engine, it should do the most for you — help you to be found in the search results. And the more content, the better.

Myth: Pay Per Click Is Where It's At

Pay per click (*PPC;* see Chapter 18) can be a very important part of a Web site's marketing strategy. It's reliable, predictable, and relatively easy to work with. But it's not the only thing you should be doing. In fact, many companies cannot use PPC because the clicks are too expensive for their particular business model (and click prices are likely to keep rising as search marketing continues to be the hot Internet marketing topic).

The growth in PPC has been partly caused by the lack of search engine optimization knowledge. Companies build a site without thinking about search engines, and then don't hire professional expertise to help them get search engine traffic, so they fall back on PPC. Many companies are now spending hundreds of thousands of dollars on PPC each month; they could complement their PPC campaigns with natural search engine traffic for a small fraction of that cost.

The wonderful thing about PPC advertising and SEO is that the two work hand in hand. If you want to know whether a word is important enough to optimize, get a hundred clicks from your favorite search engine through PPC and look at the conversion rates and the return on investment (ROI). Want to expand your PPC keyword list? No problem, look at the words that people are already using to find you as a baseline, and grow your list from these words. (For example, if they are using *rodent racing* to find you, buy the words *mouse rodent racing, rat rodent racing,* and so on.) Many companies are using PPC profitably; just don't assume it's the only way to go.

Chapter 21

Ten-Plus Useful Things to Know

*I*n this chapter, I describe a number of useful little things to know, from 301 redirects to Google's enhanced image search; from various information sources to how Google creates multi-line search result entries.

Creating Multi-Line Search Results

You've probably seen multi-line search results, such as those shown in Figure 21-1.

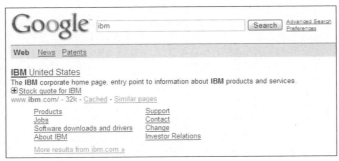

Figure 21-1: Google adds sitelinks to the results for some popular sites.

How does this happen? More important, how can you make it happen for your site?

Google calls these internal site links, um, *sitelinks,* and they're intended to help users find their way into popular pages within popular sites. Google actually analyzes the site, and tries to figure which pages are significant. At the time of writing, there's no way for you to tell Google which pages to use (though Google says that they may allow Webmaster input in the future—and because you're reading this book *after* I wrote it, the future may be now). In fact, Google only does this for very popular sites, so it's just not an option for most. Therefore, the first step in getting Google to provide these links for your site is to move your site into the list of the world's top 1,000 Web sites.

However, if you're fortunate enough to be in this happy situation but don't like one of the pages that Google is using as a sitelink, you can tell them not to use it. Log into your Webmaster account (see Chapter 11), click the Links link in the left-hand navbar, and then click the Sitelinks link.

What Is Enhanced Image Search?

Google's *enhanced image search* service is an optional service by which Google correlates labels — keywords — with images in your site. It may make your images more likely to appear in search results. One tool Google uses to label images is Image Labeler, a "game" in which people view images and race to provide as many tags as they can (see `http://images.google.com/imagelabeler/`; no, I don't know why people play this!).

How, then, to get Google to add labels to your images? You sign in to your Google Webmaster account (see Chapter 11), select the site, select Tools, and then Enable Enhanced Image Search.

Checking Your Site Rank

How do you know how well your site ranks in the search engines? You can go to a search engine, type a keyword phrase, and see what happens. If you're not on the first page, check the second; if you're not there, check the third. Then go back and do it for 50 search terms on several search engines. It's going to take a while.

Luckily there's help. Many programs can check your search engine position for you. You tell the program which keywords you're interested in, which search engines you want to check, the Web site you're looking for in the search results, and then leave it to do its work.

Most search engines don't like these automated tools. In fact, Google even mentions one of the most popular of these tools, WebPosition (available at www.webposition.com and shown in Figure 21-2), as "unauthorized software." If Google notices a computer is using one of these tools excessively, zit may ban search queries from that computer — if it can identify the computer's Internet protocol (IP) number, that is.

The problem for Google is that computers accessing the Internet through many Internet service providers (ISPs) have different IP numbers each time they log on, making it impossible for Google to know which IP number to block. On the other hand, Google now provides a special Application Programming Interface (API) that programs like WebPosition can use to send queries directly to Google, bypassing the search page. Such access *is* okay. (You can find information about the Google API at www.google.com/apis.)

You can see a typical keyword report, showing positions for each keyword in a large variety of search engines — in this case, produced by WebPosition — in Figure 21-3. Many other programs can create site-ranking reports for you — both programs installed on your computer and Web-based services, such as WebCEO (www.webceo.com) and SEO Reporter (www.seoreporter.com).

Here's a quick tip for a quick rank check. Go to Google and click the Advanced Search link. Select 100 Results from the drop-down box at the top of the page that appears, enter your keywords into the top text box, and then click the Google Search button. You'll see 100 search results, rather than the normal 10, and you can search the page looking for your site.

Figure 21-2: WebPosition being set up to check a page's rank in the search engines.

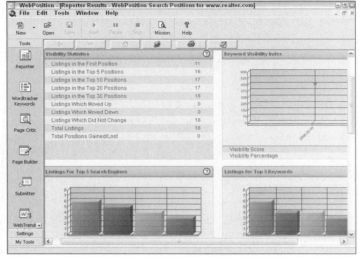

Figure 21-3:
A page
rank report
generated
by Web-
Position.

Checking for Broken Links

Link checkers are always handy, whether you're interested in optimizing your site for the search engines or not. After you've created a few pages, run a link check to make sure you didn't make any mistakes in your links.

Again, many, many link checkers are available, including paid services, such as LinkAlarm (linkalarm.com), that will automatically check links on your site and send you a report. I'm currently using a little Windows program called Xenu's Link Sleuth, as shown in Figure 21-4 (home.snafu.de/ tilman/xenulink.html). It's free, which is always nice! (The creator of Link Sleuth requests that if you like the program, support some of his favorite causes.) This program is very quick — checking tens of thousands of links in a few minutes — and very easy to use. It produces a report, displayed in your Web browser, showing the pages containing broken links. Click a link, and the page opens so you can take a look. You can use the program to check both internal and external links on your site.

Note also that your Web design software package may include a built-in link checker.

Google Toolbar

The Google toolbar (`toolbar.google.com`) is a great little tool. I mainly use it for two purposes:

- Searching Google without having to go to the Google site first.
- Seeing if a Web page is in Google's cache, as discussed in Chapter 1. To see the cache, click the *i* button and then click Cached Snapshot of Page.

The Google toolbar contains a number of other neat tools:

- The ability to quickly search Google Maps. Click the Autolink button; the toolbar searches the current page for a street address and converts it to a link that opens the appropriate map on Google Maps.
- PageRank indicator. Discussed in Chapter 14, PageRank can be useful when evaluating a potential link partner.
- Pop-up blocker.
- A way to search Google for pages similar to the one you're viewing.

The toolbar has all sorts of other useful things.

Alexa Toolbar

The Alexa toolbar (`download.alexa.com`) can be handy, too. I sometimes use it to assess the traffic of Web sites I may want to work with. For instance, if someone approaches you trying to sell advertising space on a site, how do you know whether it's a good deal? So many sites get almost no traffic that it may not be worth the expense.

The Alexa toolbar can give you a very general idea of whether the site gets any traffic at all; you can view traffic details for the site, such as the *traffic rank,* an estimate of the number of visitors to the site out of every million Internet users, and so on. Reportedly, Alexa's numbers are pretty good for the world's most popular sites, but rather inaccurate for the average site. However, you can still get a general feel. If the site is ranked 4,000,000, you can bet it doesn't get much traffic at all. If the site is ranked 4,000, it's far more popular.

Alexa also provides a list of the most popular sites in thousands of categories; a good way to track down affiliates, for instance, or link partners. Moreover, it has an interesting search function; use the Alexa toolbar to search Google, and you get different results. Sites are ranked differently, though the data comes from Google, and you get small images of the home page of the top few sites. Additionally, point at the Site Info link to see site information, such as how long the site has been online, the number of sites linking to it, similar sites, and so on.

Install Firebug

Firebug (shown in Figure 21-5) is a fantastic Firefox browser add-on. It allows you to quickly analyze a Web site. That is, to look into the site code while looking at the Web page. Click a page component, and you see the code that creates it — great for finding those pesky `nofollow` tags in links, for instance.

If you're not using Firefox, you probably should anyway. It's a great browser. So, once installed, choose Tools⇨Add-ons and then click the Get Extensions link in the Add-ons dialog box. When the Firefox Add-ons Web page appears, search for Firebug.

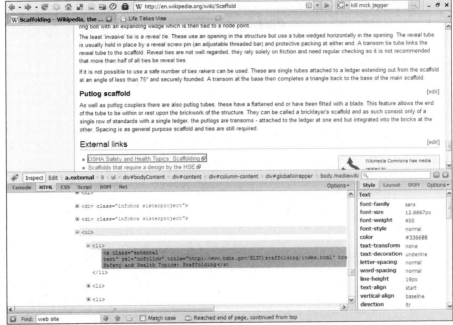

Figure 21-5:
Firebug is a great tool for analyzing Web pages.

Seeing What Search Engines See

I admit I don't often use this type of tool, but it's interesting now and then. Some utilities read a Web page and then display the content of the page in the manner in which a search engine is likely to see it; see Figure 21-6. When looking at a competitor's pages, you can sometimes see things that aren't visible to the site visitor but are on the page for the benefit of the search engines. When viewing your pages, you may want to check that all the links are readable by the search engines. These tools generally provide a list of readable links.

Here are a couple of these utilities:

- ✔ **SEO Tools Spider:** `http://www.webconfs.com/search-engine-spider-simulator.php`
- ✔ **Delorie:** `www.delorie.com/web/ses.cgi`

You can also search for *search engine simulator* or *searchbot simulator*.

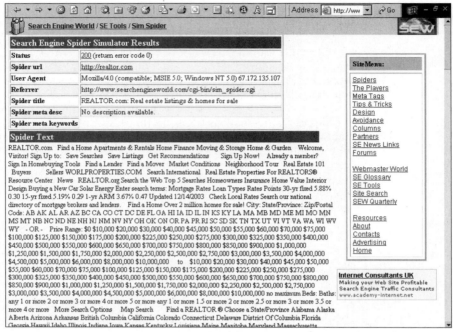

Figure 21-6:
The results
from Search
Engine
World's Sim
Spider.

Another great way to get an idea of what search engines are seeing is to turn off page "styles" in the Firefox browser. Choose View⇨Page Style⇨No Style. It's not quite the same as a spider emulator, but it's a good way to see how a stylesheet may be modifying the way in which a page appears in the browser.

Finding Your Keyword Density

As I explain in Chapter 5, you don't need to get too hung up on keyword density. You can analyze to the nth degree, and everyone has a different opinion as to exactly what the density should be. But it's sometimes interesting to check your pages for keyword density, and many tools are available to help you do so. WebPosition, mentioned earlier in this chapter, has a built-in density tool, and you can find various online tools as well, such as the following:

- ✔ **SEO Tool's Keyword Density Analyzer:** http://www.seochat.com/seo-tools/keyword-density/

- ✔ **KeywordDensity.com:** www.keyworddensity.com

Analyzing Your Site's Traffic

You really should track traffic going to your site. At the end of the day, your search engine position isn't terribly important — it's just a means to an end. What really counts is the amount of traffic coming to your site. And it's important to know *how* people get to your site, too.

The two types of traffic-analysis tools are those that read server logs, and those that tag your Web pages and track traffic by using a program on another server. In the first case, the tool analyzes log files created by the Web server — the server adds information each time it receives a request for a file. In order to use the tag systems, you have to add a little piece of code to your Web pages — each time a page from your site is requested, the program is, in effect, informed of the fact.

You quite likely have a traffic-analysis tool already installed on your site — ask your server administrator how to view your logs. Otherwise, you can use a tag-based traffic-analysis tool; in general, you have to pay a monthly fee for such a service.

Analysis tools show you all sorts of interesting (and often useless) information. But perhaps the most important things you can find are

✔ Which sites are sending visitors to your site

✔ Which search engines are sending visitors to your site

✔ What keywords are people using to reach your site

You may find that people are reaching you with keywords that you hadn't thought of, or perhaps unusual combinations of keywords that you hadn't imagined. This doesn't replace a real keyword analysis, though, as you'll only see the keywords used by people who found you, not the keywords used by people who *didn't* find you but were looking for products or services like yours. See Chapter 5 for more information about keywords.

Unfortunately, most traffic-analysis tools really aren't very good. Some don't provide much information, but the ones that do provide a lot of information are often way too complex and confusing. One log-based system I really like is ClickTracks (www.clicktracks.com). ClickTracks, shown in Figure 21-7, was created by someone who worked for one of the top log tools companies who felt that the popular tools just threw statistics at people instead of providing useful, easy-to-understand information. This is a very cool tool that uses tables and images of your Web site to make understanding your logs very easy. ClickTracks also has a tag-based tool that you can use for a monthly fee.

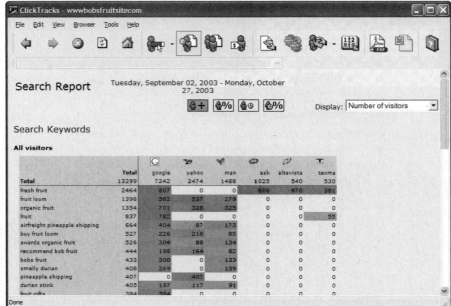

Figure 21-7:
Log analysis
from
ClickTracks.

The big news in traffic analysis, though, is Google Analytics. Google purchased one of the top traffic-analysis firms, Urchin, and then started *giving away* traffic-analysis accounts. At the time of writing, Google isn't allowing new account sign ups — they were so swamped with applications that they couldn't keep up — but by the time you read this book, you may be able to use the system. Visit `analytics.google.com`.

Checking for Duplication and Theft

Copyscape (`www.copyscape.com`) is an interesting tool that allows you to see whether anyone has stolen your site content, and to see how closely your content matches other sites. For instance, if you're quoting documents or using syndicated content, the less duplication, the better. The concern is that search engines may downgrade pages that they know duplicate other pages, so you don't want your pages to match others too closely.

Enter a URL into Copyscape, and it searches for pages that match the page referenced by the URL, to varying degrees. Copyscape returns the results, and when you click the links, you see the page with the matching text colored and, at the top, a Copyscape banner telling you how many words match. An interesting little toy; experiment and see.

More Tools

If you're looking for more tools, try these sites:

- ✔ **SEO Help:** www.seo-help.com/seo-reference/seo-resources.html
- ✔ **Webconfs.com:** www.webconfs.com
- ✔ **Pandia SEO:** www.pandia.com/optimization

Using 301 Redirects

301 redirects tell search engines that a particular URL really points to another URL. Google uses a 301, for instance, to point google.com to www.google.com (try it, you'll see).

301s are especially useful when moving pages or changing domain names. They're very easy for server administrators; about the only time you have problems with 301 redirects is when your site is a shared hosting account on a Windows server.

Search for *301 redirect* in Google, and you find plenty of information.

What Is Universal Search?

Have you heard the fuss about Google's *universal search*? Early in the summer of 2007, Google announced that it was going to create a "universal search model that will offer users a more integrated and comprehensive way to search for and view information online." Since then, not a lot has happened.

Here's how Google describes this concept:

> Google's vision for universal search is to ultimately search across all its content sources, compare and rank all the information in real time, and deliver a single, integrated set of search results that offers users precisely what they are looking for. Beginning today, the company will incorporate information from a variety of previously separate sources — including videos, images, news, maps, books, and websites — into a single set of results. At first, universal search results may be subtle. Over time, users will recognize additional types of content integrated into their search results as the company advances toward delivering a truly comprehensive search experience.

What's it mean to you? Probably not a lot. Just keep on doing what you're doing from an SEO perspective. If you have different types of content, sure, optimize them and get them indexed. But, universal search *does not,* at present, change anything dramatically.

Don't Forget the Search Engines

Don't forget that you can find just about anything through the search engines themselves. If you have a tedious procedure to work through, chances are someone has built a program to automate the procedure. So head to your favorite search engine and spend a little time tracking it down!

Appendix

Staying Out of Copyright Jail

· ·

In Chapter 9, I describe several sources of content for your Web site. Because you can get into trouble if you take copyrighted materials without permission, I feel it's important to cover a few copyright basics.

Many people think that they're allowed to take and use pretty much anything they find, especially if it can be found on the Internet. Search for *usa today,* for instance, and you discover thousands of sites that have copied articles from that newspaper. Although you can do this and may get away with it, you should be aware that you don't have the right to do this. It is, to put it bluntly, plagiarism. It's illegal, and the owner of the material has the right to sue you. Whether text, images, sounds, or whatever — if someone else created it, you don't own it!

I summarize copyright law in Chapter 9, and this appendix goes into a little more detail about the four exceptions I describe:

- ✔ If it's really old, you can use it.
- ✔ If the guvmint created it, you can use it.
- ✔ If it's *donated,* you can use it.
- ✔ It's only fair — *fair use* explained.

If It's Really Old, You Can Use It

In some cases in which you find old works that would be appropriate for your site, you can simply take content and do what you want with it. In the old days, copyrights didn't last very long — a real contrast with the situation today.

Copyright is intended to allow the creator to profit from a work, and his worthless children to live a life of drunkenness and unmerited indolence. (Luckily for my kids, computer books have a very short life.) Forget the details for works created after January 1, 1978, because you probably won't be alive when the copyright expires. (I will. Having done research for a book I'm going to call *Live Forever or Die Trying,* I've learned a few tricks.) Let me just say, by way of example, that the copyright on a work created on January 1, 1978, by a 19-year-old writer who manages to live to 89, will expire in the year 2118. (No, that's not a joke.)

The situation for works created before 1978 gets complicated because the law kept changing and seems to have been intended to confuse. I'm not going to go into details — it makes my head hurt just to think about. It all depends on whether you are Uruguayan, are quick on your toes, were 28 on January 1, 1964, and have a Swiss-born mother. However . . .

Anything copyrighted — and by that I mean either published or registered with the U.S. Copyright Office — after January 1, 1964, is out of bounds for the foreseeable future (at least until 2059).

Works copyrighted between 1923 (at the time of writing in 2008) and December 31, 1963, may have lost copyright-protection, depending on whether the copyright holder renewed it. (In those days, works had to be registered with the U.S. Copyright Office and renewed to get the full term of protection; registration, at any point, is no longer necessary.) If it was renewed, the work may still be protected. Thus, *most* works published between these dates have actually lost copyright-protection with renewals being relatively rare. The problem is figuring out *which* works.

If you really want to use a particular work, you can figure all this out. You need to contact the Copyright Office to see if the work was renewed, though unfortunately, this means you have to do the work at its offices in Washington, D.C., or pay $75 per hour for a manual search. (See www.copyright.gov for more information.)

Works copyrighted before 1923 are not copyright-protected anymore. You can take 'em and use 'em for whatever you want.

Does this help you? If you have a site selling cellphones, it almost certainly doesn't help you. If you have a site related to Victorian poetry, travelogues, or herbal medicine, it may be useful. (I have a friend who republishes old school books, many of which are now copyright free.)

This is a very quick rundown of copyright law, which should be sufficient for most people's purposes. However, I haven't covered many details — titles, short phrases, and slogans can't be copyrighted, for instance. Be careful, though — a title can be *trademarked*. (Just try publishing a book with *For Dummies* in the title and see what happens!) For the full details, visit the U.S. Copyright Office Web site at www.copyright.gov. Furthermore, www.unc.edu/~unclng/public-d.htm condenses all this complexity into a simple little chart (though it hasn't been updated since 2003). Wikipedia has an excellent article on the subject, too, at http://en.wikipedia.org/wiki/Copyright.

Before I move on, a word of warning: Be careful before you take something you think is old enough to be out of copyright. Make sure you're using a copy of the original, not a modified version, because those modifications may be protected! You can freely copy and use Charles Dickens's *Great Expectations,* but if someone has taken the original, edited it, and added notes, you can't use that. Nor can you use a version that has been translated in recent years because the translation will be copyrighted.

If the Guvmint Created It, You Can Use It

This is a good example of your tax dollars at work. The U.S. government spends many millions of dollars creating content. This content is not, in general, copyright-protected. Thus, you can take the full text of a government report and publish it on your Web site. Yep, that's right. As amazing as it may seem, you can take, for instance, all the tax forms and instructions you want, or videos created by the EPA, and post them on your site.

However, some rare exceptions exist. A government department may hold donated materials that were originally copyright-protected, and continue to hold the copyright. It may commission a private individual or company to create a work or publish the work under another arrangement, and that person or company may hold the copyright. And works created by the National Technical Information Service or the United States Postal Service may be copyright-protected.

If It's Donated, You Can Use It

Sometimes people simply give away, that is, *donate,* their work in one of two ways. In some cases, a work may be given to the *public domain,* which means the author relinquishes all rights to the work. In other cases, the author may simply allow the use of the work, but retain the copyright. For instance, sometimes you see statements similar to the one on the copyright chart at www.unc.edu/~unclng/public-d.htm:

> *Chart may be freely duplicated or linked to for nonprofit purposes. No permission needed. Please include Web address on all reproductions of chart so recipients know where to find any updates.*

The author has allowed anyone to use the chart under certain conditions. The use must be nonprofit (although this term is rather ambiguous, assume that at the very least it means you can't print the chart and sell it), and the address of the original chart should be included. (Take a look at http://en.wikipedia.org/wiki/Public_domain for more information than you ever really wanted about public-domain works.

It's Only Fair — Fair Use Explained

You can copy parts of a copyrighted work and use them on your site under an exclusion known as *fair use*. The only problem with fair use is that one man's fair use is another man's plagiarism. In other words, there are no hard and fast rules as to what *fair use* means.

I'm not going to explain this. In fact, I'm going to take some copyright-free text directly off the U.S. Copyright Office Web site and save myself a few moments:

> *Under the fair use doctrine of the U.S. copyright statute, it is permissible to use limited portions of a work including quotes, for purposes such as commentary, criticism, news reporting, and scholarly reports. There are no legal rules permitting the use of a specific number of words, a certain number of musical notes, or percentage of a work. Whether a particular use qualifies as fair use depends on the circumstances. See* `http://www.copyright.gov/fls/fl102.html`, *Fair Use, and* `http://www.copyright.gov/circs/circ21.pdf`, *Circular 21, Reproductions of Copyrighted Works by Educators and Librarians.*

The fair use exception isn't, in most cases, terribly useful for most people because you can't just take huge gobs of the work and drop them into your site. However, you can weave quotes from copyrighted works (make sure that you properly cite your sources) into original material that you've written. Of course, your interpretation of *limited portions* may not be the same as the copyright holder's, so you could still land in court.

Index

BUSINESS, CAREERS & PERSONAL FINANCE

0-7645-9847-3

0-7645-2431-3

Also available:
- Business Plans Kit For Dummies
  0-7645-9794-9
- Economics For Dummies
  0-7645-5726-2
- Grant Writing For Dummies
  0-7645-8416-2
- Home Buying For Dummies
  0-7645-5331-3
- Managing For Dummies
  0-7645-1771-6
- Marketing For Dummies
  0-7645-5600-2

- Personal Finance For Dummies
  0-7645-2590-5*
- Resumes For Dummies
  0-7645-5471-9
- Selling For Dummies
  0-7645-5363-1
- Six Sigma For Dummies
  0-7645-6798-5
- Small Business Kit For Dummies
  0-7645-5984-2
- Starting an eBay Business For Dummies
  0-7645-6924-4
- Your Dream Career For Dummies
  0-7645-9795-7

HOME & BUSINESS COMPUTER BASICS

0-470-05432-8

0-471-75421-8

Also available:
- Cleaning Windows Vista For Dummies
  0-471-78293-9
- Excel 2007 For Dummies
  0-470-03737-7
- Mac OS X Tiger For Dummies
  0-7645-7675-5
- MacBook For Dummies
  0-470-04859-X
- Macs For Dummies
  0-470-04849-2
- Office 2007 For Dummies
  0-470-00923-3

- Outlook 2007 For Dummies
  0-470-03830-6
- PCs For Dummies
  0-7645-8958-X
- Salesforce.com For Dummies
  0-470-04893-X
- Upgrading & Fixing Laptops For Dummies
  0-7645-8959-8
- Word 2007 For Dummies
  0-470-03658-3
- Quicken 2007 For Dummies
  0-470-04600-7

FOOD, HOME, GARDEN, HOBBIES, MUSIC & PETS

0-7645-8404-9

0-7645-9904-6

Also available:
- Candy Making For Dummies
  0-7645-9734-5
- Card Games For Dummies
  0-7645-9910-0
- Crocheting For Dummies
  0-7645-4151-X
- Dog Training For Dummies
  0-7645-8418-9
- Healthy Carb Cookbook For Dummies
  0-7645-8476-6
- Home Maintenance For Dummies
  0-7645-5215-5

- Horses For Dummies
  0-7645-9797-3
- Jewelry Making & Beading For Dummies
  0-7645-2571-9
- Orchids For Dummies
  0-7645-6759-4
- Puppies For Dummies
  0-7645-5255-4
- Rock Guitar For Dummies
  0-7645-5356-9
- Sewing For Dummies
  0-7645-6847-7
- Singing For Dummies
  0-7645-2475-5

INTERNET & DIGITAL MEDIA

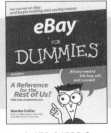

0-470-04529-9

0-470-04894-8

Also available:
- Blogging For Dummies
  0-471-77084-1
- Digital Photography For Dummies
  0-7645-9802-3
- Digital Photography All-in-One Desk Reference For Dummies
  0-470-03743-1
- Digital SLR Cameras and Photography For Dummies
  0-7645-9803-1
- eBay Business All-in-One Desk Reference For Dummies
  0-7645-8438-3
- HDTV For Dummies
  0-470-09673-X

- Home Entertainment PCs For Dummies
  0-470-05523-5
- MySpace For Dummies
  0-470-09529-6
- Search Engine Optimization For Dummies
  0-471-97998-8
- Skype For Dummies
  0-470-04891-3
- The Internet For Dummies
  0-7645-8996-2
- Wiring Your Digital Home For Dummies
  0-471-91830-X

* Separate Canadian edition also available
† Separate U.K. edition also available

Available wherever books are sold. For more information or to order direct: U.S. customers visit www.dummies.com or call 1-877-762-2974.
U.K. customers visit www.wileyeurope.com or call 0800 243407. Canadian customers visit www.wiley.ca or call 1-800-567-4797.

 WILEY

SPORTS, FITNESS, PARENTING, RELIGION & SPIRITUALITY

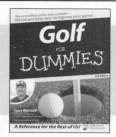

0-471-76871-5

0-7645-7841-3

Also available:

- Catholicism For Dummies
  0-7645-5391-7
- Exercise Balls For Dummies
  0-7645-5623-1
- Fitness For Dummies
  0-7645-7851-0
- Football For Dummies
  0-7645-3936-1
- Judaism For Dummies
  0-7645-5299-6
- Potty Training For Dummies
  0-7645-5417-4
- Buddhism For Dummies
  0-7645-5359-3

- Pregnancy For Dummies
  0-7645-4483-7 †
- Ten Minute Tone-Ups For Dummies
  0-7645-7207-5
- NASCAR For Dummies
  0-7645-7681-X
- Religion For Dummies
  0-7645-5264-3
- Soccer For Dummies
  0-7645-5229-5
- Women in the Bible For Dummies
  0-7645-8475-8

TRAVEL

0-7645-7749-2

0-7645-6945-7

Also available:

- Alaska For Dummies
  0-7645-7746-8
- Cruise Vacations For Dummies
  0-7645-6941-4
- England For Dummies
  0-7645-4276-1
- Europe For Dummies
  0-7645-7529-5
- Germany For Dummies
  0-7645-7823-5
- Hawaii For Dummies
  0-7645-7402-7

- Italy For Dummies
  0-7645-7386-1
- Las Vegas For Dummies
  0-7645-7382-9
- London For Dummies
  0-7645-4277-X
- Paris For Dummies
  0-7645-7630-5
- RV Vacations For Dummies
  0-7645-4442-X
- Walt Disney World & Orlando
  For Dummies
  0-7645-9660-8

GRAPHICS, DESIGN & WEB DEVELOPMENT

0-7645-8815-X

0-7645-9571-7

Also available:

- 3D Game Animation For Dummies
  0-7645-8789-7
- AutoCAD 2006 For Dummies
  0-7645-8925-3
- Building a Web Site For Dummies
  0-7645-7144-3
- Creating Web Pages For Dummies
  0-470-08030-2
- Creating Web Pages All-in-One Desk
  Reference For Dummies
  0-7645-4345-8
- Dreamweaver 8 For Dummies
  0-7645-9649-7

- InDesign CS2 For Dummies
  0-7645-9572-5
- Macromedia Flash 8 For Dummies
  0-7645-9691-8
- Photoshop CS2 and Digital
  Photography For Dummies
  0-7645-9580-6
- Photoshop Elements 4 For Dummies
  0-471-77483-9
- Syndicating Web Sites with RSS Feeds
  For Dummies
  0-7645-8848-6
- Yahoo! SiteBuilder For Dummies
  0-7645-9800-7

NETWORKING, SECURITY, PROGRAMMING & DATABASES

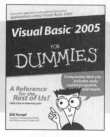

0-7645-7728-X

0-471-74940-0

Also available:

- Access 2007 For Dummies
  0-470-04612-0
- ASP.NET 2 For Dummies
  0-7645-7907-X
- C# 2005 For Dummies
  0-7645-9704-3
- Hacking For Dummies
  0-470-05235-X
- Hacking Wireless Networks
  For Dummies
  0-7645-9730-2
- Java For Dummies
  0-470-08716-1

- Microsoft SQL Server 2005 For Dummies
  0-7645-7755-7
- Networking All-in-One Desk Reference
  For Dummies
  0-7645-9939-9
- Preventing Identity Theft For Dummies
  0-7645-7336-5
- Telecom For Dummies
  0-471-77085-X
- Visual Studio 2005 All-in-One Desk
  Reference For Dummies
  0-7645-9775-2
- XML For Dummies
  0-7645-8845-1

HEALTH & SELF-HELP

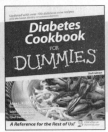

0-7645-8450-2

0-7645-4149-8

Also available:

- Bipolar Disorder For Dummies
  0-7645-8451-0
- Chemotherapy and Radiation
  For Dummies
  0-7645-7832-4
- Controlling Cholesterol For Dummies
  0-7645-5440-9
- Diabetes For Dummies
  0-7645-6820-5* †
- Divorce For Dummies
  0-7645-8417-0 †

- Fibromyalgia For Dummies
  0-7645-5441-7
- Low-Calorie Dieting For Dummies
  0-7645-9905-4
- Meditation For Dummies
  0-471-77774-9
- Osteoporosis For Dummies
  0-7645-7621-6
- Overcoming Anxiety For Dummies
  0-7645-5447-6
- Reiki For Dummies
  0-7645-9907-0
- Stress Management For Dummies
  0-7645-5144-2

EDUCATION, HISTORY, REFERENCE & TEST PREPARATION

0-7645-8381-6

0-7645-9554-7

Also available:

- The ACT For Dummies
  0-7645-9652-7
- Algebra For Dummies
  0-7645-5325-9
- Algebra Workbook For Dummies
  0-7645-8467-7
- Astronomy For Dummies
  0-7645-8465-0
- Calculus For Dummies
  0-7645-2498-4
- Chemistry For Dummies
  0-7645-5430-1
- Forensics For Dummies
  0-7645-5580-4

- Freemasons For Dummies
  0-7645-9796-5
- French For Dummies
  0-7645-5193-0
- Geometry For Dummies
  0-7645-5324-0
- Organic Chemistry I For Dummies
  0-7645-6902-3
- The SAT I For Dummies
  0-7645-7193-1
- Spanish For Dummies
  0-7645-5194-9
- Statistics For Dummies
  0-7645-5423-9

Get smart @ dummies.com®

- **Find a full list of Dummies titles**
- **Look into loads of FREE on-site articles**
- **Sign up for FREE eTips e-mailed to you weekly**
- **See what other products carry the Dummies name**
- **Shop directly from the Dummies bookstore**
- **Enter to win new prizes every month!**

* Separate Canadian edition also available
† Separate U.K. edition also available

Available wherever books are sold. For more information or to order direct: U.S. customers visit www.dummies.com or call 1-877-762-2974.
U.K. customers visit www.wileyeurope.com or call 0800 243407. Canadian customers visit www.wiley.ca or call 1-800-567-4797.